THE AMERICA'S TEST KITCHEN COOKBOOK

THE
AMERICA'S TEST
KITCHEN
COOKBOOK

BY THE EDITORS OF
COOK'S ILLUSTRATED

Photography by Carl Tremblay
Illustrations by John Burgoyne

BOSTON COMMON PRESS   BROOKLINE, MASSACHUSETTS

Boston Common Press
17 Station Street
Brookline, MA 02445

ISBN 0-936184-54-X
Library of Congress Cataloging-in-Publication Data
The Editors of Cook's Illustrated

The America's Test Kitchen Cookbook:
The Recipes, Equipment Ratings, Food Tastings, and Science Experiments from the Hit Public Television Show.
1st edition

ISBN 0-936184-54-X (hardback): $29.95
1. Cooking. 1. Title
2001

Manufactured in the United States of America

Distributed by Boston Common Press, 17 Station Street, Brookline, MA 02445

Designed by Amy Klee
Edited by Jack Bishop

CONTENTS

PREFACE

IN OUR SMALL TOWN IN VERMONT, CHARLIE BENTLEY, THE venerable selectman and local farmer, was recently injured in a farming accident involving a tractor and a disk harrow. A pancake breakfast was quickly organized to raise money to pay for his medical bills. I cooked 35 pounds of breakfast sausage, neighbors made more than 500 pancakes, the country store provided gallons of free orange juice, and we raised more than $10,000 in a town of 350 residents.

Now, that may not sound like much money to many, but that morning was an act of community. Hundreds of locals showed up—including one farmer I hadn't seen in 35 years—and everyone pitched in. The silent auction offered homemade bluebird houses, quilts, jams, candies, toy tractors, wagon rides, and even a telephone that was shaped like a duck. It was, by all accounts, a great success.

America's Test Kitchen is not unlike my small country town. It is a place where collaboration rules, where the sense of community overrides any notion of individual taste. We cook together, we test together, we taste together, and we work on the show together. But, unlike much of what is on television today, this is not a performance. The cameras give you an honest, if slightly more lively, view of how we work in our test kitchen. The set you see on the show is, in fact, a real working kitchen. This is where we live, Monday through Friday, developing recipes for *Cook's Illustrated* magazine.

It is our opinion that viewers are well served by an honest approach to cooking. To that end, we show you bad food—dry turkey meat, greasy fried chicken, and pie shells that sink when baked—as well as good food. We know what you know: Recipes rarely turn out perfectly at home. We all make mistakes, and America's Test Kitchen—through both the TV show and the cookbook—is for those of you who want to understand why recipes fail so that you can improve your chances for success.

My first day on the job at a local dairy farm, I was asked to bring in a cow with her newborn calf. Being nine years old and inexperienced, I confidently strode out through the pasture with the notion of a quick roundup. Instead, I spent the next half-hour being chased around the field, often ducking under barbed wire to escape a pair of long, untrimmed horns. That is often the story with home cooking. We set out with confidence only to quickly discover what we don't know. At America's Test Kitchen, we hope to give you the culinary knowledge to make your next trip into the kitchen a success.

America's Test Kitchen is the culmination of a dream come true for everyone on the staff here in Boston. For me, that dream began in 1980 when I founded the original *Cook's Magazine* with a lot more enthusiasm than money. My wife and partner, Adrienne, worked for the magazine for almost 20 years. Others, such as Jack Bishop (our food tasting expert) and "Doc" Willoughby (at the science desk), have been with us for more than a dozen years. Other editors—Mark Bittman and Pam Anderson in particular—have long histories with *Cook's* and have left their enthusiasm and their mark on the magazine as they have gone on to distinguished careers in the culinary world.

I would say, if asked, that the one thing that sets us apart is that we are not fancy cooks. We love good home cooking, and the show and this book have given us the opportunity to reach out into your kitchens, to start a discussion about the best way to roast a chicken or grill a hamburger. We may not always agree, but I hope that you will enjoy cooking along with us. You are part of the America's Test Kitchen community, and we welcome you into our home.

Christopher Kimball
Founder and editor, *Cook's Illustrated* magazine
Boston, Massachusetts, 2001

ACKNOWLEDGMENTS

IN ADDITION TO ALL THE PEOPLE WHO WORKED ON THE television show are the many individuals who contributed to this book.

Editor Jack Bishop took the recipes, techniques, food tastings, equipment testings, and science segments from the television show and turned them into a cookbook.

Art director Amy Klee designed a book that reflects the spirit and energy of America's Test Kitchen. Carl Tremblay spent countless hours on the set to capture the black-and-white images that appear throughout the book, and John Burgoyne's illustrations bring many key techniques to life. Thank you also to Daniel Van Ackere for the silhouette photography of equipment that appears throughout the book.

India Koopman copyedited the manuscript, and Becky Hays and Jessica Quirk shepherded the text and images through the production process.

The following individuals on the editorial and production staffs also worked on the book: Ron Bilodeau, Barbara Bourassa, Rich Cassidy, Mary Connelly, Daniel Frey, Jim McCormack, Jen McCreary, and Nicole Morris. We would also like to thank proofreader Jana Branch and indexer Diane Brenner.

And without help from members of the marketing and circulation departments, readers might never find our books. Steven Browall, Adam Dardeck, Connie Forbes, Jason Geller, Robert Lee, David Mack, and Jacqui Valerio all contributed to marketing and distribution efforts.

Thank you also to Sharyn Chabot, Henrietta Murray, Juliet Nusbaum, and Mandy Shito.

Clockwise from top left: test cooks Bridget Lancaster and Julia Collin; executive producer Geoffrey Drummond; script supervisor/makeup specialist Brenda Coffey, director/editor Herb Sevush, and technical engineer Eliat B. Goldman; host Chris Kimball; *Cook's Illustrated* editors Shannon Blaisdell and Shona Simkin; coordinating producer Kimberly Nolan and director of photography Dean Gaskill; *Cook's Illustrated* editor Becky Hays, Shona, Bridget, Julia, Herb, and chef Raquel Pelzel.

INSIDE AMERICA'S TEST KITCHEN

AMERICA'S TEST KITCHEN IS MORE THAN JUST A TELEVISION show. It's a real place—the test kitchen at *Cook's Illustrated* magazine, located just outside Boston, Massachusetts. Founded in 1980, *Cook's Illustrated* (formerly *Cook's Magazine*) is dedicated to finding the best and most foolproof methods for preparing home-cooked food. Now public television takes you inside our kitchen to give you an insider's view of how we develop recipes, test cookware, taste foods, and even perform scientific experiments. America's Test Kitchen is not, however, about celebrity chefs or restaurant cooking. The show features the staff of *Cook's Illustrated* magazine—editors, writers, test cooks, and researchers—and real food—burgers, brownies, and mashed potatoes.

Our goal is to help you make Tuesday night dinner quickly, easily, and reliably. To do this, we ask lots of questions, such as what's the best chocolate for brownies, which potato is the best choice for mashing, or what's the best pan for searing steaks. For example, to develop a recipe for brownies that are fudgy and moist, we baked more than three dozen batches. We tested cocoa (both natural and Dutch-processed), unsweetened chocolate, semisweet chocolate, and bittersweet chocolate. We tested different brands of chocolates as well as baking pans. We made brownies with melted butter and creamed butter. We tried brownies made with one egg, two eggs, and three eggs. We even tried both cake flour and all-purpose flour. In the end, we produced a fudgy brownie that we hope you will consider the "best" (or at least darn good) by your standards as well as ours.

The Four Corners

AMERICA'S TEST KITCHEN IS BUILT ON FOUR SEPARATE components: the recipe workshop, the equipment corner, the tasting lab, and the science desk. Christopher Kimball, the founder and editor of *Cook's Illustrated* magazine, acts as host, introducing the show, asking the questions, and helping to cook. Julia Collin and Bridget Lancaster demonstrate the recipes, highlighting what worked and what didn't in the recipe development process. They demonstrate the missteps (those brilliant-sounding ideas that resulted in awful, inedible food) as well as the right steps (the secret techniques and tips we discovered along the way). As you watch Julia and Bridget cook, you might learn the best way to roll out pie dough (chill the dough thoroughly and use a tapered rolling pin) or discover why an overnight rise in the refrigerator is the secret to shatteringly crisp pizza (the extra time lets the dough relax, so it can be rolled superthin).

Even the best recipes can fail if you use the wrong equipment. Adam Ried is the America's Test Kitchen cookware expert. If you need to find the best vegetable peeler, Adam will round up 25 models along with crates of potatoes, squash, and apples. After peeling all day, Adam will discover which peeler is the best choice and why. (It turns out that every home cook would be better off with two different kinds of peelers. See page 185 for details.) Because *Cook's Illustrated* magazine does not accept advertising, Adam and his colleagues in the equipment corner share their no-nonsense opinions freely. If a food processor lumbers across the counter as it attempts to knead bread dough, Adam will say so. If one saucepan really outshines the rest, Adam will quote you the model and price. And because seasoned cooks test all of this equipment, our recommendations are based on performance, not just good looks.

Jack Bishop uses the same standards when evaluating common kitchen ingredients in the tasting lab. Which brand of canned chicken broth tastes best? Does one kind of heavy cream whip up better than the rest? Are American pastas as good as Italian brands? Can anything in the supermarket beat fresh-squeezed orange juice? Which hot dog is the top dog? To answer these questions, Jack conducts blind tastings. We often invite experts from the Boston food community—

chefs, cooking teachers, owners of gourmet stores, food purveyors—to participate. Tasters write down their reactions to taste, texture, and appearance and rank the brands being tested in order of preference. No talking is allowed. Each individual vote reflects the perspective of a different palate. Results are tabulated, and the collective opinion of the tasting panel is captured in the final results. Once our tasting results have been confirmed, our reporters and researchers start talking to food scientists and manufacturers to understand the findings. Why did the beef broths with the most sodium win the tasting? Why didn't tasters object to ice creams made with artificial vanilla? What does protein content have to do with the performance of all-purpose flours?

In America's Test Kitchen, we are curious to know why something works, not just how. John "Doc" Willoughby is our resident science expert. He has spent years working with and talking to food scientists and can translate even physics and chemistry into an easy-to-understand demonstration. Don't know why your salad dressing always separates? Why

does whipped cream become grainy and curdled if beaten too long? Do marinades really tenderize meat? What you learn can be applied to all kinds of recipes, not just those featured on the show and in this cookbook. Our goal is to help you become a more informed cook, one who understands why heat tames the bitter flavors in garlic or why butter must be properly softened before creaming.

A Collective Effort

SO MANY COOKBOOKS AND TELEVISION SHOWS ARE showcases for the thoughts and creations of a single individual. At America's Test Kitchen, every recipe developed is the result of a group effort. This collaboration goes well beyond the six personalities featured on camera during the show.

Executive chefs Kay Rentschler and Dawn Yanagihara ran the "back kitchen" for the show, where all the food that appeared on camera originated. They also were responsible for turning recipes and testing information from the magazine

Left to right: Adam Ried (equipment corner), John "Doc" Willoughby (science desk), Jack Bishop (tasting lab).

Left to right: executive chefs Kay Rentschler and Dawn Yanagihara, chef Raquel Pelzel.

into lively television segments. Kay and Dawn developed many of the favorite recipes demonstrated on the show.

Dawn and Kay were not alone in the back kitchen. Chefs Matthew Card, Ian Davison, Kate Neave, Raquel Pelzel, and Meg Suzuki and assistants Ginger Hawkins, Pring Ram, and Shelley Rashotsky peeled apples, roasted turkeys, and sliced potatoes from early in the morning to late at night so that the cast of the show would have plenty of pies—good, bad, and ugly—to use in their segments. Shannon Blaisdell, Becky Hays, Raquel Pelzel, and Shona Simkin helped develop science, tasting, and equipment segments for the show. They tested ice cream scoops, ran beef broth tastings, and researched the science of emulsions.

Architect Tim Mulavey of Mulavey Studios designed the test kitchen. Jim McCormack, vice president for operations and technology at *Cook's,* and Rich Cassidy, our systems administrator, were responsible for the building of the test kitchen and for keeping it up and running. They figured out how to make the wiring in our 19th-century office building supply enough power to operate eight wall ovens, two ranges, 16 cooktop burners, three dishwashers, six refrigerators, and one chest freezer—plus all the lights, cameras, and air conditioning units brought in by the television crew.

David Mack, vice president for marketing, enjoyed his 15 minutes of television fame as a pizza delivery man.

The staff of A La Carte Communications did a wonderful job producing, directing, and filming America's Test Kitchen. Special thanks to executive producer Geoffrey Drummond; coordinating producer Kimberly Nolan; director/editor Herb Sevush; director of photography Dean Gaskill; camera operators Jan Maliszewski and Stephen Hussar; jib camera operator Michael Mulvey; alternate camera operator Michael McEachern; technical engineer Eliat B. Goldman; audio engineer Chris Bresnahan; script supervisor/makeup specialist Brenda Coffey; grip/gaffers Tommy Hamilton, Patrick Ruth, Jack McPhee, and Aaron Frutman; and production assistant Leland Drummond.

We hope that our television shows captures the spirit of the special place America's Test Kitchen has become. We invite you to come into our kitchen, pull up a stool, and watch great food being prepared. We're confident that you'll take away information and recipes that will make you a better cook and be entertained in the process. Contact us at www.americastestkitchen.com if you have questions or comments about the show. For information about *Cook's Illustrated* magazine, visit www.cooksillustrated.com.

THE AMERICA'S TEST KITCHEN COOKBOOK

PUREED vegetable soups

Soup recipes always seem so easy. Most can be boiled down to one line: Cook chopped ingredients in liquid until tender. Pureed soups have an added instruction—puree until smooth—a step that almost promises to hide any imperfections in the soup by turning the ingredients into a uniform, thickened liquid.

But as any cook knows, even the simplest of soups can go very wrong. Who hasn't had cream of tomato soup that was much too thick and devoid of tomato flavor? The same holds true for pea soup and mushroom soup. The soup looks fine—it's smooth and pretty—but tastes bland. Many pea soups are so flavorless that a blindfolded taster would be hard-pressed to identify peas as an ingredient.

As far as we are concerned, pureed vegetable soups should taste like vegetables. The trick is to coax flavor from the vegetables and then highlight that flavor—not to overwhelm it with lots of other ingredients. As for texture, pureed soups should be velvety and smooth. They should have good body without being floury or gummy.

Adam, our resident equipment guru, put nine blenders through a series of tests before deciding that simpler (and cheaper) is better when it comes to this kitchen workhorse.

TOMATO SOUP

WHAT WE WANTED: A perfectly smooth soup with rich color and great tomato flavor.

Rainy Saturdays in late winter bring to mind the grilled cheese sandwiches and tomato soup of childhood. Long after our affection for other soups wrapped in that famous red and white label has waned, our nostalgia for Campbell's cream of tomato soup persists. Few of us really eat canned tomato soup these days, but some of us do have a vision of the perfect tomato soup. Our vision was a soup of Polartec softness, rich color, and a pleasing balance of sweetness and acidity.

To get a dose of reality, we opened a can of Campbell's. Though rich and tomatoey, it was also cloyingly sweet, almost a cream of ketchup soup. So we moved on to develop a soup that would be as good as we remembered.

For our first set of tests, we used fresh out-of-season tomatoes. The tomatoes were cosmetically peerless, with gleaming red skins and crisp, upright stems. Their taste was a different matter. Without exception, the soups they produced were anemic and completely lacking in tomato flavor. Soups containing flavor boosters, such as carrots, celery, and onions, failed perhaps even more strikingly to suggest a tomato soup. One made with a *roux* (a paste of butter and flour) had the characteristics of a tomato gravy.

Not content to develop a recipe that would be worth making only during the one or two months of the year when tomatoes are in prime form, we turned to canned tomatoes. For our soup we selected fine canned organic diced tomatoes and added shallots, a bit of flour to give the finished product some body, a spoon of tomato paste and some canned chicken broth to enrich the flavor, a helping of heavy cream and a little sherry for refinement, and a pinch of sugar for good measure. Though the resulting soup was dramatically better than those made with fresh winter tomatoes, it still failed to make the cut; the flavor simply wasn't robust enough.

How do you get bigger flavor from canned tomatoes? If they were fresh and ripe, you might roast them: The caramelization of sugar that occurs during roasting concentrates flavors. In the test kitchen, where almost any experiment is considered worth trying, we decided to roast the canned tomatoes. We hoped that intense dry heat might evaporate the surface liquid and concentrate the flavor.

Leaving the above recipe otherwise unchanged, we switched from diced to whole tomatoes for ease of handling, drained and seeded them (reserving the juice for later), then laid them on a foil-covered sheet pan. We then sprinkled them with brown sugar, which we hoped would induce surface caramelization. Only minutes after sliding our tray of tomatoes into a 450-degree oven, the test kitchen was filled with real tomato fragrance, and we knew we had done something right. The roasting made an extraordinary difference, intensifying the tomato flavor and mellowing the fruit's acidity. The rest of the soup could be prepared while the tomatoes roasted, so this step didn't add to the overall preparation time.

Only one minor visual detail marred our efforts. The intense flavor we'd achieved by roasting the tomatoes was not mirrored in the soup's color. The deep coronation red we admired while the soup simmered on the stovetop gave way to a faded circus orange following a round in the blender. The mechanical action of combining solids and liquids had aerated the soup and lightened the color. This wouldn't do. We decided to leave most of the rich tomato broth behind in the saucepan while pureeing the solids with just enough liquid to result in a soup of perfect smoothness. With a finish of heavy cream, our vision of tomato soup had come to life.

WHAT WE LEARNED: For best flavor, roast canned whole tomatoes. For best color, puree the solids with a minimal amount of liquid.

CREAM OF TOMATO SOUP serves 4

Make sure to use canned whole tomatoes packed in juice. Use the packing juice as well as the liquid that falls from the tomatoes when they are seeded to obtain 3 cups of juice.

2	(28-ounce) cans whole tomatoes packed in juice, drained, 3 cups juice reserved
1½	tablespoons dark brown sugar
4	tablespoons unsalted butter
4	large shallots, minced (about ½ cup)
1	tablespoon tomato paste
	Pinch ground allspice
2	tablespoons all-purpose flour
1¾	cups homemade chicken stock or canned low-sodium chicken broth
½	cup heavy cream
2	tablespoons brandy or dry sherry
	Salt and cayenne pepper

1. Adjust oven rack to upper-middle position and heat oven to 450 degrees. Line rimmed baking sheet with foil. With fingers, carefully open whole tomatoes over strainer set in bowl and push out seeds, allowing juices to fall through strainer into bowl. Spread seeded tomatoes in single layer on foil. Sprinkle evenly with brown sugar. Bake until all liquid has evaporated and tomatoes begin to color, about 30 minutes. Let tomatoes cool slightly, then peel them off foil; transfer to small bowl and set aside.

2. Heat butter over medium heat in large saucepan until foaming. Add shallots, tomato paste, and allspice. Reduce heat to low, cover, and cook, stirring occasionally, until shallots are softened, 7 to 10 minutes. Add flour and cook, stirring constantly, until thoroughly combined, about 30 seconds. Gradually add chicken stock, whisking constantly to combine; stir in reserved tomato juice and roasted tomatoes. Cover, increase heat to medium, and bring to boil. Reduce heat to low and simmer, stirring occasionally, to blend flavors, about 10 minutes.

3. Pour mixture through strainer and into medium bowl; rinse out saucepan. Transfer tomatoes and solids in strainer to blender; add 1 cup strained liquid and puree until smooth. Place pureed mixture and remaining strained liquid in saucepan. Add cream and warm over low heat until hot, about 3 minutes. Off heat, stir in brandy and season with salt and cayenne. Serve immediately. (Soup can be refrigerated in an airtight container for up to 2 days. Warm over low heat until hot; do not boil.)

TASTING LAB: Canned Whole Tomatoes

CANNED WHOLE TOMATOES ARE THE CLOSEST PRODUCT to fresh. Whole tomatoes, either plum or round, are steamed to remove their skins and then packed in tomato juice or puree. We prefer tomatoes that are packed in juice; they generally have a fresher, more lively flavor. Puree has a cooked tomato flavor that can impart a slightly stale, tired taste to the whole can.

To find the best canned whole tomatoes, we tasted 11 brands, both straight from the can and in a simple tomato sauce. Muir Glen (an organic brand available in most supermarkets and natural foods stores) and Progresso finished at the head of the pack. Either brand is an excellent choice in cream of tomato soup or any recipe that calls for canned whole tomatoes.

TECHNIQUE:
Pureeing Hot Soup Safely
Blending hot soup can be dangerous. To prevent mishaps, don't fill the blender jar past the halfway point, and hold the lid in place with a folded kitchen towel.

PEA SOUP

WHAT WE WANTED: A velvety soup with real pea flavor, made with readily available ingredients and a minimum of tedious work.

Classic sweet pea soup was originally prepared by briefly stewing fresh blanched peas, leeks, and tendrils of lettuce in butter, moistening them with homemade veal stock, and passing them through a fine-mesh strainer. The soup was then finished with cream and seasoned with fresh chervil.

We wanted a quick and delicious version of this soup, minus the laborious techniques, so we looked at several modern versions. Some introduced new ingredients, largely dismissing the veal stock in favor of chicken stock and adding split peas or sugar snap peas to the mix. Most also moved into the arena of frozen peas. Lacking in gelatinous veal stock, these recipes were obliged to include a bit of thickener in the form of egg yolk, potatoes, or flour. Fresh mint typically replaced chervil. Of the handful of such recipes that we tried, most either completely lacked pea flavor or attained it only by sacrificing color or body.

What we were looking for was something different—an easy version of this popular soup that had the same fundamental virtues as the original. Flavor, color, and texture all bear equally on the success or failure of this soup. Our challenge was to cook the peas quickly enough to preserve their vivid color and to achieve a puree of spectacular smoothness without incurring the loss of flavor sometimes associated with sieving away vegetable bits in short-cooked soups.

The obvious starting point was the pea itself. For those of us without gardens, the long-awaited season of fresh peas is often disappointing. Grocery-store pods can conceal tough, starchy pellets worthy of neither the price they command nor the effort they occasion. So when we began this recipe, we headed not down the garden path but up the frozen foods aisle.

From the pea, we ventured to aromatics. Because the flavor of peas is delicate and easily overwhelmed, we wanted to minimize additions. After experimenting with several aromatics—onions, leeks, and shallots sautéed in butter (unquestionably the most pea-compatible fat in terms of flavor)—we found onions too strong but shallots and leeks equally agreeable. They were delicate and sweet, like the peas themselves.

The means of introducing peas to the soup now became critical. The fun of eating whole peas—breaking through the crisp, springy hull to the sweet pea paste—goes missing in a smooth pea soup, where the listless hulls become an impediment to enjoyment and so must be removed altogether. Simmering peas first to soften their skins, we invariably overcooked them. Additions of sugar snap peas or snow peas sounded interesting but actually added little flavor.

It occurred to us that if we pureed the peas before putting them in the soup and infused them briefly in the simmering liquid, we might get to the heart of the pea right off. Toward that end, we processed partially frozen peas in a food processor and simmered them briefly in the soup base to release their starch and flavor quickly. At this juncture, finding the puree a trifle thin, we doubled back and added 2 tablespoons of flour to the sautéed aromatics to give the base a little body. A few ounces of Boston lettuce added along with the peas gave the soup a marvelous frothy texture when pureed. (To achieve optimal texture, the soup still had to be passed through a strainer.) Some heavy cream, salt, and pepper were the only finishing touches required.

WHAT WE LEARNED: Frozen peas make excellent soup. For maximum pea flavor, grind the frozen peas in a food processor before adding them to the soup pot. Keep the other seasonings simple—just shallots, chicken stock, lettuce, and cream—so the focus stays on the peas.

CREAMY PEA SOUP   serves 4 to 6

A few croutons (at right) are the perfect embellishment.

4	tablespoons unsalted butter
8	large shallots, minced (about 1 cup), or
	2 medium leeks, white and light green parts
	chopped fine (about $1\frac{1}{3}$ cups)
2	tablespoons all-purpose flour
$3\frac{1}{2}$	cups homemade chicken stock or canned
	low-sodium chicken broth
$1\frac{1}{2}$	pounds frozen peas (about $4\frac{1}{2}$ cups), partially
	thawed at room temperature for 10 minutes
12	small leaves Boston lettuce (about 3 ounces)
	from 1 small head, leaves washed and dried
$\frac{1}{2}$	cup heavy cream
	Salt and ground black pepper

1. Heat butter in large saucepan over low heat until foaming. Add shallots or leeks and cook, covered, until softened, 8 to 10 minutes, stirring occasionally. Add flour and cook, stirring constantly, until thoroughly combined, about 30 seconds. Gradually add chicken stock, whisking constantly. Increase heat to high and bring to a boil. Reduce heat to medium-low and simmer 3 to 5 minutes.

2. Meanwhile, in workbowl of food processor fitted with steel blade, process partially thawed peas until coarsely chopped, about 20 seconds. Add peas and lettuce to simmering stock. Increase heat to medium-high, cover, and return to simmer; cook for 3 minutes. Uncover, reduce heat to medium-low, and continue to simmer 2 minutes longer.

3. Working in batches, puree soup in blender until smooth (see illustration on page 5). Strain soup through fine-mesh strainer into large bowl; discard solids. Rinse out and wipe saucepan clean. Return pureed mixture to saucepan and stir in cream. Warm soup over low heat until hot, about 3 minutes. Season to taste with salt and pepper and serve immediately.

BUTTERED CROUTONS   makes about 3 cups

Either fresh or stale bread can be used in this recipe, although stale bread is easier to cut and crisps more quickly in the oven. To use stale bread, reduce the baking time by about two minutes. Croutons made from stale bread will be more crisp than those made from fresh. Be sure to use regular or thick-sliced bread.

6	slices white bread (about 6 ounces), crusts
	removed and slices cut into $\frac{1}{2}$-inch cubes
	(about 3 cups)
	Salt and ground black pepper
3	tablespoons unsalted butter, melted

1. Adjust oven rack to upper-middle position and heat oven to 400 degrees. Combine bread cubes and salt and pepper to taste in medium bowl. Drizzle with butter and toss well with rubber spatula to combine.

2. Spread croutons in single layer on rimmed baking sheet or in shallow baking dish. Bake croutons, turning over at halfway mark, until golden brown and crisp, 8 to 10 minutes. After cooling, croutons can be stored in an airtight container or plastic bag for up to 3 days.

EQUIPMENT CORNER: Blenders

THE TEXTURE OF A PUREED SOUP SHOULD BE AS SMOOTH and creamy as possible. With this in mind, we tried pureeing several soups with a food mill, a food processor, a hand-held immersion blender, and a regular countertop blender.

Forget using the food mill for this purpose. We tried all three strainer plates (coarse, medium, and fine), and the liquid ran right through each plate as we churned and churned only to produce baby food of varying textures.

The food processor does a decent job of pureeing, but some small bits of vegetables can get trapped under the blade and remain unchopped. Even more troubling is the tendency of a food processor to leak hot liquid. Fill the workbowl more than halfway and you are likely to see liquid running down the side of the food processor base.

The immersion blender has appeal because it can be brought to the pot, eliminating the need to ladle hot ingredients from one vessel to another. However, we found that this kind of blender leaves unblended bits of food behind.

We found that a standard blender turns out the smoothest pureed soups. The blade on the blender does an excellent job with soups because it pulls ingredients down from the top of the container. No stray bits go untouched by the blade. And as long as plenty of headroom is left at the top of the blender, there is no leakage.

Many modern blenders have electronic touch-pad controls, a wide range of speeds, and new jar designs. We wondered how these newfangled options compared with the features on a basic blender. We put nine blenders through a series of tests to find out.

We found that blender jars with flutes (vertical protrusions on the inside of the container) were especially efficient at pureeing soups. These flutes cause the vortex created by the spinning blade to collapse, thus redirecting food matter being thrown against the jar walls back down onto the blade. A modification to the standard angled shape of the classic blender jar was not received as positively in the test kitchen. Some companies now make a wide-mouth blender with straight sides. Because these jars are wider at the base, there's more room between the blade and the walls of the jar. Extra space gives bits of food a place to hide, and the texture of soups can suffer. In contrast, the tapered bottom on the standard blender jar is quite narrow and thus promotes more contact between food and blade.

An apparent wide range of speeds (as indicated by countless buttons) did not necessarily track with the actual range of speeds observed by our test cooks. Some blenders with just two speeds (high and low) actually had more (and less) power than blenders with 15 speeds.

Our test cooks also remained unimpressed by electronic touch-pad controls. The flat touch pad is easier to clean than a control panel with raised buttons, but it is not easier to operate. On several models, we found it necessary to press down on the electronic touch pad quite forcefully.

In the end, we preferred basic models from Oster and Hamilton Beach (both around $40) to more expensive brands.

BLENDERS

Many new blenders (left) have a wide mouth with straight sides. On a classic blender (right), the jar tapers at the bottom. In our tests, we found that the classic design promotes a smoother consistency in pureed soups.

MUSHROOM SOUP

WHAT WE WANTED: A richly textured pureed soup, neither too thick nor too thin, with deep mushroom flavor.

Traditional French mushroom soups (and mushroom soups are traditionally French) use white button mushrooms sautéed in butter with onions or shallots. The sautéed mushrooms are simmered in a white veal or chicken stock, pureed, and then finished with cream and sherry. Nutmeg or thyme provides the narrow range of flavoring options. Such a soup must have a faultlessly smooth texture and taste of mushrooms. That's it. Additional "stuff" simply takes the soup off course.

We ruled out any combination of fresh wild mushrooms for the base of the soup: They are expensive and can be difficult to find. Instead, we wanted a recipe that would call on the very real virtues of the white mushroom, a readily available ingredient that is often underestimated. On the other hand, a soupçon of dried mushrooms seemed a reasonable option if the flavor needed encouragement.

We began our testing with the mushrooms themselves. In the past we had "sweated" sliced mushrooms in butter in a covered pan to soften them up and release their juices. But we were interested in seeing how roasting would affect their flavor in a soup. Roasted mushrooms appealed to us not only because they are a sublime eating experience but also because we saw them as a means of losing the chop-chop segment of the recipe altogether.

So against 2 pounds of roasted mushrooms we sliced and sautéed 2 pounds of raw mushrooms. Both batches were simmered in chicken stock and pureed, finished with cream, and tasted. To our surprise, the roasted mushroom soup was less flavorful than the soup made with sautéed mushrooms. Juices released during roasting had browned on the pan and were, for all intents and purposes, irretrievable.

Our next attempt to minimize chopping was more mundane. We pulsed the mushrooms in a food processor before sautéing them. The unevenly sliced scraps became bruised and watery; the finished soup had a blackish hue and an unfulfilled flavor. We would need to chop mushrooms by hand.

The sliced mushrooms required an initial toss in hot melted butter (which bore the translucent shimmer and perfume of sautéed shallots and garlic and had been dusted with ground nutmeg), followed by prolonged cooking over low heat in a covered Dutch oven. This half-moist/half-dry heat in close quarters brought out the flavors and was far superior to boiling a vegetable away in broth or water until softened. In contrast, a soup made with sliced mushrooms that were sautéed in an uncovered skillet, and thus stripped of their liquid and browned, suffered in much the same way as the roasted mushrooms.

After the initial cooking of the white mushrooms, we added chicken stock and a pinch of dried porcini mushrooms, which torqued up the flavor a notch or two. (Water alone, we discovered, would not produce the trophy flavor that even watery canned broth managed to impart.) Fifteen minutes of measured simmering drained every last bit of fiber and flavor from the mushrooms and fused the small family of flavors together.

Once run through the blender, the soup took on a beautiful deep taupe color, provoking tasters to fantasize about paint colors and loveseat sofa fabric (a stark contrast with the institutional flecked beige that blights most mushroom soups). With no thickening to mar its innocence, the texture of the soup was light, but it had body from the puréed mushrooms and heavy cream. The cream and the splash of Madeira added with it at the close of business rounded out the flavors and added just the right touch of sweetness.

WHAT WE LEARNED: For best flavor, slice mushrooms by hand and then sweat them in a covered pot with butter and shallots. Add dried porcini for still more mushroom flavor, and enrich the soup with cream and Madeira.

CREAMY MUSHROOM SOUP serves 6 to 8

To make sure that the soup has a fine, velvety texture, puree it hot off the stove, but do not fill the blender jar more than halfway, as the hot liquid may cause the lid to pop off the jar.

6	tablespoons unsalted butter
6	large shallots, minced (about ¾ cup)
2	small cloves garlic, minced
½	teaspoon freshly grated nutmeg
2	pounds white mushrooms, wiped clean and sliced ¼ inch thick
3½	cups homemade chicken stock or canned low-sodium chicken broth
4	cups hot water
½	ounce dried porcini mushrooms, rinsed well
⅓	cup Madeira or dry sherry
1	cup heavy cream
2	teaspoons lemon juice
	Salt and ground black pepper
1	recipe Sautéed Wild Mushrooms for garnish (recipe follows)

1. Heat butter in large stockpot or Dutch oven over medium-low heat. When foaming subsides, add shallots and sauté, stirring frequently, until softened, about 4 minutes. Stir in garlic and nutmeg and cook until fragrant, about 1 minute longer. Increase heat to medium, add sliced mushrooms, and stir to coat with butter. Cook, stirring occasionally, until mushrooms release some liquid, about 7 minutes. Reduce heat to medium-low, cover pot, and cook, stirring occasionally, until mushrooms have released all their liquid, about 20 minutes. Add chicken stock, water, and porcini mushrooms. Cover, bring to simmer, then reduce heat to low and simmer until mushrooms are fully tender, about 20 minutes.

2. Puree soup in batches in blender until smooth, filling the blender jar only halfway for each batch (see illustration on page 5). Rinse and dry pot. Return soup to pot. Stir in Madeira and cream and bring to simmer over low heat. Add lemon juice and season to taste with salt and pepper. (Soup can be refrigerated in an airtight container for up to 4 days. Warm over low heat until hot; do not boil.) Serve, garnishing each bowl with some sautéed wild mushrooms.

SAUTÉED WILD MUSHROOMS makes enough to garnish 6 to 8 bowls of soup

Float a few sautéed mushrooms in each bowl of soup for visual, textural, and flavor appeal. Delicate enoki mushrooms are also a nice addition. If you like, add an ounce or two of enoki mushrooms to the pan during the final minute of the cooking time in step 2.

2	tablespoons unsalted butter
8	ounces shiitake, chanterelle, oyster, or cremini mushrooms, stems trimmed and discarded, mushrooms wiped clean and sliced thin
	Salt and ground black pepper

1. Heat butter in medium skillet over low heat. When foam subsides, add mushrooms and sprinkle with salt and pepper to taste. Cover and cook, stirring occasionally, until the mushrooms release their liquid, about 10 minutes for shiitakes and chanterelles, about 5 minutes for oysters, and about 9 minutes for cremini.

2. Uncover and continue to cook, stirring occasionally, until liquid released by mushrooms has evaporated and mushrooms are browned, about 2 minutes for shiitakes, about 3 minutes for chanterelles, and about 2 minutes for oysters and cremini. Use mushrooms immediately as garnish for bowls of soup.

TASTING LAB:
Commercial Chicken Broth

COMMERCIAL CHICKEN BROTH WON'T MAKE VERY GOOD matzo ball soup, but it's fine in a pureed vegetable soup. That said, you want to use a broth that comes as close to homemade as possible. Unfortunately, few of the 15 commercial broths we tasted came close to the full-bodied consistency of a successful homemade stock. Many lacked even a hint of chicken flavor.

Interestingly, the top four broths were all products of the Campbell Soup Company, of which Swanson is a subsidiary. In order, they were Swanson Chicken Broth, Campbell's Chicken Broth, Swanson Natural Goodness Chicken Broth (with 33 percent less sodium than regular Swanson chicken broth), and Campbell's Healthy Request Chicken Broth (with 30 percent less sodium than regular Campbell's chicken broth). The remaining broths were decidedly inferior and hard to recommend.

We tried to find out more about why Campbell's broths were superior to so many others, but the giant soup company declined to respond to questions, explaining that its recipes and cooking techniques are considered proprietary information. Many of the answers, however, could be found in the products' ingredient lists. The top two broths happened to contain the highest levels of sodium. Salt has

been used for years in the food industry to make foods with less than optimal flavor tastier. The top two products also contained the controversial monosodium glutamate (MSG), a very effective flavor enhancer. Most of the products that had lower levels of salt and did not have the benefit of other food industry flavor enhancers tasted like dishwater.

Ingredients aside, we found one more important reason why most commercial broths simply cannot replicate the full flavor and body of a homemade stock. Most broths are sold canned, which entails an extended heating process carried out to ensure a sterilized product. The immediate disadvantage of this processing is that heat breaks down the flavorful compounds found in chicken protein. And prolonged heating, which is necessary for canning, destroys other volatile flavors at the same time that it concentrates flavor components that are not volatile, such as salt.

A few national brands of chicken broth have begun to offer the option of aseptic packaging. Compared with traditional canning, in which products are heated in the can for up to nearly an hour to ensure sterilization, the process of aseptic packaging entails a flash heating and cooling process that is said to help products better retain both their nutritional value and their flavor.

We decided to hold another tasting to see if we could detect more flavor in the products sold in aseptic packaging. We tasted Swanson's traditional and Natural Goodness chicken broths sold in cans and in aseptic packages. The results fell clearly in favor of the aseptically packaged broths; both tasted cleaner and more chickeny than their canned counterparts. So if you are truly seeking the best of the best in commercial broths, choose one of the two Swanson broths sold in aseptic packaging.

One drawback of the aseptic packages is the fact that they contain more than two cans' worth of broth, making them impractical for cooks who keep commercial broth on hand for the occasional recipe that calls for a small amount of broth. Still, an opened aseptic package will keep in the refrigerator for up to two weeks, whereas broth from a can will keep in the refrigerator for only a few days.

For great carbonara, first pour the cheese and eggs over the hot pasta. Then, add the bacon and toss again. Since the pasta is already sticky from the cheese and eggs, the bits of bacon will cling to the noodles rather than fall to the bottom of the bowl.

PESTO, CARBONARA,
CHAPTER 2
& salad

Everyone has a recipe for the classic Italian basil sauce
known as pesto. And there certainly are plenty of prepared options in
supermarkets and gourmet shops. But more often than not, this sauce
only hints at basil flavor, and the garlic takes center stage. Good pesto
should knock your socks off with a strong basil punch, and the garlic
should be muted. The test kitchen developed a clever method for
playing up the basil while toning down the garlic.

Few home cooks, however, have a well-thumbed copy of a recipe
for carbonara, a rich pasta sauce made with eggs, cheese, and bacon.
While it is popular in restaurants from Rome to Los Angeles, no one
seems to make this dish at home—even though it can be on the table 20
minutes after you walk into the kitchen. Most home cooks worry that
the sauce will turn out clumped or curdled. And even when things go
right, all the delicious bacon usually falls to the bottom of the serving
bowl. We wanted to figure out how to create a silky, rich sauce and then
get the bits of bacon to adhere to the spaghetti, not the bowl.

A leafy salad dressed with vinaigrette complements either of these
pasta dishes. (It also works with a spaghetti and meatball supper; see page
27.) After making enough salad to feed a small army, we have unlocked
the secrets of a basic oil-and-vinegar dressing and figured out the right
ratio of vinaigrette to salad greens.

PESTO

WHAT WE WANTED: **A smooth sauce with potent basil flavor and a mild hit of garlic and cheese.**

Pesto is a pounded basil sauce that comes from Liguria, a coastal area in northwestern Italy. Traditionally, the sauce is made with a mortar and pestle from basil leaves, raw garlic, extra-virgin olive oil, pine nuts, grated cheese, and salt.

In our experience, the bright herbal fragrance of basil always hinted at more flavor than it really delivered. The raw garlic can also be a problem, having a sharp, acrid taste that bites through the other flavors in the sauce. We also wondered about the nuts. Some sources suggest that only pine nuts are authentic, while others mention walnuts as an alternative. Our goals when testing pesto were simple—heighten the flavor of the basil, mellow the punch of the garlic, and figure out how to handle the nuts.

We started our tests by using a mortar and pestle to make pesto. The advantage of this method was that it produced a silky paste with an unusually full basil flavor. The disadvantage was that it required 15 minutes of constant pounding and a piece of equipment not found in many home kitchens. The blender and food processor are more practical for making pesto. Of the two, we found that the food processor makes a sauce with a finer, more consistent texture.

We decided to use the food processor for our recipe but wondered how to get the full basil flavor of pesto made with a mortar and pestle. Because the basil was completely broken down in the mortar and pestle, it released its full range of herbal and anise flavors in a way that the chopping action of a food processor alone could not accomplish. Attempting to approximate that fuller flavor, we tried separate tests of chopping, tearing, and bruising the leaves (packed in a sealable plastic bag) with a meat pounder before processing. Bruising released the most flavor from the basil leaves, so we stuck with this method.

Garlic is a star player in pesto, but we often find that this star shines a little too brightly. Wondering how to cut the raw garlic edge, we tried roasting it, sautéing it, and even infusing its flavors into olive oil, but none of these methods were ideal. Blanching whole garlic cloves in boiling water turned out to be the best solution for several reasons—it's quick (the garlic needs less than a minute in boiling water), it loosens the papery skin from cloves for easy peeling, and it eliminates the raw garlic sting.

With the basil flavor boosted and the garlic toned down, we began to experiment with nuts. We often toast nuts when using them in recipes and found that toasting the nuts in a dry skillet until fragrant also brings out their flavor in pesto. Pine nuts, walnuts, and almonds all work well. Almonds are relatively sweet, which worked beautifully with the basil, but they are also hard, so they gave pesto a coarse, granular texture. Walnuts break down a little more, but they still remained distinctly meaty in flavor and texture. Pine nuts were the favorite for the vast majority of our tasters. They became very creamy when processed and gave the pesto an especially smooth, luxurious texture.

Tasters preferred the combination of Parmesan and sharper Pecorino Romano than either cheese alone. But the pesto made with all Parmesan was a close second, so, in a nod to convenience, we made the Pecorino Romano optional. (See page 28 for information on Parmesan.)

When using pesto to sauce pasta, we found it imperative to use some of the cooking liquid to thin out the consistency. Thinning the pesto with up to ½ cup of pasta cooking water allowed for good distribution of the sauce over the noodles, it softened and blended the flavors a bit, and highlighted the creaminess of the cheese and nuts.

WHAT WE LEARNED: **Bruise the basil in a plastic bag with a meat mallet or rolling pin to unlock its flavor, and tame the sting of the garlic by blanching unpeeled cloves.**

BOW-TIE PASTA WITH PESTO serves 4

Basil usually darkens in homemade pesto, but you can boost the green color by adding the optional parsley. For sharper flavor, substitute 1 tablespoon finely grated Pecorino Romano cheese for 1 tablespoon of the Parmesan. For a change from bow-tie pasta, try long, thin pasta such as linguine or curly shapes, such as fusilli, which can trap bits of the pesto.

¼   cup pine nuts, walnuts, or almonds
3   medium cloves garlic, threaded on skewer
2   cups packed fresh basil leaves
2   tablespoons fresh flat-leaf parsley leaves (optional)
7   tablespoons extra-virgin olive oil
    Salt
¼   cup finely grated Parmesan
1   pound farfalle (bow-tie pasta)

1. Toast nuts in small, heavy skillet over medium heat, stirring frequently, until just golden and fragrant, 4 to 5 minutes.

TECHNIQUE: Blanching Garlic

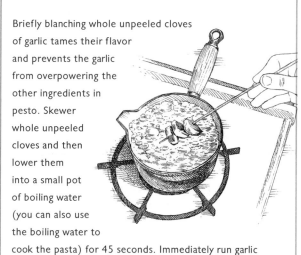

Briefly blanching whole unpeeled cloves of garlic tames their flavor and prevents the garlic from overpowering the other ingredients in pesto. Skewer whole unpeeled cloves and then lower them into a small pot of boiling water (you can also use the boiling water to cook the pasta) for 45 seconds. Immediately run garlic under cold water to stop the cooking process.

2. Meanwhile, bring 4 quarts of water to boil in large pot. Lower skewered garlic into water and boil for 45 seconds (see illustration below). Immediately run garlic under cold water. Remove from skewer; peel and mince.

3. Place basil and parsley (if using) in heavy-duty, quart-size, sealable plastic bag; pound with flat side of meat pounder or a rolling pin until all leaves are bruised (see illustration on page 16).

4. Place nuts, garlic, basil, oil, and ½ teaspoon salt in workbowl of food processor fitted with steel blade; process until smooth, stopping as necessary to scrape down sides of bowl. Transfer mixture to small bowl, stir in cheese, and adjust salt. (Surface of pesto can be covered with sheet of plastic wrap or thin film of oil and refrigerated for up to 5 days.)

5. Add 1 tablespoon salt and pasta to boiling water. Cook until al dente. Reserve ½ cup pasta cooking water; drain pasta and transfer back to cooking pot. Mix in ¼ cup reserved cooking water and pesto; use remaining ¼ cup cooking water as needed to moisten. Divide among 4 warmed pasta bowls and serve immediately.

TASTING LAB:
Supermarket Extra-Virgin Olive Oils

WHEN YOU BUY A SUPERMARKET EXTRA-VIRGIN OLIVE OIL, you're not buying a boutique oil produced and bottled in the small production plant of an olive grower just outside a quaint Tuscan village. You are buying a big-name producer's mass-marketed extra-virgin brand, usually made from olives shipped into Italy from different countries—or even different continents—for bottling. (An extra-virgin oil can be called Italian even if it is only bottled in Italy.)

This leads to differences not only in price and quality but in what you may or may not know about the oil. When you purchase an artisanal oil in a high-end shop, certain

TECHNIQUE: Bruising Herb Leaves

Bruising herb leaves in a zipper-lock plastic bag with a meat pounder (or rolling pin) is a quick but effective substitute for hand-pounding with a mortar and pestle and helps to release the herbs' flavor.

informational perks are expected (and paid for). These typically include written explanations of the character and nuances of the particular oil as well as knowledgeable staff who can assist you in your purchase. But in a supermarket, it's just you and a price tag. How do you know which supermarket extra-virgin oil best suits your needs? To provide some guidance, we decided to hold a blind tasting of the nine best-selling extra-virgin oils typically available in American supermarkets.

The label "extra-virgin" denotes the highest quality of olive oil, with the most delicate and prized flavor. (The three other grades are "virgin," "pure," and "olive pomace." "Pure" oil, often labeled simply "olive oil," is the most commonly available.) To be tagged as extra-virgin, an oil must meet three basic criteria. First, it must contain less than 1 percent oleic acid per 100 grams of oil. Second, the oil must not have been treated with any solvents or heat. (Heat is used to reduce strong acidity in some nonvirgin olive oils to make them palatable. This is where the term *cold pressed* comes into play, meaning that the olives are pressed into a paste using mechanical wheels or hammers and are then kneaded to separate the oil from the fruit.) Third, it must pass taste and aroma standards as defined by groups such as the International Olive Oil Council (IOOC), an intergovernmental olive oil regulatory committee that sets the bar for its member countries.

Tasting extra-virgin olive oil is much like tasting wine. The flavors of these oils range from citrusy to herbal, musty to floral, with every variable in between. And what one taster finds particularly attractive—a slight briny flavor, for example—another person might find unappealing. Also like wine, the flavor of a particular brand of olive oil can change from year to year, depending on the quality of the harvest and the olives' place of origin.

We chose to taste extra-virgin olive oil in its most pure and unadulterated state: raw. Tasters were given the option of sampling the oil from a spoon or on neutral-flavored French bread and were then asked to eat a slice of green apple—for its acidity—to cleanse the palate between oils. The olive oils were evaluated for color, clarity, viscosity, bouquet, depth of flavor, and lingering of flavor.

Whereas in a typical tasting we are able to identify a clear "winner" and "loser," this time around we could not draw such a distinct line. In fact, the panel seemed to quickly divide itself into those who liked a gutsy olive oil with bold flavor and those who preferred a milder, more mellow approach. Nonetheless, in both camps one oil clearly had more of a following than any other—the all-Italian-olive Davinci brand. Praised for its rounded and buttery flavor, it was the only olive oil we tasted that seemed to garner across-the-board approval with olive oil experts and in-house staff alike. Consequently, it is the only supermarket extra-virgin olive oil we could rate as "highly recommended."

Among tasters who preferred full-bodied, bold oils, Colavita and Filippo Berio also earned high marks. Tasters in the mild and delicate camp gave high scores to Pompeian and Whole Foods oils.

SPAGHETTI ALLA CARBONARA

WHAT WE WANTED: Restaurant carbonara is often an unctuous, congealed mass of cheese, eggs, and bacon. We set out to make the sauce silky and smooth.

A pasta dish quintessentially Roman in nature, carbonara taunts us with food taboos. It begins with a sauce made from eggs and cheese that cooks into velveteen consistency from only the heat of the just-drained pasta that it drapes. Shards of Italian bacon punctuate the dish with enough presence to make one give silent thanks to the pig. And just when you think that it can't get any better, the bright punch of hot garlic kicks in. This is no diet food, but the indulgent nature of carbonara is one reason it is featured on every trattoria menu.

Far from this heavenly marriage of sauce and pasta, the run-of-the-mill carbonara is a lackluster dish of spaghetti smothered in a heavy, dull, cream-laden sauce that makes you wonder if you ordered Alfredo by mistake. Even worse are variations loaded with cheese that refuses to melt and

sticks to the pasta in dry, abrasive pieces. Even a well-made carbonara can be destroyed by a waitperson. If the dish is not brought to the table immediately, the sauce congeals and the carbonara turns sticky and rubbery.

Searching Italian cookbooks for the solutions to these problems provided little help. Most recipes deviated little in the ingredient list, and the technique was similar throughout: Make a raw sauce with eggs and cheese, render bacon, cook pasta, add hot pasta to sauce and bacon, and toss until the mixture is hot and creamy. The only noticeable difference we found was in the ratio of ingredients, especially the eggs and cheese. That ratio, we reasoned, must be the key to a successful carbonara.

Eggs form the base of the lush, silky sauce that binds the other ingredients to the slender strands of pasta. Only the heat from the cooked pasta is necessary to cook the eggs to the right consistency, so we knew a precise amount of egg would be critical to both the texture and the richness of the dish. Basing our recipe on 1 pound of pasta, we started out with two eggs. Mixed with 1 cup grated cheese, this sauce was thick and clumped when introduced to the hot pasta. Four eggs made a sauce too soupy and wet to stick to the pasta. Three eggs were just right. The sauce was silky in texture, had the fortitude to cling to the spaghetti, and was moist and rich.

Next, the cheese. When in Rome, the cheese of choice is Pecorino Romano, an aged sheep's milk cheese with a distinctly sharp, tangy flavor. On its own, 1 cup of Pecorino Romano proved too strong for our taste. But reducing the amount of cheese in the hope of softening the strong flavor yielded a dish that lacked richness.

We tried substituting a cup of Parmigiano-Reggiano for the Pecorino Romano. While the Parmigiano-Reggiano gave the dish a sweet, nutty flavor that was well received, tasters now longed for a little of the potency from the Pecorino Romano. We found that a blend of cheeses—¼ cup Pecorino Romano and ¾ cup Parmesan—brought just the right amount of flavor from both. It also made for a perfect ratio of cheese to eggs to create the smooth, creamy sauce we'd been looking for.

Many carbonara recipes dictate the addition of ½ cup heavy cream to the sauce. Our tasters immediately rejected this lack of discretion. The heavy cream dulled the mouth with a fatty coating, and it deadened the flavor of the cheeses. Tablespoon by tablespoon, we reduced the amount of cream in the recipe, but tasters were satisfied only when the cream was omitted altogether.

On the other hand, the sweet punch of garlic was a welcome addition. At first we sautéed a few minced cloves in a little olive oil before adding it to the sauce, but this sautéed garlic lacked the fortitude to counterbalance the heavy weight of the eggs and cheese. Adding raw garlic to the mixture was just the trick. A brief exposure to the heat of the pasta allowed the garlic flavor to bloom and gave the dish a pleasing bite.

In Rome, carbonara is traditionally made with guanciale—salt-cured pork jowl. You can't buy this product in the United States, so we centered the testing around available bacons—pancetta (Italian bacon) and American bacon. Pancetta, like American bacon, comes from the belly of the pig, but rather than being smoked, pancetta is cured only with salt, pepper, and spice, usually cloves. American bacon is recognizably smoked and has a distinct sweetness from the sugar that's added during the curing process.

The pancetta gave the carbonara a substantial pork flavor. It was distinctly seasoned with the salt and pepper of the cure. But tasters weren't crazy about its meaty texture. Even though the pancetta was thinly sliced and fried until crisp, the pieces became chewy after a short time in the sauce. The American bacon managed to retain much of its crisp texture, and it added a pleasantly sweet and smoky flavor to the dish that tasters preferred overwhelmingly.

In an effort to find the absolutely best carbonara, we tried a dry red wine (a common ingredient in authentic recipes), vermouth (which appeared in only one recipe but piqued our interest), and a dry white wine, which was favored by the majority of the recipes we had found.

The red wine wasn't unpleasant, but the overall flavor wasn't bright enough to stand up to the smoky flavor of the bacon. The vermouth offered a distinct herbal flavor that tasters voted down. White wine created the most impact and resonance. It was full-flavored, and the acidic nature of the wine cut through the taste of the bacon, brightening the flavor of the dish.

Up to this point, we had been making the carbonara in the traditional method. We mixed the eggs and cheese in the bottom of the serving bowl along with the fried bacon, then dumped the hot, drained pasta on top and tossed the mixture thoroughly. But this method had flaws. It was difficult to distribute the egg and cheese mixture evenly throughout the pasta, and, try as we might to keep the bacon pieces afloat, gravity pulled them back to the bottom of the bowl.

Mixing the eggs and cheese together in a separate bowl, then pouring the mixture over the hot pasta, ensured even coverage. In addition, by choosing not to mix the eggs and cheese in the bottom of the serving bowl, we were able to preheat the bowl—a step that keeps the pasta warm. Finally, we found that tossing the hot pasta with the egg mixture first, then gently tossing in the bacon, worked best. The bacon adhered nicely to the sticky coating of sauce.

We found that carbonara will not maintain its creamy consistency if the cooked pasta is allowed too much time to drain. We ultimately allowed it to sit in the colander for only a few seconds before mixing it with the sauce. (To ensure that proper moisture from the pasta was not lost, we found it a good practice to reserve ⅓ cup of the pasta cooking water to add if the noodles became dry or sticky.) Even with these precautions, the carbonara thickened up considerably if left to cool for even a short time. It's best for hungry diners to wait for the carbonara, not the other way around.

WHAT WE LEARNED: **Use a blend of cheeses for the right flavor, combine the cheeses and eggs in a small bowl, and pour this mixture over the hot pasta for even coverage. Use regular American bacon, white wine, and raw garlic to balance the richness of the eggs and cheese.**

SPAGHETTI ALLA CARBONARA serves 4 to 6

Add regular table salt to the pasta cooking water, but use sea salt flakes, if you can find them, to season the dish. We like the full flavor they bring to the carbonara. Note that while either table salt or sea salt can be used when seasoning in step 3, they are not used in equal amounts.

¼ cup extra-virgin olive oil

½ pound bacon (6 to 8 slices), slices halved lengthwise, then cut crosswise into ¼-inch pieces

½ cup dry white wine

3 large eggs

¾ cup finely grated Parmesan (about 2 ounces)

¼ cup finely grated Pecorino Romano (about ¾ ounce)

3 small cloves garlic, minced to paste or pressed through garlic press

1 pound spaghetti
    Salt (see note) and ground black pepper

1. Adjust oven rack to lower-middle position, set heatproof serving bowl on rack, and heat oven to 200 degrees. Bring 4 quarts water to rolling boil in large stockpot.

2. While water is heating, heat oil in large skillet over medium heat until shimmering, but not smoking. Add bacon and cook, stirring occasionally, until lightly browned and crisp, about 8 minutes. Add wine and simmer until alcohol aroma has cooked off and wine is slightly reduced, 6 to 8 minutes. Remove from heat and cover to keep warm. Beat eggs, cheeses, and garlic together with fork in small bowl; set aside.

3. When water comes to boil, add pasta and 1 tablespoon table salt; stir to separate pasta. Cook until al dente; reserve ⅓ cup pasta cooking water and drain pasta for about 5 seconds, leaving pasta slightly wet. Transfer drained pasta to warm serving bowl; if pasta appears dry, add some reserved cooking water and toss to moisten. Immediately pour egg mixture over hot pasta, sprinkle with 1 teaspoon sea salt flakes or ¾ teaspoon table salt; toss well to combine. Pour bacon mixture over pasta, season generously with black pepper, and toss well to combine. Serve immediately.

LEAFY SALAD WITH VINAIGRETTE

WHAT WE WANTED: A basic dressing that is neither harsh nor oily and salad greens that glisten with dressing but are not wilted.

A leafy salad sounds simple. Take some lettuce and dress with oil and vinegar. But this is a case where little adjustments in the recipe can make a big difference in the results. We've all had soggy, overdressed salads as well as salads ruined by poorly made dressings.

Vinaigrette is the most popular dressing for salads. While it is possible to dress a salad by adding the oil and vinegar separately, the results are quite different when the ingredients are combined before being poured over greens. To demonstrate this difference, try this test we conducted in the test kitchen. Dress a simple green salad first with oil, then with a mixture of vinegar, salt, and pepper. The result will be harsh, with a prominent vinegar bite. If you are using a good vinegar, you may like this result.

For the sake of comparison, take another batch of greens and the same dressing ingredients. Mix the salt and pepper into the vinegar and then whisk in the oil until the dressing is translucent. When this emulsified dressing is poured over greens, the flavor will be smoother, with a greater emphasis on the oil.

The science of emulsions explains why the same ingredients can taste so different. In the first oil-then-vinegar salad, the oil and vinegar don't mix, so both race up the tongue. The less viscous vinegar wins, hence this salad tastes more acidic. In the emulsion, the oil is whipped into tiny molecules that surround dispersed droplets of vinegar. The oil is in the so-called continuous phase of the emulsion and is tasted first. The tongue is coated with fat droplets that cushion the impact of the acid.

The best ratio of oil to vinegar is open to much discussion and can depend on the acidity of the vinegar as well as the flavor of the oil. In general, we prefer a ratio of 4 parts oil to 1 part acid, but this can vary, especially when using citrus juices or rice vinegar, both of which are much less acidic than common vinegars.

We find that either a fork or small whisk generates the whipping action necessary to break up the oil and vinegar into small droplets. (You can also shake ingredients together in a sealed jar.) In any case, the emulsion will break rather quickly, so it is necessary to rewhisk (or reshake) the dressing just before pouring it over salad greens. We like to add the salt and pepper to the vinegar because the vinegar mutes these flavors a bit and prevents them from becoming too overpowering. On the other hand, we prefer to add herbs to the finished dressing to maximize their impact.

We find that ¼ cup of vinaigrette is sufficient to dress 2 quarts of salad greens, enough for four servings. Any more dressing turns the salad greens soggy. Salad greens can be tricky to measure. We lightly pack a 4-cup plastic measure to obtain consistent amounts.

Because they grow so close to the ground, salad greens are often quite sandy. Thorough washing in a deep bowl or sink filled with cold water is a must. Swish the greens in the water to loosen any sand, then lift them out of the dirty water. Once the bottom of bowl is free of grit (you may need to drain the bowl and add clean water several times), dry greens in a salad spinner and then use paper or kitchen towels to blot off any remaining moisture. It's imperative to remove all visible moisture. Dressing slides off damp greens and pools at the bottom of the salad bowl.

Once a leafy salad is dressed, the clock is ticking. Our tests showed that waiting even 15 minutes to eat the salad causes significant loss in freshness and crispness.

WHAT WE LEARNED: In most cases, 4 parts oil to 1 part vinegar produces the best balance of flavors in a vinaigrette. The ingredients can be mixed with a fork or small whisk or shaken together in a jar.

BASIC VINAIGRETTE makes about ½ cup, enough to dress 4 quarts (8 servings) of salad greens

Salt and pepper are mixed first with the vinegar, which subdues their sometimes harsh bite. If you like, you can adjust the seasonings after the salad has been dressed by sprinkling additional salt and pepper directly onto the greens. Extra dressing can be refrigerated for several days. Variations that contain fresh herbs should be used within several hours for maximum freshness.

1½ tablespoons red wine vinegar
¼ teaspoon salt
⅛ teaspoon ground black pepper
6 tablespoons extra-virgin olive oil

Combine vinegar, salt, and pepper in bowl with fork. Add oil, then whisk or mix with fork until smooth, about 30 seconds. The dressing will separate after 5 to 10 minutes, so use immediately or cover and refrigerate; mix again before tossing with greens.

VARIATIONS

BALSAMIC VINAIGRETTE

Follow recipe for Basic Vinaigrette, reducing red wine vinegar to 1½ teaspoons and combining with 1½ tablespoons balsamic vinegar.

WALNUT VINAIGRETTE

Follow recipe for Basic Vinaigrette, replacing vinegar with 2 tablespoons lemon juice and replacing olive oil with 4 tablespoons canola oil mixed with 2 tablespoons walnut oil.

MEDITERRANEAN VINAIGRETTE

Follow recipe for Basic Vinaigrette, replacing vinegar with 2¼ teaspoons lemon juice, increasing pepper to ¼ teaspoon, and decreasing oil to 4 tablespoons. Whisk 1 tablespoon drained and minced capers, 1 tablespoon minced fresh parsley leaves, 1 teaspoon minced fresh thyme leaves, and 1 medium garlic clove, minced fine, into finished dressing.

MIXED HERB VINAIGRETTE

Follow recipe for Basic Vinaigrette, adding 1 tablespoon minced fresh basil leaves, 1½ teaspoons minced fresh parsley leaves, and 1 teaspoon minced fresh oregano leaves to finished dressing.

TASTING LAB: Vinegars and Citrus Juices in Salad Dressings

WE FIND THAT THE FOLLOWING VINEGARS WORK BEST IN salad dressings. Lower-acidity vinegars work best with mild greens, such as Bibb or Boston lettuce; higher-acidity vinegars can be matched with stronger greens, such as arugula or mizuna. Citrus juice and zest add a distinct flavor and less acid.

red wine vinegar: The most versatile choice in salads. Its flavor is sharp but clean. Domestic brands tend to have an acidity around 5 percent, imported red brands often about 7 percent. In our tasting of red wine vinegars, Heinz beat other domestic brands as well as imports, some of which cost 10 times as much.

white wine vinegar: Similar to red wine vinegar but often not quite as complex. Our choice when a pink-colored vinaigrette made with red wine vinegar might seem odd.

balsamic vinegar: This rich, sweet, oaky vinegar is best used in combination with red wine vinegar in salads. Real balsamic vinegar is aged at least a dozen years and can cost $50 an ounce. Cheaper supermarket versions vary tremendously in quality. Some are nothing more than caramel-colored red wine vinegar. Others follow the traditional process (unfermented white grape juice, called must, is fermented in wood casks) but cut back on the aging time. Our advice is to avoid products with artificial colors and flavors—they were deemed harsh and unpleasant in our tasting of leading brands. It's usually a good sign if the word "must" appears on the label.

rice vinegar: A natural choice in Asian dressings, this low-acidity (about 4.5 percent), clear vinegar is quite mild. Use it when you want to keep acidity in check but also want to avoid the distinctive flavor of citrus juices.

sherry vinegar: This Spanish vinegar is usually quite strong (often with 7 percent acidity) but has a rich, oaky, nutty flavor.

citrus juices: Orange, lime, and lemon juices can all be used in salad dressing. They add acidity (although not as much as most vinegars) as well as flavor. Lemon and lime juices are more acidic and can stand on their own. Orange juice is usually combined with vinegar. To add more citrus flavor without disturbing the ratio of acid to oil, stir in some grated zest.

LEAFY GREEN SALAD   serves 4

For best results, use at least two kinds of greens. A blend of mild, delicate greens, such as Boston and leaf lettuces, and peppery greens, such as arugula and watercress, is ideal. Romaine adds crunch and texture and is welcome in most salads. If you like, add mild fresh herbs, such as chives, tarragon, or basil, in small amounts.

> 2   quarts salad greens, washed and dried
> ¼   cup Basic Vinaigrette or any variation
>   (page 21)

Place greens in large salad bowl. Drizzle dressing over greens and toss to coat evenly, about 1 minute. Serve immediately.

VARIATIONS
TRICOLOR SALAD WITH BALSAMIC VINAIGRETTE

Dress 4 cups arugula, 1 small head radicchio, cored and leaves torn, and 2 small heads Belgian endive, stems trimmed and leaves cut crosswise into thirds, with ¼ cup Balsamic Vinaigrette.

ARUGULA SALAD WITH WALNUT VINAIGRETTE

We prefer to toast nuts in a dry skillet over medium heat until fragrant, which takes four or five minutes. Make sure to shake the pan occasionally to turn the nuts.

Dress 2 quarts arugula and 3 tablespoons toasted and coarsely chopped walnuts with ¼ cup Walnut Vinaigrette.

EQUIPMENT CORNER: Salad Spinners

THE BASIC DESIGN OF ALL SALAD SPINNERS IS SIMILAR. A perforated basket is fitted into a larger outer bowl, and gears connected to the mechanism in the lid spin the basket rapidly, creating centrifugal force that pulls the greens to the sides of the basket and the water on the leaves through the perforations into the outer bowl. Beyond this, however, there are three important ways in which various models can differ.

First is the lid. Some are solid, and some have a hole that lets water run directly into the basket while it spins. Second is the outer bowl. Some, like the lids, are solid, while others are perforated so water can flow through. Third is the mechanism that makes the basket spin: pull cord, turning crank, lever crank, or pump knob.

BEST SALAD SPINNERS
With its non-skid base and push-button brake, the Oxo Good Grips spinner (left) requires just one hand to operate. The Zyliss Salad Spinner (right) is especially sturdy and dried greens exceptionally well in our tests.

To be fair, all of the eight spinners we tested did a reasonably good job of drying wet lettuce leaves and parsley, though none dried the greens so thoroughly that they wouldn't benefit from a quick blotting with paper towels before being dressed. Since the differences between them in terms of drying performance are not terribly dramatic, what you really want in your kitchen is a spinner that is well designed, easy to use, and sturdy.

We didn't like the spinners with flow-through lids. The greens we cleaned by running water into the basket tended to bruise from the rushing water and never got clean enough. We also didn't like models with bowls that had holes in the bottom so the water could flow right out. Again, we did not consider this a benefit, in part because it assumes you have an empty sink in which to place the spinner. Second, we like to use the outer bowl of the spinner to soak the leaves clean, something you can't do if there are holes in the bowl.

As for the turning mechanism, the real standout in terms of design and ease of use was the spinner made by Oxo. You can use the Oxo with just one hand because of its clever no-skid base and the pump knob by which it operates. Pushing the pump down both makes the basket spin and pushes the whole unit down onto the counter.

Among the other models tested, the pull cord on the Zyliss model was the easiest to grip, and it did in fact get the greens a tad drier than other spinners, including the Oxo. The Zyliss and the Oxo, each of which can be purchased for about $25, were also the sturdiest of the bunch.

SPAGHETTI & meatballs

CHAPTER 3

A spaghetti and meatball dinner is an American classic, beloved by children and adults alike. Start with spaghetti, coated with thick tomato sauce and topped with savory meatballs. Add garlic bread, crusty and heady with garlic and butter. You might round out the meal with a leafy green salad (see page 22).

Although this meal sounds simple (and it is), much can go wrong. Who hasn't tasted leaden meatballs capable of sinking the *Titanic* or squishy garlic bread devoid of crunch or character?

Our goals for this hearty supper were clear: Produce moist, creamy meatballs and a quick, robust tomato sauce for the pasta. Figure out how to make crisp garlic bread that's neither bland nor so strong tasting that it overpowers everything else on the table.

With the right techniques and recipes, a spaghetti supper can rival any fancy meal. This is honest, good food.

We tested whole, diced, and crushed canned tomatoes before determining that spaghetti and meatballs requires the kind of smooth sauce that only crushed tomatoes can deliver.

SPAGHETTI AND MEATBALLS

WHAT WE WANTED: Moist, light meatballs and a tomato sauce that's easy to prepare yet packed with flavor.

Many cooks think of meatballs as hamburgers with seasonings (cheese, herbs, garlic) and a round shape. This is partly true. However, unlike hamburgers, which are best cooked rare or medium-rare, meatballs are cooked until well-done—at which point they've often turned into dry, tough golf balls.

Our goal was to create meatballs that were moist and light. We also wanted to develop a quick tomato sauce that was loaded with flavor. We focused on the meatballs first.

Meatballs start with ground meat but require additional ingredients to keep them moist and lighten their texture. Meatballs also require binders to keep them from falling apart in the tomato sauce.

A traditional source of moisture in meatballs is egg. We tested meatballs made with and without egg and quickly determined that the egg was a welcome addition. It made the meatballs both moister and lighter.

The list of possible binders included dried bread crumbs, fresh bread crumbs, ground crackers, and bread soaked in milk. We found that bread crumbs and ground crackers soaked up any available moisture, making the meatballs harder and drier when cooked to well-done. In comparison, the meatballs made with bread soaked in milk were moist, creamy, and rich. Milk was clearly an important part of the equation.

We liked the milk but wondered if we could do better. We tried adding yogurt but had to thin it with some milk in order to mix it with the bread. Meatballs made with thinned yogurt were even creamier and more flavorful than those made with plain milk. We also tried buttermilk, and the results were just as good, with no need to thin the liquid.

With the dairy now part of our working recipe, we found the meatball mixture a tad sticky and hard to handle. By eliminating the egg white (the yolk has all the fat and emulsifiers that contribute smoothness), we eliminated the stickiness.

It was finally time to experiment with the crucial ingredient: the meat. Ground round was too lean. We preferred fattier chuck in this recipe. We tried blending in some ground veal but decided it was not worth the bother; these meatballs tasted bland. Ground pork was another matter. It added another flavor dimension.

With our ingredients in order, it was time to test cooking methods. We tried roasting, broiling, and the traditional pan-frying. Roasting yielded dry, crumbly meatballs, while broiling was extremely messy and also tended to produce dry meatballs. Pan-frying produced meatballs with a rich, dark crust and moist texture.

We wondered if we could save some cleanup time and build more flavor into the tomato sauce by making it in the same pan used to fry the meatballs. We emptied out the vegetable oil used to fry the meatballs (olive oil is too expensive for this task and doesn't add much flavor), then added a little fresh olive oil (olive oil is important to the flavor of the sauce) before adding garlic and tomatoes. Not only did this method prove convenient, but it gave the sauce depth, as the browned bits that had formed when the meatballs were fried loosened from the pan bottom and dissolved in the sauce.

Meatballs need a thick, smooth sauce—the kind produced by canned crushed tomatoes. Sauces made with whole or diced tomatoes were too chunky and more liquidy; they didn't meld with the meatballs and made them soggy.

WHAT WE LEARNED: White bread soaked in buttermilk is the best binder for meatballs, giving them a creamy texture and an appealing tang. An egg yolk keeps meatballs moist and light, and a mixture of ground beef and ground pork tastes best. Pan-frying browns the exterior of the meatballs while keeping the interior moist. Finally, building the tomato sauce on top of the browned bits left in the pan after frying the meatballs makes for a hearty, robust-tasting sauce.

SPAGHETTI AND MEATBALLS serves 4 to 6

The shaped meatballs can be covered with plastic wrap and refrigerated for several hours ahead of serving time, if you like. Fry the meatballs and make the sauce at the last minute.

meatballs

2 slices white sandwich bread (crusts discarded), torn into small pieces
½ cup buttermilk or 6 tablespoons plain yogurt thinned with 2 tablespoons whole milk
1 pound ground meat (preferably ¾ pound ground chuck and ¼ pound ground pork)
¼ cup freshly grated Parmesan cheese
2 tablespoons finely minced fresh parsley leaves
1 large egg yolk
1 teaspoon finely minced garlic
¾ teaspoon salt
  Ground black pepper
  About 1¼ cups vegetable oil for pan-frying

smooth tomato sauce

2 tablespoons extra-virgin olive oil
1 teaspoon minced garlic
1 (28-ounce) can crushed tomatoes
1 tablespoon minced fresh basil leaves
  Salt and ground black pepper

1 pound spaghetti
  Freshly grated Parmesan cheese

1. FOR THE MEATBALLS: Combine bread and buttermilk in small bowl and let stand, mashing occasionally with fork, until smooth paste forms, about 10 minutes.

2. Place ground meat, cheese, parsley, egg yolk, garlic, salt, and pepper to taste in medium bowl. Add bread-milk mixture and combine until evenly mixed. Shape 3 tablespoons of mixture into 1½-inch-round meatball. (When forming meatballs use a light touch. If you compact the meatballs too

much, they can become dense and hard.) You should be able to form about 14 meatballs.

3. Pour vegetable oil into 10- or 11-inch sauté pan to depth of ¼ inch. Turn flame to medium-high. After several minutes, test oil with edge of meatball. When oil sizzles, add meatballs in single layer. Fry, turning several times, until nicely browned on all sides, about 10 minutes (see illustration below). Regulate heat as needed to keep oil sizzling but not smoking. Transfer browned meatballs to plate lined with paper towels and set aside.

4. Bring 4 quarts water to a boil in large pot for pasta.

5. FOR THE SAUCE: Meanwhile, discard oil in pan but leave behind any browned bits. Add olive oil for tomato sauce along with garlic and sauté over medium heat, scraping up browned bits, just until garlic is golden, about 30 seconds. Add tomatoes, bring to boil, and simmer gently until sauce thickens, about 10 minutes. Stir in basil and salt and pepper to taste. Add meatballs and simmer,

---

TECHNIQUE: Browning Meatballs

We found that meatballs taste best when browned evenly on all sides. Their round shape makes this a challenge. Our solution is to brown the two broader sides of the meatballs first and then use tongs to stand the meatballs on their sides. If necessary, lean the meatballs up against one another as they brown.

turning them occasionally, until heated through, about 5 minutes. Keep warm over low flame.

6. Meanwhile, add 1 tablespoon salt and pasta to boiling water. Cook until al dente, drain, and return to pot. Ladle several large spoonfuls of sauce (without meatballs) over spaghetti and toss until noodles are well coated. Divide pasta among individual bowls and top each with a little more tomato sauce and 2 or 3 meatballs. Serve immediately with grated cheese passed separately.

VARIATION

SPAGHETTI AND CHICKEN MEATBALLS

If you want to trim some fat from this recipe, ground chicken is a decent alternative to ground beef and pork. We found that meatballs made from chicken are a tad soft, so they must be refrigerated for an hour before being fried to keep them from sticking to the pan or falling apart.

Follow recipe for Spaghetti and Meatballs, replacing ground meat with 1 pound ground chicken. After shaping meatballs in step 2, place on platter, cover with plastic wrap, and refrigerate until firm, about 1 hour. Proceed as directed.

TASTING LAB: Parmesan Cheese

WHEN IT COMES TO GRATED PARMESAN CHEESE, THERE'S A wide range of options—everything from the whitish powder in green jars to imported cheese that costs $14 a pound. You can buy cheese that has been grated, or you can pick out a whole hunk and grate it yourself. We wondered if the "authentic" Parmigiano-Reggiano imported from Italy would be that much better when tasted side by side with a domestic Parmesan at half the price.

Parmesan is a *grana,* a hard, grainy cheese. The grana cheese category is composed mostly of Italian grating cheeses. Parmigiano-Reggiano is the most famous (and expensive) of the granas, and its manufacture dates back 800 years. Parmigiano-Reggiano has become an increasingly regulated product; in 1955 it became what is known as a certified name (not a brand name). Since that time the name has indicated that the cheese was made within a specific region of northern Italy and approved by a certifying consortium.

American cheese makers have been making Parmesan only since the beginning of the century and need not abide by any more stringent regulations than basic U.S. Department of Agriculture standards. There is no lack of pregrated products, but only a handful of domestic Parmesans come in wedges. Other granas considered Parmesan types are Grana Padano (from Italy) and Reggianito (from Argentina).

The samples in our tasting included five pregrated Parmesan cheeses (domestic and imported), three wedges of domestic Parmesan, a wedge of Grana Padano, one of Reggianito, and two of Parmigiano-Reggiano. To see if differences in storage and handling could affect the quality of the latter two, we purchased one at a specialty cheese store, where the humidity and temperature of the storage room are controlled and the wedges are cut from the wheel per order, and the other at a large supermarket, where the cheese is sold precut and wrapped in plastic. All of the cheeses were tasted grated, at room temperature.

To get an idea of what tasters might want to look for when tasting the different cheeses, we spoke to a number of cheese experts. All recommended that the tasters rate the cheeses on the basics: aroma, flavor (particularly depth of flavor and saltiness versus sweetness), and overall texture. The experts also said the Parmesans should be left to sit on tasters' tongues to see if they would melt smoothly into creaminess in the mouth. All of the experts we spoke to expressed confidence that Parmigiano-Reggiano would be the hands-down winner. This time the experts were correct. Parmigiano-Reggiano had a depth and complexity of flavor and a smooth, melting texture that none of the others could match.

Parmigiano-Reggiano owes much of its flavor to the unpasteurized milk used to produce it. It is a "controlled-district" cheese, which means not only that it must be made within the boundaries of this zone but also that the milk

weighs 75 to 90 pounds; domestic Parmesan wheels average 24 pounds.)

The low-salt content of Parmigiano-Reggiano makes it more perishable than other cheeses once cut from the wheel. Once cut, the cheese will also begin to dry out. This was evident in the Parmigiano-Reggiano sample purchased at the grocery store. Tasters rated this a few tenths of a point lower than the sample purchased at the specialty cheese store because of a chalky finish. This drying effect was even more glaring with the chalky pregrated products, which received consistently poor ratings.

Another benefit of the larger wheel is that it gives the cheese more time to age. Parmigiano-Reggiano ages for about 24 months, while domestic Parmesan ages for about 10 months. The longer aging allows more complex flavors and aromas to develop. The aging also makes a difference in texture, creating a distinctive component that tasters described as "crystal crunch." The crunch stems from proteins breaking down into free amino acid crystals during the latter half of the aging process. The crystals are visible, appearing as white dots in the cheese. No other Parmesan showed this effect.

Other textural differences are created by the fact that the curds for Parmigiano-Reggiano are cut into fragments the size of wheat grains, which is much finer than the fragments cut in the manufacture of domestic Parmesan. The benefit of smaller curds is that they drain more effectively. Domestic Parmesans are mechanically pressed to rid them of excess moisture. The consequence, as our tasting panel discovered with several domestic Parmesans that were not pregrated, is a cheese that is much more dense. Tasters characterized these cheeses as "rubbery," "tough," and "squeaky."

One domestic Parmesan scored well enough to be recommended. This was Wisconsin-made DiGiorno. The other less expensive options paled in comparison with the real thing. The pregrated cheeses received especially low ratings and harsh comments from our panel. Most were much too salty and marred by odd off flavors. Most everyone agreed that these poor imitations could actually ruin a dish.

used to make it and even the grass, hay, and grain fed to the cows that make the milk must come from the district. Consequently, just like good wine, a lot of character comes from the soil and climate where the cheese was made. In the tasting we found that none of the other cheeses had the sweet, nutty, creamy flavor of Parmigiano-Reggiano.

Most of the cheeses in the tasting—except the Parmigiano-Reggiano—were extremely salty. In fact, Parmigiano-Reggiano contains about two-thirds less sodium than the other Parmesans. This is because the wheels of Parmigiano-Reggiano are so large that they do not become as saturated with salt during the brining process that is one of the final steps in making the cheese. (The average wheel is about 9 inches high and 16 to 18 inches in diameter and

TASTING LAB: Jarred Tomato Sauces

WE WONDERED IF ANY TOMATO SAUCE FROM A JAR could compete with a simple homemade recipe. We assembled a sampling of 11 leading brands of marinara-style sauces containing tomatoes, garlic, herbs (usually basil and/or oregano), and sometimes onions and tasted them blind against our sauce.

While tasters clearly expressed varied preferences when it came to the ideal consistency of the sauces, they all agreed on the driving component—freshness of flavor. In this department, our homemade sauce was the only one considered to taste "extremely fresh" and the only one that tasters really liked. Several jarred sauces were deemed acceptable, but we judged the rest not worth eating.

We found several probable reasons for the stale taste of most of the jarred sauces. Apart from those which placed first and second (Barilla and Classico, respectively), all of the supermarket jarred tomato sauces listed tomato puree as their main ingredient and diced tomatoes second. We find that tomato puree diminishes the fresh tomato flavor. This results from the fact that puree is a concentrate requiring higher temperatures and longer cooking times to process than simple cooked tomatoes, whether whole or diced.

The freshness and purity of other ingredients in a sauce also contribute to the success of the final product. Barilla, a market leader in pasta and jarred sauces in Italy, uses primarily fresh ingredients that are diced at the plant. Some other producers use dried spices and even dried vegetables. Barilla's sauce is minimally cooked, really just enough to prevent the growth of bacteria. The problem for many manufacturers, however, is not excessive cooking but the prolonged time that a sauce stays hot before it is jarred and cooled. To avoid this, Barilla expedites the final stage by rapidly cooling the sauce and filling the jars.

A few of the sauces tried to make up for their deficiency in tomato flavor with excessive sweetness. These efforts failed. Our tasters typically labeled these sauces as

"kids' food." Notably, Barilla and Classico were the only supermarket brands to put onions before sugar (or corn syrup in some cases) on their list of ingredients.

In the end, most jarred tomato sauces don't taste very good. Some are acceptable; most are not.

GARLIC BREAD

WHAT WE WANTED: Crisp toasted bread with sweet, nutty garlic flavor.

So simple to make, yet so often a soggy, greasy disappointment, garlic bread should have a lightly toasted surface with a crisp crust that shatters when bitten. The bread within should be warm and chewy, light and yet substantial. Butter, which we chose over olive oil for this American-style bread, should be plentiful but not excessive, and the garlic flavor should be full and prominent without being harsh. But garlic bread rarely lives up to this ideal. Sometimes there is so much garlic you can taste it for days; other times there is so little you can't taste it at all. Worse yet, the bread is often completely saturated with butter.

We started out by tasting several garlic breads made according to different recipes and methods. From this came an interesting revelation: Even though most of the breads had too little garlic oomph (they ranged from a single clove to six cloves per 1-pound loaf of bread), all the tasters complained about the raw garlic flavor in every recipe. We definitely had to deal with this. Tasters made several other helpful observations. First, there was unanimous preference for wide loaves of bread, such as Italian, which yielded large slices. Second, tasters preferred their loaf sliced with the insides exposed to the oven to crisp up rather than cut in vertical slices left attached at the bottom, as specified in many recipes. The latter method left the slices soggy and a bit harsh-tasting.

The cry for a full, resonant garlic flavor necessitated the use of many more cloves than the usual two or three. But upping the ante created another problem—near overpowering harshness from all that raw garlic. Because the flavor of garlic mellows with heat, precooking seemed like a good plan.

To keep the testing consistent, we used six medium garlic cloves (about two tablespoons), minced, per 1-pound loaf of bread and tried two methods of precooking the garlic. First, we sautéed minced garlic in butter, but the resulting bread lacked character and depth, failing to win over any of the tasters. Next, we tried toasting unpeeled cloves in a dry skillet over medium heat until they were just fragrant. This cooked the garlic just enough to highlight its rich, sweet, nutty flavor, and the resulting bread was judged a unanimous winner. After a few experiments, we settled on 8 minutes of toasting; at 10 minutes the garlic was a little too docile, and at 5 minutes it still had more raw punch than we liked.

Toasting allowed us to use far more garlic than recipes generally allow. Most tasters favored 10 medium cloves, which equaled three generous tablespoons, minced, for each 1-pound loaf.

Not surprising for a dish largely about bread, the type of bread used makes a huge difference. The whole wheat and sourdough loaves we tried tasted out of place, and the long, narrow shape and relatively open texture of French bread produced slices that were too small to be truly satisfying. So we stuck with football-shaped loaves of hearty white Italian bread. We found it worthwhile to buy the highest quality loaf available to us. The sturdy texture, satisfying chew, and well-developed yeasty flavor of the bakery-purchased, artisan Italian loaves we tried made the supermarket variety seem fluffy, unsubstantial, and bland.

The right amount of butter would make the garlic bread moist, not soggy or saturated. Many recipes call for a stick or more, which made the bread spongy and slightly greasy. Less butter—6 tablespoons—did the trick, giving the bread ample richness without marring its texture. Melting the butter proved unnecessary, while also adding to the process an unnecessary step and utensil (a brush to distribute it on the bread). Softened butter that we could spread easily with a rubber spatula worked best.

We also checked out an arsenal of additional ingredients common to many recipes. Red wine, olive oil, paprika, hot pepper sauce, cayenne, garlic powder, garlic salt, mustard, and lemon juice all failed to impress, but 2 tablespoons of grated Parmesan cheese added depth and complexity without interfering with the garlic flavor. Even for the basic recipe, we recommend the cheese. You won't even know it's there but for the subtle flavor boost it gives the bread.

The last areas of inquiry were the cooking method and temperature. Many recipes recommend wrapping the loaf in foil for all or part of the baking time. Our tests proved foil wrapping to be a counterproductive extra step. We consistently found the wrapped breads to be soggy, with a slightly harsh flavor and an unwelcome steamed taste. It turned out that exposing the cut-and-buttered surface to the oven heat helped to mellow the garlic's flavor by dehydrating the molecules somewhat. This changes their structure and, with it, their flavor. Wrapping the loaf in foil, or for that matter reassembling it so the cut sides faced each other, deprived

the garlic of some heat, thereby diminishing the desirable flavor change.

The oven setting most commonly listed in the recipes we looked at was 350 degrees, but that wasn't hot enough to give the bread the supercrisp, toasted exterior layer we were after. We tested and retested, increasing the temperature by 25 degrees each time until getting to 500 degrees, which produced a beautifully crunchy crust and a nicely browned surface in just nine minutes or so, with no broiling involved. We did find it necessary to set the bread on a baking sheet, though, to avoid scorching the bottom.

WHAT WE LEARNED: Toast whole garlic cloves to tame their harshness. Use softened butter rather than melted butter. Add a bit of Parmesan cheese for depth and complexity of flavor. Select a football-shaped loaf of Italian bread, slice it horizontally, and then leave the bread unwrapped as it bakes to achieve the crispiest crust.

AMERICAN GARLIC BREAD serves 6 to 8

Plan to pull the garlic bread from the oven when you are ready to serve the other dishes. Garlic bread is best served piping hot.

9–10 medium cloves garlic (about the size of a plump cashew nut), skins left on
6 tablespoons unsalted butter, softened
2 tablespoons grated Parmesan cheese
½ teaspoon salt
1 whole loaf high-quality Italian bread (about 1 pound, football-shaped), halved lengthwise
Ground black pepper

1. Adjust oven rack to middle position and heat oven to 500 degrees. Meanwhile, toast garlic cloves in small skillet over medium heat, shaking pan occasionally, until fragrant and color of cloves deepens slightly, about 8 minutes (see illustration at right). When cool enough to handle, skin and mince cloves (you should have about 3 tablespoons). Using dinner fork, mash garlic, butter, cheese, and salt in small bowl until thoroughly combined.

2. Spread cut sides of loaf evenly with butter mixture; season to taste with pepper. Transfer loaf halves, buttered side up, onto rimmed baking sheet; bake, reversing position of baking sheet in oven from front to back halfway through baking time, until surface of bread is golden brown and toasted, 5 to 10 minutes. Cut each half into 2-inch slices; serve immediately.

VARIATIONS
CHIPOTLE GARLIC BREAD

Canned chipotle chiles packed in adobo sauce add a smoky, spicy flavor that made this the hands-down favorite of everyone who tasted these variations.

Follow recipe for American Garlic Bread, mashing 1½ chipotle chiles en adobo (about 1 tablespoon) and 1 teaspoon adobo sauce into garlic butter mixture. Increase baking time by a minute or two.

HERB GARLIC BREAD

Follow recipe for American Garlic Bread, mashing 1 tablespoon each minced fresh basil and chives and ½ tablespoon each minced fresh thyme and oregano into garlic butter mixture.

PARMESAN AND ASIAGO CHEESE GARLIC BREAD

Follow recipe for American Garlic Bread, decreasing salt to ¼ teaspoon, increasing Parmesan cheese to ¼ cup, and mashing ¼ cup grated Asiago cheese and 2 teaspoons Dijon mustard into butter along with garlic.

EQUIPMENT CORNER: Bread Knives

A BREAD KNIFE SHOULD EASILY BREAK THROUGH THE top crust on a loaf, no matter how thick that crust is. It should also slice neatly through the crumb, clean through to the bottom of the loaf. Finally, the handle should provide enough space for fingers, especially as you get close to the bottom of the loaf. Ideally, you won't scrape your knuckles

TECHNIQUE: Dry-Toasting Garlic

Place unpeeled garlic cloves in a dry skillet over medium heat. Toast, shaking the pan occasionally, until the skins are golden brown, about 8 minutes.

against the cutting board every time you cut through bread.

To find out which features really matter, we tested 10 bread knives, slicing through 30 loaves of crusty peasant bread, five dozen bagels, and 25 pounds of tomatoes, whose surprisingly tough skin is a perfect subject for serrated knives. Here's what we learned.

When it comes to a bread knife, we found that longer is better. Knives with 10-inch blades could cut through the entire width of a medium-sized peasant bread. The 8-inch blades were particularly frustrating because the tips of their blades tended to catch in the crumb of loaves.

There are two different styles of serration—pointed and wavy. On blades with pointed serrations, the points touch the food first. Between each point is an arched cutting edge that helps the knife cut through foods once the points have made contact. Wavy serrations are just the opposite—the arched cutting edges make up most of the cutting blade.

We found that pointed serrations give a blade a good grip on tough crusts, allowing the knife to cut into loaves easily. The points also preserve overall blade sharpness because they are the first part of the knife to touch all surfaces—be it a bread crust or a cutting board—thereby minimizing the contact the rest of the edge has with any surface. Our favorite knives had pointed serrations, although knives with extremely pronounced serrations caught on tomato skins and soft bread and caused some ripping.

With wavy serrations, more of the cutting edge comes into contact with the food. In our tests on crusty bread, this blade type failed to get the same sure grip as knives with pointed serrations. The wavy serrations tended to slide a little more than we liked, especially when trying to make that initial cut into a crusty loaf.

Another important aspect of blade design is the curvature of the cutting edge. We found that curved cutting edges allow for a gentle rocking motion that helps cut through tough bottom crusts and separates each slice neatly. By contrast, knives with straight cutting edges required more manipulation—sometimes sawing with the tip of the blade, twisting, and even ripping—to get through the bottom crust and free the slice. A slightly curved blade also allows a little extra room under the handle for fingers.

In terms of flexibility, we found that knives with very flexible blades can be unsteady when trying to slice through thick crusts. Rigid blades are more stable and easier to work with.

Finally, our test cooks preferred textured plastic handles to wood because the former felt especially stable in the hand. More important, our testers liked knives with handles that were offset, or raised above the blade. This design keeps fingers above the level of the cutting board, preventing knuckle scrapes even when cutting through the bottom crust.

BREAD KNIVES

Bread knives can have curved (top) or straight (bottom) cutting edges. In our tests, we found that a curved cutting edge allows for a gentle rocking motion that helps cut through tough bottom crusts. Knives with straight cutting edges require more sawing, twisting, and tearing to separate slices of bread.

SCIENCE DESK: Taming Garlic

HUNDREDS OF CHEMICAL COMPOUNDS ARE RESPONSIBLE for the flavor and odor of garlic. The two harshest tasting and smelling chemical groups, glucose inolates and sulfur-containing isothiocyanates, are activated when the garlic cloves are cut, but they are also the first to dissipate when the garlic is heated. Heat, therefore, tames the harshness of garlic, eliminating its unpleasant raw edge and helping to accentuate its sweet, nutty flavors.

Raquel uses a long-handled peel to slide a thin-crust pizza into a hot oven. If you don't own a peel, use a rimless baking sheet or the back of a rimmed baking sheet to move thin-crust pizza in and out of the oven.

PIZZA *night*

CHAPTER 4

Good pizza can be defined largely by what it is not. A good pizza is neither puffy, bland white bread under a sea of overly sweet tomato sauce nor tough cardboard stamped into a circle and topped with a mountain of blistering, rubbery, tasteless cheese. A good pizza is not damp, molten, saucy, greasy, or messy. Unfortunately, most pizza parlor pies fall into at least one of the above categories. Matters become even worse once you start talking about takeout pizza. Sure, it's nice to have a hot pizza delivered to your door in 30 minutes. But when that pizza tastes like a chemical-laden sponge, we think convenience has come at too high a price.

Thankfully, good pizza can be made at home. As long as you invest $15 in a large ceramic pizza stone, a regular home oven can turn out remarkably good pies. In the test kitchen, we are evenly divided into two camps—those who like their pizza thick and rich and those who like it light and lean. To satisfy everyone, we've developed two pizza recipes—a deep-dish pizza that bakes in a pan as well as a cracker-thin pie that's in and out of the oven in just 10 minutes.

DEEP-DISH PIZZA

WHAT WE WANTED: Something better than take-out pizza that wouldn't require Herculean effort.

Deep-dish pizza is about 75 percent crust, so the crust must be great. We wanted it to be rich, substantial, and moist, with a tender, yet slightly chewy crumb and a well-developed flavor, like that of a good loaf of bread. We also thought a crust should be crisp and nicely browned without being dry or tough. Knowing how time-consuming pizza making can be, we also wanted a pizza dough that could be made in as little time as possible without sacrificing quality.

After scouring various cookbooks, the test kitchen made five different pizza doughs and baked them in deep-dish pans. To our disappointment, none delivered the flavorful, crisp brown crust that we felt was needed.

After these initial tests, we tried dozens of variations. We played around with the ratio of water to flour, the amount of oil, the type of flour, and just about every other variable we could think of. But we weren't satisfied until we finally widened the field and tried a recipe for focaccia that used boiled, riced potatoes to add moisture and flavor to the dough. This dough was just what we were hoping for: very wet and yet easy to handle, light, and smooth. When baked, it was soft and moist, yet with a bit of chew, sturdiness, and structure that was not present in the previous doughs.

Now that we had found a dough that we liked, the challenge was to come up with a rising and baking method suited to deep-dish pizza. We placed the pizza dough in a barely warmed oven for the first rise, reducing the initial rising time from 1 hour to 35 minutes and producing dough that tasted no different from the dough that rose at room temperature for a full hour.

Next we tried reducing—even eliminating—the amount of time allowed for the second rise. The dough given a full 30 minutes of rising time was vastly better than doughs given a second rise of only 15 minutes or given no second rise at all. The flavor was more complex, and the texture of the pizza crust was softer and lighter, making this second rise too important to pass up or shorten.

After some testing, we discovered that a crust baked at 425 degrees in a pan placed on a baking stone was almost perfect; the bottom and sides of the pizza were well-browned, and the interior crumb was moist, light, and evenly cooked through. The exterior of this crust was, however, slightly tough. To combat this, we began lining the pizza pan with oil. After some experimentation, we found that the pizzas made with a generous amount of oil lining the pan (¼ cup was optimal) had a far more desirable crust than those made with little or no oil in the pan. Lightly "frying" the dough in the pan made for a rich, caramelized exterior; this added a good amount of flavor and a secondary texture to the crust, without drying it out or making it tough.

Now it was time for the toppings. On most pizzas, the toppings can simply be placed on raw dough and baked, since the crust bakes in about the same amount of time as the toppings. But we found that the weight of the toppings prevented the crust from rising in the oven, resulting in a dense, heavy crust, especially in the center of the pie. So we tried prebaking crusts from 5 minutes up to 15 minutes to develop some structure before adding the toppings. The pizza prebaked for 15 minutes, then topped, was perfect. This scheme gave the pizza a chance at an initial rise in the oven without the weight or moisture of the toppings, and the toppings had just enough time to melt and brown by the time the crust was baked through.

WHAT WE LEARNED: Add potato to the dough for a soft, chewy crust and prebake the crust before adding the toppings to encourage maximum rise.

DEEP-DISH PIZZA makes one 14-inch pizza, serving 4 to 6

Prepare the topping while the dough is rising so the two will be ready at the same time. Baking the pizza in a deep-dish pan on a hot pizza stone will help produce a crisp, well-browned bottom crust. If you don't have a pizza stone, use a heavy rimless baking sheet (do not use an insulated baking sheet). If you have only a rimmed baking sheet, turn it upside down and bake the pizza on the rimless side. The amount of oil used to grease the pan may seem excessive, but it helps brown the crust while also preventing sticking.

1	medium baking potato (about 9 ounces), peeled and quartered
3½	cups (17.5 ounces) unbleached all-purpose flour
1½	teaspoons rapid-rise or instant yeast
1¾	teaspoons salt
1	cup (8 ounces) warm water (105 to 115 degrees)
6	tablespoons extra-virgin olive oil, plus more for oiling bowl
1	recipe topping (recipes follow)

1. Bring 1 quart water and potato to boil in a small saucepan over medium-high heat; cook until tender, 10 to 15 minutes. Drain and cool until potato can be handled comfortably; press through fine disk on potato ricer or grate through large holes on box grater. Measure 1⅓ cups lightly packed potato; discard remaining potato.

2. Adjust one oven rack to highest position, other rack to lowest; heat oven to 200 degrees. Once oven reaches 200 degrees, maintain heat for 10 minutes, then turn off heat.

3. Combine flour, yeast, and salt in workbowl of food processor fitted with steel blade. With motor running, add water and process until dough comes together in a shaggy ball. Add 2 tablespoons oil and process several more seconds, until dough is smooth and slightly sticky. Transfer dough to

lightly oiled medium bowl, turn to coat with oil, and cover tightly with plastic wrap. Place in warm oven until dough is soft and spongy and doubled in size, 30 to 35 minutes.

4. Oil bottom of 14-inch deep-dish pizza pan with remaining 4 tablespoons olive oil. Remove dough from oven and gently punch down; turn dough onto clean, dry work surface and pat into 12-inch round. Transfer round to oiled pan, cover with plastic wrap, and let rest until dough no longer resists shaping, about 10 minutes.

5. Place pizza stone or rimless baking sheet on low oven rack (do not use insulated baking sheet; see note) and heat oven to 500 degrees. Uncover dough and pull up into edges and up sides of pan to form 1-inch-high lip. Cover with plastic wrap; let rise in warm draft-free spot until doubled in size, about 30 minutes. Uncover dough and prick generously with fork. Reduce oven temperature to 425, place pan with pizza on preheated stone or baking sheet, and bake until dry and lightly browned, about 15 minutes. Add desired toppings; bake on stone or baking sheet until cheese melts, 10 to 15 minutes (5 to 10 minutes for 10-inch pizzas). Move pizza to top rack and bake until cheese is spotty golden brown, about 5 minutes longer. Let cool 5 minutes, then, holding pizza pan at angle with one hand, use wide spatula to slide pizza from pan to cutting board. Cut into wedges and serve.

VARIATIONS

10-INCH DEEP-DISH PIZZAS
If you don't own a 14-inch deep-dish pizza pan, divide the dough between two 10-inch cake pans.

Follow recipe for Deep-Dish Pizza through step 3. Grease bottom of two 10-inch cake pans with 2 tablespoons olive

oil each. Turn dough onto clean, dry work surface and divide in half. Pat each half into 9-inch round; continue with recipe, reducing initial baking time on lowest rack to 5 to 10 minutes and dividing topping evenly between pizzas.

FRESH TOMATO TOPPING WITH MOZZARELLA AND BASIL

    4   medium ripe tomatoes (about 1½ pounds),
        cored, seeded, and cut into 1-inch pieces
    2   medium cloves garlic, minced
        Salt and ground black pepper
    6   ounces whole milk mozzarella cheese, shredded
        (about 1½ cups)
 1¼   ounces Parmesan cheese, grated (about ½ cup)
    3   tablespoons shredded fresh basil leaves

1. Mix together tomatoes and garlic in medium bowl; season to taste with salt and pepper and set aside.

2. Top partially baked crust evenly with tomato mixture, followed by mozzarella, then Parmesan. Bake as directed in step 5 of recipe for Deep-Dish Pizza. Scatter basil over fully baked pizza before cutting into wedges.

FOUR-CHEESE TOPPING WITH PESTO
For the pesto, follow the recipe on page 15 for Bow-Tie Pasta with Pesto through step 4.

    ½   cup pesto
    6   ounces mozzarella cheese, shredded
        (about 1½ cups)
    4   ounces provolone cheese, shredded (about 1 cup)
 1¼   ounces grated Parmesan cheese (about ½ cup)
 1¼   ounces blue cheese (about ¼ cup, crumbled)

Spread partially baked crust evenly with pesto; sprinkle with mozzarella, followed by provolone, Parmesan, and blue cheese. Bake as directed in step 5 of recipe for Deep-Dish Pizza.

TASTING LAB: Mozzarella Cheese

IF YOU'RE GOING TO THE TROUBLE OF MAKING YOUR own pizza, you certainly don't want to wreck things by using inferior mozzarella. We wondered if you could use preshredded cheese or whether premium buffalo mozzarella (made from water buffalo milk and imported from Italy) was worth the added expense. Could you even compare these cheeses?

To find out which kinds of mozzarella work best in pizza, tasters sampled six different brands, including three shrink-wrapped low-moisture cheeses from the supermarket (two made from whole milk, one from part skim milk), a preshredded part-skim cheese also from the supermarket, one salted fresh mozzarella made at a local cheese shop, and one salted fresh buffalo mozzarella imported from Italy. We sampled each cheese raw and cooked on a deep-dish pizza. Tasters were asked to rate each cheese on overall flavor (both raw and melted), texture, and melting properties.

When tasted raw, the results were quite clear. Tasters liked the gamey, barnyard flavor of the buffalo mozzarella. The fresh cow's milk mozzarella also performed quite well. Among the supermarket cheeses, there was a clear bias for the whole milk cheeses over those made with part skim milk. The preshredded cheese had a rubbery texture and grainy mouthfeel. (Most tasters noted that even when cooked it was chalky or grainy.) Preshredded cheese is coated with powdered cellulose to prevent clumping. Some tasters felt that the preshredded cheese was drier, attributable to the cellulose or from having been shredded months ago.

Tasted on pizzas, the cheeses produced the same results (at least in terms of flavor), but moisture was now a factor. The fresh cheeses exuded a lot of liquid that flooded the surface of the pizza. Unless the fresh mozzarella is pressed of excess liquid before cooking (we had success weighting the shredded cheese for an hour prior to cooking in a strainer set in a bowl), it is unsuitable for pizza.

Because most cooks (ourselves included) don't want to weight cheese, we think the shrink-wrapped supermarket cheeses make more sense for sprinkling on pizzas. Stick with a whole milk cheese and try to choose a brand with a bit more moisture than the rest of the pack. Our favorite supermarket cheese was Calabro brand whole milk mozzarella (from Connecticut), which was softer and moister than the other supermarket offerings. Certainly, don't use preshredded cheese. The convenience is simply not worth the sacrifice in taste and texture.

SCIENCE DESK: How Yeast Works

YEAST IS A PLANT-LIKE LIVING ORGANISM. ITS FUNCTION in a bread dough is to consume sugars and starches in the flour and convert them into carbon dioxide and alcohol, which give bread its lift and flavor. This process is known as fermentation. Flavor compounds and alcohol—byproducts of fermentation—give bread its characteristic aroma and flavor.

A small amount of honey or sugar is sometimes added to bread dough to enhance the fermentation process—yeast grows faster and better when it has enough sugar to feed on. Warm water (about 110 degrees) is also necessary to activate dry yeast. Very warm water (in excess of 130 degrees) will kill the yeast, and yeast will not activate well in cool water.

Heat is generated during fermentation and rising, and punching the dough down mixes the warmer dough (in the center) with the cooler dough (on the outside edges), thus normalizing the overall temperature. Punching down also releases any excess carbon dioxide, breaks apart yeast particles that are clinging together, and redistributes the sugars, giving the yeast a refreshed food source. After punching down, the dough is often given a second rise, which happens more quickly since there is more yeast at work.

During the first few minutes of baking, the alcohol (formed earlier during fermentation) evaporates, gasses expand, and bubbles enlarge, fostering more rise. This is referred to as oven spring. The yeast cells are killed off during the first few minutes in the oven.

THIN-CRUST PIZZA

WHAT WE WANTED: A crackling-crisp pizza with big flavor that could be rolled superthin with a minimum of effort.

We think a pizza should be thick, soft, and chewy (like our deep-dish pizza) or thin and crisp—not in between. Our goal for thin-crust pizza was simple: a shatteringly crisp, wafer-thin crust with a deeply caramelized flavor and no trace of raw yeast or flour and toppings that were sleek, light, and off the charts in flavor.

We knew that this crust must not only taste remarkably good, it must be easy to produce and cooperative as well. Pizza is casual fare and should shape up easily. Our first inclination, therefore, was to advance to the food processor and give it a whirl against the standing mixer and hand methods. It buried the competition for ease and speed, producing gorgeous, supple doughs in about 30 seconds, or faster than you could say "large pepperoni."

We were keen to make a big, free-form pizza, and we knew that a thin crust would need every bit of conventional oven heat it could get in the 10 minutes or so it would take to bake. That meant 500 degrees and a giant pizza stone with an hour's head start to preheat. (Though we tested a slightly lower oven heat as well, the extra minutes the pizza needed to brown left the finished crust more tough than crisp.) Wanting the crackerlike simplicity of a rich burnished crust, we dressed the pizzas with sauce and mozzarella only.

A handful of the pizza recipes we reviewed offered ideas that contributed significantly to the success of our final recipe. Overnight fermentation (the dough's first long rise) in the refrigerator was a key first precept. The dough is put to bed in chilly quarters—where it rises at its leisure—and is then stretched and baked the following day.

The chilled, rested dough handled easily, having become more pliant and less sticky in the intervening hours. Even better, we could toss the dough into the fridge and forget about it altogether until the next day—we didn't need to wait around to punch it down after a two- or three-hour rise at room temperature. By letting the dough rest overnight, we were also able to use less yeast and gain more flavor from fermentation. As a result of using warm water to make the dough, the yeast got enough of a jump to take off in the cold climate of the refrigerator. The refrigerated dough holds for up to two days without depleting the energy of just ½ teaspoon of yeast. (Granted, this approach removes home pizza making from the world of whimsy and impulse, but the fact that the dough was so easy to handle and the baked pizza so flavorful and crisp more than made up for the delay.)

The second precept was that a soft, supple, and frankly moist dough produces a light, crisp crust. This proved true time after time. Surprisingly, and to our everlasting relief, moist doughs were also easier to work with than drier ones.

Having long been fans of the neo-Neapolitan-style pizza, which is just a couple of hairs thinner than the original thin-crust pizza of Naples, we knew the only instrument equal to the task of achieving a crust as thin as a credit card was a rolling pin. Armed with our overnight-rested, food-processor dough and a tapered French rolling pin, we lightly dusted a large sheet of parchment paper with flour and commenced rolling as one would with a pie dough.

The dough was fully compliant under the pin until we made an effort to turn it like a regular pie dough. At that point, the dough gripped the parchment for dear life. Though it continued to roll thinner and wider, we could not shake it loose from the parchment. A potentially maddening situation morphed into a saving grace when we realized the parchment could accompany the dough to the oven. As the pizza baked, it loosened from the paper automatically, and the stone remained clean. Best yet, the tackiness of the dough held it securely to the parchment, preventing it from springing and shrinking back and eliminating the need for excess flouring when rolling out.

Eventually, we refined this technique by positioning an 18-inch piece of plastic wrap directly onto the top surface of the dough during rolling. Thus insulated, the dough could be rolled effortlessly and flipped about like a sandwich. It did not dry out. Once the dough was rolled, the plastic wrap peeled off easily; the thin round could be dressed and hurried into the oven without further ado.

While Americans have a propensity for using high-protein flour in breads, our research indicated that Italians use fairly soft flour. Here at the test kitchen, King Arthur all-purpose is generally our flour of choice. A fairly strong all-purpose flour with no chemical additives, King Arthur has outstanding flavor. We had been using it throughout testing, occasionally in combination with softer flours such as cake or rye to lighten the dough (these flour combinations produced unexceptional pizzas). But doughs made exclusively with King Arthur were occasionally less than cracker-crisp, especially during damp weather.

At the suggestion of Maggie Glezer, a baker certified by the American Institute of Baking and a wizard with yeast, we switched from King Arthur all-purpose flour at 11.7 percent protein to Gold Medal unbleached all-purpose flour at 10.5 percent protein. Flours with a higher protein content require more vigorous kneading to create structure in the dough and more water to achieve proper hydration. The lower-protein Gold Medal flour yielded uniformly light doughs that were as full-flavored as those made with King Arthur.

Working initially with measures of volume—2 cups flour to ¾ cup water—the results became unpredictable enough to convince us to switch to weights. We discovered stunning discrepancies between liquid measuring cups at that volume (up to a tablespoon), and with our meager dough ball, a few drops of water more or less made quite an impact.

We found that thin-crust pizzas are best topped simply—tomato sauce and good mozzarella are sufficient. If you want to get fancier, tread carefully. A thin crust cannot bear the weight and water of raw vegetables or a stifling canopy of four cheeses. During their stay in the oven, the crust and topping must become one, sustaining temperatures

that drive off moisture as they toast the crust mahogany, bake the sauce to a lacquer, and graft cheese to the top. If you want to add some embellishments, try caramelized onions, roasted mushrooms, or strips of roasted red peppers added before baking. Thin-crust pizza can also be "flavored" after baking with a thin layer of pesto or tapenade, arugula tossed with olive oil, or thin medallions of goat cheese.

A final note or two: Force of habit persuaded us to transfer the hot, sliced pizza to a cooling rack. Though the pizza rarely survived long enough to underscore the merits of this method, on the occasions that it did, the air circulating under the crust kept it crisp. In fact, the crusts generally became more crisp in the few minutes after being removed from the oven—like a cookie might. And although a 14-inch pizza may sound extra-large, one of these will satisfy only two restrained, polite adults.

WHAT WE LEARNED: Use a low-protein, unbleached all-purpose flour, let the dough rise slowly overnight in the refrigerator, and roll the dough between parchment and plastic to prevent sticking and the need for additional flour.

CRISP THIN-CRUST PIZZA makes two 14-inch pizzas

All-purpose unbleached flour with a protein percentage no higher than 10.5, such as Gold Medal, makes the lightest, crispiest pizzas. We recommend weighing the flour and water, but because many factors affect the flour's capacity to absorb water, heed visual and tactile clues to achieve a dough with the proper consistency. For rolling out the dough, we prefer commercial-sized parchment paper sheets, though parchment sold in rolls 14 inches wide also works. Keep in mind that it is more important for the rolled dough to be of even thinness than to be a perfect circle. For topping the pizzas, we recommend buying whole milk mozzarella and shredding it by hand with a box grater; do not use fresh or prepackaged shredded mozzarella, and resist the temptation to sprinkle on more cheese than is recommended.

2	cups (10 ounces) unbleached all-purpose flour, preferably Gold Medal or Pillsbury, protein content no higher than 10.5 percent
½	teaspoon rapid-rise or instant yeast
½	teaspoon honey
½	teaspoon salt
¾	cup plus 2 teaspoons (6.2 ounces) water, preferably filtered or spring, 100 to 105 degrees
¼	cup olive oil
1	cup Quick Tomato Sauce for Pizza (recipe follows)
8	ounces whole milk mozzarella, shredded (about 2 cups)

day 1

1. Combine flour, yeast, honey, and salt in workbowl of food processor fitted with steel blade. With machine running, add all but 2 teaspoons water through feed tube. With machine still running, add olive oil through feed tube and process until dough forms ball, about 30 seconds. Turn dough out onto work surface. Use technique recommended on page 45 to see if dough needs more water and to finish kneading.

2. Divide dough in half and place each piece in gallon-sized, heavy-duty zipper-lock plastic bag and seal. Refrigerate overnight or up to 48 hours.

day 2

1. Adjust oven rack to lowest position, set baking stone on rack, and heat oven to 500 degrees. Heat baking stone 1 hour before proceeding.

2. Remove dough from plastic bags. Set each half in center of lightly floured large sheet parchment paper. Cover each with two 18-inch lengths plastic wrap overlapping in center (alternatively, use one 18-inch length of extrawide plastic wrap); let doughs rest 10 minutes.

3. Setting one dough aside, roll the other into 14-inch round with even thinness of ⅟₃₂ inch, using tackiness of dough against parchment to help roll. If parchment wrinkles, flip dough sandwich over and smooth wrinkles with metal dough scraper.

4. Peel plastic wrap off top of rolled dough. Use soup spoon to spread and smooth ½ cup tomato sauce to edges of dough. Sprinkle with about 1 cup cheese. With scissors, trim excess parchment so that it is just larger than dough.

5. Slip dough with parchment onto pizza peel, inverted rimmed baking sheet, or rimless baking sheet. Slide pizza, parchment and all, onto hot baking stone. Bake until deep golden brown, about 10 minutes. Remove from oven with pizza peel or pull parchment with pizza onto baking sheet. Transfer pizza to cutting board, slide parchment out from under pizza; cut pizza into wedges and slide onto wire rack. Let cool 2 minutes until crisp; serve.

6. While first pizza is baking, repeat steps 3 and 4 to roll and sauce second pizza; allow baking stone to reheat 15 minutes after baking first pizza, then repeat step 5 to bake second pizza.

CRISP THIN-CRUST PIZZA WITH ARUGULA

Since dressed arugula will wilt, it's best to prepare the topping for each pizza as needed. For two pizzas, double the amounts listed below.

Toss 5 ounces arugula, stemmed (about 1 cup lightly packed), with 1 tablespoon extra-virgin olive oil and salt and pepper to taste. Follow recipe for Crisp Thin-Crust Pizza, preparing pizza as directed and baking for 8 minutes. Sprinkle arugula over pizza and return to oven for 2 minutes more. Slice as directed and cool.

CRISP THIN-CRUST PIZZA WITH TAPENADE

For best presentation, spoon eight equal portions of tapenade (each about 1 teaspoon) evenly over baked pizza and cut so each slice has one portion. You can do the same thing with pesto (see recipe on page 15 and follow steps 1 through 4).

Follow recipe for Crisp Thin-Crust Pizza, spooning 8 teaspoons Tapenade (recipe follows) over each pizza as soon as it comes out of the oven.

QUICK TOMATO SAUCE FOR PIZZA

makes about 1 ½ cups

For pizza, you want the smoothest possible sauce. Start with crushed tomatoes and puree them in a food processor before cooking the tomatoes with garlic and oil. This recipe makes a bit more sauce than needed to sauce two thin-crust pizzas.

1   can (14.5 ounces) crushed tomatoes
1   large clove garlic, minced or pressed through garlic press
1   tablespoon olive oil
    Salt and ground black pepper

1. Process tomatoes in workbowl of food processor fitted with steel blade until smooth, about five 1-second pulses.

2. Heat garlic and oil in medium saucepan over medium heat until garlic is sizzling, about 40 seconds. Stir in tomatoes; bring to simmer and cook, uncovered, until sauce thickens enough to coat wooden spoon, about 15 minutes. Season to taste with salt and pepper.

TECHNIQUE: How to Achieve the Proper Dough Consistency

  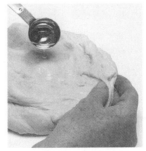 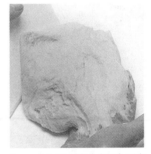

A freshly processed dough with adequate water will look shaggy and stick to the counter. A few "throws" against the counter will help the dough become supple and fine-textured.

A freshly processed dough that is too dry will form a clean ball, feel more oily than moist, and look slightly curdy on the surface.

To moisten a processed dough that is too dry, add 1 teaspoon water and throw the dough against the counter 10 times. The dough may take up to 2 teaspoons additional water.

A properly kneaded dough with enough water will be supple and fine-textured. Though moist and sticky, the dough should have structure and not feel "batter-like."

TAPENADE *makes 1 cup*

Spread extra tapenade on small toasts for a quick appetizer or use tapenade as a sandwich spread—it works especially well with fresh mozzarella and either sliced tomatoes or roasted peppers.

3	tablespoons extra-virgin olive oil
1½	cups pitted kalamata olives
2	tablespoons shredded fresh basil leaves
2	teaspoons fresh rosemary leaves
1	tablespoon capers, rinsed
4	anchovy fillets, rinsed

Place ingredients in workbowl of food processor. Process, stopping as necessary to scrape down sides of bowl, until mixture is finely minced and forms a chunky paste, about 1 minute. Transfer mixture to small bowl. (Surface of tapenade can be covered with plastic wrap or film of olive oil and refrigerated for up to 3 days.)

THIN-CRUST PIZZA ON HOLD

OUR RECIPE MAKES TWO PAPER-THIN 14-INCH PIZZAS. If you're hungry for just one pizza, make the full recipe anyway. Roll out both doughs, but roll one of them to 15 inches. Dress the dough rolled to the standard 14 inches with sauce and topping and bake it; poke the larger dough everywhere with a fork, but leave it undressed. Bake the undressed dough on the stone for 2 minutes, then remove it from the parchment and cool it on a rack. (The dough will look like a large flour tortilla and will have shrunk to 14 inches.) Wrap well and freeze on a baking sheet (yes, it is pretty big, but the sheet can be balanced on top of other frozen goods). When you're in the mood for pizza, heat up the stone for an hour, defrost and dress the frozen dough, slide it onto parchment, and bake it for nine minutes. Pizzas done this way were so good our tasters could not distinguish them from fresh. A frozen crust will keep nicely for up to three weeks in the freezer—but can you wait that long to have another pizza?

EQUIPMENT CORNER: Box Graters

A BOX GRATER IS ONE OF THOSE UNFORTUNATE KITCHEN tools—it occupies significant cabinet or counter space, is used infrequently, yet is absolutely essential. While food processors come complete with a grater attachment, not everyone has one, and it's doubtful that those who do would dirty the entire contraption to grate a handful of mozzarella. That said, there are a number of graters on the market, from nonstick to heavy-grade stainless steel. We wanted to find out if there was a significant difference between these models. Did we need to spend $20 on a grater, or would a $6 grater do the job?

We tested eight different box graters, ranging in price from $6.48 to $19.99. We grated items of varying texture and firmness, all of which we grate frequently in the test kitchen—mozzarella cheese, celeriac, carrots, and ginger.

The winning box grater would need to rate well in all categories. It would be fast (efficient and sharp, requiring little effort and pressure), stable (no rocking or sliding), comfortable (a good grip on the handle), and easy to clean (a single trip through the dishwasher or a quick scrub with soapy water—all models were dishwasher-safe). With those standards in mind, we grated and rated.

We soon found that most graters had little problem with speed and sharpness. From carrots to cheese, the shreds were clean and uniform, falling quickly from the grater. Ginger proved a problem for two models, which sported only the punched, raised-spike holes for grating smaller items. Those spiked teeth grabbed onto the ginger fibers, leaving juice on the counter and negligible scrapings of actual ginger meat. Graters with miniature versions of the large-holed side were much more successful with ginger.

Stability proved an essential component of a quality box grater. While many models slid a bit if set atop a smooth countertop, testers found sliding to be the lesser of evils. Grated knuckles, the unwelcome result of tipping and rocking, were a common (and unacceptable) occurrence with poorly balanced, flimsy graters. The graters with the largest bases sat

firmly on the countertop, allowing fast, safe grating.

Several graters boasted "slipfree" rubber bases, which we found to be both a help and a hindrance. When grating soft items that required little pressure (such as cheese), the bases indeed kept the grater firmly in place. But when grating firmer items (such as carrots) that required more pressure, the immovable graters tipped, endangering fingers. Additionally, testers preferred a smooth surface for making uninterrupted passes with the cheese or vegetable. The models with rubber or plastic bases and tops were not composed of a single piece of metal, so the grated item had to pass over or be halted by the attached base or top. The attached base also acted as a trap for juices or tiny bits of grated material.

Comfort was similarly affected by the size of the grater's base; there was no need for a tight grip as long as the grater was well-balanced. The most stable graters required merely a hand resting on the top. As a bonus, larger bases offered wider openings at the top, enabling a clear view of the progress.

Most of the graters were easy to clean. A simple scrub by hand or a single run through the dishwasher removed all traces of cheese or vegetables. However, the two models that trapped the ginger fibers had significant problems. The fibers were thoroughly enmeshed in the teeth, proving a true challenge for washing by hand, and they remained firmly in place after a heavy-duty dishwasher run, quickly drying into an intractable mess. The fibers had to be delicately plucked by hand from the sharp teeth.

On your next trip to the kitchen store, look for box graters with extra wide bases, preferably composed of a single piece of metal, with one side offering tiny raised holes for smaller items. We found the more expensive graters tended to be better. The top-rated graters were the Küchenprofi 6-Sided ($15; see photo on page 49), Amco Professional Performance ($19.99), and Progressive International Perfect Prep ($16.99). You can justify the extra expense and cabinet space with the savings you'll reap in Band-Aids.

SIMPLE sandwiches

Although the sandwich was named in England for the Earl of Sandwich, we rightly think of sandwiches as particularly American creations. Packed in a lunch box, eaten at a picnic table, or nibbled in front of the television, there's something comforting about a sandwich.

Of course, just because Mom used to make sandwiches doesn't mean that this humble American mainstay is always shown the proper respect today. Mushy, bland tuna salad is the rule rather than the exception. Individually wrapped cheese singles have all but ruined the grilled cheese sandwich.

But there's something special about a well-made sandwich. It shows that you care about the details and can enjoy life's small pleasures. With good ingredients and some easy-to-master techniques, great sandwiches are within reach.

Lunch is ready in the test kitchen. Two classics—tuna salad and grilled cheese—along with a fancy steak sandwich are being served. Bring on the chips and pickles.

When making grilled cheese sandwiches, we found that grated cheese melts better than sliced and also covers the bread more evenly.

TUNA SALAD SANDWICHES

WHAT WE WANTED: A technique that would elimi-nate the twin problems that plague most tuna salad: watery texture and bland flavor.

Grade-school lunches, hospital cafeterias, and second-rate delis have given tuna salad a bad name with mixtures that are typically mushy, watery, and bland. But these poor examples should not cause cooks to lose hope for this old standard. We tackled tuna salad in the test kitchen and came up with three simple preparation and flavoring tricks that guarantee a tuna salad that is evenly moist, tender, flaky, and well-seasoned every time.

A first-rate tuna salad begins with the best canned tuna. All comers favored solid white tuna over chunk light for its meaty texture and delicate flavor. Among the five brands we tried, StarKist reigned supreme, so we made it the basis of all our subsequent testing. (See the Tasting Lab on page 52 for more details.)

In a dish as simple as tuna salad, the finer points of preparation make a real difference. For instance, most cooks simply squeeze out a bit of the packing water by pressing the detached can lid down lightly on the fish. Tasters con-sistently deemed all of the salads made with tuna prepared in this manner "soggy" and "watery." Taking the minor extra step of draining the tuna thoroughly in a colander before mixing it with other ingredients gave the salads a tooth-some, less watery texture.

Breaking the tuna apart with a fork was another standard procedure we dumped. In salads made with tuna prepared this way, we'd invariably bite into a large, dry, unseasoned chunk that the fork had missed. With the tuna in the colander, we decided to break down the larger chunks with our fingers until the whole amount was fine and even in texture. This gave the finished salad a smooth, even, flaky texture that all of our tasters appreciated.

Seasoning was the last problem we addressed. All too often, tuna salad tastes dull and lifeless because of careless seasoning or, even worse, no seasoning at all. Salt and pep-per were critical to making the most of tuna's delicate flavor. An acidic seasoning, such as lemon or lime juice or vinegar, was equally important, adding some much needed bright-ness to the flavor.

We also found that the order in which we mixed the ingredients made a difference. We first tried mixing the basic seasonings and flavorings with the tuna alone before adding the mayonnaise. Next we tried adding the seasonings, flavorings, and mayonnaise all at once. Our tasters agreed that preseasoning the tuna resulted in a more deeply fla-vored, lively tuna salad.

After settling on these three basic techniques, we were unanimous in finding mayonnaise to be the binder of choice and found other salad ingredients to be largely a matter of taste. We nonetheless agreed that trace amounts of garlic and mustard added dimension to the overall flavor and that a modest amount of minced pickle provided a touch of piquancy, not to mention a link to tradition. (In fact, tuna takes well to a wide range of flavorings; see some of our variations for inspiration.)

So forget the sopping, mushy salad you ate in your last beleaguered, institutional tuna sandwich. The next time the cold cuts run out, or even before, reach for the canned tuna that graces even the emptiest pantry, take a little extra care with the contents, and find out how satisfying a well-made tuna salad sandwich can be.

WHAT WE LEARNED: Thoroughly drain the tuna in a colander and break it up with your fingers for the optimal texture. For the best flavor and even distribution of ingredi-ents, season the tuna and add flavorings before mixing with mayonnaise.

CLASSIC TUNA SALAD
makes about 2 cups, enough for 4 sandwiches

See the Tasting Lab on page 52 for information on brands of tuna and the one we recommend.

2 (6-ounce) cans solid white tuna in water
2 tablespoons juice from 1 lemon
½ teaspoon salt
¼ teaspoon ground black pepper
1 small rib celery, minced (about ¼ cup)
2 tablespoons minced red onion
2 tablespoons minced dill or sweet pickles
½ small clove garlic, minced or pressed through garlic press (about ⅛ teaspoon)
2 tablespoons minced fresh parsley leaves
½ cup mayonnaise
¼ teaspoon Dijon mustard

Drain tuna in colander and shred with fingers until no clumps remain and texture is fine and even. Transfer tuna to medium bowl and mix in lemon juice, salt, pepper, celery, onion, pickles, garlic, and parsley until evenly blended. Fold in mayonnaise and mustard until tuna is evenly moistened. (Can be covered and refrigerated up to 3 days.)

VARIATIONS

TUNA SALAD WITH BALSAMIC VINEGAR AND GRAPES
Follow recipe for Classic Tuna Salad, omitting lemon juice, dill (or pickles), garlic, and parsley and adding 2 tablespoons balsamic vinegar, 6 ounces halved red seedless grapes (about 1 cup), ¼ cup lightly toasted slivered almonds, and 2 teaspoons minced thyme leaves to tuna along with salt and pepper.

CURRIED TUNA SALAD WITH APPLES AND CURRANTS
Follow recipe for Classic Tuna Salad, omitting dill (or pickles), garlic, and parsley and adding 1 medium firm, juicy apple, cut into ¼-inch dice (about 1 cup), ¼ cup currants, and 2 tablespoons minced fresh basil leaves to tuna along with lemon juice, salt, and pepper; mix 1 tablespoon curry powder into mayonnaise before folding into tuna.

TUNA SALAD WITH LIME AND HORSERADISH
Follow recipe for Classic Tuna Salad, omitting lemon juice, dill (or pickles), and garlic and adding 2 tablespoons juice and ½ teaspoon grated zest from 1 lime and 3 tablespoons prepared horseradish to tuna along with salt and pepper.

TUNA SALAD WITH CAULIFLOWER, JALAPEÑO, AND CILANTRO
Follow recipe for Classic Tuna Salad, omitting dill (or pickles), garlic, and parsley and adding 4 ounces cauliflower florets cut into ½-inch pieces (about 1 cup), 1 medium jalapeño chile, minced (about 2 tablespoons), 2 medium scallions, minced (about ¼ cup), and 2 tablespoons minced fresh cilantro leaves to tuna along with lemon juice, salt, and pepper.

EQUIPMENT CORNER: Can Openers

WE PURCHASED FOUR MANUAL CAN OPENERS LABELED "safety" can openers and six standard can openers with varying grips and features. We tested these can openers on standard 14.5 ounce cans of beans. We judged each opener on its comfort, ease of operation, and safety.

In terms of comfort, we took into account both the grip and the turning mechanism. Can openers having an ergonomic grip and a comfortable turning mechanism were preferred over models that pinched our fingers or forced an uncomfortable hand angle.

Ease of operation hinged on time—if more than one rotation around the can was necessary, or if we had to pause and restart turning, the opener was downgraded.

Determining safety was clear-cut. If the opened can had smooth edges and little handling of sharp-edged tops was necessary, the opener earned the top rating. If the operation endangered fingers or produced ragged edges on the can or its top, the opener received a poor rating.

In the end, the simplest models won. Perhaps it was our lifelong use of standard can openers, but we simply could not get used to a different hand position, a two-part operation, or a locking handle—particularly if the opener in question was stiff and difficult to operate, which most of them were. Standard, simple models may not result in perfectly smooth edges, but we're willing to use a bit of extra caution in exchange for ease, speed, and comfort.

Our favorite models were the Oxo Good Grips ($9.95), with a great grip and comfortable turning mechanism, and Swing Away ($6.99), a classic stainless steel opener with plastic coated handles for extra comfort. Of the safety-oriented models, the Culinare MagiCan Auto Release ($9.99) received the best marks. This all-plastic opener magnetically attaches itself to the lid and then ejects the lid with the push of a button. However, testers found this model messy to use (liquid spilled out as cans were opened), and we can only recommend it with reservations.

TASTING LAB: Canned Tuna

WE SELECTED THE 10 BEST-SELLING CHUNK-LIGHT AND solid white tunas packed in water and assembled 25 tasters in the test kitchen. We drained the tuna and lightly blended it with mayonnaise. No seasonings were added.

In most of our blind taste tests, taste has predictably reigned. But when it came to canned tuna, texture set the pace. Most canned tuna is bland—that's why tuna salad is so heavily seasoned. But some brands could be chewed, while others were more suitable to gumming.

Chunk light was the least expensive of the two varieties in our tasting, costing about 41 cents a can less than solid white. This may explain why it is also the top-selling type of canned tuna. Certainly our tasting results do not explain it, since tasters found only one of the five chunk-light samples (Geisha) acceptable. In general, chunk light tuna is made of skipjack tuna or yellowfin tuna or both; skipjack contributes a stronger flavor than yellowfin. Each can contains several small pieces of tuna as well as some flakes.

While our tasters were not wild about the more pronounced flavor of chunk light (which often included an aftertaste of tin), what really upset the balance between the white and light tunas was texture. White tuna you could eat, even pierce, with a fork; the light version was more appropriately scooped with a spoon. When blended with mayonnaise, the small flakes of chunk light tuna quickly broke down even further, taking on a texture that reminded many tasters of cat food. Tasters not only disliked this lack of chew but found that the small shreds of fish held moisture too well, which created a sopping, mushy consistency.

Solid white, on the other hand, consists of one large piece of loin meat from albacore tuna. Though known as "white" tuna, albacore can vary from nearly white to light pink or even beige. Solid white was the tuna of choice among tasters for its mild flavor, milky-white appearance, and chunky texture. StarKist took top honors, followed by 3 Diamonds, Chicken of the Sea, Bumble Bee, and Geisha.

GRILLED CHEESE SANDWICHES

WHAT WE WANTED: Buttery, golden sandwiches with a lacy-crisp exterior and perfectly melted, oozing cheese.

Anyone with kids makes a lot of grilled cheese sandwiches. Rarely are they as good as they could be. Quite simply, most parents are often rushed. The skillet's too hot, the butter is cold, and the cheese is difficult to slice—especially when the block has been whittled down to a nub.

We set some time aside to figure out exactly how to make consistently great grilled cheese sandwiches—hot and buttery, with a golden, lacy-crisp exterior and a tender interior oozing with melted cheese.

What we've come to understand is that making a grilled cheese sandwich with an evenly golden, crispy exterior and a molten interior has less to do with your choice of cheese, bread, and skillet than with what you do with your cheese, bread, and skillet. What's most important is how (pardon the expression) to cut the cheese, how and where to apply the fat, and what level of heat to use when cooking the sandwich.

When it comes to grilled cheese sandwiches, the filling is largely a question of personal taste. What tradition does firmly suggest is that the cheese be cut into thin, even slices for even melting. Unfortunately, achieving such perfectly sliced cheese can be problematic. Cheese planes don't work well on soft, rubbery cheeses. (Besides, not everyone has a cheese plane.) Achieving thin slices with a knife requires patience, practice, and a relatively hard block of cheese. We usually end up with a pile of small, uneven pieces, suitable for placing together like a mosaic.

With all this in mind, we opted for the common box grater. Grating is quick and efficient, and it always delivers a uniform mass of cheese, whether it's hard or soft, from a big hunk or a tiny nub. And grated cheese covers the entire slice of bread in one even layer.

Choosing the right bread is like choosing the right pillow. Some people like theirs soft, while others prefer theirs firm. The test kitchen's favorite is Pepperidge Farm Toasting White Bread for its ½-inch-thick slices, delicate flavor, tender yet firm texture, and crumb with craterlike pockets that cradle the melted cheese perfectly.

Having tried the full range of fats, from vegetable spray to mayonnaise to clarified butter, we chose to work with (salted) butter for its superior flavor and ability to turn the bread deeply golden. We also preferred buttering the bread instead of adding butter to the skillet, where the butter tends to burn and is absorbed unevenly by the bread. For this approach, melted butter was the logical choice. This method eliminates any risk of tearing the bread's tender crumb and allows the entire surface to be evenly coated, thus ensuring a uniform toasty golden-brown color.

A heavy-gauge skillet with a flat bottom is your best choice for cooking grilled cheese sandwiches. The real key when it comes to cooking, though, is low heat. We found we could leave the sandwich in the skillet over low heat for an astonishing 30 minutes on one side before the bread became too dark. Few of us have that kind of time to spend making a simple sandwich. But the fact is, the longer it takes the bread to turn golden, the more developed and crispy the exterior will be. The level of heat may be raised slightly, but no higher than medium-low. The least amount of time you can get away with to achieve a golden-crisp exterior is about five minutes per side, though eight to ten minutes is optimal. At higher temperatures, the bread will burn long before the cheese melts.

WHAT WE LEARNED: To make sure the cheese is evenly distributed, grate rather than slice it. For a uniformly golden crust, brush the bread with melted butter rather than melting butter in a hot pan. To make sure that the crust is also lacy-crisp, cook the sandwich over low heat.

CLASSIC GRILLED CHEESE SANDWICHES

serves 2

The traditional grilled cheese sandwich usually uses a mild cheddar cheese, but our technique for this sandwich works with most any cheese. Grilled cheese sandwiches are best served hot out of the pan, though in a pinch they can be held, unsliced, for about 20 minutes in a warm oven. If you want to make more than two sandwiches at once, get two skillets going or use an electric griddle, set at medium-low (about 250 degrees), grilling 10 minutes per side. The possible variations on the basic grilled cheese sandwich are endless, but the extras are best sandwiched between the cheese. Try a few very thin slices of baked ham, prosciutto, turkey breast, or ripe, in-season tomato. Two to three tablespoons of caramelized onions also make a nice addition. Condiments such as Dijon mustard, pickle relish, or chutney can be spread on the bread instead of sandwiched in the cheese.

> 3   ounces cheese (preferably mild cheddar) or combination of cheeses, grated on large holes of box grater (about ¾ cup)
> 4   slices (½ inch-thick) firm white sandwich bread, such as Pepperidge Farm Toasting White
> 2   tablespoons butter (preferably salted), melted

1. Heat heavy 12-inch skillet over low to medium-low heat. Meanwhile, sprinkle a portion of cheese over two bread slices. Top each with a remaining bread slice, pressing down gently to set.

2. Brush sandwich tops completely with half of melted butter; place each sandwich, buttered-side down, in skillet. Brush remaining side of each sandwich completely with remaining butter. Cook until crisp and deep golden brown, 5 to 10 minutes per side, flipping sandwiches back to first side to reheat and crisp, about 15 seconds. Serve immediately.

VARIATION

GRILLED FRESH MOZZARELLA SANDWICHES WITH BLACK OLIVE PASTE AND ROASTED RED PEPPERS

If you prefer not to roast fresh peppers, use jarred; for the olive paste, try our recipe for tapenade on page 46 or use a prepared paste.

Cut 2 ounces roasted red peppers into ½-inch strips; set aside. Follow recipe for Classic Grilled Cheese Sandwiches, substituting European-style country bread for sandwich white and 3 ounces fresh mozzarella for cheddar. Spread 1 teaspoon tapenade on each slice of bread. Sprinkle half of cheese over two bread slices; top each with portion of roasted pepper strips and few grinds of black pepper, then remaining cheese. Continue with recipe, substituting extra-virgin olive oil for butter and rubbing toasted sandwiches with clove raw garlic.

FLANK STEAK SANDWICHES

WHAT WE WANTED: An upscale steak sandwich that would be easy to execute.

We love flank steak. It's relatively inexpensive, lean, and tender as long as the meat is cooked and sliced correctly. (For more information on this cut, see the Tasting Lab on page 158.) Although we usually grill flank steak, for sandwiches we like to pan-sear the meat—it seems a shame to limit this recipe to the grill, which is dependent on warm weather.

We found that searing flank steak is easy as long as you follow a couple of basic rules. You must use a heavy-bottomed pan that has been preheated over high heat for four minutes. (A 12-inch cast-iron skillet is the ideal choice.) The meat won't brown properly in cooler, lighter pans. Although many steaks have enough fat to pan-sear with little or no oil, we discovered that lean flank steak requires a tablespoon of vegetable oil. Once the steak is well browned on both sides, it's imperative to let the meat rest (see the Science Desk on page 158) before slicing. To make the sandwiches easy to eat, slice the meat very thin across the grain; thicker slices will be unpleasantly tough and chewy.

With the meat element of our sandwich ready, we focused on the bread and greens. A baguette was our first choice, and it tested well in the kitchen. We tried both mild and spicy greens, and most tasters preferred the latter, especially arugula, watercress, or mizuna. Tasters also responded well to a little thinly sliced red onion, which added crunch and bite.

Mayonnaise is the classic dressing for this kind of sandwich. It is usually spiked with herbs and/or spices. After testing several possibilities, we decided on Asian-inspired seasonings—soy sauce, garlic, ginger, and sesame oil.

We experimented with both homemade and commercial mayonnaise. (For information on our favorite brands, see the Tasting Lab on page 96.) Although commercial mayonnaise was fine, it could not compete with the richness and silky texture of homemade. We decided to do some testing to perfect our recipe for homemade mayonnaise.

The old-fashioned way of making mayonnaise is to whisk together oil, lemon juice, and egg yolk into a thick creamy sauce known as an emulsion. The egg yolk stabilizes the emulsion and prevents the oil and lemon juice from reverting to their liquid form. At least this is what is supposed to happen. But homemade mayonnaise often separates into a greasy mess as the cook attempts to stretch as much as ¾ cup oil around a single egg yolk and teaspoon of lemon juice. We found that whisking the egg yolk and lemon juice thoroughly (the egg yolk itself contains liquid and fat materials that must be emulsified) helps to stabilize the mayonnaise. Adding the oil very, very slowly is also key.

Given the perils of whisking, many modern cooks turn to the food processor when making mayonnaise. We wondered how the two methods would compare. Although we eventually perfected a whisk method, the food processor is more foolproof, in part because it's easier to add the oil slowly through the feed tube when both hands are free. (When whisking, you must balance the measuring cup with oil in one hand, while whisking constantly with the other. This takes some practice.)

But making mayonnaise in a food processor necessitates some changes to the basic recipe. Because of the size of the workbowl, it's not possible to make a small amount, using just one egg yolk. Many sources suggest using one whole egg and twice as much oil, while others recommend two egg yolks and twice as much oil. We tested both methods and preferred the whole-egg mayonnaise for its lightness and creaminess. Rather than doubling the oil to 1½ cups, we found we could use just 1¼ cups oil.

WHAT WE LEARNED: Sear the flank steak in an extremely hot, heavy skillet for maximum browning. Use the food processor to make an especially stable, creamy mayonnaise.

about 5 minutes longer. Transfer steak to cutting board, tent with foil, and let rest 10 minutes. Cut steak into ¼-inch slices on the bias against the grain.

2. Spread each baguette piece with 1 tablespoon mayonnaise; portion out steak over bottom pieces of bread and sprinkle with salt and pepper. Add portion of red onion and arugula; place tops of baguette on top and serve.

QUICK FOOD PROCESSOR MAYONNAISE

makes about 1½ cups

Extra mayonnaise can be refrigerated in an airtight container for up to several days.

      2   teaspoons juice from 1 lemon
          Salt
     ¼   teaspoon Dijon mustard
          Dash Tabasco sauce
          Dash Worcestershire sauce
          Pinch ground black pepper
      1   large egg
   1¼   cups vegetable, canola, or light olive oil

1. Process lemon juice, generous ¼ teaspoon salt, mustard, Tabasco, Worcestershire, pepper, and egg in food processor until combined and mixture turns light yellow, about 30 seconds.

2. With machine running, pour oil in thin, steady stream through feed tube until fully incorporated, thick, and emulsified, about 1 minute.

VARIATION

GARLIC-SOY MAYONNAISE   makes ½ cup

If you prefer, start with commercial mayonnaise instead of homemade.

     ½   cup Quick Food Processor Mayonnaise
      1   tablespoon soy sauce
     ½   teaspoon honey

FLANK STEAK AND ARUGULA SANDWICHES WITH RED ONION   serves 4

If you prefer, grill the flank steak according to the directions on page 157.

   1½   pounds flank steak, trimmed of excess fat and
          patted dry with paper towels
          Salt and ground black pepper
      1   tablespoon vegetable oil
      1   baguette, cut into four 5-inch lengths, each
          piece split into top and bottom pieces
     ½   cup Garlic-Soy Mayonnaise (recipe follows)
     ½   small red onion, sliced thin
      1   bunch arugula, stemmed, washed, and dried
          (about 3 cups)

1. Heat heavy-bottomed, 12-inch skillet over high heat until very hot, about 4 minutes. While skillet is heating, season steak generously with salt and pepper. Add oil to pan and swirl to coat bottom. Lay steak in pan and cook without moving it until well browned, about 5 minutes. Using tongs, flip steak; cook until well browned on second side,

1 very small clove garlic, minced or pressed through garlic press (about ½ teaspoon)
1 piece (⅓ inch) ginger, minced (about 1 teaspoon)
½ teaspoon Asian sesame oil

Mix all ingredients together in small bowl. (Can be covered and refrigerated for up to 1 day.)

SCIENCE DESK:
Mayonnaise Emulsification

AN EMULSION IS A MIXTURE OF TWO OR MORE THINGS that don't ordinarily mix, such as oil and water, or the stuffed monster and Barbie doll that Doc is using to demonstrate this phenomenon in the photo above. The only way to mix them is to stir or whisk so strenuously that one of the two ingredients breaks down into tiny droplets. In the case of mayonnaise, the oil is broken down into tiny droplets (called the dispersed phase of the emulsion) that are suspended in the lemon juice (called the continuous phase). Light cannot make its way through the many suspended droplets, and this is why the mixture appears to be creamy.

Such a mixture will start to fall out of emulsion (or separate) because the droplets move around. As they move around, they run into each other and stick, becoming bigger and bigger, until the oil and lemon juice return to their previously separate states.

One way to sustain an emulsion is to add some sort of emulsifier. Egg yolks act as an emulsifier by preventing the oil droplets from sticking together. The active emulsifying ingredient in egg yolks is lecithin. Whereas most substances are either attracted to water (hydrophilic) or repelled by water (hydrophobic), lecithin is both. One end of the lecithin molecule is hydrophilic, and the other end is hydrophobic. The hydrophobic ends coat the oil droplets, preventing the oil droplets from coming together and falling out of suspension.

The combined forces of cognac and flame bring out the deepest, sweetest flavor in shrimp and imbue our fra diavolo recipe with the spirit's richness and complexity.

SHRIMP classics

CHAPTER 6

Cooking shrimp is a relatively straightforward process.
As soon as the meat turns pink (which can happen in just two to three minutes in the presence of intense heat), the shrimp are done. How the shrimp are handled before cooking actually generates more confusion. Should they be peeled? Should the vein that runs down the back of each shrimp be removed?

Shopping for shrimp is equally thought-provoking. Are some shrimp varieties better than others? Is it worth the extra money to buy larger shrimp? Are frozen shrimp a viable option?

We cooked pound after pound of shrimp to answer these questions and to develop recipes for classic dishes such as shrimp cocktail, shrimp scampi, shrimp fra diavolo, and grilled shrimp. Our recipes are easy to follow, but they do rely on some unusual techniques to obtain optimal results. Step into the test kitchen and learn how to become the shrimp expert in your home.

IN THIS CHAPTER

THE RECIPES

Herb-Poached Shrimp
Cocktail Sauce

Shrimp Scampi
Shrimp Fra Diavolo with Linguine
Scallops Fra Diavolo with Linguine
Monkfish Fra Diavolo with Linguine

Grilled Shrimp
Grilled Shrimp with Spicy Garlic
    Paste
Grilled Shrimp with Lemon,
    Garlic, and Oregano Paste
Grilled Shrimp with
    Southwestern Flavors
New Orleans–Style Grilled
    Shrimp

EQUIPMENT CORNER

Garlic Presses

SCIENCE DESK

Why Shrimp Turn Pink
Changing Garlic's Flavor

TASTING LAB

Buying Shrimp
Dried Pasta

SHRIMP COCKTAIL

WHAT WE WANTED: Plump, tender, flavorful shrimp accompanied by a zesty cocktail sauce.

Nothing is more basic than shrimp cocktail: "boiled" shrimp served cold with "cocktail" sauce, typically a blend of bottled ketchup or chili sauce spiked with horseradish. Given its simplicity, few dishes are more difficult to improve. Yet we set out to do just that and believe we succeeded.

It's easy enough to change the basic pattern to produce a more contemporary cold shrimp dish; you could, for example, grill shrimp and serve them with a fresh tomato salsa. But there is something refreshing and utterly classic about traditional shrimp cocktail.

We saw two ways to challenge the traditional method of preparing shrimp cocktail to produce the best-tasting but still recognizable version of this dish. One, work on the flavor of the shrimp; two, produce a great cocktail sauce.

The shrimp in shrimp cocktail can be ice-cold strings of protein, chewy or mushy, or they can be tender, flavorful morsels that barely need sauce. To achieve the latter, you need to start with the best shrimp you can find and give them as much flavor as they can handle without overwhelming them.

If you start with good shrimp and follow a typical shrimp cocktail recipe—that is, simmer the shrimp in salted water until pink—the shrimp will have decent but rarely intense flavor. The easiest way to intensify the flavor of shrimp is to cook them in their shells. But, as we found out, this method has its drawbacks. First of all, it's far easier to peel shrimp when they are raw than when they have been cooked in liquid. More important, however, the full flavor of the shells is not extracted during the relatively short time required for the shrimp to cook through. It takes a good 20 minutes for the shells to impart their flavor, and this is far too long to keep shrimp in a pot.

It's better, then, to make shrimp stock, using just the shrimp shells, and then cook the shrimp in that stock. To improve on the results of this process, every time you use shrimp for any purpose, place the peels in a pot with water to cover, then simmer them for 20 minutes. Cool, strain, and freeze the resultant stock. Use this stock as the cooking liquid for your next batch of shrimp peels. Naturally, this stock will become more and more intensely flavored each time you add to it.

Next, we thought, it would be best to see what other flavors would complement the shrimp without overpowering it. Our first attempt was to use beer and a spicy commercial seasoning, but this was a near disaster; the shrimp for cocktail should not taste like a New Orleans crab boil. Next we tried a classic court bouillon, the traditional herb-scented stock for poaching fish, but quickly discovered that the result wasn't worth the effort; we wanted a few quick additions to our shrimp stock that would add complexity of flavor without making a simple process complicated. Court bouillon was a good idea, but we wanted to reduce the laundry list of ingredients called for in classic recipes.

After trying about 20 different combinations, involving wine, vinegar, lemon juice, and a near-ludicrous number of herbs and spices, we settled on the mixture given in the recipe here. It contains about 25 percent white wine, a dash of lemon juice, and a more-or-less traditional herb combination. Variations are certainly possible, but we caution against adding more wine or lemon juice; both were good up to a point, but after that their pungency became overwhelming.

Although we were pleased at this point with the quality of the shrimp's flavor, we thought it could be still more intense. We quickly learned, however, that the answer to this problem was not to keep pouring flavorings into the cooking liquid; that was self-defeating because we eventually lost the flavor of the shrimp. We decided to keep the shrimp in contact with the flavorings for a longer period of time.

We tried several methods to achieve this, including

starting the shrimp in cold water with the seasonings and using a longer cooking time at a lower temperature. But shrimp cook so quickly that these methods only served to toughen the meat. What worked best, we found, was to bring the cooking liquid to a boil, turn it off, and add the shrimp. Depending on their size, we could leave them in contact with the liquid for up to 10 minutes (even a little longer for jumbo shrimp), during which time they would cook through without toughening, while taking on near perfect flavor.

Improving traditional cocktail sauce proved to be a tricky business. We wanted to make a better sauce, but we still wanted it to be recognizable as cocktail sauce. Starting with fresh or canned tomatoes, we discovered, just didn't work. The result was often terrific (some might say preferable), but it was not cocktail sauce. It was as if we had decided to make a better version of liver and onions by substituting foie gras for veal liver—it might be "better," but it would no longer be liver and onions.

We went so far as to make American-style ketchup from scratch, an interesting project but not especially profitable in that the effect was to duplicate something sold in near-perfect form in the supermarket. Again, there are more interesting tomato-based sauces than ketchup, but they're not ketchup.

So we decided the best thing we could do was to find the bottled ketchup or chili sauce we liked best and season it ourselves. First we had to determine which made the better base, ketchup or chili sauce. The answer to this question was surprising but straightforward: ketchup. Bottled chili sauce is little more than vinegary ketchup with a host of seasonings added. The less expensive chili sauces have the acrid, bitter taste of garlic powder, monosodium glutamate, and other dried seasonings. The more expensive ones have more honest flavors but still did not compare with the cocktail sauce we whipped up in three minutes using basic store-bought ketchup. In addition, chili sauce can be four to eight times as expensive as ketchup.

Our preference in cocktail sauce has always been to emphasize the horseradish. But ketchup and horseradish, we knew, were not enough. Cocktail sauce benefits from a variety of heat sources, none of which overpower the other, and the sum of which still allow the flavor of the shrimp to come through. We liked the addition of chili powder. We also liked some bite from cayenne. Black pepper plays a favorable role as well (as does salt, even though ketchup is already salty). Finally, after trying high-quality wine vinegar, balsamic vinegar, rice vinegar, sherry vinegar, and distilled vinegar, we went back to lemon, the gentlest and most fragrant acidic seasoning. In sum, the keys to good cocktail sauce include ordinary ketchup, fresh lemon juice, horseradish (fresh is best—even month-old bottled horseradish is dim when compared with a just-opened bottle), and chili powder.

WHAT WE LEARNED: For best flavor, cook the shrimp in a potent but not overpowering liquid. We used shrimp shells to make stock and then flavored the stock with herbs and wine. To maximize flavor absorption, bring the liquid to a boil, turn off the heat, and add the shrimp. Stick with ketchup as the base for cocktail sauce but liven things up with horseradish, chili powder, cayenne pepper, and lemon juice.

HERB-POACHED SHRIMP serves 4

When using larger or smaller shrimp, increase or decrease cooking times for shrimp by one to two minutes, respectively. When using such large shrimp, we find it wise to remove the large black vein.

  1 pound very large (16 to 20 per pound) shrimp, peeled, deveined, and rinsed, shells reserved
  1 teaspoon salt
  1 cup dry white wine
  4 peppercorns
  5 coriander seeds
  ½ bay leaf
  5 sprigs fresh parsley
  1 sprig fresh tarragon
  1 teaspoon juice from 1 small lemon

1. Bring reserved shells, 3 cups water, and salt to boil in medium saucepan over medium-high heat; reduce heat to low, cover, and simmer until fragrant, about 20 minutes. Strain stock through sieve, pressing on shells to extract all liquid.

2. Bring stock and remaining ingredients except shrimp to boil in 3- or 4-quart saucepan over high heat; boil 2 minutes. Turn off heat and stir in shrimp; cover and let stand until firm and pink, 8 to 10 minutes. Drain shrimp, reserving stock for another use. Plunge shrimp into ice water to stop cooking, then drain again. Serve shrimp chilled with cocktail sauce.

COCKTAIL SAUCE makes about 1 cup

Use horseradish from a freshly opened bottle and mild chili powder for the best flavor.

  1 cup ketchup
  2½ teaspoons prepared horseradish
  ¼ teaspoon salt
  ¼ teaspoon ground black pepper
  1 teaspoon ancho or other mild chili powder
     Pinch cayenne pepper
  1 tablespoon juice from 1 small lemon

Stir all ingredients together in small bowl; adjust seasonings as necessary.

TECHNIQUE: Easy Shrimp Peeling

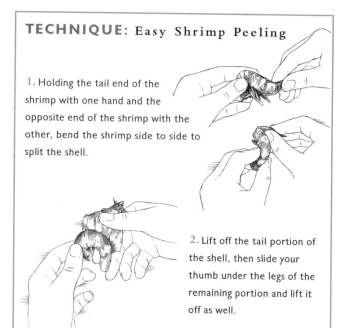

1. Holding the tail end of the shrimp with one hand and the opposite end of the shrimp with the other, bend the shrimp side to side to split the shell.

2. Lift off the tail portion of the shell, then slide your thumb under the legs of the remaining portion and lift it off as well.

TASTING LAB: Buying Shrimp

IT'S SAFE TO SAY THAT ANY SHRIMP YOU BUY HAVE BEEN frozen (and usually thawed by the retailer), but not all shrimp are the same—far from it. The Gulf of Mexico supplies about 200 million pounds of shrimp annually to the United States, but three times that amount is imported, mostly from Asia and Central and South America.

After tasting all of the commonly available varieties of shrimp several times, we had little trouble declaring two winners: Mexican whites *(Panaeus vannamei),* from the Pacific coast, are usually the best. A close second, and often just as good, are Gulf whites *(P. setiferus)*. Either of these may be wild or farm-raised. Unfortunately, these are rarely the shrimp you're offered in supermarkets. The shrimp most commonly found in supermarkets is Black Tiger, a farmed shrimp from Asia. Its quality is inconsistent, but it can be quite flavorful and firm. And even if you go to a fishmonger and ask for white shrimp, you may get a farm-raised, less expensive, and decidedly inferior shrimp from China *(P. chinensis)*. (There are more than 300 species of shrimp in the world and not nearly as many common names.)

All you can do is try to buy the best shrimp available, and buy it right. Beyond choosing the best species you can find, there are a number of factors to consider.

Because almost all shrimp are frozen after the catch, and thawed shrimp start losing their flavor in just a couple of days, buying thawed shrimp gives you neither the flavor of fresh nor the flexibility of frozen. We recommend buying frozen shrimp rather than thawed. We found that shrimp stored in the freezer retain peak quality for several weeks, deteriorating very slowly after that until about the three-month point, when we detected a noticeable deterioration in quality. If you do buy thawed shrimp, they should smell of saltwater and little else, and they should be firm and fully fill their shells.

Avoid prepeeled and deveined shrimp; cleaning before freezing unquestionably deprives shrimp of some of their flavor and texture; everyone we asked to sample precleaned shrimp found them to be nearly tasteless. In addition, precleaned shrimp may have added tripolyphosphate, a chemical that aids in water retention and can give shrimp an off flavor.

Shrimp should have no black spots, or melanosis, on their shells, which indicate that a breakdown of the meat has begun. Be equally suspicious of shrimp with yellowing shells or those that feel gritty. Either of these conditions may indicate the overuse of sodium bisulfite, a bleaching agent sometimes used to retard melanosis.

Despite the popularity of shrimp, there are no standards for size. Small, medium, large, extra-large, jumbo, and other size classifications are subjective and relative. Small shrimp of 70 or so to the pound are frequently labeled "medium," as

are those twice that size and even larger. It pays, then, to judge shrimp size by the number it takes to make a pound, as retailers do. Shrimp labeled "16/20," for example, require 16 to 20 (usually closer to 20) individual specimens to make a pound. Those labeled "U-20" require fewer than 20 to make a pound. Large shrimp (21 to 25 per pound) usually yield the best combination of flavor, ease of preparation, and value (really big shrimp usually cost more).

One more note about size: Larger shrimp generally have larger veins, which should be removed. The veins in smaller shrimp are often so negligible that it's not worth removing them. Either way, we find the issue of removing the vein to be one of aesthetics. It neither harms nor improves the flavor of the shrimp. We tested several shrimp deveiners and found that some models work better than others but none beats a regular paring knife. We recommend that you save money (and drawer space) and live without this gadget that is of little real use.

SCIENCE DESK: Why Shrimp Turn Pink

MOST COOKS KNOW THAT WHEN YOU THROW A BATCH of shrimp into a pot of boiling water or a hot skillet, they change color almost immediately. The gray-white shells and flesh are transformed into a bright red/orange/pink. The color comes from a carotene-like pigment called astaxanthin, found not only in shrimp but also in salmon, lobster, crabs, crawfish, red sea bream, and some fish eggs.

Usually astaxanthin is the reddish color we associate with salmon and most crustaceans. But in shrimp, astaxanthin is bound to a protein that masks the color, making the shrimp appear gray, not pink, when raw. When heat is applied, a chemical reaction occurs, and the bond between the protein and the pigment is broken, allowing the reddish color to show through.

Astaxanthin does more than provide a pretty pink hue—it is also a powerful antioxidant. In aquatic species, it plays a role in immune system functions and reproduction.

SHRIMP SCAMPI AND SHRIMP FRA DIAVOLO

WHAT WE WANTED: Two Italian-American favorites with tender shrimp and plenty of delicious sauce.

The perfect shrimp scampi is surrounded by an ample amount of sauce flavored with garlic and lemon. We find that most recipes are too oily and that the garlic (which generally goes into the pan first) burns by the time the shrimp have cooked through. Most sauces are too thin, and there's not nearly enough to sop up with a chewy piece of bread. In addition, most recipes overcook the shrimp.

To start, we sautéed the shrimp quickly in batches. This prevented them from overcooking and becoming rubbery. With the shrimp cooked and reserved, we built a sauce in the sauté pan. Beginning with butter, we simply heated the garlic through before adding the lemon juice and a little vermouth, which gave the sauce a nice depth of flavor. Adding the liquid also kept the garlic from burning.

The sauce was delicious but thin. We mounted the sauce with more butter and finished it with parsley, both of which gave the sauce body, and added a pinch of cayenne. We returned the shrimp and their juices to the pan and the dish was done. Nothing complicated, but perfect nonetheless.

Shrimp fra diavolo, a seriously garlicky, spicy, winey tomato sauce studded with shrimp and served over pasta, is an Italian restaurant standard that's easy to make at home. But all too often, the garlic flavor is unpleasantly sharp, even acrid. In this dish, the garlic needs to be mellower than in scampi. And all too often the shrimp themselves contribute little to the overall flavor of the sauce, serving merely as a bulky, lifeless garnish.

Most fra diavolo recipes add raw shrimp to the almost finished sauce. While the shrimp remain tender, our tasters agreed that their flavor was barely developed. We improved the situation by seasoning the shrimp with some olive oil, salt, and red pepper flakes and searing them quickly in a very hot pan. Then we set the seared shrimp aside while making the sauce and added the shrimp back to heat through in the sauce just before serving. Every taster noted that both the shrimp and the sauce had much more flavor. The sear also benefited the red pepper flakes on the shrimp, as they now offered not only heat but a notably earthy, toasty note as well.

Shrimp and cognac have a well-established culinary affinity, and a number of fra diavolo recipes call for stirring cognac in with the other liquid sauce ingredients. We thought we might bring out still more flavor from the shrimp if we flambéed them in the cognac. As we'd hoped, the combined forces of cognac and flame brought out the shrimp's deepest, sweetest flavor and imbued our fra diavolo with the spirit's own richness and complexity.

We wanted enough garlic to make the devil proud, and we were frankly surprised to find that tasters agreed, preferring sauces that packed the wallop of 10 large cloves. But there was a caveat: We had to mitigate the bitterness. We experimented with cutting the garlic in slices and slivers, grating it, pureeing it, and adding it to the sauce at varying times, none of which eliminated the bitterness completely. Then we tried sautéing the garlic slowly, over low heat, until it turned golden, sticky, mellow, and nutty. The bitterness was gone, and the sauce had acquired an even sweeter, deeper dimension. We reserved a tablespoon of raw garlic to add to the sauce at the end of cooking, along with a splash of raw olive oil. Tasters appreciated the bright, fruity, high flavor notes that these raw ingredients added to the dish.

Tasters were united behind white wine for this sauce, preferring it to red wine and vermouth. All along, though, we had been bothered by the compounded acidity of the tomatoes and wine, so we tried adding a little brown sugar, which we found balanced the acidity perfectly.

WHAT WE LEARNED: Bring out the flavor of the shrimp and keep them tender by sautéing them separately, and tame the harshness of the garlic by treating it gently.

SHRIMP SCAMPI serves 4 to 6

Serve scampi with plenty of chewy bread to soak up extra juices.

    2 tablespoons olive oil
    2 pounds large shrimp (21 to 25 per pound),
       peeled and deveined if desired
    3 tablespoons unsalted butter
    4 medium cloves garlic, minced
    2 tablespoons juice from 1 lemon
    1 tablespoon dry vermouth
    2 tablespoons minced fresh parsley leaves
       Pinch cayenne
       Salt and ground black pepper

1. Heat 12-inch skillet over high heat until hot, 2 to 3 minutes. Add 1 tablespoon oil and swirl to coat bottom of pan. Add 1 pound shrimp and cook, stirring occasionally, until just opaque, about 1 minute; transfer to medium bowl. Return pan to heat and repeat process with remaining oil and shrimp.

2. Return empty skillet to medium-low heat; melt 1 tablespoon butter. Add garlic and cook, stirring constantly, until fragrant, about 30 seconds. Off heat, add lemon juice and vermouth. Whisk in remaining 2 tablespoons butter; add parsley and cayenne, and season to taste with salt and pepper. Return shrimp and accumulated juices to skillet. Toss to combine; serve immediately.

SHRIMP FRA DIAVOLO WITH LINGUINE

serves 4 to 6

Tongs are the ideal tool for moving the shrimp in the pan. One teaspoon of red pepper flakes will give the sauce a little kick, but you may want to add more depending on your taste for fire.

    1 pound medium shrimp (31 to 35 per pound),
       peeled and deveined if desired
    1 teaspoon crushed red pepper flakes
       (or more, to taste)
    6 tablespoons extra-virgin olive oil
  1½ tablespoons salt
    ¼ cup cognac or brandy
    ¼ cup minced garlic (about 20 small, 12 medium,
       10 large, or 5 extra-large cloves) from
       1 or 2 heads
    ½ teaspoon sugar
    1 (28-ounce) can diced tomatoes, drained
    1 cup dry white wine, such as Sauvignon Blanc
    1 pound dried linguine or spaghetti
    ¼ cup minced fresh parsley leaves

1. Bring 4 quarts water to a boil in large Dutch oven or stockpot.

2. While water is heating, heat 12-inch heavy-bottomed skillet over high heat for 4 minutes. Meanwhile, toss shrimp with half of red pepper flakes, 2 tablespoons olive oil, and

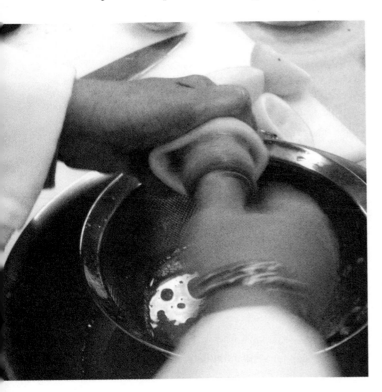

until garlic foams and becomes sticky and straw colored, 7 to 10 minutes. Add remaining red pepper flakes and ¾ teaspoon salt, sugar, tomatoes, and wine, increase heat to medium-high, and simmer until thickened and fragrant, about 8 minutes longer. Stir in reserved shrimp (with accumulated juices), remaining 1 tablespoon garlic, and parsley and simmer until shrimp have heated through, about 1 minute longer. Off heat, stir in remaining 1 tablespoon olive oil.

4. Meanwhile, add linguine or spaghetti and 1 tablespoon salt to boiling water, stir to separate pasta, and cook until al dente; reserve ⅓ cup pasta cooking water and drain pasta. Transfer drained pasta back to now empty Dutch oven or stockpot; add about ½ cup sauce (sauce only, no shrimp) and 2 to 3 tablespoons reserved pasta cooking water; toss to coat. Divide pasta among warm serving plates, top with a portion of sauce and shrimp, and serve immediately.

VARIATIONS

SCALLOPS FRA DIAVOLO WITH LINGUINE

The scallops, as well as the monkfish in the recipe below, leave more *fond*—dark, sticky drippings—in the pan than do the shrimp. This is good, because fond is flavorful, but it can make the garlic appear straw colored before it has really finished cooking. Make sure that the garlic is fragrant, looks sticky, and has cooked for the full 7 to 10 minutes.

Follow recipe for Shrimp Fra Diavolo with Linguine, substituting 1 pound sea scallops, with small, crescent-shaped muscles removed, for shrimp.

MONKFISH FRA DIAVOLO WITH LINGUINE

See the note above for Scallops Fra Diavolo.

Follow recipe for Shrimp Fra Diavolo with Linguine, substituting 1-pound monkfish fillet, cut into 1-inch pieces, for shrimp.

¾ teaspoon salt. Add shrimp to hot skillet and quickly arrange in single layer; sear until bottom of shrimp forms small spot of crust, about 30 seconds. Remove skillet from heat, turn shrimp over, and add cognac; pause until cognac has warmed slightly, about 5 seconds, and return to high heat. Wave lit match over pan until cognac ignites, shaking pan. When flames subside, 15 to 30 seconds later, remove shrimp to medium bowl and set aside.

3. Allow empty skillet to cool, off heat, for 2 minutes; return to burner over low heat; add 3 tablespoons olive oil and 3 tablespoons garlic and cook, stirring constantly,

TASTING LAB: Dried Pasta

IN THE NOT-SO-DISTANT PAST, AMERICAN PASTA HAD A poor reputation, and rightly so. It cooked up gummy and starchy, and experts usually touted the superiority of Italian brands. We wondered if this was still the case.

To find out, we tasted eight leading brands of spaghetti—four American and four Italian. American brands took two of the three top spots, while two Italian brands landed at the bottom of the rankings. It seems that American companies have mastered the art of making pasta.

American-made Ronzoni was the top finisher, with tasters praising its "nutty, buttery" flavor and superb texture. Mueller's, another American brand, took third place. Tasters liked its "clean," "wheaty" flavor.

DeCecco was the highest-scoring Italian brand, finishing second in the tasting. It cooked up "very al dente" (or with a good bite) and was almost chewy. Other Italian brands did not fare quite so well. Martelli, an artisanal pasta that costs nearly $5 a pound, finished in next-to-last place, with comments like "gritty" and "mushy" predominating on tasters' score sheets. Another Italian brand, Delverde, sank to the bottom of the ratings.

Our conclusion: Save your money and don't bother with most imported pasta—American pastas are just fine. If you must serve Italian pasta in your home, stick with DeCecco.

EQUIPMENT CORNER: Garlic Presses

MOST COOKS DISLIKE THE CHORE OF MINCING GARLIC, and many turn to garlic presses. We know that many professional cooks sneer at this tool, but we have a different opinion. In hundreds of hours of use in our test kitchens, we have found that this little tool delivers speed, ease, and a comfortable separation of garlic from fingers.

And there are other advantages. First is flavor, which changes perceptibly depending on how the cloves are broken down. The finer a clove of garlic is cut, the more flavor is released from its broken cells (see the Science Desk on page 68 for more on this reaction). Fine mincing or pureeing, therefore, results in a fuller, more pungent garlic flavor. A good garlic press breaks down the cloves more than the average cook would with a knife. Second, a good garlic press ensures a consistently fine texture, which in turn means better distribution of the garlic throughout the dish.

The question for us, then, was not whether garlic presses work but which of the many available presses work best. Armed with 10 popular models, we pressed our way through a mountain of garlic cloves to find out.

Most garlic presses share a common design, consisting of two handles connected by a hinge. At the end of one handle is a small perforated hopper; at the end of the other is a plunger that fits snugly inside that hopper. The garlic cloves in the hopper get crushed by the descending plunger when the handles are squeezed together; the puree is extruded through the perforations in the bottom of the hopper.

Some presses employ a completely different design—a relatively large cylindrical container with a tight-fitting screw-down plunger. These presses are designed for large capacity, but this unusual design failed to impress us. The screw-type plungers required both pressure and significant repetitive motion, which we felt contributed to hand fatigue. This seemed like a lot of work just to press garlic. Matters did not improve when the hoppers were loaded

BEST GARLIC PRESS
We found that this Zyliss press can handle two cloves at once, producing very finely pureed garlic in a flash.

with multiple garlic cloves. Even greater effort was required to twist down the plungers, and the texture of the garlic puree produced was coarse and uneven.

A good garlic press should not only produce a smooth, evenly textured puree but should also be easy to use. To us, this means that different users should be able to operate it without straining their hands. With several notable exceptions, all of our presses performed reasonably well in this regard.

Several of our test cooks wondered if we could make an easy task even easier by putting the garlic cloves through the presses without first removing their skins. Instructions on the packaging of the Zyliss and Bodum presses specified that it was OK to press unpeeled cloves, and our tests bore out this assertion. Though the directions for several other presses did not address this issue specifically, we found that the Oxo and the Endurance also handled unpeeled garlic with ease. We did note, however, that the yield of garlic puree was greater across the board when we pressed peeled cloves. While we were at it, we also tried pressing chunks of peeled, fresh ginger. The Zyliss, Kuhn Rikon, and Oxo were the only three to excel in this department, and we found that smaller chunks, about ½ inch, were crushed much more easily than larger, 1-inch pieces.

When all was said and pressed, the traditionally designed, moderately priced Zyliss ($12.99) turned out to be comfortable and consistent, and it produced the finest, most even garlic puree. In addition, it handled unpeeled garlic and small chunks of fresh ginger without incident. While other presses got the job done, the Zyliss just edged out the field in terms of both performance and design.

SCIENCE DESK: Changing Garlic's Flavor

IT MAY SEEM UNLIKELY, BUT THE WAY IN WHICH GARLIC IS prepared—whether sliced, chopped, or minced—influences the flavor it contributes to a dish. Raw garlic cloves contain a sulfur-based compound called alliin and an enzyme called alliinase. These two compounds are not in contact in raw garlic, which is why a head of garlic has almost no aroma. When the garlic is cut, the enzyme comes into contact with the alliin and converts it to allicin, a new and very pungent compound that gives garlic its typical aroma. This compound also gives garlic its characteristic bite.

When you slice garlic, only a small amount of enzyme and sulfur-compound come into contact with each other, so just a small amount of allicin is produced. The result is a mild garlic flavor. When you mince garlic, however, more allicin is produced because there's more contact between the sulfur-compound and the enzyme. More allicin means more aroma and flavor.

For the strongest garlic flavor, put the cloves through a press or mince them into a smooth paste. Doc is making just this point to Chris in the photo on the opposite page, by using packing peanuts to represent the amount of allicin that is released when the garlic is pressed or minced fine.

Because heat breaks down the enzyme alliinase, roasting or toasting garlic cloves before adding them to a dish will pretty much eliminate the development of any harsh garlic flavor.

TECHNIQUE: Mincing Garlic to a Paste

Mince the garlic as you normally would on a cutting board with a chef's knife. Sprinkle the minced garlic with salt and then drag the side of the chef's knife over the garlic-salt mixture to form a fine puree. Continue to mince and drag the knife as necessary until the puree is smooth. If possible, use kosher or coarse salt; the larger crystals do a better job of breaking down the garlic than fine table salt.

GRILLED SHRIMP

WHAT WE WANTED: Tender, juicy shrimp that tastes like it was cooked on the grill.

Throwing some shrimp on the barbie sounds easy. But even the simplest grilled dish requires proper technique. More often than not, grilled shrimp are tough and dry. And grilled shrimp rarely pick up the tantalizing flavors of wood or smoke.

After some initial tests, we concluded that shrimp destined for the grill should not be peeled. The shell shields the meat from the intense heat and helps to keep the shrimp moist and tender. Try as we might, we found it impossible to grill peeled shrimp without overcooking them and making the meat dry and tough, especially the exterior layers. The only method that worked was to intentionally undercook the shrimp; but that left the inside a little gooey, something that no one enjoyed.

Another reason to grill shrimp with the shells on is flavor. Peeled shrimp cooks so quickly that it doesn't have much time

to pick up any grill flavor. With the peel on, the grilling time is slightly longer; hence the shrimp tastes a bit smokier. Also, the shell contributes a lot of flavor to the shrimp meat as it cooks. If the shells are discarded before cooking, the transfer of flavor from shell to meat cannot occur.

To make it easier to eat the unpeeled, grilled shrimp, we found it useful to slit the shell open prior to cooking with a pair of manicure scissors. The shell still protects the meat as the shrimp cook, but the shell comes right off at the table.

Even with the shell on, though, tasters found the shrimp a tad too dry. We wondered if brining the shrimp before cooking would help. (We have found that soaking other delicate foods, especially chicken, in a mixture of water, salt, and sugar before cooking helps them to retain moisture.) It did. Our tests revealed that brined shrimp may gain as much as 10 percent in water weight. At its most successful, brining turns mushy shrimp into plump, juicy specimens with the chewy texture of a lobster tail. Even top-quality shrimp are improved by this process. We tested various concentrations of salt and brining times and in the end settled on soaking shrimp in a strong salt solution (1 cup kosher salt dissolved in 2 quarts water) for 30 minutes.

Once the shrimp have been brined, they can be threaded onto skewers and grilled. We found that shrimp should be cooked quickly to prevent them from toughening. This means using a very hot fire. Thankfully, grilling is simple—as soon as the shrimp turn pink, they are done.

We like to coat the shrimp with a paste or marinade before grilling. The flavorings adhere to the shell beautifully. When you peel the shrimp at the table, the seasonings stick to your fingers and are in turn transferred directly to the meat as you eat it. Licking your fingers also helps.

WHAT WE LEARNED: Shrimp must be grilled in their shells to prevent dryness. To increase flavor, firmness, and moisture, brine shrimp before grilling them.

CHARCOAL-GRILLED SHRIMP   serves 4 to 6

We recommend that you brine the shrimp before grilling. This makes them especially plump and juicy. To keep the shrimp from dropping through the grill rack onto the hot coals, thread them onto skewers. This recipe (and the one that follows) are rather plain but still delicious. The variations on pages 72 and 73 are more complex-tasting and require only minimal additional work.

  1   cup kosher salt or ½ cup table salt
  ½   cup sugar
  2   pounds large shrimp (21 to 25 per pound)
  2   tablespoons extra-virgin olive oil
      Lemon wedges

1. Pour 2 quarts very cold water into large bowl. Add salt and sugar and stir until dissolved. Add shrimp and let stand in refrigerator for 30 minutes. Drain shrimp. Open shells with manicure scissors (see illustration 1 at right) and devein if desired (see illustration 2 at right). Toss shrimp and oil in medium bowl to coat.

2. Meanwhile, light large chimney starter filled with hardwood charcoal (about 2½ pounds) and allow to burn until charcoal is covered with layer of fine gray ash. Spread coals evenly over grill bottom for medium-hot fire. (See how to gauge heat level on page 133.) Set cooking rack in place, cover grill with lid, and let rack heat up, about 5 minutes. Scrape rack clean with wire brush.

3. Thread shrimp on skewers (see illustration on page 73). Grill shrimp, uncovered, turning skewers once, until shells are barely charred and bright pink, 4 to 6 minutes. Serve hot or at room temperature with lemon wedges.

TECHNIQUE: Preparing Shrimp

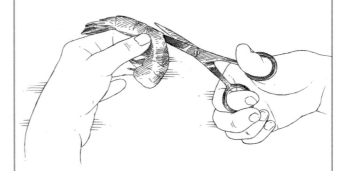

1. When grilling shrimp, we find it best to keep the shrimp in their shells. The shells hold in moisture and also flavor the shrimp as they cook. However, eating shrimp cooked in their shells can be a challenge. As a compromise, we found it helpful to slit the back of the shell with manicure or other small scissors with a fine point. When ready to eat, each person can quickly and easily peel away the shells.

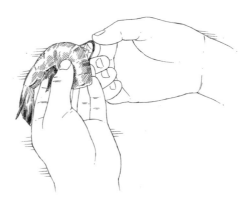

2. Slitting the back of the shell makes it easy to devein the shrimp as well. Except when the vein is especially dark and thick, we found no benefit to deveining in our testing. If you choose to devein shrimp, slit open the back of the shell as in step 1. Invariably you will cut a little into the meat and expose the vein as you do this. Use the tip of the scissors to lift up the vein and then grab it with your fingers and discard.

GAS-GRILLED SHRIMP serves 4 to 6

There's only one difference between grilling shrimp over char-coal and gas—in the latter, the lid is kept down to concentrate the heat.

   1   cup kosher salt or ½ cup table salt
   ½   cup sugar
   2   pounds large shrimp (21 to 25 per pound)
   2   tablespoons extra-virgin olive oil
       Lemon wedges

1. Pour 2 quarts very cold water into large bowl. Add salt and sugar and stir until dissolved. Add shrimp and let stand for 30 minutes. Drain shrimp. Open shells with manicure scissors (see illustration 1 on page 71) and devein if desired (see illustration 2 on page 71). Toss shrimp and oil in medium bowl to coat.

2. Preheat grill with all burners set to high and lid down until grill is very hot, about 15 minutes. Scrape cooking rack clean with wire brush. Leave burners on high.

3. Thread shrimp on skewers (see illustration on page 73). Grill shrimp, covered, turning skewers once, until shells are barely charred and bright pink, 5 to 6 minutes. Serve hot or at room temperature with lemon wedges.

VARIATIONS

GRILLED SHRIMP WITH SPICY GARLIC PASTE

The garlic paste adheres perfectly and will coat your fingers as you peel and eat the grilled shrimp.

Mince 1 large garlic clove with 1 teaspoon salt to form smooth paste (see illustration on page 68). Combine garlic paste with ½ teaspoon cayenne pepper, 1 teaspoon sweet paprika, 2 tablespoons extra-virgin olive oil, and 2 teaspoons lemon juice in medium bowl. Follow recipe for Charcoal-Grilled or Gas-Grilled Shrimp, tossing brined and drained shrimp with garlic mixture instead of oil to coat well. Thread shrimp on skewers and grill as directed.

GRILLED SHRIMP WITH LEMON, GARLIC, AND OREGANO PASTE

The fresh oregano in this recipe can be replaced with other fresh herbs, including chives, tarragon, parsley, or basil.

Mince 1 large garlic clove with 1 teaspoon salt to form smooth paste (see illustration on page 68). Combine garlic paste with 2 tablespoons extra-virgin olive oil, 2 teaspoons lemon juice, and 2 teaspoons chopped fresh oregano leaves in a medium bowl. Follow recipe for Charcoal-Grilled or Gas-Grilled Shrimp, tossing brined and drained shrimp with garlic mixture instead of oil to coat well. Thread shrimp on skewers and grill as directed.

GRILLED SHRIMP WITH SOUTHWESTERN FLAVORS

Serve these shrimp with warm cornbread.

Heat 2 tablespoons extra-virgin olive oil in small skillet over medium heat. Add 2 minced garlic cloves, 2 teaspoons chili powder, and ¾ teaspoon ground cumin and sauté until

---

TECHNIQUE: Skewering Shrimp

Thread shrimp on a skewer by passing the skewer through the body near the tail, folding the shrimp over, and passing the skewer through the body again near the head end. Threading the shrimp twice keeps them in place (they won't spin around) and makes it easy to cook them on both sides by turning the skewer just once.

---

garlic is fragrant, 30 to 45 seconds. Scrape mixture into heat-proof bowl and cool to room temperature. Mix in 2½ table-spoons lime juice and 2 tablespoons minced fresh cilantro leaves. Follow recipe for Charcoal-Grilled or Gas-Grilled Shrimp, tossing brined and drained shrimp with garlic mixture instead of oil to coat well. Thread shrimp on skewers and grill as directed. Serve with lime wedges instead of lemon wedges.

NEW ORLEANS–STYLE GRILLED SHRIMP

Shrimp are tossed with a spicy paste, grilled, and drizzled with a rich butter-garlic mixture. For a classic Creole meal, serve with steamed white rice.

1	teaspoon dried thyme
1	teaspoon dried oregano
1	teaspoon sweet paprika
1	teaspoon garlic powder
	Pinch cayenne pepper
½	teaspoon salt
4	tablespoons unsalted butter
2	medium cloves garlic, minced
1	recipe Charcoal-Grilled or Gas-Grilled Shrimp (omit olive oil)
1½	tablespoons vegetable oil

1. Mix thyme, oregano, paprika, garlic powder, cayenne, and salt together in small bowl.

2. Melt butter in small saucepan over medium heat. When butter begins to sizzle, add garlic and cook for 30 seconds. Remove pan from heat, cover, and keep warm.

3. Prepare shrimp as directed in recipe for Charcoal-Grilled or Gas-Grilled Shrimp, tossing them with vegetable oil and spice mixture instead of olive oil. Grill shrimp and arrange skewers on platter. Drizzle with butter mixture and serve with lemon wedges.

STEAK frites

CHAPTER 7

When bistro food is as good as seared steak with red wine sauce and a piping-hot pile of extra-crisp fries, who needs haute cuisine? Nothing could be simpler or more satisfying.

So why, then, do steaks seared at home often turn out pallid? And why do restaurant sauces taste so much better than sauces made at home?

When it comes to searing steaks, most home cooks are timid about the heat. We found that you need a really hot pan to brown steaks properly. As for sauces, home cooks don't have the arsenal of gelatinous stocks that chefs rely on for so much of their cooking. But there must be a way to turn canned broth into a memorable sauce. In the test kitchen, we were determined to find out.

Despite what you may think, French fries really are best made at home, where you can control the timing and enjoy the fries the minute they emerge from the hot oil. Good fries aren't pale blondes, like those served at fast-food restaurants. They have a rich golden brown color and are crisp—really crisp. You'll learn how to make fries worthy of the finest Parisian bistro, and it's surprisingly easy.

For great French fries, we discovered that you must soak the cut potatoes in ice-cold water for at least 30 minutes. The water chills the exterior of each piece so that when the potatoes are drained and fried the interior has plenty of time to cook through before the exterior starts to brown.

PAN-SEARED STEAKS

WHAT WE WANTED: Steaks cooked on the stove that were every bit as good as those cooked on the grill.

Steaks must be cooked so that the entire surface caramelizes to form a rich, thick crust. The intense heat of the grill makes it easy to obtain such a crust. But sometimes grilling is impractical. We wanted to get the same result from pan-searing.

We decided to focus on boneless steaks. Bone-in steaks, such as T-bones and porterhouses, really should be grilled; when pan-seared it's the bone, not the meat, that makes contact with the pan, and the result is poor coloring and no crust development. We tested a dozen boneless steaks and found two that everyone in the test kitchen could agree on—rib-eye and strip steaks.

Rib steaks are cut from the rib roast (or prime rib) and come with the curved bone attached. More often, you will see boneless steaks from the rib, called rib-eye steaks. Rib-eyes are tender and smooth-textured, with a distinctive, robust, beefy taste. They are very rich, with good-sized pockets of fat. Rib eye is also known as Delmonico steak in New York or Spencer steak in the West.

The strip steak is cut from the short loin area of the cow. Also called shell, Kansas City strip, New York strip, or top loin, strip steak has a noticeable grain and a moderate amount of chew. The flavor is excellent and the meat a bit less fatty than in rib-eye steaks. Strips steaks are also slightly more expensive than rib-eyes.

It was obvious to us from the beginning that the key to browning the steaks was going to be preheating the pan, so that when the steaks hit the pan, the surface would be hot enough to sear the steaks before they overcooked. In this regard, we wondered if different types of pans would heat and cook differently.

We found that a cast-iron skillet did an excellent job of browning the steaks, but we feared pan sauces would suffer.

Many sources discourage the use of cast-iron pans because of the iron's tendency to react with acidic foods, giving them a metallic, off flavor. Sure enough, when we prepared a red wine pan sauce in a cast-iron skillet, it tasted tinny.

Next, we tried searing steaks in a nonstick skillet, but the browned bits that a good sear leaves behind in the pan and that make sauces so delicious did not materialize. The resulting sauces were anemic and weakly flavored. Pan sauces made in regular nonreactive pans were rich both in flavor and color. We had good results with heavy-bottomed pans made by All-Clad and Calphalon.

We had been searing the steaks over high heat to promote browning, but tasters noticed that the sauces tasted bitter. To avoid this problem, we heated the pan over high heat and then reduced the heat to medium-high once the steaks went into the pan. This worked fine as long as the pan was fully preheated (three minutes over high heat worked best) before the steaks were added. We found that strip and rib-eye steaks had enough fat to be seared without oil.

Over the course of testing, we noticed a few more factors that ensured the formation of a good crust on the steak and of richly flavored brown bits in the pan. (Called *fond*, these brown bits are crucial to the flavor of the sauce.) There should be at least ¼ inch of space between each steak if they are to sear, not steam. At the same time, the pan should not be too large because that encourages burning. A 12-inch skillet is the right size for four steaks. We also noticed that it was not a good idea to move the steaks around in the pan. This interrupted the browning process and resulted in steaks that lacked good caramelization. The steaks browned much better when moved only once, just to turn them over to the other side.

WHAT WE LEARNED: Sear boneless strip or rib-eye steaks in a preheated, heavy-bottomed, nonreactive 12-inch skillet, reducing the heat once the steaks go into the pan to keep the fond from burning.

PAN-SEARED STEAKS   serves 4

Serve these steaks with either the red wine or shallot butter sauce on page 79.

> 4 boneless strip or rib-eye steaks, 1 to 1¼ inches thick (about 8 ounces each), thoroughly dried with paper towels
> Salt and ground black pepper

1. Heat heavy-bottomed, nonreactive 12-inch skillet over high heat until very hot, about 3 minutes. Meanwhile, season both sides of steaks with salt and pepper.

2. Lay steaks in pan, leaving ¼ inch of space between them; reduce heat to medium-high, and cook, not moving steaks until well browned, about 4 minutes. Using tongs, flip steaks; cook 4 minutes more for rare, 5 minutes more for medium-rare, and 6 minutes more for medium. Transfer steaks to large plate, tent with foil, and let rest 5 minutes while preparing pan sauce (recipes follow).

TASTING LAB: Prime, Choice, or Select Beef

THE U.S. DEPARTMENT OF AGRICULTURE (USDA) RECOG-nizes eight grades of beef, but most everything available to consumers falls into the top three: Prime, Choice, and Select. The grades classify meat according to fat marbling and age, which are relatively accurate predictors of palatability; they have nothing to do with freshness or purity. Grading is voluntary on the part of the meat packer. If the meat is graded, it should bear a USDA stamp indicating the grade, but it may not be visible. Ask the butcher when in doubt.

We pan-seared rib-eye steaks from all three grades and tasted them blind. Prime ranked first for its tender, buttery texture and rich beefy flavor; it was discernibly fattier. Choice came in second, with solid flavor and a little more chew. The Select steak was tough and stringy, with flavor that was only "acceptable." The lesson here is that you get what you pay for. Prime steaks are worth the extra money, but Choice steaks that exhibit a moderate amount of marbling are a fine and more affordable option.

CONSUMER BEEF GRADES

PRIME

Prime meat is heavily marbled with intra-muscular fat (seen as white streaks within the meat in this drawing), which makes for a tender, flavorful steak. About 2 percent of graded beef is considered Prime. Prime meats are most often served in restaurants or sold in high-end butcher shops.

CHOICE

The majority of graded beef is Choice. While the levels of marbling in Choice beef can vary, it is generally moderately marbled with intramuscular fat.

SELECT

Select beef has little marbling. The small amount of intramuscular fat can make Select meats drier, tougher, and less flavorful than the two higher grades.

PAN SAUCES FOR STEAK

WHAT WE WANTED: **Two great sauces for steak— one heady with red wine and stock, the other a simple emulsion of butter and shallots.**

Ever wonder how restaurants make the thick, rich red wine sauce they pour over a seared rib-eye steak? How about that creamy shallot-butter sauce drizzled over a seared strip steak? Chances are these sauces are made in the pan used to cook the steak. They begin with fond, the caramelized browned bits that sit on the bottom of the pan after the meat is seared.

Pan sauces are generally made by adding liquid (usually stock) to the pan and dissolving the fond (a process known as deglazing), reducing the liquid, then enriching and thickening the sauce with butter. These sauces are heavenly when made well—full-bodied, complex, balanced in flavor, rich in color, and thick enough to coat the steak and form a nice pool of sauce into which you can dip the meat. If you've properly seared the steak (see recipe on page 77), there will be plenty of browned bits to start a pan sauce.

A great red wine pan sauce starts with the right wine (see Tasting Lab on page 79). But even the right wine can produce a poor sauce. We found that wine doesn't react well to changes in temperature, making it a tricky ingredient to handle. As wine is heated, delicate flavor compounds known as esters break apart, turning fruity flavors and aromas sour and bitter. The higher the heat, the more rapidly the esters break down.

Transferring this knowledge to cooking, it would seem reasonable to assume that low, slow heat is better for wine than hot and fast heat. To test this assumption, we made two classic steak pan sauces, one made with rapidly simmered wine and the other made with slowly reduced wine. The results were so radically different that tasters thought the sauces had been made from different wines altogether. The rapidly simmered wine was tart and edgy, while the slowly

reduced wine was smooth and round. This surprised many of us who have learned to cook pan sauces the traditional way.

Classically, wine is added to a hot pan (the same pan in which the meat was just cooked) and reduced quickly over high heat while scraping up the tasty browned bits off the pan's bottom. We found that deglazing the hot pan with stock, not wine, and finishing the sauce with wine that had been slowly reduced in a separate pan, made a much better pan sauce—one unlike any we had made before. It was rich and voluptuous, with complex layers of flavor.

As we tested a few more pan sauces using this method, we discovered another trick. The wine reduction takes on an extra dimension and polished texture when small amounts of aromatic vegetables are added. Treating the wine almost like a stock, we steeped shallots, carrots, mushrooms, and herbs in the reducing wine, then strained them out before adding the reduction to the sauce.

By comparison, a shallot butter sauce is easy to prepare. It makes sense to think of this sauce as a melted version of compound butter. Compound butters are made by rolling butter (seasoned with shallots, herbs, spices, mustard, etc.) into a log, chilling the log, and then slicing off a round to melt over a cooked steak. Although delicious, a compound butter does not take advantage of the browned bits left in the pan used to sear the steaks.

For this reason, we like to add shallots to the empty skillet, then throw in the cold butter to create a quick, light sauce. Some lemon juice and parsley round out the flavor. Make sure the butter is cold when it goes into the pan. We found that cold butter gives a sauce more body than softened butter.

WHAT WE LEARNED: **When making a red wine pan sauce, reduce the wine separately over low heat to preserve its delicate flavors. When making a shallot butter sauce, add cold, not softened, butter to the sautéed shallots to give the sauce body.**

RED WINE SAUCE (FOR PAN-SEARED STEAKS)

makes enough for 4 steaks

Start cooking the steaks when the wine has almost fin-ished reducing, then keep the steaks warm on a plate in a 200-degree oven as you make the pan sauce. Use a smooth, medium-bodied, fruity wine, preferably made from a blend of grapes, such as a Côtes du Rhône. For more information about choosing a red wine for cooking, see the Tasting Lab below.

wine reduction

1 small carrot, peeled and chopped fine (about 2 tablespoons)
1 medium shallot, minced (about 2 tablespoons)
2 white mushrooms, chopped fine (about 3 tablespoons)
1 small bay leaf
3 sprigs fresh parsley
1 cup red wine

sauce

1 medium shallot, minced (about 2 tablespoons)
½ cup canned low-sodium chicken broth
½ cup canned low-sodium beef broth
3 tablespoons unsalted butter, cut into 6 pieces
½ teaspoon fresh thyme leaves
   Salt and ground black pepper

1. FOR THE WINE REDUCTION: Heat carrot, shallot, mushrooms, bay leaf, parsley, and wine in 12-inch nonstick skillet over low heat; cook, without simmering (liquid should be steaming but not bubbling) until entire mixture reduces to 1 cup, 15 to 20 minutes. Strain through fine-mesh strainer and return liquid (about ½ cup) to clean skillet. Continue to cook over low heat, without simmering, until liquid is reduced to 2 tablespoons, 15 to 20 minutes. Transfer reduction to bowl.

2. FOR THE SAUCE: Follow recipe for Pan-Seared Steaks, transferring plate with steaks to 200-degree oven to keep warm. To same skillet used to cook steaks (do not clean skil-let or discard accumulated fat), add shallot and cook over low heat until softened, about 1 minute. Turn heat to high; add chicken and beef broths. Bring to a boil, scraping up browned bits on pan bottom with wooden spoon until liq-uid is reduced to 2 tablespoons, about 6 minutes. Turn heat to medium-low, gently whisk in reserved wine reduction and any accumulated juices from plate with steaks. Whisk in butter, one piece at a time, until melted and sauce is thick-ened and glossy; add thyme and season with salt and pepper. Spoon sauce over steaks and serve immediately.

SHALLOT BUTTER SAUCE (FOR PAN-SEARED STEAKS)

makes enough for 4 steaks

2 large shallots, minced (about ⅓ cup)
4 tablespoons cold unsalted butter, cut into 4 pieces
1 teaspoon lemon juice from 1 lemon
1 teaspoon minced fresh parsley leaves
   Salt and ground black pepper

Follow recipe for Pan-Seared Steaks. To same skillet used to cook steaks (do not clean skillet or discard accumulated fat), add shallots and cook over low heat until softened, about 1 minute. Turn heat to medium-low; stir in butter, scraping up browned bits on pan bottom with wooden spoon. When butter is just melted, stir in lemon juice and parsley; season to taste with salt and pepper. Spoon sauce over steaks and serve immediately.

TASTING LAB: Red Wines for Cooking

WHEN A RECIPE CALLS FOR RED WINE, THE TENDENCY IS to grab whatever is inexpensive, close at hand, or already open on the counter. But as with any ingredient, the type of wine you cook with can make a big difference. The wrong wine can turn a good sauce bad. Yet because wines range enormously in flavor, body, and astringency, choosing a good one for the kitchen can be a shot in the dark.

What defines a good red cooking wine? It is appropriate for a wide range of recipes, easy to find at the local store, and consistent through the years. To help determine which red wines are good cookers, we set up a series of three cooking tests—a quick tomato sauce, a long-cooked beef stew, and a pan sauce for steak—through which we could test numerous bottles.

Organizing the overwhelming body of red wine into manageable groups, we assigned four categories based on flavor, body, and style: light/fruity, smooth/mellow, hearty/robust, and nondescript jug wine. Ironically, the only type of wine not represented is the "cooking wine" found on most supermarket shelves. In the past, we found that these low-alcohol concoctions have no flavor, a high-pitched acidity, and an enormous amount of salt, which renders them both undrinkable and a very poor choice for cooking.

We began by cooking with a representative from each category: a light/fruity Beaujolais, a smooth/mellow Merlot, a hearty/robust Cabernet Sauvignon, and a jug of Paul Mason Mountain Burgundy. The results were drastically different. The Beaujolais made refreshingly fruity but wimpy sauces, while the Merlot made for balanced sauces with an overcooked, jamlike flavor. The Cabernet Sauvignon produced an astringent, woody bite that bullied other ingredients out of the way, and the Paul Masson made sweet, simple sauces that neither offended nor impressed anyone.

Although none of the four groups "won" this first round of testing, what emerged were some important attributes of a good cooking wine and some characteristics to be wary of. The light wine made weak sauces, and the hearty wine made sauces that were too muscular. Oak flavors (from barrel aging) did not soften as they cooked but wound up tasting bitter and harsh. Fruity characteristics, on the other hand, mingled well with the other sauce ingredients and complemented their flavors.

Narrowing our focus to smooth, fruity, medium-bodied wines with little oak influence, we put four more types of

wine through the trio of recipes: a Chianti, a Zinfandel, a Pinot Noir, and a Côtes du Rhône. The Chianti tasted great in the tomato sauce but made an astringent pan sauce and cardboard-tasting stew. The Zinfandel tasted overcooked and jammy in the tomato sauce and turned the pan sauce bitter. While both the Côtes du Rhône and Pinot Noir turned in impressive results across the board, the Côtes du Rhône was stellar. When compared with the sauces made with Pinot Noir (a wine made from just one type of grape), the Côtes du Rhône (a blend of grapes) had a fuller, more even-keeled flavor. Varietals within the blend compensated for each others' shortcomings. The resulting sauces were potent but well-rounded. Besides Côtes du Rhône, there are many fruity, medium-bodied, blended wines, including wines from the greater Rhône Valley, Languedoc (near the Mediterranean), Australia, and the United States.

We found a strong correlation between price and quality when it comes to red wine. Tests demonstrated that a $5 bottle cooked much differently from bottles costing $10, $20, or $30. As a wine cooks and reduces, it becomes a more intensely flavored version of itself, and defining characteristics become unbearably obvious. The sweet, bland, $5 wines cooked down to candy-like sauces, while the $10, $20, and $30 bottles were increasingly smooth, with multiple layers of flavor. Although the higher-end wines tasted more balanced and refined, none of the tasters thought the flavor difference between the $10 and $20 or $30 bottles was worth the extra money. What's more, limiting the price to around $10 does not restrict your options when shopping. We found plenty of good blends from California, Australia, and France.

EQUIPMENT CORNER: Corkscrews

YOU WANT A CORKSCREW THAT REQUIRES A MINIMUM OF force to operate. A corkscrew should work just as well with fresh, tight-fitting corks as with dry, older corks that may crumble. Most of all, a corkscrew must be reliable. It should remove the cork each and every time.

We tested 18 different corkscrews on a variety of wine bottles. Some bottles had standard rims; others the wider rims common on flanged bottles. We worked with corks that were brittle and falling apart as well as firm, newer corks. There are three basic designs for a corkscrew—worm, air pump, and prong—and we tested several versions of each.

Most corkscrews have a spiraling metal shaft called a worm. The worm has a pointed end that can be driven through the cork. Air pump corkscrews have a syringe-like needle that pierces the cork and allows the user to pump air into the bottle. Once enough air has been pumped into the bottle, the pressure pushes the cork up and out with a pop. Prong corkscrews have thin prongs, usually of uneven length, that the user is supposed to insert between the cork and the glass. Once the prongs are inserted, a twisting motion pulls up the cork.

We quickly dismissed the corkscrews without the familiar worm. The air pump models were easy enough to use but felt odd. It took a fair amount of strength to pierce the cork with the needle, followed by an average of 16 pumps per bottle to lift up the cork.

We also dismissed the corkscrews with two prongs. One of our testers consistently pushed corks into bottles when trying to wiggle the prongs between cork and glass. Though other testers had better luck, none felt that these corkscrews were reliable. Practice made the process more comfortable, but we preferred the models with worms.

The best worm-style corkscrews had several traits in common. First and foremost, models that operate by continually turning after the worm fully penetrates the cork are preferable to models that stop turning once the worm is in the cork. The latter rely on a lever to lift up the impaled cork. For example, the classic waiter's corkscrew, with a hinged arm that swings out to brace against the rim of the bottle, works fine but it takes some practice to master.

In contrast, novices can uncork a bottle the first time they use a corkscrew with a continuously turning worm (often called a screwpull). These corkscrews rely on continued turning action (called torque) after the worm has already gone all the way through the cork. The cork rides up the worm, so there's no yanking involved. These models have an extra-long shaft so that the cork has some place to go.

We also liked the nonstick surface on the continuously turning models we tested. The slick coating reduces resistance as the worm works its way through the cork. Finally, most models that operate by continuous turning usually have worms encased in frames, which slip over the bottle neck and guide the worm straight into the cork.

As for worm-style corkscrews with neither lever nor continuous turning, the less said the better. Even if you can jab the worm into the cork, most people don't have the strength necessary to pull out the cork.

FRENCH FRIES

WHAT WE WANTED: Long, straight, crisp fries with sides neatly cut at right-angles; golden brown fries with a nice crunch on the outside and an earthy potato taste.

A good French fry requires the right potato. Would it be starchy (like a baking potato) or waxy (like a boiling potato)? We tested two of the most popular waxy potatoes, and neither was even close to ideal, both being too watery. During frying, the water inside the potato evaporated, leaving hollows that would fill with oil, making the finished fries greasy.

Next we tested the starchy potato most readily available nationwide, the russet. This potato turned out to be ideal, frying up with all the qualities that we were looking for.

Many sources suggest chilling the sliced potatoes in ice water before frying them, and we found this step was crucial. With a 30-minute chill, the potatoes are nearly frozen when they first enter the hot oil; this allows for a slow, thorough cooking of the inner potato pulp. When we tried making fries without prechilling, the outsides started to brown well before the insides were fully cooked.

What is the right fat for making perfect French fries? To find out, we experimented with lard, vegetable shortening, canola oil, corn oil, and peanut oil. Lard and shortening make great fries, but we assumed that many cooks wouldn't want to use these products. Canola oil, the ballyhooed oil of the 1990s, produced bland, almost watery fries. Corn oil rebounded well from temperature fluctuations, and the fries tasted very good. Potatoes fried in peanut oil, however, were even better: light, with a flavor that was rich but not dense. The earthy flavor of the potato was there, too. Although corn oil is fine for frying potatoes, tasters gave the edge to the peanut oil.

At this point, we were very close to the perfect fry, and yet there was still something missing. The high flavor note, which is supplied by the animal fat in lard, was lacking. We tried a dollop of strained bacon grease in peanut oil, about

two generous tablespoons per quart of oil. The meaty flavor came through. At last, an equivalent to lard.

Now it was time to get down to the frying, which actually means double-frying. First, we par-fried the potatoes at a relatively low temperature to release their rich and earthy flavor. The potatoes are then quick-fried at a higher temperature until nicely browned and served immediately.

The garden variety cookbook recipe calls for par-frying at 350 degrees and final frying at 375 to 400 degrees. We found these temperatures to be far too aggressive. We prefer an initial frying at 325 degrees, with the final frying at 350 degrees. Lower temperatures allowed for easier monitoring; with higher temperatures the fries can get away from the cook.

For the sake of convenience, we also attempted a single, longer frying. Like many cooks before us, we found that with standard French fries (as opposed to the much thinner shoestring fries), we could not both sear the outside and properly cook the inside with a single visit in the hot fat.

WHAT WE LEARNED: Use russet potatoes, soak them in ice water, and fry in peanut oil twice—first to cook the potatoes through, then to make them crisp and golden brown. For an old-fashioned, meaty flavor, add a little strained bacon grease to the pot.

FRENCH FRIES serves 4

We prefer to peel the potatoes. A skin-on fry keeps the potato from forming those little airy blisters that we like. Peeling the potato also allows removal of any imperfections and greenish coloring. Once the potatoes are peeled and cut, plan on at least an hour before the fries are ready to eat.

4 large russet potatoes, peeled and cut into
   ¼ inch by ¼-inch lengths (reserve nonuniform
   pieces for another use)
2 quarts peanut oil
4 tablespoons strained bacon grease (optional)
   Salt and ground black pepper

1. Place cut fries in large bowl, cover with at least 1 inch of water, then cover with ice cubes. Refrigerate at least 30 minutes or up to 3 days.

2. In 5-quart pot or Dutch oven fitted with clip-on candy thermometer, or in larger electric fryer, heat oil over medium-low heat to 325 degrees. (Oil will bubble up when you add fries, so be sure you have at least 3 inches of room at top of pot.) Add bacon grease, if using.

3. Pour off ice and water, quickly wrap potatoes in clean kitchen towel, and thoroughly pat dry. Increase heat to medium-high and add fries, one handful at a time, to hot oil. Fry, stirring with Chinese skimmer or large-hole slotted spoon, until potatoes are limp and soft and have turned from white to gold, about 10 minutes. (Oil temperature will drop 50 to 60 degrees during this frying.) Use skimmer or slotted spoon to transfer fries to triple thickness of paper towels to drain; let rest at least 10 minutes. (Can stand at room temperature up to 2 hours or be wrapped in paper towels, sealed in zipper-lock bag, and frozen up to 1 month.)

4. When ready to serve fries, reheat oil to 350 degrees. Using paper towels as funnel, pour potatoes into hot oil. Discard paper towels and line wire rack with another triple thickness of paper towels. Fry potatoes, stirring fairly constantly, until medium brown and puffed, about 1 minute. Transfer to paper towel–lined rack to drain. Season to taste with salt and pepper. Serve immediately.

SCIENCE DESK: Storing Potatoes

SINCE POTATOES SEEM ALMOST INDESTRUCTIBLE COMpared with other vegetables, little thought is generally given to their storage. But because various problems can result from inadequate storage conditions, we decided to find out how much difference storage really makes. We stored all-purpose potatoes in five environments: in a cool (50–60 degrees), dark place; in the refrigerator; in a basket near a sunlit window; in a warm (70–80 degrees), dark place; and in a drawer with some onions at room temperature. We checked all the potatoes after four weeks.

As expected, the potatoes stored in the cool, dark place were firm, had not sprouted, and were crisp and moist when cut. There were no negative marks on the potatoes stored in the refrigerator, either. Although some experts say that the sugar level dramatically increases in some potato varieties under these conditions, we could not see or taste any difference between these potatoes and the ones stored in the cool, dark but unrefrigerated environment.

Our last three storage tests produced unfavorable results. The potatoes stored in sunlight, in warm storage, and with onions ended up with a greenish tinge along the edges. When potatoes are stressed by improper storage, the level of naturally occurring toxins increases, causing the greenish tinge known as solanine. Because solanine is not destroyed by cooking, any part of the potato with this greenish coloring should be completely cut away before cooking. In addition, the skin of the potatoes stored in sunlight became gray and mottled, while the potatoes stored in a warm place and those stored with onions sprouted and became soft and wrinkled. Sprouts also contain increased levels of solanine and should be cut away before cooking.

A Dutch oven may seem like an unlikely choice for frying chicken. But this pot is deep enough to prevent splatters and comes with a lid that traps moisture during the first half of the cooking time, helping to keep the chicken moist.

FRIED CHICKEN,
& fixin's

CHAPTER 8

Fried chicken is so patently American, so perennially "in," that it travels with a band of icons. It's not possible to think of biscuits or gravy, coleslaw or ham, or Grandma without thinking about fried chicken.

But making good fried chicken is harder than it seems. There's a reason why the Colonel kept his recipe a secret. Not only must you get the chicken right—it should be juicy, tender, and incredibly well seasoned—but the coating has to be perfect. For us, the ultimate fried chicken is shatteringly crisp. Softness and sogginess have no place in this recipe.

Our fried chicken recipe is the result of five years' work and incorporates many unusual techniques. We soak the chicken in a mixture of buttermilk, salt, sugar, and spices; air-dry the pieces to make the skin taut; coat them with flour; and then fry them in a Dutch oven rather than a skillet. The results put fast-food chicken to shame.

Our oven-fried chicken—designed for those cooks who are trying to reduce fat content or want to avoid creating a mess in the kitchen—is pretty darn good, too.

Coleslaw is the classic accompaniment to fried chicken. Coleslaw should be crisp and tangy. The dressing should coat the cabbage lightly and not become watery as the coleslaw sits on the picnic table.

CRISPY FRIED CHICKEN

WHAT WE WANTED: Chicken with a crackling crisp crust and tender, moist, seasoned meat.

What makes fried chicken great? First come, first served: the crust. Crisp and crackling with flavor, the crust must cleave to the chicken itself, not balloon away or flake off in chips like old radiator paint. In addition, it should carry a deep, uniform mahogany without spots or evidence of greasiness. As for the chicken itself, tender, moist, and flavorful are the descriptors of the day. Served hot, it should be demonstrably juicy; served room temperature, it should be moist. On no account should it be punishingly dry or require a salt shaker as a chaperone.

The truth is that frying chicken at home is a daunting task, a messy tableau of buttermilk dip and breading, hot fat, and splatters one hopes will end at the stove's edge. The results are often tantamount to the mess: greasy, peeling chicken skin and dry, unseasoned meat that's a long way from Grandma's.

It was no surprise to us that the chicken we were frying had to be premium quality to be worth the effort. Packaged chicken parts were irregular and disappointing, containing mismatched pieces in shabby dress with tattered skin, cut without a nod to basic anatomy. Given this situation, we thought it wise to spend a few minutes cutting a whole 3½-pound broiler into 12 manageable pieces (see page 89).

In our first stove-side excursion, we fried up several batches of chicken with different coatings, oils, and so on. But our real interest resided beneath the skin: half of the chickens had been brined for two hours; the other half had not. A brine is at minimum a mixture of salt and water. When soaked in a brine, chicken (as well as other poultry and meat) absorbs some of the salt and some of the water, thereby becoming more flavorful and more juicy once cooked. The tasting results bore out these benefits of brining: However glorious the crust, however perfectly fried the piece, the unbrined chicken earned marks far below its brined competition. Who wants to bite through a crisp, rich, seasoned crust only to hit dry, white Styrofoam? Another benefit of brining presented itself during cooking. Our brined chicken parts fried at equal rates, relieving us of the need to baby-sit the white meat or pull the wings out of the fat early.

While brining per se may not be common practice when preparing fried chicken, soaking the pieces in some kind of liquid—particularly buttermilk—is traditional. This process is thought to tenderize the meat (a mistaken assumption) and add flavor. We examined a number of soaking solutions and found the bright acidic flavor and clinging viscosity of buttermilk to produce the best flavor accents and richest browning during cooking.

Appreciating the tang of a buttermilk soak but unwilling to forgo the succulence of brined chicken, we found ourselves whispering "buttermilk brine." Instead of soaking the chicken in buttermilk alone, why not add the saline blast of a brine, doubling the rewards and minimizing the number of steps? To get a leg up on the idea, we made it a flavored brine, adding a mountain of crushed garlic, a couple of crushed bay leaves, and some sweet paprika.

This remarkable "twofer" won high marks indeed, well above those garnered by a unilateral soak or brine. The buttermilk and paprika showed spirit, garlic and bay crept into the crust, and the meat was tender and seasoned. We also spiked the brine with ¼ cup of sugar—not enough to sweeten but enough to bring other flavors out of hiding.

Fried foods taste irresistibly good when dressed in crumbs or flour, not only because their insides are protected from damaging temperatures but also because hot, enveloping fat performs minor miracles on the flavor of the flour or crumbs. But what kind of coating is best?

To find out, we tested straight flour against a panoply of contenders: matzo crumbs, ground saltines, cornflakes, Melba toast, cornmeal, and panko (Japanese) bread crumbs.

In the end, plain flour—requiring in this instance no seasoning whatsoever since the chicken had been brined—surpassed all other options for the integrity and lightness of the crust it produced.

Many fried chicken recipes use a single breading process in which the chicken is dipped first into beaten egg, then into flour or crumbs. A double, or bound, breading dips the chicken into flour first, then into egg, and finally into flour or crumbs. In side-by-side tests, we found that the double breading offered a superior base coat—more tenacious in its grip, more protective in its bearing—without being overly thick or tough.

Another practice that has made its way into many fried chicken recipes is that of air-drying breaded chicken before frying it. Rather than becoming soggy in the refrigerator, as might be expected, the breading toughens up over time to produce a fried chicken of superior crispiness.

We were also curious about the effect of air-drying on unbreaded chicken. We have come to favor the laser-crisp and taut skin of roasted birds that have been air-dried and wanted to see if an analogous effect could be achieved by refrigerating our brined, unbreaded chicken on a rack for a couple of hours. We were reasonably confident this would allow the buttermilk to dry just enough to maintain a protective and flavorful posture and the chicken to bread nicely without first being dabbed or dried, frying up dry and crisp.

We tested the effects of air-drying the chicken before and after breading and compared the results with chicken that underwent no air-drying. Both air-dried versions were superior in terms of crust, but each was distinctly different from the other. The chicken that was breaded and then air-dried had a heartier, more toothsome crust—crunchy to some, hard to others. The chicken that was air-dried and then breaded was lighter and crispier, flaky, more shattery. We preferred this traditionally Southern crust. Though it initially seemed ideal, we noticed that its delicate crispiness succumbed to sandiness and porosity over the course of a few hours. This was not acceptable.

The memory of a particularly light but resilient crust on a chicken-fried steak recipe we had made persuaded us to add baking soda and baking powder to an egg wash bolstered with buttermilk. We hoped the sandiness in the crust that developed over time might thus be offset. Stirred into the wash, ½ teaspoon of soda and 1 teaspoon of powder produced just enough carbon dioxide to lighten the breading to perfection. Not only did it bronze to a shattery filigree in the hot fat, it also remained crisp as it cooled.

One of the most important requirements of fat as a frying medium is that it offer nothing of its own flavor—and, in fact, have none to offer. This means that the oil must be refined—in other words, cleansed and sanitized. Another requirement is that the oil perform at temperatures below its smoke point (the temperature at which it emits smoke and acrid odors) to maintain thermal stability. With the relatively moderate temperatures required by our recipe, all refined vegetable oils stayed well below their smoke points. In the end, peanut oil edged out Crisco shortening by virtue of its marginally more neutral and clean flavor.

A cast-iron Dutch oven covered during the first half of the frying reduced splatters to a fine spray, maintained the oil temperature impeccably, and fried the chicken through in about 15 minutes total versus the 20 minutes per side recommended in many recipes.

Drying the gleaming, bronzed statuettes was the most satisfying test. Paper bags are simply not porous enough to keep the chicken out of a gathering pool of grease. We found that paper towels absorbed excess fat quickly and that rolling the pieces over onto a bare rack thereafter kept them crisp.

WHAT WE LEARNED: Soak chicken parts in a seasoned buttermilk brine for ultimate flavor and juiciness. Air-dry the brined chicken parts before coating with crumbs to create a light, crisp crust. Flour makes the crispest coating. Peanut oil can withstand the demands of frying and has the most neutral flavor of all the oils tested. Shortening was a close runner-up. With its high sides and lid, a Dutch oven minimizes splatters and retains heat that helps the chicken cook through.

CRISPY FRIED CHICKEN serves 4 to 6

Maintaining an even oil temperature is key to the success of this recipe. An instant-read thermometer with a high upper range is perfect for checking the temperature; a clip-on candy/deep-fry thermometer is fine, though it can be clipped to the pot only for the uncovered portion of frying.

1¼ cups kosher salt or ½ cup plus 2 tablespoons table salt
¼   cup sugar
2   tablespoons paprika
3   medium heads garlic, cloves separated
3   bay leaves, crumbled
2   quarts low-fat buttermilk
1   whole chicken (about 3½ pounds), giblets discarded, cut into 12 pieces (see illustrations on page 89)
4   cups all-purpose flour
1   large egg
1   teaspoon baking powder
½   teaspoon baking soda
3–4 cups refined peanut oil or vegetable shortening

1. In large zipper-lock plastic bag, combine salt, sugar, paprika, garlic cloves, and bay leaves. With rubber mallet or flat meat pounder, smash garlic into salt and spice mixture thoroughly. Pour mixture into large plastic container or nonreactive stockpot. Add 7 cups buttermilk and stir until salt is completely dissolved. Immerse chicken, cover with plastic wrap, and refrigerate until fully seasoned, 2 to 3 hours. Remove chicken from buttermilk brine and shake off excess; place in single layer on large wire rack set over rimmed baking sheet. Refrigerate uncovered for 2 hours. (After 2 hours, chicken can be covered with plastic wrap and refrigerated up to 6 hours longer.)

2. Measure flour into large shallow dish. Beat egg, baking powder, and baking soda in medium bowl; stir in remaining 1 cup buttermilk (mixture will bubble and foam). Working in batches of 3, drop chicken pieces in flour and shake pan to coat. Shake excess flour from each piece. Then, using tongs, dip chicken pieces into egg mixture, turning to coat well and allowing excess to drip off. Coat chicken pieces with flour again, shake off excess, and return to wire rack.

3. Adjust oven rack to middle position, set second wire rack over second rimmed baking sheet, and place on oven rack; heat oven to 200 degrees. Line large plate with double layer of paper towels. Meanwhile, heat oil (oil should have 2½-inch depth in pan) to 375 degrees over medium-high heat in large 8-quart cast-iron Dutch oven with a diameter of about 12 inches. Place half of chicken pieces skin-side down in oil, cover, reduce heat to medium, and fry until deep golden brown, 6 to 8 minutes; after about 3 minutes, lift chicken pieces with tongs to check for even browning; rearrange if some pieces are browning faster than others. (Spot-check oil temperature; after first 6 minutes of frying, oil should be about 325 degrees. Adjust burner if necessary.) Turn chicken pieces over and continue to fry, uncovered, until chicken pieces are deep golden brown on second side, 6 to 8 minutes longer. Using tongs, transfer chicken to paper towel–lined plate; let stand 2 minutes to drain, then transfer to rack in warm oven. Replace paper towel lining on plate. Return oil to 375 degrees and fry remaining pieces, transferring pieces to paper towel–lined plate to drain, then transferring to wire rack. Cool chicken pieces on wire rack (outside oven) about 5 minutes and serve.

TECHNIQUE: Cutting Up a Chicken for Frying

Chicken destined for the fry pot should be cut into fairly small pieces. Instead of the standard eight pieces (two breasts, two wings, two thighs, and two legs), we cut each breast piece in half and sever the wing at the main joint (the skin cooks better when thus separated, and the wings pieces are easier to eat) to yield a total of 12 pieces.

1. With a sharp chef's knife, cut through the skin around the leg where it attaches to the breast.

2. Using both hands, pop the leg joint out of its socket.

3. Use a chef's knife to cut through the flesh and skin to detach the leg from the body.

4. A line of fat separates the thigh and drumstick. Cut through the joint at this point. Repeat steps 1 through 4 with the other leg.

5. Bend the wing out from the breast and use a boning knife to cut through the joint. Repeat with the other wing.

6. Cut through the cartilage around the wing tip to remove it. Discard the tip. Cut through the joint to split. Repeat with the other wing.

7. Using poultry shears, cut along the ribs to completely separate the back from the breast. Discard backbone.

8. Place the knife on the breast-bone, then apply pressure to cut through and separate the breast into halves.

9. Cut each breast in half crosswise.

SCIENCE DESK: Successful Frying

MANY COOKS SHY AWAY FROM FRYING, THINKING THAT the technique adds loads of fat to their food. Taking nothing for granted, we put this notion to the test. We heated 3 cups of peanut oil to 375 degrees in a 12-inch Dutch oven and pan-fried a whole chicken in two batches. To our delight, we poured back almost exactly three cups of fat after frying. Each time the test was repeated, we ended up with virtually the same amount of fat before and after.

The explanation is simple: If the water in the food you are frying is kept above the boiling point (212 degrees), the outward pressure of the escaping water vapor keeps oil from soaking into the hot food. If the frying oil is not hot enough, the oil will seep into the food, making it greasy. The key is to get the oil hot enough before adding food (375 degrees worked well) so that you maintain a temperature (around 325 degrees) that keeps the moisture in the food boiling.

EQUIPMENT CORNER: Best Pots for Frying Chicken

A SKILLET MIGHT SEEM THE NATURAL CHOICE FOR FRYING CHICKEN, BUT THE DEEP SIDES OF A DUTCH OVEN MINIMIZE splattering and create a veil of condensation that tenderizes the chicken. (All-Clad refers to its pan as a stockpot, but it functions well as a Dutch oven.)

CAST-IRON SKILLET
The lid for this squat skillet basically sat on top of the chicken, giving the hot, moist air nowhere to go. After turning, the top of the chicken became soggy.

LODGE CAST-IRON DUTCH OVEN
The thick walls of this pot took 10 minutes to heat, but once they did, the pot maintained the oil's temperature and fried the chicken to perfection.

ALL-CLAD STOCKPOT
This sturdy entry took on heat quickly but lost it, and failed to recover it, once the chicken entered the fat. The chicken did not color easily.

LE CREUSET ENAMELED DUTCH OVEN
The thinner cast-iron walls of this beauty heated up fast and stayed that way. Cleanup was a cinch with its slick enamel surface.

OVEN-FRIED CHICKEN

WHAT WE WANTED: "Fried" chicken with real crunch and good flavor.

We've always thought of oven-fried chicken as ersatz fried chicken—only for those who were afraid to mess up their kitchen or consume too much fat. Depending on the liquid or crumb coating, this chicken could be bland, soggy, rubbery-skinned, greasy, artificially flavored, dry, or crumbly. Was it possible, we wondered, to make a decent alternative to the real thing?

After reading many recipes, we realized that the coatings—both the moist one that helps the crumbs stick and the dry one that provides crunch—were the key issues to examine.

Since the moist coating comes first, we started there. (For information on dry coatings, see page 92.) Before testing, we assumed this wet dunk did little more than help the crumbs adhere to the chicken. After testing, however, it became clear that this initial coat plays a larger role. A good first coat, we discovered, should offer flavor, attract the right proportion of crumbs to form an impressive, uniform crust, and, finally, help the crust stay crunchy during baking.

To find the best moist coating, we baked 13 drumsticks, keeping the dry coating constant while varying the moist coating: water, whole milk, evaporated milk, cream, buttermilk, yogurt, sour cream, milk beaten with egg, egg beaten with lemon juice, and egg with Dijon mustard. In addition, we tried legs coated with ranch dressing, mayonnaise, and butter.

Because many recipes for oven-fried chicken start by rolling chicken parts in butter, we thought the fat coatings would perform well. Not so. All of them—butter, mayonnaise, and ranch dressing—created a slick surface that prevented the crumbs from adhering properly. In addition, none of the fats did anything to crisp up the crumbs.

With the exception of buttermilk and evaporated milk, moreover, none of the dairy coatings impressed us. Buttermilk and evaporated milk did attract decent crusts and give a subtle flavor dimension to the chicken, but they didn't result in the crispness we wanted.

The egg beaten with lemon did result in a crisp coating. Unfortunately, it also contributed too much lemon flavor with an overcooked egg aftertaste. But a change of just one ingredient made all the difference. Chicken coated with beaten egg and Dijon mustard was our favorite. This not-too-thick, not-too-thin moistener not only attracted a uniform, impressive layer of crumbs, it also gave the meat a wonderfully subtle flavor. Unlike many of the wet coatings, which made the crumbs either soggy or barely crisp, this one took the crumbs to an almost crunchy level.

Over the course of testing, we found that we much preferred legs and thighs to breasts because they don't dry out as quickly. As expected, the buttermilk brine that worked so well in our crispy fried chicken recipe did wonders here, too. The meat was more moist and better seasoned after a two-hour brine. We also discovered that we didn't like the skin on oven-fried chicken. Unlike fried chicken, in which hot oil causes the fat to render and the skin to crisp up, oven heat simply softens the skin and makes it rubbery. We decided to remove the skin before coating the pieces.

Oven temperature was a simple matter. We started baking at 400 degrees, and all of the chicken pieces were cooked through and rich golden brown in about 40 minutes. A wire rack set over a rimmed baking sheet allows heat to circulate around the chicken during baking, allowing the chicken to crisp without being turned.

In the end, this "fried" chicken was pretty darn good. Perhaps not as crispy as the real thing, but a close runner-up.

WHAT WE LEARNED: Soak chicken legs and thighs in buttermilk brine to achieve maximum juiciness and flavor in the meat. A mixture of eggs and mustard helps the crumbs stick to the chicken and encourages the formation of a crunchy crust. Melba toast crumbs make the crispest coating.

OVEN-FRIED CHICKEN serves 4

To make Melba toast crumbs, place the toasts in a heavy-duty plastic freezer bag, seal, and pound with a meat pounder or other heavy blunt object. Leave some crumbs in the mixture the size of pebbles, but most should resemble coarse sand.

chicken

1¼	cups kosher salt or ½ cup plus 2 tablespoons table salt
¼	cup sugar
2	tablespoons paprika
3	medium heads garlic, cloves separated
3	bay leaves, crumbled
7	cups low-fat buttermilk
4	whole chicken legs, separated into drumsticks and thighs (see illustration 4 on page 89) and skin removed

coating

¼	cup vegetable oil
1	box (about 5 ounces) plain Melba toast, crushed
2	large eggs
1	tablespoon Dijon mustard
1	teaspoon dried thyme
¾	teaspoon salt
½	teaspoon ground black pepper
½	teaspoon dried oregano
¼	teaspoon garlic powder
¼	teaspoon cayenne (optional)

1. FOR THE CHICKEN: In large zipper-lock plastic bag, combine salt, sugar, paprika, garlic cloves, and bay leaves. With rubber mallet or flat meat pounder, smash garlic into salt and spice mixture thoroughly. Pour mixture into large plastic container or nonreactive stockpot. Add buttermilk and stir until salt is completely dissolved. Immerse chicken and refrigerate until fully seasoned, 2 to 3 hours. Remove chicken from buttermilk brine and shake off excess; place in single layer on large wire rack set over rimmed baking sheet. Refrigerate uncovered for 2 hours. (After 2 hours, chicken can be covered with plastic wrap and refrigerated up to 6 hours longer.)

2. Adjust oven rack to upper-middle position and heat oven to 400 degrees. Line sheet pan with foil and set large flat wire rack over sheet pan.

3. FOR THE COATING: Drizzle oil over Melba toast crumbs in a shallow dish or pie plate; toss well to coat. Mix eggs, mustard, thyme, salt, pepper, oregano, garlic powder, and optional cayenne with a fork in a second shallow dish or pie plate.

4. Working one piece at a time, coat chicken on both sides with egg mixture. Set chicken in Melba crumbs, sprinkle crumbs over chicken, and press to coat. Turn chicken over and repeat on other side. Gently shake off excess and place on rack. Bake until chicken is deep nutty brown and juices run clear, about 40 minutes.

TASTING LAB: Dry Coatings

WE STARTED WITH 20 DRY COATINGS OR COMBINATIONS, all from published recipes. After baking and tasting them all, there wasn't a single one we thought was perfect.

Of the cereal coatings, cornflakes were the best, offering good color and crunch, but they also had too much sweet corn flavor. Ditto for bran flakes, but their distinct flavor was even more pronounced. Unprocessed bran looked like kitty litter, while Grape-Nuts looked (worse) like hamster food.

Crackers didn't work, either. Both saltines and Ritz were too soft; the Ritz, in addition, were too sweet. Cracker meal delivered a bland blond shell. In the bread department, stuffing mix scored well in crunch but struck out in flavor. Fresh bread crumbs, on the other hand, tasted great but lacked the crunch we had come to like.

The meals and flours, as to be expected, did not show well. Cornmeal tasted raw, and it chipped off the chicken like flecks of old paint. Our grocery store's house brand of Shake 'n Bake was vile, tasting of liquid smoke and bad hot dogs.

Although this first round of tests did not produce a strong winner, it did help us to clarify what it was that we wanted—a coating that was crunchy (not just crisp) and flavorful (but not artificial tasting) and that baked up a rich copper brown.

With a clear ideal in mind, we found a whole new range of coating possibilities in the specialty/international cracker section of our grocery store, including Melba toast, pain grillé (French crisp toast), Swedish crisps, lavash (crisp flat bread), bread sticks, bagel chips, Italian toasts, and pita chips.

This series of tests delivered oven-fried chicken that was much closer to our ideal. The rather surprising winner, it turned out, was Melba toast. It scored the best in all three major categories—texture, flavor, and color.

EQUIPMENT CORNER: Cutting Boards

WHAT SEPARATES GOOD CUTTING BOARDS FROM BAD ones? Is it material? Size, thickness, or weight? Whether the board warps or retains odors with use?

To sort all of this out, we gathered boards made from wood, polyethylene (plastic), acrylic, glass, and Corian (the hard countertop material) and used them daily in our test kitchen for eight weeks. We found the two most important factors to be size and material.

In terms of size, large boards provide ample space for both cutting and pushing aside cut foods and waste. The disadvantage of really large boards is that they may not fit in the dishwasher. We are willing to make that sacrifice for the extra work area. If you are not, buy the largest board that will fit in your dishwasher. No matter the dimensions, a board should be heavy enough for stability but not so heavy (or thick and bulky) to impede its easy movement around the kitchen. We found boards in the range of 3 to 4 pounds to be ideal.

Material is important primarily in terms of the way the board interacts with the knife, but it is also relevant to odor retention and warping. We disliked cutting on hard acrylic, glass, and Corian boards because they don't absorb the shock of the knife strike. Plastic and wood boards are softer and therefore cushion the knife's blow, making for more controlled cutting.

There is one advantage to hard boards—they don't retain odors like plastic and wood can. A dishwasher will remove odors from plastic boards as well as specially treated dishwasher-safe wood boards. (Unless treated by the manufacturer with a waterproof coating, wood boards should never go in the dishwasher.)

If your boards are too large to fit in the dishwasher, use one for onions, garlic, and the like; another for raw poultry, fish, and meat; and a third for other foods. To remove most odors and bacteria, wash with hot soapy water after each use and then sanitize with a light bleach solution (1 tablespoon of bleach to 1 gallon of water).

Many plastic and wood boards will warp over time. Makers of wood boards advise consumers to season their boards with mineral oil to build up water resistance and, thereby, resist warping. As none of the cooks we know will go this extra mile, plastic boards probably make the most sense for home cooks. Keep plastic boards away from the dishwasher's heating element to prevent warping.

COLESLAW

WHAT WE WANTED: A crisp salad with creamy dressing that would be neither watery nor harsh-tasting.

Despite its simplicity, coleslaw has always bothered us for two reasons: the pool of watery dressing that appears at the bottom of the bowl after a few hours, and the salad's sharp flavor, no matter what kind or quantity of vinegar is used. Our slaw always seemed to taste better when we tried it again the next day, but by then the dressing was the consistency of skim milk.

While most recipes instruct the cook to toss the shredded cabbage immediately with dressing, a few add an extra step. Either the shredded (or merely quartered) cabbage is soaked in ice water for crisping and refreshing, or it is salted, drained, and allowed to wilt.

We soaked cabbage in ice water and found it to be crisp, plump, and fresh. If looks were all that mattered, this cabbage would have scored high next to the limp, salted cabbage in the neighboring colander. But its good looks were deceiving. Even though we drained the ice water–soaked cabbage and dried it thoroughly, the dressing didn't really adhere. Within minutes, the cabbage shreds started to lose their recently acquired water, making for not a small but a large puddle of water to dilute the creamy dressing. The stiff cabbage shreds were strawlike, making them difficult to get onto a fork and even more difficult to get into the mouth without leaving a creamy trail.

Quite unlike the ice-water cabbage, the salted shreds lost most of their liquid while sitting in the salt, leaving the cabbage wilted but pickle-crisp. Because the cabbage had already lost most of its own liquid, there was little or no liquid for the salt in the dressing to draw out. We had found the solution to the problem of watery dressing. In addition, we found that this cabbage, having less water in it, absorbed more flavor from the dressing, and, unlike the stiff, icy shreds, this limp cabbage was also easier to eat.

We did discover that the salting process leaves the cabbage a bit too salty, but a quick rinse washes away the excess. After the cabbage has been rinsed, just pat it dry with paper towels and refrigerate until ready to combine with the dressing. If the coleslaw is to be eaten immediately, rinse it quickly in ice water rather than tap water, then pat it dry. Coleslaw, at least the creamy style, should be served cold.

Having figured out how to keep the cabbage from watering down the dressing, we were ready to tackle the problem of acidity in the dressing. We found a few creamy coleslaw recipes in which the cabbage was tossed with sour cream only, or a combination of mayonnaise and sour cream—no vinegar. Although we were looking for ways to tone down the tang, a mix of sour cream and mayonnaise proved too mild for our taste. Other recipes called for lemon juice rather than vinegar. Although the lemon juice–flavored coleslaw was pleasantly tart, it lacked the depth that vinegar could offer. We decided to give low-acidity rice vinegar a try. We drizzled a bit of rice vinegar over the mayonnaise-tossed cabbage and found its mild acidity to be perfect for coleslaw.

Although there are several styles of coleslaw, the two that follow are classics—one mild and creamy, the other sweet-and-sour. Adjust either recipe to your taste. If sour cream is a must for your creamy slaw, then substitute it for some or all of the mayonnaise. And feel free to embellish our recipe. Add green pepper or celery, red onions, or apples. Try caraway seeds or fresh dill, radishes, or nuts.

WHAT WE LEARNED: Don't soak the shredded cabbage; that just makes the dressing watery. Do salt the shredded cabbage; removing excess water keeps the dressing thick and creamy. A combination of mayonnaise and low-acidity rice vinegar creates a dressing that's flavorful but not harsh.

CREAMY COLESLAW serves 4

If you like caraway or celery seeds, add 1/4 teaspoon of either with the mayonnaise and vinegar. You can shred, salt, rinse, and pat the cabbage dry a day ahead, but dress it close to serving time. If you like a tangier slaw, replace some or all of the mayonnaise with an equal amount of sour cream. For tips on handling cabbage, see illustrations at right.

- 1 pound (about 1/2 medium head) red or green cabbage, shredded fine or chopped (6 cups)
- 1 large carrot, peeled and grated
- 2 teaspoons kosher salt or 1 teaspoon table salt
- 1/2 small onion, minced
- 1/2 cup mayonnaise
- 2 tablespoons rice vinegar
  Ground black pepper

1. Toss cabbage and carrots with salt in colander set over medium bowl. Let stand until cabbage wilts, at least 1 hour and up to 4 hours.

2. Dump wilted cabbage and carrots into bowl. Rinse thoroughly in cold water (ice water if serving slaw immediately). Pour vegetables back into colander, pressing, but not squeezing, to drain. Pat dry with paper towels.

3. Pour cabbage and carrots back again into bowl. Add onion, mayonnaise, and vinegar; toss to coat. Season with pepper to taste. Cover and refrigerate until ready to serve. (Can be refrigerated for up to 2 days.)

SWEET-AND-SOUR COLESLAW serves 4

The presence of the sugar in this recipe makes it unnecessary to rinse the salt from the cabbage, as is ordinarily the case. For tips on handling cabbage, see illustrations at right.

- 1 pound (about 1/2 medium head) red or green cabbage, shredded fine or chopped (6 cups)
- 1 large carrot, peeled and grated

TECHNIQUE: Shredding Cabbage

1. Cut a whole head of cabbage in quarters. Cut away the hard piece of the core attached to each quarter.

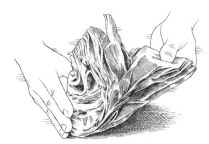

2. Separate the cored cabbage quarters into stacks of leaves that flatten when pressed lightly.

3. Use a chef's knife to cut each stack of cabbage diagonally into long, thin pieces. Or, roll the stacked leaves crosswise to fit them into the feed tube of a food processor fitted with the shredding disk.

½ cup sugar
2 teaspoons kosher salt or 1 teaspoon table salt
¼ teaspoon celery seeds
6 tablespoons vegetable oil
¼ cup rice vinegar
Ground black pepper

1. Toss cabbage and carrots with sugar, salt, and celery seeds in colander set over medium bowl. Let stand until cabbage wilts, at least 1 hour and up to 4 hours.

2. Pour draining liquid from bowl; rinse bowl and dry. Dump wilted cabbage and carrots from colander into bowl.

3. Add oil and vinegar; toss to coat. Season with pepper to taste. Cover and refrigerate until ready to serve. (Can be refrigerated for up to 2 days.)

VARIATION

CURRIED COLESLAW WITH APPLES AND RAISINS serves 6
Follow recipe for Sweet-and-Sour Coleslaw, adding 1 teaspoon curry powder, 1 medium apple, peeled and cut into small dice, and ¼ cup raisins (optional) with oil and vinegar.

SCIENCE DESK:
Where There's Salt, There's Water

VEGETABLES THAT SOAK IN ICE WATER CRISP UP, WHILE salted and drained vegetables go limp. These phenomena are evidence of the cell structure of most foods, including vegetables. Cells are filled with liquid, and their walls are semipermeable, meaning they allow some things, like water, to flow into and out of the cell. The water will flow to whichever side of the wall has a higher concentration of salt.

Cabbage is a pretty tough vegetable, but when soaked in ice water, its shreds become even stiffer and crisper. In this case, the cabbage cells have a greater concentration of salt than the ice water. The ice water is drawn into the cabbage cells, causing the shreds to plump up. Watching a scored radish blossom into a radish rose when soaked in ice water is an even more dramatic example of this principle.

When shredded cabbage is salted, on the other hand, the concentration of salt is greater outside the cabbage than inside the cells. The cell water is drawn out by the clinging salt. This partially dehydrated cabbage is limp but still crisp.

TASTING LAB: Mayonnaise

WHILE HOMEMADE MAYONNAISE IS A DELICIOUS ADDItion to salads, many cooks prefer the convenience and safety of commercial brands made without raw eggs. In dishes such as coleslaw, good commercial mayonnaise is a fine addition.

Two brands dominate the mayo market—Hellmann's (also known as Best Foods in some parts of the country) and Kraft. Each company makes several products—full fat, reduced fat, and low- or no-fat. We tasted six kinds of mayonnaise (three from each company) and tasters were unanimous in their first choice.

Hellmann's Real Mayonnaise was the creamiest in the bunch, with an excellent balance of flavors. Many tasters felt it was as good, if not better, than most homemade mayonnaise. Hellmann's Light (a reduced-calorie product with about half the fat of Hellmann's Real) took second place. Most tasters thought this product was almost as creamy as the winner.

Kraft Real Mayonnaise finished in third place, right behind Hellmann's Light. It was a bit less creamy and not as flavorful as the top finishers.

The remaining reduced-fat and no-fat products fared poorly in our tasting. Most were too acidic and lacked the sheen of a good mayonnaise. If you want to cut calories and fat, Hellmann's Light is a fine option, but don't try to trim any more fat grams—what you lose in calories just isn't worth what you lose in flavor.

Spaghetti and Meatballs page 27

Deep-Dish Pizza page 39 with Fresh Tomato Topping page 40

Spaghetti alla Carbonara **page 19**

Grilled Fresh Mozzarella Sandwiches with Black Olive Paste and Roasted Red Peppers page 54

Breaded Chicken Cutlet page 119

Herb-Poached Shrimp with Cocktail Sauce **page 62**

104

Stuffed Chicken Cutlets **page 122** with Broiled Asparagus and Smoked Mozzarella Cheese Filling **page 123**

Grilled Hamburger page 128

French Fries page 83

107

Chunky Guacamole page 155

108

Classic Fajitas **page 157** and Grilled Corn **page 135**

Green Beans with Toasted Hazelnuts and Brown Butter **page 187**

Pommes Anna **page** 184

CHICKEN cutlets 101

It's no secret that most Americans prefer white meat to dark meat chicken. Meat from the breast is lean and tender. Since most Americans don't like to deal with skin and bones, it makes sense that cutlets (otherwise known as boneless, skinless breasts) have become the preferred cut of chicken.

Although cutlets can be delicious, they can also be tough and dry. Because white meat contains very little fat, it can be the trickiest part of the bird to prepare.

For this episode, we take three classic preparations—Marsala, breaded, and stuffed—and explore ways to make these dishes really good. Chicken should be more than just serviceable. It should be something you look forward to and enjoy.

Bridget gathers flour, eggs, and fresh bread crumbs to make the crisp coating for our breaded cutlets.

CHICKEN MARSALA

WHAT WE WANTED: A rich, potent sauce to coat browned mushrooms and perfectly cooked chicken cutlets.

Marsala has never been a glamorous wine. It bears the name of its hometown, a seaport on the western coast of Sicily, once mockingly dubbed "the dump" by Italians from neighboring wine-making regions. In the early 1800s, a marketing campaign touted Marsala as a less expensive alternative to Madeira and sherry. As sales soared, it quickly made its way into Italian kitchens, where classic dishes such as chicken Marsala were created. Nowadays, chicken Marsala is an Italian restaurant staple. After having several disappointing encounters with this dish involving watery sauces, flaccid mushrooms, and pale, stale chicken, we realized that chicken Marsala was being taken for granted. It was in need of a rescue.

While all of the recipes we found listed the same three ingredients—breast of chicken, mushrooms, and Marsala—the cooking methods differed. Some called for simmering the chicken and mushrooms in Marsala, which resulted in flavors that were waterlogged and bland. Others recommended cooking everything in separate pans, creating not only a messy kitchen but a dish with disjointed flavors. Yet others had the cook sauté everything in the same pan, but sequentially. The clear winner turned out to be the classic, in which the meat is sautéed first and then moved to a warm oven while the browned bits left in the pan are splashed with wine and mounted with butter to create a sauce. With this decided, we focused on perfecting the sautéed chicken and developing the sauce.

When sautéing, the most important steps include getting the skillet incredibly hot and patting the chicken dry with paper towels before dusting with a light coating of flour. Using these pointers as a guide, we sautéed with a variety of oils and with butter to find that vegetable oil was the least likely to burn and splatter.

Our next task was to figure out how to get the mushrooms crisp and brown without burning the drippings left from the sautéed chicken. One way to do this, we thought, would be to add more fat to the pan and scrape the browned bits off the bottom before cooking the mushrooms. One way to add both fat and flavor was to cook small pieces of pancetta (Italian bacon that has been cured but not smoked) directly after the chicken. Just as we had thought, the fat rendered from the pancetta prevented the chicken drippings from burning while providing the oil necessary for sautéing the mushrooms—not to mention adding a meaty, pepper-flavored punch to the sauce.

Because several types and grades of Marsala wine can be found on the market, we conducted a taste test before doing any cooking, trying imported and California brands of both the sweet and dry varieties. We favored an imported wine, Sweet Marsala Fine, for its depth of flavor, smooth finish, and reasonable price tag. By reducing the wine, we found the silky, plush texture we were looking for in the final sauce. Knowing that stock is traditionally added to pan sauces for depth of flavor and body, we tested a variety of stock-to-Marsala ratios. Again and again, tasters preferred a sauce made only from wine, slightly reduced. The stock simply got in the way of the Marsala's distinctive zip.

All we needed to do now was round out the final flavors. Some lemon juice tempered the Marsala's sweetness, while one clove of garlic and a teaspoon of tomato paste rounded out the middle tones. Last, we found that 4 tablespoons of unsalted butter whisked in at the end added a dreamlike finish and beautiful sheen. Here was a chicken Marsala Sicilians could be proud of.

WHAT WE LEARNED: Add pancetta to help moisten the mushrooms as they cook and to add meatiness to the sauce. Use sweet Marsala wine (without any stock) for the richest-tasting sauce.

CHICKEN MARSALA serves 4

Our wine of choice for this dish is Sweet Marsala Fine, an imported wine that gives the sauce body, soft edges, and a smooth finish.

  1   cup all-purpose flour
  4   boneless, skinless chicken breasts (5 to 6 ounces each), fat trimmed (see illustration below)
       Salt and ground black pepper
  2   tablespoons vegetable oil
 2½   ounces pancetta (about 3 slices), cut into pieces 1 inch long and ⅛ inch wide
  8   ounces white mushrooms, sliced (about 2 cups)
  1   medium clove garlic, minced (about 1 teaspoon)
  1   teaspoon tomato paste
 1½   cups sweet Marsala
 1½   tablespoons juice from 1 small lemon
  4   tablespoons unsalted butter, cut into 4 pieces
  2   tablespoons minced fresh parsley leaves

1. Adjust oven rack to lower-middle position, place large heatproof dinner plate on oven rack, and heat oven to 200 degrees. Heat 12-inch heavy-bottomed skillet over medium-high heat until very hot (you can hold your hand 2 inches above pan surface for 3 to 4 seconds), about 3 minutes. Meanwhile, place flour in shallow baking dish or pie plate. Pat chicken breasts dry. Season both sides of breasts with salt and pepper; working one piece at a time, coat both sides with flour. Lift breast from tapered end and shake to remove excess flour; set aside. Add oil to hot skillet and heat until shimmering. Place floured cutlets in single layer in skillet and cook until golden brown, about 3 minutes. Using tongs, flip cutlets and cook on second side until golden brown and meat feels firm when pressed with finger, about 3 minutes longer. Transfer chicken to heated plate and return plate to oven.

2. Return skillet to low heat and add pancetta; sauté, stirring occasionally and scraping pan bottom to loosen browned bits until pancetta is brown and crisp, about 4 minutes. With slotted spoon, transfer pancetta to paper towel–lined plate. Add mushrooms and increase heat to medium-high; sauté, stirring occasionally and scraping pan bottom, until liquid released by mushrooms evaporates and mushrooms begin to brown, about 8 minutes. Add garlic, tomato paste, and cooked pancetta; sauté while stirring until tomato paste begins to brown, about 1 minute. Off heat, add Marsala; return pan to high heat and simmer vigorously, scraping browned bits from pan bottom, until sauce is slightly syrupy and reduced to about 1¼ cups, about 5 minutes. Off heat, add lemon juice and any accumulated juices from chicken; whisk in butter 1 tablespoon at a time. Season to taste with salt and pepper, and stir in parsley. Pour sauce over chicken and serve immediately.

TECHNIQUE: Trimming Cutlets

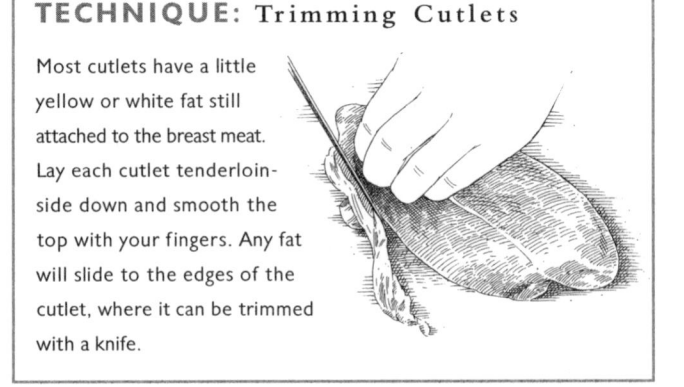

Most cutlets have a little yellow or white fat still attached to the breast meat. Lay each cutlet tenderloin-side down and smooth the top with your fingers. Any fat will slide to the edges of the cutlet, where it can be trimmed with a knife.

EQUIPMENT CORNER: Pepper Mills

PEPPER MILLS COME IN A VAST RANGE OF STYLES AND materials, but what really matters to us and other serious home cooks is performance. Is the fine-ground pepper truly fine? Is the medium grind really medium, or are there coarse particles mixed in? And how about output? Will you have to turn and turn and turn until your arm needs a brace to produce a teaspoon of ground pepper? To answer these questions, we rounded up 12 widely available mills.

Most pepper mills work by similar means. Peppercorns are loaded into a central chamber, through which runs a metal shaft. Near the bottom of the mill, the shaft is connected to a grinding mechanism that consists of a rotating, grooved "male" head that fits into a stationary, grooved "female" ring. Near the top of the male piece, large grooves crack the peppercorns and then feed the smaller pieces downward to be ground between the finer grooves of the male and female components.

Generally, the finer the grind, the more even the distribution of pepper throughout a dish. Thus the quality of a mill's fine grind is more important than options for an endless range of grinds beyond fine, medium, and coarse.

The industry experts we queried explained that the specifics of the grinding mechanism are key to grind quality. Jack Pierotti, president of Chef Specialties, maker of the Windsor mill, named the size, number, and angle of teeth in both male and female grinder components as factors in performance. A related consideration, according to Tom David, president of Tom David, Inc., maker of the Unicorn Magnum Plus mill, is how well the male and female grinding pieces are machined (the process used to cut the grooves). Sharper teeth combined with a very tight tolerance between the pieces yields a better grind, which to us means finer fine-ground pepper. Unfortunately, none of these details is evident upon inspecting a pepper mill in a kitchen store.

In addition to having an excellent grind quality, Unicorn Magnum Plus managed an awesome output. In one minute

of grinding, the Magnum produced an incredible average of 7.3 grams, or about 3½ teaspoons, of fine-ground pepper. By comparison, honors for the next highest average output went to the Oxo Grind It, at 5.1 grams, while about half the pack hovered around the two-grams-or-less mark (which, at roughly one teaspoon in volume, is perfectly acceptable).

Grind quality and speed are only half the battle—especially if most of your peppercorns land on the floor when you try to fill the mill. So we appreciated mills with wide, unobstructed filler doors that could accommodate the tip of a wide funnel or, better yet, the lip of a bag or jar so that we could dispense with the funnel altogether.

The ease of adjusting the grind was another factor we considered. Changing the grind from fine to coarse involves changing the tolerances of, or distances between, the male and female grinding components. The more space between them, the larger the pepper particles and the coarser the grind. Traditionally, a knob at the top of the mill called the finial is used to adjust the grind. This was our least favorite design for two reasons. First, the finial must be screwed down very tight for a fine grind, which not only requires

BEST PEPPER MILLS
The Unicorn Magnum Plus (far left) has a huge capacity and awesome speed. The East Hampton Industries Peppermate (second from left) has a detachable cup that captures ground pepper and makes measuring easy. The Oxo Good Grips Grind It (second from right) is lightning-fast, but it can be tricky to adjust the grind on this mill. The Zyliss Large Mill (far right) has a huge capacity and excellent range of grinds but is slower than the other top mills.

significant finger strength but also makes the head (or the crank) of the mill more difficult to turn. Second, the finial usually has to be removed entirely to fill the mill, which means you have to readjust the grind with each filling. We preferred mills like the Unicorn Magnum Plus, which use a screw or dial at the base of the grinding mechanism.

More than half of the mills tested did their jobs well, but the Unicorn Magnum Plus was the superstar. At $45, however, this mill was one of the two most expensive in the test (the second-place EHI Peppermate was $40). If your budget is a bit more restricted, we recommend both the Oxo Grind It ($19.99) and the Zyliss Large Pepper Mill ($27.50).

SCIENCE DESK:
The Role of Fond in Pan Sauces

EVER WONDER HOW RESTAURANTS MAKE THICK, RICH sauces to accompany sautéed cutlets and steaks? Chances are it's a pan sauce, made with the delicious caramelized browned bits (called fond) that sit on the bottom of the pan after the meat has been sautéed or pan-seared.

Pan sauces are usually made by adding liquid (stock, wine, or juice) to the pan once the cooked cutlets or steaks have been transferred to a plate to rest. The liquid dissolves the fond (a process known as deglazing) and incorporates it into the sauce.

So what makes those browned bits so delicious, so valuable? When meat or chicken browns, a process called the Maillard reaction occurs. This process is named after the French chemist who first described this reaction about one hundred years ago. When the amino acids (or protein components) and natural sugars in meat are subjected to intense heat, like that found in a skillet, they begin to combine and form new compounds. These compounds in turn break down and form yet more new flavor compounds, and so on and so on. The process is like rabbits multiplying. The browned bits left in the pan once the meat has been cooked are packed with complex flavors, which in turn are carried over to the pan sauce once the fond has been dissolved.

BREADED CHICKEN CUTLETS

WHAT WE WANTED: Tender, well-seasoned chicken with an evenly browned, crisp crust.

Tender boneless chicken breast pan-fried with a cloak of mild-flavored crumbs has universal appeal. Chicken Milanese, with grated Parmesan cheese added to the coating, is arguably the most popular incarnation of this technique. Yet this simple dish can fall prey to a host of problems. The chicken itself may be rubbery and tasteless, and the coating—called a bound breading and arguably the best part of the dish—often ends up uneven, greasy, pale, or even burnt.

For a breaded chicken cutlet to be great, the chicken itself better hold up its end of the bargain. According to our tasters, that means starting with a premium chicken cutlet rather than a mass-market supermarket brand. Since the test kitchen is fiercely devoted to the benefits of brining poultry, we wondered what effect soaking the cutlets in a mixture of salt, sugar, and water would have. The brined cutlets were a hit, exceptionally juicy and seasoned all the way to the center. The brining step is easy to execute and takes just 30 minutes, during which time you can pull together other components of the recipe. It's not often that so little work yields such big benefits.

Throughout this first series of tests, we noticed that the thin tip of the cutlet and the opposite end, which was much more plump, cooked at different rates. This problem was a cinch to fix—all we had to do was pound the chicken breasts gently to an even ½-inch thickness with a meat pounder or the bottom of a small saucepan. To promote even cooking, we also found it best to remove the floppy tenderloin from the underside of each cutlet before pounding.

During the crumb testing (see Tasting Lab on page 120), we made several important observations about the breading process. First, we learned that the cutlets had to be thoroughly dried after brining. We also learned that we could not dispense with the coating of flour that went onto the chicken before the egg wash and crumbs. If the cutlets were even slightly moist, or if we skipped the flour coat, the breading would peel off the finished cutlets in sheets. Dry cutlets also produced the thinnest possible coating of flour, which mitigated any floury taste when the cutlets were cooked and served. In addition, we found that it was essential to press the crumbs onto the cutlets to assure an even, thorough cover. Finally, we discovered that it was best to let the breaded cutlets rest for about five minutes before frying them, again to help bind the breading to the meat.

The bread crumbs are attached to the floured cutlets by means of a quick dip into beaten egg. But beaten eggs are thick and viscous, and they tend to form too heavy a layer on the meat, giving the breading a thick, indelicate quality. Thinning the egg with oil, water, or both is a common practice that allows excess egg to slide off the meat more easily, leaving a thinner, more delicate coat. We tried all three routines, and honestly, we couldn't detect much difference in the flavor or texture of the finished breading. In repeated tests we did notice that the breading made with oil-thinned egg wash seemed to brown a little more deeply than that made with water-thinned wash, so we added a tablespoon of oil to our two beaten eggs and moved on.

Last we explored the details of pan-frying. In any breaded preparation, the oil in the pan should reach one-third to one-half way up the food for thorough browning. We pitted pure olive oil against vegetable oil, and top billing went to the vegetable oil for its light, unobtrusive presence. The olive oil contributed too much of its own flavor.

WHAT WE LEARNED: Brine the cutlets for 30 minutes to make them moist and juicy; pound to an even thickness for even cooking; and dip in flour, egg wash, and fresh bread crumbs, then fry in batches in vegetable oil, for the crispiest coating.

BREADED CHICKEN CUTLETS *serves 4*

If you'd rather not prepare fresh bread crumbs, use panko, extra-crisp Japanese bread crumbs. The chicken is cooked in batches of two because the crust is noticeably more crisp if the pan is not overcrowded. We found it pays to use a premium brand of chicken. We particularly like Bell & Evans cutlets.

4	boneless, skinless chicken breasts (5 to 6 ounces each), tenderloins removed and reserved for another use, fat trimmed (see illustration on page 115)
½	cup kosher salt or ¼ cup table salt
½	cup sugar
5–8	slices high-quality white bread, such as Pepperidge Farm, crusts removed and torn into rough 1½-inch pieces
	Ground black pepper
¾	cup all-purpose flour
2	large eggs
1	tablespoon plus ¾ cup vegetable oil
	Lemon wedges for serving

1. Use rubber mallet, meat pounder, or rolling pin to pound chicken breasts to even ½-inch thickness. Dissolve salt and sugar in 1 quart cold water in gallon-sized zipper-lock plastic bag. Add cutlets and seal bag, pressing out as much air as possible; refrigerate 30 minutes. Line rimmed baking sheet with triple layer of paper towels.

2. Remove cutlets and lay in single layer on baking sheet; cover with another triple layer paper towels and press firmly to absorb moisture. Allow cutlets to dry for 10 minutes. Process bread in food processor until evenly fine-textured, 20 to 30 seconds (you should have about 1¼ cups fresh bread crumbs). Transfer crumbs to pie plate. Carefully peel paper towels off cutlets, sprinkle cutlets with pepper, and set aside.

3. Adjust oven rack to lower-middle position, set heatproof plate on rack, and heat oven to 200 degrees. Spread flour in second pie plate. Beat eggs with 1 tablespoon oil in third pie plate.

4. Working one at a time, dredge cutlets thoroughly in flour, shaking off excess. Using tongs, dip both sides of cutlets in egg mixture, taking care to coat thoroughly, allowing excess to drip back into pie plate to ensure very thin coating. Dip both sides of cutlets in bread crumbs, pressing crumbs with fingers to form even, cohesive coat. Place breaded cutlets in single layer on wire rack set over baking sheet and allow coating to dry about 5 minutes.

5. Meanwhile, heat 6 tablespoons remaining oil in heavy-bottomed 10-inch nonstick skillet over medium-high heat until shimmering but not smoking, about 2 minutes. Lay two cutlets gently in skillet; cook until deep golden brown and crisp on first side, gently pressing down on cutlets with wide metal spatula to help ensure even browning, about 2½ minutes. Using tongs, flip cutlets, reduce heat to medium, and continue to cook until meat feels firm when pressed gently and second side is deep golden brown and crisp, 2½ to 3 minutes longer. Line warmed plate with double layer paper towels and set cutlets on top; return plate to oven.

6. Discard oil in skillet and wipe skillet clean using tongs and large wad paper towels. Repeat step 5 using remaining 6 tablespoons oil and now-clean skillet to cook remaining cutlets; serve along with first batch with lemon wedges.

VARIATIONS
CHICKEN MILANESE
Though Parmesan is classic in this dish, use Pecorino Romano if you prefer a more tangy flavor. Keep a close eye on the cutlets as they brown to make sure the cheese does not burn.

Follow recipe for Breaded Chicken Cutlets, substituting ¼ cup finely grated Parmesan cheese for an equal amount of bread crumbs.

PECAN-CRUSTED CHICKEN CUTLETS WITH INDIAN SPICES
Keep a close eye on the cutlets as they cook to make sure the nuts in the coating do not burn. If you prefer the pure flavor of pecans, feel free to leave out the spice mixture.

Mix 1 teaspoon garam masala, ¼ teaspoon ground cumin, and ¼ teaspoon ground coriander in small bowl. Follow recipe for Breaded Chicken Cutlets, rubbing each side of each cutlet with scant ¼ teaspoon of spice mixture before dredging in flour, and substituting 6 tablespoons very finely ground pecans for an equal amount of bread crumbs.

BREADED CHICKEN CUTLETS WITH GARLIC AND OREGANO
Follow recipe for Breaded Chicken Cutlets, beating 3 tablespoons very finely minced fresh oregano leaves and 8 medium garlic cloves, pressed through garlic press, grated, or minced to puree, into egg mixture in step 3.

DEVILED BREADED CHICKEN CUTLETS
Follow recipe for Breaded Chicken Cutlets, rubbing each side of each cutlet with generous pinch cayenne before dredging in flour, and beating 3 tablespoons Dijon mustard, 1 tablespoon Worcestershire sauce, and 2 teaspoons very finely minced fresh thyme leaves into egg mixture in step 3.

TASTING LAB: Bread Crumbs

THE IDEAL BREADING SHOULD TASTE MILD AND comforting, but not dull, and certainly not greasy. To explore the possibilities, we pan-fried cutlets coated with fine, fresh bread crumbs (made from fresh sliced sandwich bread ground fine in the food processor), dry bread crumbs, and Japanese panko crumbs.

The dry bread crumbs had an unmistakably stale flavor, while the panko crumbs rated well for their shattering crispness and wheaty flavor. But the fresh bread crumbs swept the test, with a mild, subtly sweet flavor and a light, crisp texture. We went on to test crumbs made from different kinds of white bread, including premium sliced sandwich bread, Italian, French, and country style. The sliced bread was the sweetest, and therefore, the favorite.

STUFFED CHICKEN CUTLETS

WHAT WE WANTED: A filling that is creamy without being runny, flavorful without overpowering the chicken. A crust that is crisp all over, without burnt spots, and that completely seals in the filling so that none leaks out.

Cutlets that are stuffed and breaded are special-occasion food. The filling coats the chicken from the inside with a creamy, tasty sauce, while the crust makes a crunchy counterpoint. They can be very good, but these little bundles pose a number of problems for the cook.

We first focused on the cooking method. We wanted to develop a technique that would crisp the exterior without overbrowning it before the center was fully cooked. Deep-frying was the obvious answer, but this option is really better suited to restaurants than home kitchens. We tested roasting, broiling, sautéing, and combinations of these methods. We found that two approaches warranted further exploration: Complete cooking in a skillet on the stovetop and stovetop browning followed by roasting.

We ran our next test on the stovetop, sautéing the breasts in just enough vegetable oil to generously coat the bottom of a sauté pan. This test revealed a number of problems. First, it was difficult to arrive at a heat level that would cook the chicken through without burning it. And the cutlets often stuck to the pan. Furthermore, even though the breasts in the pan were of only slightly different weights, their rates of cooking were different enough to be worrisome.

It seemed logical that the two-step method—a preliminary pan-frying on top of the stove followed by roasting in the even heat of the oven—would solve the twin problems of overbrowning and undercooking. We sautéed the next batch in oil that came one-third to halfway up the sides of the chicken, cooking until the chicken was well-browned all over. Then, to combat the sogginess we had observed in roasted breasts during the initial round of testing, we baked the chicken on a rack in a rimmed baking sheet so that hot air could circulate underneath the breasts.

The results were much improved: The breasts didn't stick to the pan; they came out of the oven evenly browned, with an excellent, crunchy coating; and the meat inside was not soggy but instead almost uniformly moist, with only the skinny tips of the breasts slightly dry. Because the time in the oven didn't significantly darken the crust, we could rely on this method for a perfect crust every time as long as we carefully supervised the stovetop browning.

We turned our attention to the stuffing. After several false starts, we concluded that pounding the breasts thin and rolling them up around the filling produced the most even distribution of filling and the most even cooking of the meat.

As for the content of the filling, we wanted something creamy but thick. Cheese was the obvious choice. After several tests, we concluded that beaten cream cheese provided the creamy consistency we wanted. It was thick and smooth. For flavor, we turned to more potent cheeses, such as cheddar and gorgonzola, along with seasonings such as browned onions, garlic, and herbs.

But there was still a problem. These stuffed cutlets had to be secured with toothpicks—sometimes multiple toothpicks in a single breast—all of which then had to be removed before the cutlets were sliced into medallions.

Luckily, getting over this hurdle turned out to be easier than we anticipated. We found that wrapping the breasts in aluminum foil and refrigerating them for one hour before breading and cooking cooled the cheese enough to hold the roll together. It also kept the cheese from seeping out of the crust during baking, all without any toothpicks.

WHAT WE LEARNED: Pound chicken breasts thin, then roll them up around a cheese filling. Refrigerate the filled cutlets before breading and cooking to prevent leaks. Sauté the stuffed cutlets to brown and crisp them, but finish them in the oven for even, thorough cooking.

STUFFED CHICKEN CUTLETS   serves 4

The cutlets can be filled and rolled in advance, then refrigerated for up to 24 hours. To dry fresh bread crumbs, spread them out on a baking sheet and bake in a 200-degree oven, stirring occasionally, for 30 minutes. Removing some moisture from the crumbs cuts down on splattering when the breaded cutlets are pan-fried.

4	boneless, skinless chicken breasts (5 to 6 ounces each), tenderloins removed and reserved for another use, fat trimmed (see illustration on page 115)
	Salt and ground black pepper
1	recipe filling (recipes follow)
¾	cup all-purpose flour
2	large eggs
1	tablespoon plus ¾ cup vegetable oil
1½	cups fresh bread crumbs, dried (see note)

1. Place each chicken breast on large sheet of plastic wrap, cover with second sheet, and pound with rubber mallet, meat pounder, or rolling pin until ¼ inch thick throughout. Each pounded breast should measure roughly 6 inches wide and 8¼ inches long. Cover and refrigerate while preparing filling.

2. Place cutlets smooth-side down on work surface; season with salt and pepper. Fill, roll, and wrap each breast (see illustrations on page 123). Refrigerate until filling is firm, at least 1 hour.

3. Adjust oven rack to lower-middle position; heat oven to 450 degrees. Spread flour in pie plate. Beat eggs with 1 tablespoon oil in second pie plate. Spread bread crumbs in third pie plate. Unwrap chicken breasts and roll in flour; shake off excess. Using tongs, roll breasts in egg mixture; let excess drip off. Transfer to bread crumbs; shake pan to roll breasts in crumbs, then press with fingers to help crumbs adhere. Place breaded cutlets on large wire rack set over baking sheet and allow coating to dry about 5 minutes.

4. Heat remaining ¾ cup oil in heavy-bottomed 10-inch nonstick skillet over medium-high heat until shimmering, but not smoking, about 4 minutes; add chicken, seam-side down, and cook until medium golden brown, about 2 minutes. Turn each roll and cook until medium golden brown on all sides, 2 to 3 minutes longer. Transfer chicken rolls, seam-side down, to wire rack set over rimmed baking sheet; bake until deep golden brown and instant-read thermometer inserted into center of a roll registers 155 degrees, about 15 minutes. Let stand 5 minutes before slicing each roll crosswise diagonally with serrated knife into 5 medallions; arrange on individual dinner plates and serve.

HAM AND CHEDDAR CHEESE FILLING
enough to stuff 4 cutlets

1	tablespoon unsalted butter
1	small onion, minced
1	small clove garlic, minced
4	ounces cream cheese, softened
1	teaspoon minced fresh thyme leaves
2	ounces cheddar cheese, shredded (about ½ cup)
	Salt and ground black pepper
4	slices (about 4 ounces) thin-sliced cooked deli ham

1. Heat butter in medium skillet over low heat until melted; add onion and sauté, stirring occasionally, until deep golden brown, 15 to 20 minutes. Stir in garlic and cook until fragrant, about 30 seconds longer; set aside.

2. In medium bowl using hand mixer, beat cream cheese on medium speed until light and fluffy, about 1 minute. Stir in onion mixture, thyme, and cheddar; season with salt and pepper and set aside. To stuff cutlets, place one slice ham on top of cheese on each cutlet, folding ham as necessary to fit onto surface of cutlet.

VARIATIONS

ROASTED MUSHROOMS AND PROVOLONE CHEESE FILLING WITH ROSEMARY

To cook mushrooms, toss 10 ounces stemmed and quartered white mushrooms with 2 tablespoons olive oil and salt and pepper to taste on large rimmed baking sheet, then roast in 450-degree oven, turning once, until mushrooms are well browned, 20 to 25 minutes.

Follow recipe for Ham and Cheddar Cheese Filling, replacing cheddar cheese with 2 ounces shredded provolone (about ½ cup) and adding 1 tablespoon chopped fresh rosemary to cheese mixture. Replace ham with roasted mushrooms.

BROILED ASPARAGUS AND SMOKED MOZZARELLA CHEESE FILLING

To cook asparagus for this filling, toss trimmed spears with 2 teaspoons olive oil and salt and pepper to taste on a rimmed baking sheet, then broil until tender and browned, 6 to 8 minutes, shaking pan to rotate spears halfway through cooking time.

Follow recipe for Ham and Cheddar Cheese Filling, replacing cheddar cheese with 2 ounces shredded smoked mozzarella (about ½ cup). Replace ham with 16 medium asparagus, trimmed to 5-inch lengths and broiled. Place 4 asparagus spears horizontally on top of cheese on each cutlet, spacing them about 1 inch apart and trimming off ends if necessary.

GORGONZOLA CHEESE FILLING WITH WALNUTS AND FIGS

Two tablespoons of dried cherries or cranberries can be substituted for the figs.

Follow recipe for Ham and Cheddar Cheese Filling, replacing cheddar cheese with 2 ounces crumbled gorgonzola (about ½ cup). Stir in ¼ cup chopped toasted walnuts, 3 medium dried figs, stemmed and chopped (about 2 tablespoons), and 1 tablespoon dry sherry along with gorgonzola. Omit ham.

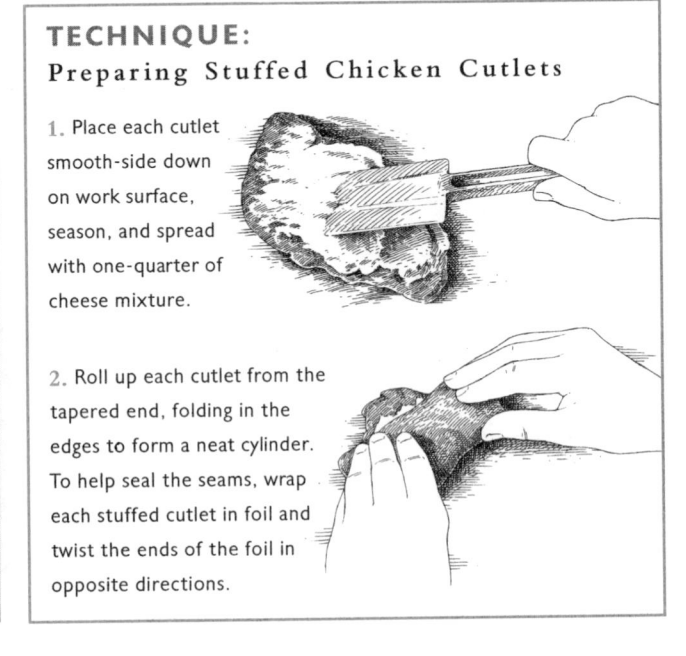

TECHNIQUE:
Preparing Stuffed Chicken Cutlets

1. Place each cutlet smooth-side down on work surface, season, and spread with one-quarter of cheese mixture.

2. Roll up each cutlet from the tapered end, folding in the edges to form a neat cylinder. To help seal the seams, wrap each stuffed cutlet in foil and twist the ends of the foil in opposite directions.

ALL-AMERICAN cookout

The backyard cookout is a ritual of summer. You light the grill, gather friends and family, and throw some burgers and dogs over the coals. While this scene may conjure up visions of American life circa 1955, the food often pales in comparison to the memory.

Who hasn't made burgers that were overcooked or, worse still, glued to the grill rack? Even if you manage to remove the burgers from the grill safely and at the right time, they can puff up into round balls that roll right off the buns. How can something so simple be so hard to cook right?

Ever notice how the hot dogs disappear long before the burgers? That said, lots of hot dogs have a mushy texture or just don't taste good. In our Tasting Lab, we figure out which brands are the top dogs.

Finally, what's a summer cookout without some grilled veggies? But which vegetables respond best to grilling, and how do you keep delicate vegetables from scorching or sticking to the grill?

Take a deep breath. Summer cooking is supposed to be fun. We've moved the test kitchen out back and made these favorite dishes foolproof.

The alley behind the test kitchen was turned into the staging ground for our outdoor cooking segments. Julia reads through her notes, Shannon readies the burgers, and Dawn tends the fire, while the television crew takes a breather.

GRILLED HAMBURGERS

WHAT WE WANTED: A juicy, meaty tasting burger that cooks up level, not puffy.

If you have the right ground beef, a perfect hamburger can be ready in less than 15 minutes, assuming you season, form, and cook it right. The biggest difficulty for many cooks, though, may be finding the right beef.

To test which cut or cuts of beef cook into the best burger, we ordered chuck, round, rump, sirloin, and hanging tenderloin, all ground to order with 20 percent fat. (Although we would question fat percentages in later testing, we needed a standard for these early tests. From past experience, this percentage seemed right.) After a side-by-side taste test, we quickly concluded that most cuts of ground beef are pleasant but bland when compared with the robust flavored ground chuck. Pricier ground sirloin, for example, cooked up into a particularly boring burger.

So pure ground chuck—the cut of beef that starts where the ribs end and moves up to the shoulder and neck, ending at the foreshank—was the clear winner. We were ready to race ahead to seasonings, but before moving on we stopped to ask ourselves, "Will cooks buying ground chuck straight out of the supermarket meat case agree with our choice?" Our efforts to determine whether supermarket ground chuck and ground-to-order chuck were even remotely similar took us along a culinary blue highway from kitchen to packing plant, butcher shop, and supermarket.

According to the National Live Stock and Meat Board, the fat content of beef is checked and enforced at the retail level. If a package of beef is labeled 90 percent lean, then it must contain no more than 10 percent fat, give or take a point. Retail stores are required to test each batch of ground beef, make the necessary adjustments, and keep a log of the results. Local inspectors routinely pull ground beef from a store's meat case for a fat check. If the tested meat is not within 1 percent of the package sticker, the store is fined.

Whether a package labeled ground chuck is, in fact, 100 percent ground chuck is a different story. We surveyed a number of grocery store meat department managers, who said that what was written on the label did match what was in the package. For instance, a package labeled "ground chuck" would contain only chuck trimmings. Same for sirloin and round. Only "ground beef" would contain mixed beef trimmings.

We got a little closer to the truth, however, by interviewing a respected butcher in the Chicago area, who spoke candidly. Of the several grocery stores and butcher shops he had worked at over the years, he had never known a store to segregate meat trimmings. In fact, in his present butcher shop, he sells only two kinds of ground beef—sirloin and chuck. He defines ground sirloin as ground beef (mostly but not exclusively sirloin) that's labeled 90 percent lean and chuck as ground beef (including a lot of chuck trimmings) that's labeled 85 percent lean.

Only meat ground at federally inspected plants is guaranteed to match its label. At these plants, an inspector checks to see if labeled ground beef actually comes from the cut of beef named on the label and if the fat percentage is correct.

Since retail ground beef labeling can be deceptive, we suggest buying a chuck roast and having the butcher grind it for you. Even at a local grocery store, the butcher was willing to grind to order. Some meat always gets lost in the grinder, so count on losing a bit (2 to 3 percent).

Because mass-ground beef also stands a greater chance of being contaminated by bacteria than nonground beef, it made theoretical sense to recommend grinding beef at home for those who want to reduce their odds of eating beef tainted with the bacterium E. coli. It doesn't make much practical sense, though. Not all cooks own a grinder. And even if they did, we thought home grinding demanded far too much setup, cleanup, and effort for a food meant to be so simple.

To see if there was an easier way, we tried chopping by

hand and grinding in the food processor. The hibachi-style (two knives, one in each hand) method of chopping was just as time-consuming and more messy than the traditional grinder. The food processor, however, did a good job grinding meat. We thought the steel blade would raggedly chew the meat, but to our surprise, the meat was evenly chopped and fluffy. (See the Equipment Corner on page 130.)

For those who buy a chuck roast for grinding, we found the average chuck roast to be about 80 percent lean. To check its leanness, we bought a chuck roast—not too fatty, not too lean—and ground it in the food processor. We took our ground chuck back to the grocery store for the butcher to check its fat content in the Univex Fat Analyzer, a machine the store uses to check the beef it grinds. A plug of our ground beef scored an almost perfect 21 percent fat when tested in the fat analyzer.

Up to this point, all of our beef had been ground with approximately 20 percent fat. A quick test of burgers with less and more fat helped us decide that 20 percent fat, give or take a few percentage points, was good for burgers. Any higher, and the burgers are just too greasy. Any lower, and you start compromising the beef's juicy, moist texture.

Working with fresh-ground chuck, seasoned with salt and pepper, we now moved into shaping and cooking. To test the warnings against overpacking and overhandling that you see in many recipes, we thoroughly worked a portion of ground beef before cooking it. The resulting burger had a well-done exterior that was nearly as dense as a meat pâté; its less well-done interior was compact and pasty.

All the same, it's actually pretty hard to overhandle a beef patty, especially if you're trying not to overhandle it. After dividing the meat into portions, we found that tossing the meat from one hand to another helped bring it together into a ball without overworking it. We made one of our most interesting discoveries when we tested various shaping techniques for the patties. A divot in the center of each burger ensures that they come off the grill with an even thickness instead of puffed up like a tennis ball. (See the Science Desk on page 130.)

We were now nearly done with our testing. We simply needed to perfect our grilling method. Burgers require a real blast of heat if they are to form a crunchy, flavorful crust before the interior overcooks. While many of the recipes we looked at advise grilling burgers over a hot fire, we suspected we'd have to adjust the heat because our patties were quite thin in the middle. Sure enough, a superhot fire made it too easy to overcook the burgers. We found a medium-hot fire formed a crust quickly while also providing a wider margin of error in terms of cooking the center. Nonetheless, burgers cook quickly—needing only 2 to 4 minutes per side. Don't walk away from the grill when cooking burgers.

One last finding from our testing: Don't ever press down on burgers as they cook. Rather than speeding their cooking, pressing on the patties serves only to squeeze out their juices and make the burgers dry.

WHAT WE LEARNED: Don't buy beef that's already been ground. Instead, grind your own chuck in the food processor, or ask the butcher to do this for you. Make a divot in the center of each burger to prevent puffing. Grease the cooking rack to prevent sticking and grill over a medium-hot fire.

CHARCOAL-GRILLED HAMBURGERS serves 4

For those who like their burgers well-done, we found that poking a small hole in the center of the patty before cooking helped the center to cook through before the edges dried out. See illustrations on page 129 for tips on shaping burgers.

1½ pounds 100 percent ground chuck (about 80 percent lean)
1 teaspoon salt
½ teaspoon ground black pepper
Vegetable oil for grill rack
Buns and desired toppings

1. Light large chimney starter filled with hardwood charcoal (about 2½ pounds) and allow to burn until all charcoal is covered with layer of fine gray ash. Spread coals evenly over bottom of grill for medium-hot fire. (See how to gauge heat level on page 133.) Set cooking rack in place, cover grill with lid, and let rack heat up, about 5 minutes. Scrape cooking rack clean with wire brush.

2. Meanwhile, break up chuck to increase surface area for seasoning. Sprinkle salt and pepper over meat; toss lightly with hands to distribute. Divide meat into four equal portions (6 ounces each); with cupped hands, toss one portion back and forth to form loose ball. Pat lightly to flatten meat into ¾-inch-thick burger that measures about 4½ inches across. Press center of patty down with your fingertips until about ½ inch thick, creating well in center of patty. Repeat with remaining portions of meat.

3. Lightly dip a wad of paper towels in vegetable oil; holding wad with tongs, wipe grill rack (see illustration on page 130). Grill burgers, uncovered and without pressing down on them, until well seared on first side, about 2½ minutes. Flip burgers with wide metal spatula. Continue grilling to desired doneness, about 2 minutes for rare, 2½ minutes for medium-rare, 3 minutes for medium, or 4 minutes for well-done. Serve immediately.

GAS-GRILLED HAMBURGERS serves 4

1½ pounds 100 percent ground chuck (about 80 percent lean)
1 teaspoon salt
½ teaspoon ground black pepper
Vegetable oil for grill rack
Buns and desired toppings

1. Preheat grill with all burners set to high and lid down until grill is very hot, about 15 minutes. Scrape cooking rack clean with wire brush. Leave both burners on high.

2. Meanwhile, break up chuck to increase surface area for seasoning. Sprinkle salt and pepper over meat; toss lightly with hands to distribute. Divide the meat into four equal portions (6 ounces each); with cupped hands, toss one portion back and forth to form loose ball. Pat lightly to flatten meat into ¾-inch-thick burger that measures about 4½ inches across. Press center of patty down with your fingertips until about ½ inch thick, creating well in center of patty. Repeat with remaining portions of meat.

3. Lightly dip a wad of paper towels in vegetable oil; holding wad with tongs, wipe grill rack (see illustration on page 130). Grill burgers, covered and without pressing down on them, until well seared on first side, about 3 minutes. Flip burgers with wide metal spatula. Continue grilling, covered, to desired doneness, about 3 minutes for rare, 3½ minutes for medium-rare, 4 minutes for medium, or 5 minutes for well-done. Serve immediately.

VARIATIONS

GRILLED CHEESEBURGERS

We like grating cheese into the raw beef. Since the cheese is evenly distributed, a little goes much further than when a big hunk of cheese is melted on top.

Follow recipe for Charcoal-Grilled Hamburgers or Gas-Grilled Hamburgers, sprinkling 3½ ounces cheddar, Swiss, Monterey Jack, or blue cheese, shredded or crumbled as necessary, over ground chuck along with salt and pepper.

GRILLED HAMBURGERS WITH GARLIC, CHIPOTLES, AND SCALLIONS

Toast 3 medium unpeeled garlic cloves in small dry skillet over medium heat, shaking pan occasionally, until fragrant and color deepens slightly, about 8 minutes. When cool enough to handle, skin and mince garlic. Follow recipe for Charcoal-Grilled Hamburgers or Gas-Grilled Hamburgers, mixing garlic, 1 tablespoon minced chipotle chile in adobo sauce, and 2 tablespoons minced scallions into meat along with salt and pepper.

GRILLED HAMBURGERS WITH COGNAC, MUSTARD, AND CHIVES

Mix 1½ tablespoons cognac, 2 teaspoons Dijon mustard, and 1 tablespoon minced fresh chives in small bowl. Follow recipe for Charcoal-Grilled Hamburgers or Gas-Grilled Hamburgers, mixing cognac mixture into meat along with salt and pepper.

GRILLED HAMBURGERS WITH PORCINI MUSHROOMS AND THYME

Cover ½ ounce dried porcini mushroom pieces with ½ cup hot tap water in small microwave-safe bowl; cover with plastic wrap, cut several steam vents with paring knife, and microwave on high power for 30 seconds. Let stand until mushrooms soften, about 5 minutes. Lift mushrooms from liquid with fork and mince using chef's knife (you should

---

TECHNIQUE: Shaping Hamburgers

1. With cupped hands, toss one portion of meat back and forth from hand to hand to shape it into a loose ball.

2. Pat lightly to flatten the meat into a ¾-inch-thick burger that measures about 4½ inches across. Press the center of the patty down with your fingertips until it is about ½ inch thick, creating a well in the center. Repeat with the remaining portions of ground meat.

have about 2 tablespoons). Follow recipe for Charcoal-Grilled Hamburgers or Gas-Grilled Hamburgers, mixing porcini mushrooms and 1 teaspoon minced fresh thyme leaves into meat along with salt and pepper.

EQUIPMENT CORNER:
Food Processor as Grinder

EVEN THOUGH WE HAVE A MEAT GRINDER IN THE kitchen, we don't regularly grind meat ourselves. The setup, breakdown, and washing up required to grind a 2-pound chuck roast just isn't worth the effort. Besides, hamburgers are supposed to be impromptu, fast, fun food.

To our surprise, though, the food processor does a respectable grinding job, and it's much easier to use than a grinder. The key is to make sure the roast is cold, cut into small chunks, and processed in small batches.

For a 2-pound roast, cut the meat into 1-inch chunks. Divide the chunks into four equal portions. Place one portion of meat in the workbowl of a food processor fitted with a steel blade. Pulse the cubes until the meat is ground, fifteen to twenty 1–second pulses. Repeat with the remaining portions of beef. Then shape the ground meat as directed.

SCIENCE DESK: Why Hamburgers Puff

ALL TOO OFTEN, BURGERS COME OFF THE GRILL WITH A domed, puffy shape that makes it impossible to keep condiments from sliding off. Fast-food restaurants produce burgers with an even surface, but these burgers are usually extremely thin. We wondered if there was a way to produce a heftier burger at home that was the same thickness from edge to edge, with no puffing.

We shaped 6-ounce portions of ground beef into patties that were 1 inch, ¾ inch, and ½ inch thick. Once cooked, all these burgers looked like tennis balls. After talking to several food scientists, we understood why this happens.

The culprit responsible for puffy burgers is the connective tissue, or collagen, ground up along with the meat. When the connective tissue in the patty heats up to roughly 130 degrees, it shrinks. This happens on the top and bottom flat surfaces first, and then on the sides, where the tightening acts like a belt. When the sides tighten, the interior meat volume is forced up and out, so the burger puffs.

One of the cooks in the test kitchen suggested a trick she had picked up when working in a restaurant. We shaped patties ¾ inch thick but then formed a slight depression in the center of each one so that the edges were thicker than the center. On the grill, the center puffed so that it was now the same height as the edges. Finally, a level burger that could hold onto toppings.

TECHNIQUE: Oiling the Grill Rack

We find it helpful to oil the grill rack just before cooking foods that are prone to sticking, such as burgers, fish, and some vegetables. Dip a large wad of paper towels in vegetable oil, grab the wad with tongs, and wipe the grill rack thoroughly to lubricate it and prevent sticking. Wiping the grill rack also cleans off any residue you may have missed when scraping it with a wire brush—something we recommend that you do each time you grill.

TASTING LAB: Ketchup

FOR MANY PEOPLE, A BURGER ISN'T DONE UNTIL IT HAS been coated liberally with ketchup. This condiment originated in Asia as a salty, fermented medium for pickling or preserving ingredients, primarily fish. Early versions were made with anchovies and generally were highly spiced.

Tomato-based ketchup has its origins in 19th-century America. We now consume more than 600 million pints of ketchup every year, much of it landing on top of burgers. But as any ketchup connoisseur knows, not all brands are created equal. To find out which is the best, we tasted 13 samples, including several fancy mail-order ketchups and one that we made from scratch in our test kitchen.

It wasn't much of a surprise that the winner was Heinz. For all tasters but one, Heinz ranked first or second and was described as "classic" and "perfect." A tiny bit sweeter than Heinz, Del Monte took second place, while Hunt's (the other leading national brand, along with Heinz and Del Monte) took third place.

What about the mail-order, organic, fruit-sweetened, and homemade ketchups? Most tasters felt these samples were overly thick and not smooth enough. Some were too spicy, others too vinegary. Our homemade ketchup was too chunky, more like "tomato jam" that ketchup. In color, consistency, and flavor, none of these interlopers could match the ketchup archetype, Heinz.

EQUIPMENT CORNER: Hamburger Presses

WE HAVE FORMED PLENTY OF HAMBURGERS IN OUR TEST kitchen. While we don't consider patting a burger out by hand to be a problem, we wondered about all the gadgets specifically designed for this task. Could they make a simple task even simpler?

We rounded up four models and began testing. All of the presses easily accommodated 6-ounce portions of ground meat. That said, the only general advantage we could find to these gadgets was that they kept your hands from becoming overly greasy by limiting contact with the meat. As advantages go, this was pretty weak. You still have to touch the meat and thus wash your hands well. We suggest that you save your money and cabinet space for something more useful.

TASTING LAB: Hot Dogs

WHAT'S A BACKYARD BARBECUE WITHOUT SOME HOT dogs? We tasted nine brands of nationally available all-beef hot dogs, along with a deli-style hot dog sold in links at a local supermarket and made with natural casings. Since kids are such a big market for hot dogs, we departed from tradition with this tasting and assembled two panels instead of one. The first comprised 15 adults; the second a dozen third- and fifth-grade children. To make things easier for the kids, we served them just three brands of hot dogs—the top two finishers from the adult tasting and one of the adults' lowest rated dogs.

Hot dogs are made from meat trimmings, the same meat that would go into hamburger or other sausages. Trimmings should not be confused with variety meats—hearts, kidney, liver, etc. If variety meats are used, which nowadays is uncommon for hot dogs, the manufacturer is required by federal law to state on the front of the package "with variety meats" or "with meat byproducts." Hot dogs can contain nonmeat binders, such as nonfat dry milk,

cereal, dried whole milk, or isolated soy protein. These must also be identified in the ingredients list.

Other hot dog ingredients include water (added in the form of ice) and curing or preserving agents—salt, nitrite, sugar, spices, and seasonings (typically coriander, garlic, ground mustard, nutmeg, and white pepper). Nitrite is a chemical that interacts with muscle pigment, myoglobin, to create the hot dog's characteristic pink color. It also lends a characteristic flavor. Most important, though, it prevents the growth of organisms that can cause botulism.

The process of making hot dogs is a source of intrigue for most eaters. Basically, meat trimmings are ground into a paste and then placed in a high-speed mixer along with spices, ice chips (to keep the meat cold), and curing ingredients. This forms a thick liquid that is pumped into casings. Most brands use inedible plastic casings, which are later removed. Traditional natural casings are costly and therefore less common. The filled casings are then moved to a smokehouse, where they are fully cooked. Finally, they are showered in cool water, sent to an automatic peeler to be stripped of the casings (if not natural casings), and vacuum-sealed.

What seemed to make or break a hot dog for our panels of tasters was meaty flavor with a balance of seasonings. They also required decent chewability. The deli-style dog was indisputably the top pick among the adult tasters. The manufacturer, a supermarket chain in the Northeast, was reluctant to give away any recipe secrets as to what made this hot dog stand out. A spokesman did say it was formulated after an old-fashioned hot dog with natural casings and "quality ingredients." The children were not quite as enthusiastic about the deli-style dog. The flavor and chew were a little too adult for their tastes.

The kids chose Ball Park franks as their favorite (the second-place finisher among adults). For similar reasons as the adults, the kids decisively rejected the dog that received the worst rating from adults.

All but one of the hot dogs that received poor ratings were unpalatably mushy and weak on beef flavor. The very worst of all the dogs was a brand purchased at a large natural foods chain store. The meat was uncured and contained no nitrites. Unlike its cohorts in the reject bin, it had chew. This was not much help, however, as tasters likened it to both leather and a spicy rubber sausage.

Aside from the obvious differences in products, such as the amount and type of spices used, there are more complex differences. The heart of a hot dog's flavor intensity is carried in the fat, so less fat often means less flavor. This was obvious in the flavorless low-fat product we tasted, but we found no particular correlation between fat and flavor in the regular dogs. As for texture, the addition of nonmeat binders, such as nonfat dry milk and cereal starches, seem to make a hot dog less firm. Significantly, the leading two hot dogs did not contain any such binders.

Cooking hot dogs is remarkably simple as long as you avoid the most common pitfall—burning the dogs. We found it best to grill hot dogs over a medium-hot fire (the same temperature we use to cook burgers). Avoid a scorching hot fire, which is likely to singe hot dogs. Let the hot dogs cook for two minutes, or until they plump and begin to show grill marks. At this point, start turning the hot dogs every 30 seconds to promote even browning. After a total of about four minutes over a medium-hot fire, hot dogs will be plump, lightly browned, and ready to serve.

TECHNIQUE:
Judging the Heat Level of a Grill Fire

Test the temperature of the grill by holding your hand 5 inches above the grill rack. If you can hold your hand there for three to four seconds, the fire is medium-hot. If you can hold your hand there for only three seconds, the fire is hot. If you can hold your hand there for two seconds or less, the fire is very hot.

GRILLED VEGETABLES

WHAT WE WANTED: Vegetables that are lightly streaked with grill marks and cooked just until crisp-tender.

Grilling vegetables should be easy. You've made a fire to grill a couple of steaks, some swordfish, or maybe a few burgers and hot dogs. There are some vegetables in the fridge, and you want to turn them into a side dish without having to heat up your kitchen. It sounds simple, but a number of questions immediately arise. Do you have to precook the vegetables? How thick should each vegetable be sliced? What's the best temperature for grilling them?

We decided at the outset that we wanted to develop guidelines for grilling as many kinds of vegetables as possible without precooking them. Blanching, baking, or microwaving is not hard, but each does add an extra step and time to what should be a simple process. In addition, blanching and baking heat up the kitchen. We wanted to blanch only when absolutely necessary.

Vegetables don't respond well to blazing fires—incineration is a real possibility. We found that most vegetables are best cooked over a medium or medium-hot fire. We played around with wood chips (both hickory and mesquite) and found no perceptible change in flavor. Vegetables do not cook long enough to pick up any wood flavor. If you happen to have chips on the grill to cook something else, they won't do any harm, but don't expect them to add great flavor to the vegetables.

A better way to season vegetables is to brush them with flavored oil just before grilling. (Marinating is not advised because the acids will make vegetables soggy; portobello mushrooms are the one exception.) Make sure to use a good-quality olive or peanut oil. (We found that vegetables brushed with canola, corn, or other bland oils were boring.) Try adding fresh herbs, garlic, and/or grated citrus zest to the oil, or purchase one that is already flavored. Seasoning with salt and pepper both before and after grilling is another way to maximize flavor.

A lot of equipment exists out there for grilling, much of it designed for vegetables. We tried grilling vegetables in a hinged metal basket and didn't find it to be very practical. One part of the grill is always hotter or colder than another, and, invariably, some vegetables are ready to be turned before others. Large vegetables (everything from asparagus spears to sliced zucchini) are best cooked right on the grill rack.

You can skewer smaller items (like cherry tomatoes and white mushrooms) to keep them from falling through the rack. Wooden skewers are generally quite thin (which is good), but they can burn. Metal skewers are a better option. Just make sure they are thin. Thick metal skewers are fine for meat but will tear mushrooms and cherry tomatoes.

The other option is to grill small vegetables on a grill grid or vegetable grid. This gadget prevents the vegetables from falling through the rack but allows you to turn each piece of food individually when it has browned sufficiently. A grill grid is typically made out of crosshatched wires or a single sheet of perforated metal. The grid goes right on top of the cooking rack. Once the grid is hot, small vegetables can be cooked on it.

Whether cooking vegetables on the grill surface or a grid, make sure the surface is clean. Vegetables will pick up any off flavors from the grill, so scrape the surface with a wire brush just before placing the vegetables on the grill.

If using a charcoal grill, cook the vegetables with the cover off to prevent them from picking up any stale smoke odors. If using a gas grill, cook the vegetables with the cover down to concentrate the heat.

WHAT WE LEARNED: Cook vegetables over a moderate fire to prevent burning, coat them with olive oil or peanut oil to boost flavor and prevent sticking, and don't bother with a hinged vegetable basket.

GRILLED CORN serves 4 to 8

While grilling husk-on corn delivers great pure corn flavor, it lacks the smokiness of the grill; essentially, the corn is steamed in its protective husk. By leaving only the innermost layer, we were rewarded with perfectly tender corn graced with the grill's flavor. Prepared in this way, the corn does not need basting with oil.

    8   ears fresh corn, prepared according to illustrations below
        Salt and ground black pepper
        Butter (optional)

TECHNIQUE: Preparing Corn

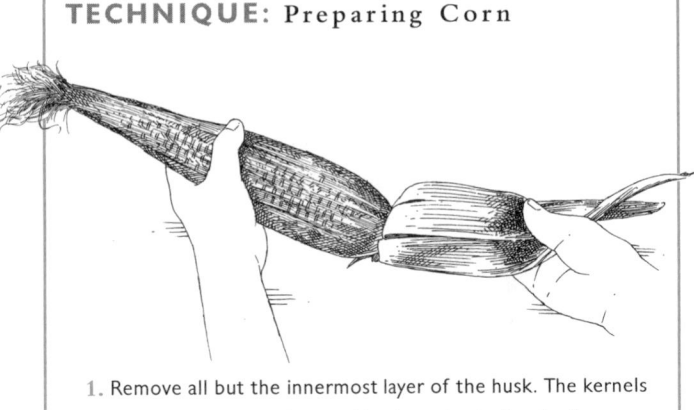

1. Remove all but the innermost layer of the husk. The kernels should be covered by, but visible through, the last husk.

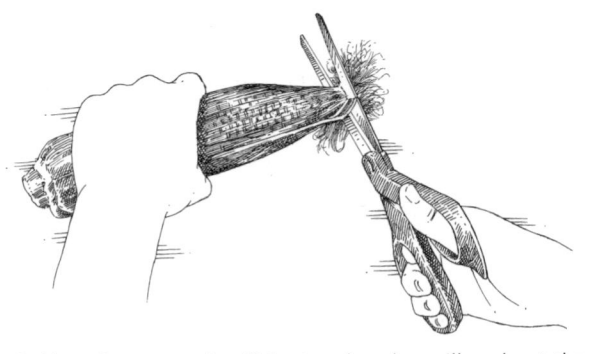

2. Use scissors to snip off the tassel, or long silk ends, at the tip of the ear.

---

1. Grill corn over a medium–hot fire (see how to gauge heat level on page 133), turning ears every 1½ to 2 minutes, until dark outlines of kernels show through husk and husk is charred and beginning to peel away from tip to expose some kernels, 8 to 10 minutes.

2. Transfer corn to platter; carefully remove and discard charred husk and silk. Season corn with salt and pepper to taste and butter, if desired. Serve immediately.

VARIATIONS

GRILLED CORN WITH HERB BUTTER
Brush with herb butter just before serving.

Melt 6 tablespoons unsalted butter in small saucepan. Add 3 tablespoons minced fresh parsley, thyme, cilantro, basil, and/or other fresh herbs and salt and pepper to taste; keep butter warm. Follow recipe for Grilled Corn, brushing herb butter over grilled corn in step 2.

GRILLED CORN WITH GARLIC BUTTER AND CHEESE
The buttery, nutty flavor of Parmesan cheese works surprisingly well with the flavor of grilled corn.

Melt 6 tablespoons unsalted butter in small saucepan over medium heat until bubbling. Add 1 minced garlic clove and cook until fragrant, about 30 seconds. Remove pan from heat and stir in ¼ teaspoon salt. Follow recipe for Grilled Corn, brushing butter over grilled corn in step 2. Sprinkle with ¼ cup grated Parmesan cheese and serve immediately.

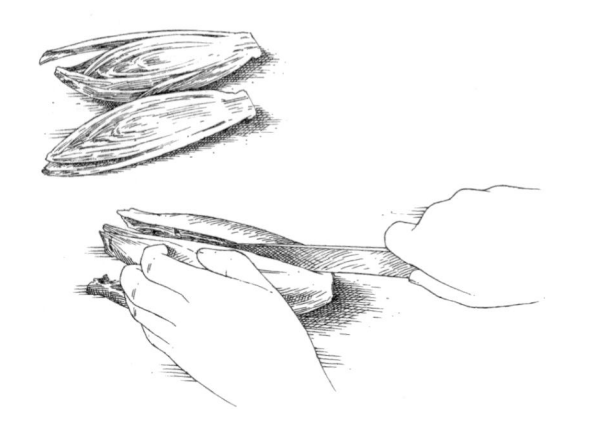

With a knife, shave off the discolored end of the endive. Cut the endive in half lengthwise through the core. Cut this way, the halves stay intact for easy grilling.

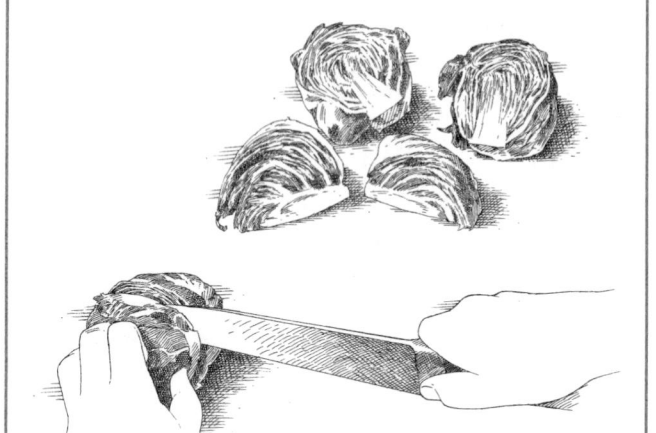

Remove any brown outer leaves. Cut the radicchio in half through the core. Cut each half again through the core to make four wedges.

GRILLED BELGIAN ENDIVE serves 8

Although we generally think of crisp and crunchy Belgian endive in terms of salads, it grills beautifully. The texture softens, but the vegetable holds its shape. Best of all, the bitter flavor mellows a bit when exposed to intense heat.

8 medium heads Belgian endive, prepared according to illustration at left
3 tablespoons extra-virgin olive oil or basting oil (see page 138)
Salt and ground black pepper

1. Toss endive halves in large bowl with oil and season with salt and pepper to taste.

2. Grill endive over medium-hot fire (see how to gauge heat level on page 133), turning once, until dark grill marks appear and center of each is crisp-tender, 5 to 7 minutes. Serve hot, warm, or at room temperature.

GRILLED RADICCHIO serves 4

To prevent radicchio from burning, it is necessary to brush the pieces with a fair amount of olive oil. For maximum grill flavor, turn each wedge of radicchio twice so that each side spends some time facing the fire.

3 medium heads radicchio, cut into quarters with core intact (see illustration at left)
4 tablespoons extra-virgin olive oil or basting oil (see page 138)
Salt and ground black pepper

1. Place radicchio wedges on large rimmed baking sheet and brush all sides with oil. Season with salt and pepper to taste.

2. Grill radicchio over a medium-hot fire (see how to gauge heat level on page 133), turning every 1½ minutes, until edges are browned and wilted but centers remain slightly firm, about 4½ minutes total. Serve immediately.

GRILLED FENNEL serves 4

Fennel grills beautifully. Its anise flavor is complemented by the caramelization of natural sugars on the surface of the vegetable. The trickiest part is cutting the fennel so that it does not fall through the rack. We found that slicing it vertically into sections 1/4 inch thick, with a piece of the core still attached, keeps the layers intact.

2 medium fennel bulbs (about 2 pounds), prepared according to illustrations below
3 tablespoons extra-virgin olive oil or basting oil (see page 138)
Salt and ground black pepper

1. Toss fennel and oil together in large bowl. Season with salt and pepper to taste.

2. Grill fennel over medium-hot fire (see how to gauge heat level on page 133), turning once, until tender and streaked with dark grill marks, 7 to 9 minutes. Serve hot, warm, or at room temperature.

GRILLED PORTOBELLO MUSHROOMS serves 4

Because of their dense, meaty texture, portobellos—unlike other vegetables—can be marinated. If you can find only smaller portobellos (say, about 4 inches across), use six mushrooms (and six pieces of foil) and reduce the grilling time wrapped in foil to 9 minutes.

1/2 cup extra-virgin olive oil
3 tablespoons juice from 1 lemon
6 medium cloves garlic, minced fine (about 2 tablespoons)
1/4 teaspoon salt
4 medium portobello mushrooms, each 5 to 6 inches (or about 6 ounces each), stems removed and discarded, caps wiped clean

1. Combine oil, lemon juice, garlic, and salt in large zipper-lock bag. Add mushrooms; seal bag and gently shake to coat mushrooms with marinade. Refrigerate until seasoned, about 1 hour.

2. Cut four 12-inch-square pieces of foil. Remove mushrooms from marinade and place foil squares on work surface. Set one mushroom on top of each piece of foil, gill-side up, and fold foil edges over to enclose mushroom and seal edges.

TECHNIQUE: Preparing Fennel

1. Cut off the stems and feathery fronds.

2. Trim a very thin slice from the base of the bulb and remove any tough or blemished outer layers.

3. Slice the bulb vertically through its base into 1/4-inch-thick pieces that resemble fans.

3. Grill mushrooms, with sealed sides of foil packets facing up, over medium-hot fire (see how to gauge heat level on page 133), until juicy and tender, 10 to 12 minutes. Using tongs, unwrap mushrooms and discard foil; set unwrapped mushrooms on rack gill-side up and cook until grill-marked, 30 to 60 seconds. Serve mushrooms hot.

VARIATION

GRILLED PORTOBELLO MUSHROOMS WITH TARRAGON

This variation is great served with burgers.

Combine 2 teaspoons rice vinegar, 1 minced garlic clove, 1 tablespoon chopped fresh tarragon leaves, ¼ teaspoon salt, and 2 tablespoons vegetable oil in medium bowl. Add Grilled Portobello Mushrooms and ground black pepper to taste. Toss to coat and serve immediately or cover with plastic wrap and let stand at room temperature for up to 30 minutes.

GARLIC BASTING OIL FOR VEGETABLES

makes about ½ cup

For extra flavor, use this basting oil, or the one that follows, instead of plain olive oil when cooking endive, fennel, or radicchio. These flavored oils work well with other vegetables, too, including peppers, onions, mushrooms, asparagus, and zucchini.

  ½ cup extra-virgin olive oil
  1 small clove garlic, minced to a paste or pressed through garlic press

Combine ingredients in small bowl; let stand to infuse flavors, about 10 minutes. Use while fresh and discard any unused oil.

LEMON-ROSEMARY BASTING OIL FOR VEGETABLES   makes about ½ cup

  ½ cup extra-virgin olive oil
  1 teaspoon minced fresh rosemary leaves
  1 teaspoon grated zest plus 1 tablespoon juice from 1 lemon

Combine ingredients in small bowl; let stand to infuse flavors, about 10 minutes. Use while fresh and discard any unused oil.

EQUIPMENT CORNER: Gas Grills

GAS GRILLS NOW ACCOUNT FOR 6 OUT OF 10 GRILLS sold in this country. The reasons for their increasing popularity are clear: The fire is easy to light and control. While there are few options when buying a charcoal grill, there are dozens and dozens of gas grills on the market. We tested six from the leading manufacturers and came to the following conclusions.

In general, we found that you get what you pay for. Inexpensive gas grills, priced at $200 or less, are generally inferior. If you are willing to spend more money (about $400), you can buy a gas grill that works extremely well, with results that can compete with a charcoal grill.

There are several features and design elements that separate a good grill from a poor one. A built-in thermometer that registers real numbers (not just low, medium, and hot) is essential. A gauge that tells you how much gas is left in the tank is also a plus.

As you might expect, a large grill offers the cook more possibilities. Unless the cooking surface has an area of at least 400 square inches, you will need to cook one slab of ribs at a time. (If the grill comes with a warming rack, you can cook a second slab there.)

In addition to size, the number of burners is critical. It's not possible to cook by indirect heat on a grill with only one burner, because the burner is usually positioned in the center of the grill and the "cool" parts of the grill are too small to fit most foods. You need a grill with at least two burners. With one burner on and one burner off, at least half of the grill will be cool enough for slow cooking.

The heat should be evenly distributed across the entire surface of the grill. We found that most gas grills are plenty hot. A bigger problem is that gas grills are often unable to sustain temperatures low enough for barbecuing. Many of the cheaper grills we tested were unable to barbecue a brisket without burning the exterior before the meat was tender. A good grill will heat up to 600 degrees and maintain a temperature of 250 degrees when the lid is down and just one burner is lit and turned to low.

Perhaps the most shocking conclusion we came to during our testing of gas grills concerns the cause of flare-ups. We found that lava rocks soak up dripping fat and catch fire as soon as there is some sort of flare-up. Several times we moved flaming chicken parts to the cool side of the grill (without a lit burner), and they still flamed from below for several minutes. It wasn't the chicken that was on fire, rather, the lava rocks had caught fire even though the burner underneath those rocks was cool.

Lava rocks are not the sole reason for flare-ups. Poor design that traps grease on the bottom of the grill doesn't help either. We consider a drainage system mandatory. The bottom of the cooking chamber should be sloped so that fat runs through an opening in the center and into a drip pan below.

Weber grills do not have lava rocks. Bars, made from steel coated with porcelain-enamel and shaped like an upside down V, channel fat down into the bottom of the grill and eventually into a drip pan attached to the underside of the cooking chamber. We find this drainage system far superior to others. For this (and the reasons stated above), these grills are our favorites.

If you entertain a lot, you will want the bigger and more expensive Weber Genesis Silver B with three burners. If your needs (or budget) are more modest, the two-burner Weber Genesis Silver A is an excellent choice.

Most gas grills come with two temperature controls, each regulating a separate burner. You can use the dials to change the heat level on the entire grill, turning it from high to medium once food has been seared. The dials can also be manipulated to create two heat levels on the cooking surface at the same time. For instance, you may set one burner at high for searing and set the other at medium to cook foods through or to have a place to move foods if they ignite.

Another note about gas grills. Unlike charcoal grills, the inside of the cover stays fairly clean because there is no buildup of resinous smoke. The grill cover can thus be used in recipes that call for a cover to cook foods through, such as grilled chicken breasts.

To make sure a gas grill is good and hot, always preheat with all burners turned to high and the lid down for 15 minutes. Then adjust the burners as directed in recipes, scrape the grill surface clean with a wire brush, and place the food on the grill to cook.

Unless you know you are going to need it, you may want to remove the warming rack before lighting the grill. On most grills, the rack is very close to the cooking surface, and it can be hard to reach foods on the back of the grill without burning your hands on the hot metal.

MIDDLE EASTERN
barbecue

CHAPTER II

The backyard barbecue always seems so familiar, so American. But grilling is practiced in almost every country around the globe. Shish kebab—skewers of lamb and vegetables—is perhaps the greatest "barbecue" dish from Turkey and the Middle East. When done right, the lamb is well browned but not overcooked, and the vegetables are crisp and tender. Everything is perfumed with the flavor of smoke.

When we make shish kebab, we like to offer other popular Middle Eastern dishes. Rice is a natural partner for shish kebab, and we think rice pilaf is the best choice. If you've only had rice pilaf from a box, you don't know how good this dish can be. Real rice pilaf is fluffy and fragrant. The grains are long and separate, tender but not mushy. The flavors of warm spices, nuts, and dried fruits take "plain rice" to new heights.

To start the meal, we serve baba ghanoush—the region's famous eggplant dip. Although this dip ends up in a bowl, the recipe begins on the grill, where the eggplant is cooked and flavored. The challenge here is to keep the focus on the eggplant, complementing it by adding just the right amount of garlic, sesame, and lemon.

Trays of eggplants are ready to be grill-roasted and then made into baba ghanoush.

SHISH KEBAB

WHAT WE WANTED: Lamb that cooks at the same rate as the vegetables on the skewer so that neither is raw or charred.

Shish kebab's components cook at different rates—either the vegetables are still crunchy when the meat is cooked perfectly to medium-rare, or the lamb is long overdone by the time the vegetables have been cooked properly. Our efforts to resolve this dilemma led us to explore which cut of lamb and which vegetables serve the kebab best. Getting the grill temperature just right was another challenge. Too hot, and the kebabs charred on the outside without being fully cooked; too cool, and they cooked without the benefit of flavorful browning.

Lamb can be expensive, so we searched for a cut that would give us tender, flavorful kebabs without breaking the bank. We immediately ruled out high-end cuts like loin and rib chops, which fetch upward of $14.99 per pound. Sirloin and shoulder chops are meatier and far more reasonable at $4.99 per pound. Each of these, however, requires cutting the meat off the bone before trimming and cubing. The best cut turned out to be the shank end of a boneless leg of lamb. It requires little trimming, yields the perfect amount of meat for four to six people, and can be purchased for about $6.99 per pound.

Lamb has a supple, chewy texture that behaves best when cut into small pieces. We found 1-inch pieces of lamb to be the optimal size for kebabs. With the meat cut and ready to go, we could now focus on the vegetables.

Many vegetables don't cook through by the time the lamb reaches the right temperature. This can be particularly ugly if you're using eggplant, mushrooms, or zucchini. We tried precooking the vegetables, but they turned slimy and were difficult to skewer. We thought about cooking them separately alongside the lamb on the grill, but that's just not shish kebab. Other vegetables, such as cherry tomatoes, initially looked great on the skewer but had a hard time hanging on once cooked.

As we worked our way through various vegetables, we came up with two that work well within the constraints of this particular cooking method. Red onions and bell peppers have a similar texture and cook through at about the same rate. When cut fairly small, these two vegetables were the perfect accompaniments to the lamb, adding flavor and color to the kebab without demanding any special attention.

What these handsome kebabs needed now was a little seasoned help, so we tried a variety of spices, dry rubs, and marinades on the meat. Spice rubs tasted good but left the surface of the meat chalky and dry; kebabs just aren't on the fire long enough for their juices to mix with the dried spices and form a glaze. Marinades, on the other hand, added a layer of moisture that kept the kebabs from drying out on the grill while their flavors penetrated the meat. Two hours in the marinade was sufficient time to achieve some flavor, but it took a good eight hours for these flavors to really sink in. Marinating for 12 hours, or overnight, was even better.

We were aware of the pitfalls of a mismanaged grill. The idea was to get a nice caramelization around the edges of the kebab without overcooking the interior of the small pieces of meat. A medium fire didn't work, turning the lamb an unappealing gray while leaving no grill marks behind. By the time the medium-hot fire turned out some decent grill marks, the meat was overcooked and a bit dry. A sizzling hot fire turned out to be the ticket, cooking the kebabs perfectly in only seven to eight minutes, about two minutes per side for medium-rare to medium. Tasters agreed that these kebabs tasted best when the meat was cooked to medium-rare; well-done lamb tasted "too muttony."

WHAT WE LEARNED: Use boneless leg of lamb, marinate for best flavor, limit vegetables to onions and peppers, and cook quickly over high heat.

CHARCOAL-GRILLED SHISH KEBAB serves 6

Cutting up the onion so the pieces will stay together on skewers is a little tricky. After substantial testing, we found that this method works best: Trim away stem and root end and cut the onion into quarters. Peel the three outer layers of the onion away from the inner core. Working with the outer layers only, cut each quarter—from pole to pole—into three strips of equal width. Cut each of the 12 strips crosswise into three pieces. (You should have 36 small stacks of three layers each.)

   1   recipe marinade (recipes follow)
2¼   pounds boneless leg of lamb (shank end), trimmed of fat and silver skin and cut into 1-inch pieces
   3   medium bell peppers, 1 red, 1 yellow, and 1 orange (about 1½ pounds), each cut into twenty-four 1-inch pieces
   1   large red onion (about 12 ounces), cut into thirty-six ¾-inch pieces (see note)
       Lemon or lime wedges for serving (optional)

1. Toss marinade and lamb in gallon-sized zipper-lock plastic bag or large, nonreactive bowl; seal bag, pressing out as much air as possible, or cover bowl and refrigerate until fully seasoned, at least 2 hours and up to 24 hours.

2. Ignite about 6 quarts (1 large chimney, or 2½ pounds) hardwood charcoal and burn until covered with light gray ash, 20 to 30 minutes. Spread coals over grill bottom, then spread 6 more quarts unlit charcoal over lit coals. Position grill rack over coals and heat until very hot, about 15 minutes. (See how to gauge heat level on page 133.)

3. Meanwhile, starting and ending with meat, thread 4 pieces meat, 3 pieces onion (three 3-layer stacks), and 6 pieces pepper in mixed order on 12 metal skewers.

4. Grill kebabs, uncovered, until meat is well browned all over, grill-marked, and cooked to medium-rare, about 7 minutes (or 8 minutes for medium), turning each kebab one-quarter turn every 1¾ minutes to brown all sides. Transfer kebabs to serving platter, squeeze lemon or lime wedges over kebabs if desired, and serve immediately.

GAS-GRILLED SHISH KEBAB serves 6

   1   recipe marinade (recipes follow)
2¼   pounds boneless leg of lamb (shank end), trimmed of fat and silver skin and cut into 1-inch pieces
   3   medium bell peppers, 1 red, 1 yellow, and 1 orange (about 1½ pounds), each cut into twenty-four 1-inch pieces
   1   large red onion (about 12 ounces), cut into thirty-six ¾-inch pieces (see note under Charcoal-Grilled Shish Kebab)
       Lemon or lime wedges for serving (optional)

1. Toss marinade and lamb in gallon-sized zipper-lock plastic bag or large, nonreactive bowl; seal bag, pressing out as much air as possible, or cover bowl and refrigerate until fully seasoned, at least 2 hours and up to 24 hours.

2. Turn all burners on gas grill to high, close lid, and heat grill until hot, 10 to 15 minutes.

3. Meanwhile, starting and ending with meat, thread 4 pieces meat, 3 pieces onion (three 3-layer stacks), and 6 pieces pepper in mixed order on 12 metal skewers.

4. Grill kebabs, covered, until meat is well browned all over, grill-marked, and cooked to medium-rare, about 8 minutes (or 9 minutes for medium), turning each kebab one-quarter turn every 2 minutes to brown all sides. Transfer kebabs to serving platter, squeeze lemon or lime wedges over kebabs if desired, and serve immediately.

WARM-SPICED PARSLEY MARINADE WITH GINGER   enough for 1 recipe of shish kebab

- ½   cup (packed) fresh parsley leaves
- 1   jalapeño chile, seeded and chopped coarse
- 1   (2-inch) piece fresh ginger, peeled and chopped coarse
- 3   medium cloves garlic, peeled
- 1   teaspoon ground cumin
- 1   teaspoon ground cardamom
- 1   teaspoon ground cinnamon
- ½   cup olive oil
- 1   teaspoon salt
- ⅛   teaspoon ground black pepper

Process all ingredients in workbowl of food processor fitted with steel blade until smooth, about 1 minute, stopping to scrape sides of workbowl with rubber spatula as needed.

GARLIC AND CILANTRO MARINADE WITH GARAM MASALA   enough for 1 recipe of shish kebab

- ½   cup (packed) fresh cilantro leaves
- 3   medium cloves garlic, peeled
- ¼   cup dark raisins
- ½   teaspoon garam masala
- 1½   tablespoons juice from 1 lemon
- ½   cup olive oil

- 1   teaspoon salt
- ⅛   teaspoon ground black pepper

Process all ingredients in workbowl of food processor fitted with steel blade until smooth, about 1 minute, stopping to scrape sides of workbowl with rubber spatula as needed.

SWEET CURRY MARINADE WITH BUTTERMILK   enough for 1 recipe of shish kebab

- ¾   cup buttermilk
- 1   tablespoon juice from 1 lemon
- 3   medium cloves garlic, minced
- 1   tablespoon brown sugar
- 1   tablespoon curry powder
- 1   teaspoon crushed red pepper flakes
- 1   teaspoon ground coriander
- 1   teaspoon chili powder
- 1   teaspoon salt
- ⅛   teaspoon ground black pepper

Combine all ingredients in gallon-sized, zipper-lock plastic bag or large, nonreactive bowl in which meat will marinate.

ROSEMARY-MINT MARINADE WITH GARLIC AND LEMON   enough for 1 recipe of shish kebab

- 10   large fresh mint leaves
- 1½   teaspoons chopped fresh rosemary
- 2   tablespoons juice plus ½ tablespoon minced zest from 1 lemon
- 3   medium cloves garlic, peeled
- ½   cup olive oil
- 1   teaspoon salt
- ⅛   teaspoon ground black pepper

Process all ingredients in workbowl of food processor fitted with steel blade until smooth, about 1 minute, stopping to scrape sides of workbowl with rubber spatula as needed.

SCIENCE DESK: Do Marinades Work?

CAN TOUGH CUTS OF BEEF, LAMB, AND PORK YIELD TENDER results if marinated long enough? Many cookbooks suggest tenderizing meat in acidic marinades, often for several days. The theory here is pretty straightforward: Acids, such as lemon juice, vinegar, and wine, cause protein strands to break apart. Over time, as more and more proteins disassemble, the meat softens. What actually happens in the refrigerator under real-life conditions is another question. We went into the test kitchen to find out.

We took a cut of steak from the round that is often used for London broil (a particularly lean cut and therefore prone to being tough when cooked), cut it into 2-inch cubes, and marinated the cubes in various solutions for 24 hours. Marinades with little or no acid had no affect on the texture of the meat. (Above, Doc is setting up toy cowboys and Indians to explain the standoff that occurs as meat soaks in a non-acidic marinade.) When we used more acid, the outer layer of the meat turned gray and dry—it had "cooked."

While some might call the texture tender, we found the meat to be mushy and the flavor of the acid to be overpowering. Our conclusion was simple—if you want tender meat, you must pay attention to the cut you purchase and the cooking method and forget about tenderizing with marinades.

Although marinades may not tenderize meat, they can give it a delicious flavor, as long as you soak the food for an appropriate amount of time. We marinated cubes of beef, lamb, and pork, as well as chicken parts, flounder, and tuna in low-acid marinades for varying amounts of time. As might be expected, fish picked up flavor rather quickly, in as little as 15 minutes for flounder and 30 minutes for the firmer tuna. Chicken was somewhat slower to become fully flavored, with skinless pieces taking about three hours and skin-on pieces taking at least eight hours. Dense meat takes even more time to absorb marinades. It took eight hours for the flavor to penetrate beyond the surface of beef, lamb, and pork, and meat marinated for 24 hours absorbed even more flavor. After a day, we found that meat gained little extra flavor. Although you can leave meat in a low-acid marinade for days, we don't see the point.

BABA GHANOUSH

WHAT WE WANTED: A smoky, creamy dip with real eggplant flavor.

The driving force behind baba ghanoush is grill-roasted eggplant, sultry and rich. Its beguiling creaminess and haunting flavor come from sesame tahini paste, cut to the quick with a bit of garlic, brightened with lemon juice, and flounced up with parsley. In Middle Eastern countries baba ghanoush is served as part of a mezze platter—not unlike an antipasto in Italy—which might feature salads, various dips, small pastries, meats, olives, other condiments, and, of course, bread.

There is no doubt that the eggplant is a majestic fruit—shiny, sexy, brilliantly hued. But its contents can be difficult to deal with. Baba ghanoush can be bitter and watery, green and raw, metallic with garlic, or occluded by tahini paste.

The traditional method for cooking eggplant for baba ghanoush is to scorch it over a hot, smoky grill. There the purple fruit grows bruised, then black, until its insides fairly slosh within their charred carapace. The hot, soft interior is scooped out with a spoon and the outer ruins discarded.

We realized that baba made with eggplant not cooked to the sloshy soft stage simply isn't as good. Undercooked eggplant, while misleadingly soft to the touch (eggplant has, after all, a yielding quality), will taste spongy-green and remain unmoved by additional seasonings.

Another question was whether a decent baba ghanoush could be made without a grill. Taking instruction from the hot fire we had used, we roasted a few large eggplants in a 500-degree oven. It took about 45 minutes to collapse the fruit and transform the insides to pulp. Though the babas made with grill-roasted eggplant were substantially superior to those made with oven-roasted, the latter were perfectly acceptable.

Eggplant suffers from persistent rumors that it is bitter. Most baba ghanoush recipes call for discarding the seedbed. But the insides of the eggplants we were roasting were veritably paved with seeds. We thought it impractical and wasteful to lose half the fruit to mere rumor, so we performed side-by-side tests comparing versions of the dip with and without seeds. We found no tangible grounds for seed dismissal. The dip was not bitter. The seeds stayed.

Other sources suggest one variety of eggplant over another, so we made baba ghanoush with standard large globe eggplants, with compact Italian eggplants, and with long, lithe Japanese eggplants. All were surprisingly good. The globe eggplants made a baba that was slightly more moist. The Italian eggplants were drier and contained fewer seeds. The Japanese eggplants were also quite dry. Their very slenderness allowed the smoke to permeate the flesh completely, and the resulting dip was meaty and delicious. (Given a choice, we would definitely select Italian or Japanese eggplant.)

Once the eggplants are roasted and scooped, you are about five minutes away from removing your apron. The eggplant can be mashed with a fork, but we prefer the food processor, which makes it a cinch to add the other ingredients and to pulse the eggplant, leaving the texture slightly coarse.

As for the proportions of said ingredients, tests indicated that less was always more. Minced garlic gathers strength on-site and can become aggressive when added in abundance. Many recipes we saw also called for tahini in amounts that overwhelmed the eggplant. Likewise with lemon juice: Liberal amounts dash the smoky richness of the eggplant with astringent tartness.

If you're serving a crowd, the recipe can easily be doubled or tripled. Time does nothing to improve the flavor of baba ghanoush, either. An hour-long stay in the refrigerator for a light chilling is all that's needed.

WHAT WE LEARNED: For the best flavor, grill-roast eggplant until it has completely collapsed. Don't bother discarding the seeds, but do use a gentle hand with the garlic, tahini, and lemon juice.

BABA GHANOUSH, CHARCOAL-GRILL METHOD *makes about 2 cups*

When buying eggplants, select those with shiny, taut, and unbruised skins and an even shape (eggplants with a bulbous shape won't cook evenly). We prefer to serve baba ghanoush only lightly chilled. If yours is cold, let it stand at room temperature for about 20 minutes before serving. Baba ghanoush does not keep well, so plan to make it the day you want to serve it. Pita bread, black olives, tomato wedges, and cucumber slices are nice accompaniments.

2   pounds eggplant (about 2 large globe eggplants, 5 medium Italian eggplants, or 12 medium Japanese eggplants), each eggplant poked uniformly over entire surface with fork to prevent it from bursting
1   tablespoon juice from 1 lemon
1   small clove garlic, minced
2   tablespoons tahini paste
    Salt and ground black pepper
1   tablespoon extra-virgin olive oil, plus extra for serving
2   teaspoons chopped fresh parsley leaves

1. Ignite about 6 quarts (1 large chimney, or 2½ pounds) hardwood charcoal and burn until completely covered with thin coating of light gray ash, 20 to 30 minutes. Spread coals evenly over grill bottom, then spread additional 6 quarts unlit charcoal over lit coals. Position grill rack and heat until very hot, about 20 minutes. (See how to gauge heat level on page 133.)

2. Grill eggplants until skins darken and wrinkle on all sides and eggplants are uniformly soft when pressed with tongs, about 25 minutes for large globe eggplants, 20 minutes for Italian eggplants, and 15 minutes for Japanese eggplants, turning every 5 minutes and reversing direction of eggplants on grill with each turn. Transfer eggplants to rimmed baking sheet and cool 5 minutes.

3. Set small colander over bowl or in sink. Trim top and bottom off each eggplant. Slit eggplants lengthwise and use spoon to scoop hot pulp from skins and place pulp in colander (you should have about 2 cups packed pulp); discard skins. Let pulp drain 3 minutes.

4. Transfer pulp to workbowl of food processor fitted with steel blade. Add lemon juice, garlic, tahini, ¼ teaspoon salt, and ¼ teaspoon pepper; process until mixture has coarse,

choppy texture, about eight 1-second pulses. Adjust seasoning with salt and pepper; transfer to serving bowl, cover with plastic wrap flush with surface of dip, and refrigerate 45 to 60 minutes. To serve, use spoon to make trough in center of dip and spoon olive oil into it; sprinkle with parsley and serve.

VARIATIONS

BABA GHANOUSH, GAS-GRILL METHOD
Turn all burners on gas grill to high, close lid, and heat grill until hot, 10 to 15 minutes. Follow recipe for Baba Ghanoush, Charcoal-Grill Method, from step 2.

BABA GHANOUSH, OVEN METHOD
Adjust oven rack to middle position and heat oven to 500 degrees. Line rimmed baking sheet with foil, set eggplants on baking sheet, and roast, turning every 15 minutes, until eggplants are uniformly soft when pressed with tongs, about 60 minutes for large globe eggplants, 50 minutes for Italian

eggplants, and 40 minutes for Japanese eggplants. Cool eggplants on baking sheet 5 minutes, then follow recipe for Baba Ghanoush, Charcoal-Grill Method, from step 3.

BABA GHANOUSH WITH SAUTÉED ONION
Sautéed onion gives the baba ghanoush a sweet, rich flavor.

Heat 1 tablespoon extra-virgin olive oil in small skillet over low heat until shimmering; add 1 small onion, chopped fine, and cook, stirring occasionally, until edges are golden brown, about 10 minutes. Follow recipe for Baba Ghanoush, Charcoal-Grill, Gas-Grill, or Oven Method, stirring onion into dip after processing.

EQUIPMENT CORNER: Grill Tongs

GRILLING TODAY CAN BE COMPLICATED. EACH GRILLING season brings with it a truckload of snazzy new barbecue utensils. We wondered if any of these often expensive gadgets was worth a second look.

Testing all manner of tongs, we groped and grabbed kebabs, asparagus, chicken drumsticks, and 3-pound slabs of ribs and found tong performance differed dramatically. Grill tongs by Progressive International, Charcoal, Lamson, Oxo Good Grips, and AMC Rosewood were heavy and difficult to maneuver, and their less delicate pincers couldn't get a grip on asparagus. Other problems included sharp, serrated edges that nicked the food, flimsy arms that bent under the strain of heavy food, and pincers whose spread could not even accommodate the girth of a chicken leg. A new tong on the scene, the Lamson multipurpose, had a spatula in place of one pincer, rendering its grasp almost useless.

The winner was a pair of 16-inch stainless steel kitchen tongs by Amco. Not only did they grip, turn, and move food around the grill easily, but they also were long enough to keep the cook a safe distance from the hot coals. So forget about all those flashy new grill utensils and simply bring your kitchen tongs outside.

RICE PILAF

WHAT WE WANTED: Perfectly steamed, fragrant, fluffy rice that is tender while still retaining an al dente quality.

According to most culinary sources, rice pilaf is simply long-grain rice that has been cooked in hot oil or butter before being simmered in hot liquid, typically either water or stock. In Middle Eastern cuisines, however, the term pilaf also refers to a more substantial dish in which the rice is cooked in this manner and then flavored with other ingredients—spices, nuts, dried fruits, and/or chicken or other meat. To avoid confusion, we decided to call the simple master recipe for our dish "pilaf-style" rice, designating the flavored versions as rice pilaf.

The logical first step in this process was to isolate the best type of rice for pilaf. We immediately limited our testing to long-grain rice, since medium and short-grain rice inherently produce a rather sticky, starchy product, and we were looking for fluffy, separate grains. Searching the shelves of our local grocery store, we came upon a number of different choices: plain long-grain white rice, converted rice, instant rice, jasmine, basmati, and Texmati (basmati rice grown domestically in Texas). We took a box or bag of each and cooked them according to a standard, stripped-down recipe for rice pilaf, altering the ratio of liquid to rice according to each variety when necessary.

Each type of rice was slightly different in flavor, texture, and appearance. Worst of the lot was the instant rice, which was textureless and mushy and had very little rice flavor. The converted rice had a very strong, off-putting flavor, while the jasmine rice, though delicious, was a little too sticky for pilaf. Plain long-grain white rice worked well, but basmati rice was even better: Each grain was separate, long, and fluffy, and the rice had a fresh, delicate fragrance. Though the Texmati produced similar results, it cost three times as much as the basmati per pound, making the basmati rice the logical choice. That said, we would add that you can use plain long-grain rice if basmati is not available.

Most sources indicate that the proper ratio of rice to liquid for long-grain white rice is 1 to 2, but many cooks use less water. After testing every possibility, from 1:1 to 1:2, we found that we got the best rice using 1⅔ cups of water for every cup of rice. To make this easier to remember, as well as easier to measure, we increased the rice by half to 1½ cups and the liquid to 2½ cups.

With our rice/water ratio set, we were ready to test the traditional methods for making pilaf, which called for rinsing, soaking, or parboiling the rice before cooking it in fat and simmering it to tenderness. Each recipe declared one of these preparatory steps to be essential in producing rice with distinct, separate grains that were light and fluffy.

We began by parboiling the rice for three minutes in a large quantity of water, as you would pasta, then draining it and proceeding to sauté and cook it. This resulted in bloated, waterlogged grains of rice. To be sure that we weren't adding more liquid than necessary, we weighed the rice before and after parboiling to measure the amount of water the rice had absorbed, then subtracted that amount from the water in which the final cooking was done. After trying this with both basmati and domestic long-grain white rice and still coming up with waterlogged rice, we eliminated parboiling as part of our cooking method.

Rinsing the rice, on the other hand, made a substantial difference, particularly with basmati rice. We simply covered 1½ cups of rice with water, gently moved the grains around using our fingers, and drained the water from the rice. We repeated this process four or five times until the rinsing water was clear enough for us to see the grains distinctly. We then drained the rice and cooked it in oil and liquid (decreased to 2¼ cups to compensate for the water that had been absorbed by or adhered to the grains during rinsing). The resulting rice was less hard and more tender, and it had a slightly shinier, smoother appearance.

We also tested soaking the rice before cooking it. We rinsed three batches of basmati rice and soaked them for five minutes, one hour, and overnight, respectively. The batch that soaked for five minutes was no better than the one that had only been rinsed. Soaking the rice for an hour proved to be a still greater waste of time, since it wasn't perceptibly different from the rinsed-only version. Soaked overnight, however, the rice was noticeably better. It was very tender, less starchy, and seemed to have longer, more elegant grains than the other batches we'd prepared. Though the difference was subtle, this batch of rice was definitely more refined than the others. (Keep in mind that rice soaked overnight needs to be cooked in only 2 cups of liquid, compensating for the amount of water absorbed while it soaks overnight). Soaking overnight takes some forethought, of course, so if you don't think of it a day ahead of time, simply rinse the rice well; this also delivers a good pilaf.

Thus far, we had allowed the rice to steam an additional 10 minutes after being removed from the heat to ensure that the moisture was distributed throughout. We wondered if a longer or shorter steaming time would make much of a difference in the resulting pilaf. We made a few batches of pilaf, allowing the rice to steam for 5 minutes,

10 minutes, and 15 minutes. The rice that steamed for 5 minutes was heavy and wet. The batch that steamed for 15 minutes was the lightest and least watery. We also decided to try placing a clean dish towel between the pan and the lid right after we took the rice off the stove. We found this produced the best results of all, while reducing the steaming time to only 10 minutes. It seems that the towel prevents condensation and absorbs the excess water in the pan during steaming, producing drier, fluffier rice.

We were surprised to see that many Middle Eastern recipes called for as much as ¼ cup butter per cup of rice. Using butter (since we like the extra flavor that it lends to the rice), we tried from 1 to 4 tablespoons per 1½ cups rice. Three tablespoons turned out to be optimal. The rice was rich without being overwhelmingly so, and each grain was shinier and more distinct than when cooked with less fat.

We also wondered if sautéing the rice for different amounts of time would make a difference, so we sautéed the rice over medium heat for one minute, three minutes, and five minutes. The pan of rice that was sautéed for five minutes was much less tender than the other two. It also had picked up a strong nutty flavor. When sautéed for one minute, the rice simply tasted steamed. The batch sautéed for three minutes was the best, with a light nutty flavor and tender texture.

At the end comes the fun part—adding the flavorings, seasonings, and other ingredients that give the pilaf its distinctive character. We found that dried spices, minced ginger, and garlic, for example, are best sautéed briefly in the fat before the raw rice is added to the pan. Saffron and dried herbs are best added to the liquid as it heats up, while fresh herbs and toasted nuts should be added to the pilaf just before serving to maximize freshness, texture (in the case of nuts), and flavor. Dried fruits such as raisins, currants, or figs can be added just before steaming the rice, which gives them enough time to heat through and plump up without becoming soggy.

WHAT WE LEARNED: Use basmati rice, rinse well, sauté in plenty of butter, and then steam, with a dish towel under the lid, once the rice is done.

BASIC PILAF-STYLE RICE serves 4

If you like, olive oil can be substituted for the butter depending on what you are serving with the pilaf. Soaking the rice overnight in water results in more tender, separate grains. If you'd like to try it, add enough water to cover the rice by 1 inch after the rinsing process in step 1, then cover the bowl with plastic wrap and let it stand at room temperature 8 to 24 hours; reduce the amount of water to cook the rice to 2 cups. For the most evenly cooked rice, use a wide-bottomed saucepan with a tight-fitting lid.

1½	cups basmati or long-grain rice
2½	cups water
1½	teaspoons salt
	Ground black pepper
3	tablespoons unsalted butter
1	small onion, minced (about ½ cup)

1. Place rice in medium bowl and add enough water to cover by 2 inches; using hands, gently swish grains to release excess starch. Carefully pour off water, leaving rice in bowl. Repeat four or five times, until water runs almost clear. Using a colander or fine-mesh strainer, drain water from rice; place colander over bowl and set aside.

2. Bring water to boil, covered, in small saucepan over medium-high heat. Add salt and season with pepper; cover to keep hot. Meanwhile, heat butter in large saucepan over medium heat until foam begins to subside; add onion and sauté until softened but not browned, about 4 minutes. Add rice and stir to coat grains with butter; cook until edges of rice grains begin to turn translucent, about 3 minutes. Stir hot seasoned water into rice; return to boil, then reduce heat to low, cover, and simmer until all liquid is absorbed, 16 to 18 minutes. Off heat, remove lid, and place kitchen towel folded in half over saucepan (see illustration at right); replace lid. Let stand 10 minutes; fluff rice with fork and serve.

VARIATIONS

RICE PILAF WITH CURRANTS AND PINE NUTS

Toast ¼ cup pine nuts in small dry skillet over medium heat until golden and fragrant, about 5 minutes; set aside. Follow recipe for Basic Pilaf-Style Rice, adding ½ teaspoon turmeric, ¼ teaspoon ground cinnamon, and 2 medium garlic cloves, minced, to sautéed onion; cook until fragrant, about 30 seconds longer. When rice is off heat, before covering saucepan with towel, sprinkle ¼ cup currants over rice in pan (do not mix in). When fluffing rice with fork, toss in toasted pine nuts.

INDIAN-SPICED RICE PILAF WITH DATES AND PARSLEY

Follow recipe for Basic Pilaf-Style Rice, adding 2 medium garlic cloves, minced, 2 teaspoons grated fresh ginger, ⅛ teaspoon ground cinnamon, and ⅛ teaspoon ground cardamom to sautéed onion; cook until fragrant, about 30 seconds longer. When rice is off heat, before covering saucepan with towel, add ¼ cup chopped dates and 2 tablespoons chopped fresh parsley (do not mix in); continue with recipe.

TECHNIQUE: Steaming Rice

After the rice is cooked, cover the pan with a clean dish towel and allow it to sit on a cool burner for 10 minutes.

FAJITAS &margaritas

CHAPTER 12

Guacamole, fajitas, and margaritas are standard-issue fare, even at non-Mexican restaurants, which might explain why they are generally so terrible. Who hasn't been served watery or gray guacamole overpowered by onions and an array of seasonings?

Fajitas is another dish often ruined by unnecessary complexity. The meat must be perfectly cooked, with a rosy interior and browned crust. The accompaniments must be flawless—strips of grilled vegetables, warm tortillas, and guacamole.

Finally, what's a Cinco de Mayo celebration or night out on the town without some margaritas? Too bad most Americans have never tasted the real thing—made with fresh citrus juice. Most bartenders rely on low-quality mixes and compensate with a surfeit of alcohol and the froth added by the blender. We wanted something more refined.

This Mexican meal, simple enough to prepare on a weeknight, is the real thing. The flavors are clean, crisp, and totally appealing.

After a long day of margarita testing, Ian uses a wine bottle to mash leftover lemons and limes to make lemon-limeade.

GUACAMOLE

WHAT WE WANTED: A chunky dip with an emphasis on the avocado, not the seasonings.

Guacamole has traveled a long road. Once a simple Mexican avocado relish, it has become one of America's favorite party dips. It's also an essential element when making fajitas, which is perhaps America's favorite Mexican entrée. Unfortunately, the journey has not necessarily been kind to this dish. The guacamole we are served in restaurants, and even in the homes of friends, often sacrifices the singular, extraordinary character of the avocado—the culinary equivalent of velvet—by adding too many other flavorings. Even worse, the texture of the dip is usually reduced to an utterly smooth, listless puree.

We wanted our guacamole to be different. First, it should highlight the dense, buttery texture and loamy, nutty flavor of the avocado. Any additions should provide bright counterpoints to the avocado without overwhelming it. Just as important, the consistency of the dip should be chunky.

Since good guacamole must begin with good avocados, we began our research with an avocado tasting. We focused on the two most familiar market varieties, the small, rough-skinned Hass (also spelled Haas), grown primarily in California and Mexico, and the larger, smooth-skinned Fuerte, grown mostly in Florida. The tasters were unanimous in their preference for Hass, compared with which the Fuerte tasted "too fruity," "sweet," and "watery."

Regardless of their origin, many supermarket avocados are sold rock hard and unripe. Because these fruits ripen off the tree, that's fine; in two to five days, your avocados are ready to eat. We tested all the supposed tricks to accelerate ripening, from burying the avocados in flour or rice to enclosing them in a brown paper bag, with and without another piece of fruit. We also tried putting them in different areas in the kitchen: light spots and dark, cool spots and warm. In the end, we found that most of these efforts made little difference. The fastest ripening took roughly 48 hours and occurred in a warm, dark spot, but the advantage was minor. From now on, we won't think twice when tossing hard avocados into the fruit bowl on the counter.

Determining ripeness was also straightforward. The skins of Hass avocados turn from green to dark, purply black when ripe, and the fruit yields slightly to a gentle squeeze when held in the palm of your hand.

Now having the proper ripe avocados, we turned to the mixing method. Most guacamole recipes direct you to mash all the avocados, and some recipes go so far as to puree them in a blender or food processor. After making dozens of batches, we came to believe that neither pureeing nor simple mashing was the way to go. Properly ripened avocados break down very easily when stirred, and we were aiming for a chunky texture. To get it, we ended up mashing only one of the three avocados in our recipe lightly with a fork and mixing it with most of the other ingredients, then dicing the remaining two avocados into substantial ½-inch cubes and mixing them into the base using a very light hand. The mixing action breaks down the cubes somewhat, making for a chunky, cohesive dip.

Other problems we encountered in most recipes were an overabundance of onion and a dearth of acidic seasoning. After extensive testing with various amounts of onion, tasters found that 2 tablespoons of finely minced or grated onion gave guacamole a nice spike without an overwhelming onion flavor. We also tried guacamoles with various amounts of fresh lemon and lime juice. The acid was absolutely necessary, not only for flavor but also to help preserve the mixture's green color. Tasters preferred two tablespoons of lime juice in our three-avocado guacamole.

WHAT WE LEARNED: Use ripe, pebbly-skinned avocados. Mash just one with a fork, and dice the other two. Keep the onion to a minimum, but don't skimp on lime juice.

CHUNKY GUACAMOLE makes 2½ to 3 cups

To minimize the risk of discoloration, prepare the minced ingredients first so they are ready to mix with the avocados as soon as they are cut. Ripe avocados are essential here. To test for ripeness, try to flick the small stem off the end of the avocado. If it comes off easily and you can see green underneath it, the avocado is ripe. If it does not come off or if you see brown underneath after prying it off, the avocado is not ripe. If you like, garnish the guacamole with diced tomatoes and chopped cilantro just before serving.

3	medium, ripe avocados (preferably pebbly-skinned Hass)
2	tablespoons minced onion
1	medium clove garlic, minced
1	small jalapeño chile, stemmed, seeded, and minced
¼	cup minced fresh cilantro leaves
	Salt
½	teaspoon ground cumin (optional)
2	tablespoons lime juice

1. Halve one avocado, remove pit, and scoop flesh into medium bowl. Mash flesh lightly with onion, garlic, chile, cilantro, ¼ teaspoon salt, and cumin (if using) with tines of fork until just combined.

2. Halve, pit, and cube remaining two avocados, following illustrations at right. Add cubes to bowl with mashed avocado mixture.

3. Sprinkle lime juice over diced avocado and mix entire contents of bowl lightly with fork until combined but still chunky. Adjust seasonings with salt, if necessary, and serve. (Guacamole can be covered with plastic wrap, pressed directly onto surface of mixture, and refrigerated up to 1 day. Return guacamole to room temperature, removing plastic wrap at last moment, before serving.)

VARIATION

GUACAMOLE WITH BACON, SCALLIONS, AND TOMATO

Follow recipe for Chunky Guacamole, substituting 3 large scallions, sliced thin (about ⅓ cup), for onion and adding 6 slices cooked, drained, and crumbled bacon with 1 teaspoon rendered fat and ½ medium tomato, seeded and diced small.

TECHNIQUE: Dicing an Avocado

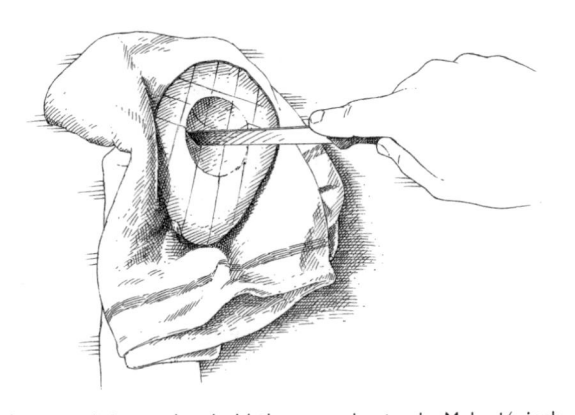

1. Use a dish towel to hold the avocado steady. Make ½-inch crosshatch incisions in the flesh of each avocado half with a dinner knife, cutting down to but not through the skin.

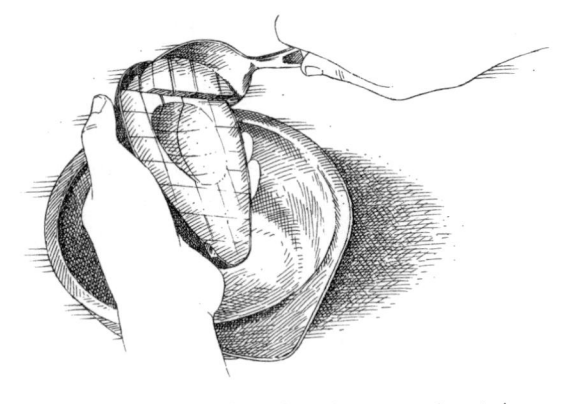

2. Separate the diced flesh from skin using a spoon inserted between the skin and flesh, gently scooping out the avocado cubes.

FAJITAS

WHAT WE WANTED: Perfectly cooked flank steak accompanied by grilled onions and peppers, warm tortillas, and great guacamole.

Thanks to fajitas, flank steak has become the darling of Tex-Mex fans from New York to California and everywhere in between. Although this dish was originally made with skirt steak (see page 158 for more information), flank steak is much more available and has become the steak of choice for this recipe.

But there are good reasons for the popularity of flank steak in addition to mere culinary fashion. Like other steaks cut from the chest and side of the cow, flank has a rich, full, beefy flavor. Also, because it is very thin, it cooks quickly.

Although the idea of grilling flank steak is a pretty straightforward proposition, we still had some questions about what was exactly the best way to go about it. All of them were directed at the achievement of two very simple goals: getting a good sear on the outside of this thin cut of meat before overcooking on the inside, and keeping it tender. We wondered whether the meat should be marinated or rubbed with spices, how hot the fire should be, and how long the meat should be cooked.

Virtually every recipe we found for flank steak called for marinating. Most sources ballyhooed the marinade as a means of tenderizing the meat as well as adding flavor. We found that marinades with a lot of acid eventually made this thin cut mushy and unappealing. If we left out the acid, we could flavor the meat, but this took at least 12 hours.

We eventually decided that the easiest, most effective way to flavor this cut of meat was with a squeeze of lime juice just before grilling and a generous seasoning with salt and pepper. With grilled vegetables and guacamole, this dish has plenty going on without the addition of spicy distractions. Everyone in the kitchen felt it was best to play up the beefy flavor of the meat.

To achieve tenderness (the reason many sources recommend marinating in the first place), we found that cutting the cooked steaks thinly and against the grain did the trick. When the steaks were cut up this way, there was virtually no difference between those that were marinated and those that were not. We concluded that flank steak can be seasoned in seconds, without compromising tenderness.

Every source we checked was in the same camp when it came to cooking the flank steak, and it is the right camp. These steaks should be cooked over high heat for a short period of time. We tried lower heat and longer times, but the meat inevitably ended up being tough.

Flank steak is so thin that it's impossible to check its temperature with a meat thermometer, so you need to resort to the most primitive (but ultimately the most effective) method of checking for doneness: Cut into the meat and see if it is done to your liking. Remember that carryover heat will continue to cook the steak after it comes off the grill for a much-needed rest (see the Science Desk on page 158). So if you want the steak medium-rare, take it off the heat when it looks rare, and so on. Because cooking flank steak beyond medium-rare toughens it, we advise against it. In fact, if you like your meat more than medium, you might want to choose another cut.

With the flank steak cooked and guacamole in hand, the rest of the recipe goes quickly. As the meat rests, the onions and peppers can be grilled. At the last minute, the tortillas are warmed around the edges of the fire (which should have cooled, if using charcoal, or which can be lowered, if using gas).

WHAT WE LEARNED: Don't bother marinating flank steak; it will be plenty tender as long as you slice it thin across the grain. Do let the meat rest (it will be juicier and more tender) before slicing, and grill the vegetables while the steak reposes.

CLASSIC FAJITAS serves 8

The ingredients go on the grill in order as the fire dies down: steak over a medium-hot fire, vegetables over a medium fire, and tortillas around the edge of a medium to low fire just to warm them. (Alternatively, the tortillas can be wrapped together in a clean, damp dish towel and warmed in a microwave oven for about 3 minutes at full power; keep them wrapped until you're ready to use them.) Flank steak is best when cooked rare or medium-rare at most. Because flank is a thin cut, it is very important for the meat to rest after it comes off the grill. Make sure to cover the grilled but unsliced flank steak with foil; it will take you at least 10 minutes to get the vegetables and tortillas ready. If you can find skirt steak (see Tasting Lab on page 158), it can be grilled just like flank steak.

1	flank steak (about 2½ pounds)
¼	cup lime juice
	Salt and ground black pepper
1	very large onion, peeled and cut into ½-inch rounds
2	very large red or green bell peppers, prepared following illustration at right
16	flour tortillas (each 10 to 12 inches in diameter)
1	recipe Chunky Guacamole (page 155)

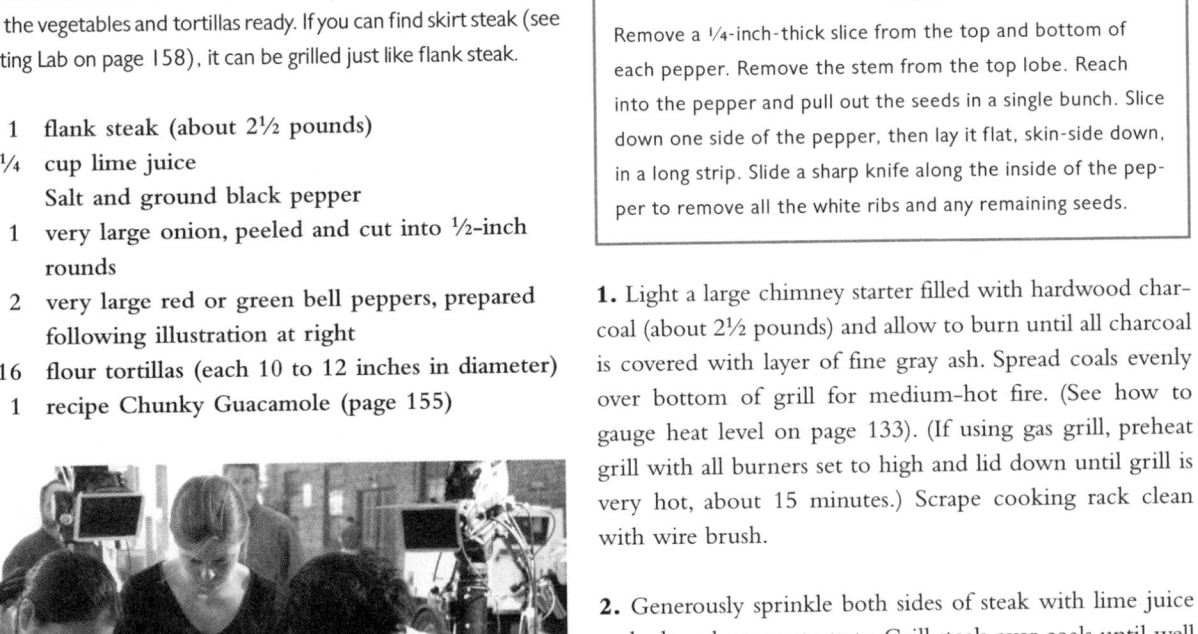

TECHNIQUE: Cutting Peppers

Remove a ¼-inch-thick slice from the top and bottom of each pepper. Remove the stem from the top lobe. Reach into the pepper and pull out the seeds in a single bunch. Slice down one side of the pepper, then lay it flat, skin-side down, in a long strip. Slide a sharp knife along the inside of the pepper to remove all the white ribs and any remaining seeds.

1. Light a large chimney starter filled with hardwood charcoal (about 2½ pounds) and allow to burn until all charcoal is covered with layer of fine gray ash. Spread coals evenly over bottom of grill for medium-hot fire. (See how to gauge heat level on page 133). (If using gas grill, preheat grill with all burners set to high and lid down until grill is very hot, about 15 minutes.) Scrape cooking rack clean with wire brush.

2. Generously sprinkle both sides of steak with lime juice and salt and pepper to taste. Grill steak over coals until well seared and dark brown on one side, 5 to 7 minutes. Flip steak using tongs; continue grilling on other side until interior of meat is slightly less done than you want it to be when you eat it, 2 to 5 minutes more for medium-rare (depending on heat of fire and thickness of steak). (If using gas grill, grill steak, covered, until well seared and brown, 4 to 6 minutes. Flip and continue grilling another 2 to 5 minutes.) Transfer meat to cutting board; cover loosely with foil, and let rest for 10 minutes.

3. While meat rests and charcoal fire has died down to medium or gas burners have been adjusted to medium, grill onions and peppers, turning occasionally, until onions are lightly charred, about 6 minutes, and peppers are streaked with grill marks, about 10 minutes. Remove vegetables from grill and cut into long, thin strips; set aside. Arrange tortillas around edge of grill; heat until just warmed, about 20 seconds per side. Wrap tortillas in towel to keep warm and place in a basket.

4. Slice steak very thin on bias against grain; adjust seasonings with additional salt and pepper. Arrange sliced meat and vegetables on large platter; serve immediately with tortillas and guacamole passed separately.

TASTING LAB: Three Flat Steaks

LIKE FLANK STEAKS, THE OTHER TWO CUTS MOST SIMILAR to it—skirt steak and hanger steak—have also recently become fashionable. These three popular steaks share the distinction of coming from the chest and side of the animal. Hanger and flank both come from the rear side, while skirt comes from the area between the abdomen and the chest cavity. In addition to location, these steaks share certain other basic qualities: All are long, relatively thin, quite tough, and grainy, but with rich, deep, beefy flavor.

Of course, these flavorful steaks also have their individual distinctions. Hanger, a thick muscle that is attached to the diaphragm, derives its name from the fact that when a cow is butchered, this steak hangs down into the center of the carcass. Because it is a classic French bistro dish, this cut is highly prized in restaurants and therefore difficult to find in butcher shops. We don't think this is a great loss since the hangers we sampled had the toughest texture and least rich flavor of these three cuts.

Fortunately, flank steak is easy to find in any supermarket. It has a great beef flavor and is quite tender if cooked rare or medium-rare and sliced thin against the grain. Because of the popularity of fajitas, flank steak has become somewhat expensive, often retailing for $7 a pound.

Skirt steak, which was the cut originally used for fajitas, can be hard to locate, even in butcher shops. This is a real pity because skirt steak has more fat than flank steak, which makes it juicier and richer tasting. At the same time, it has a deep, beefy flavor that outdoes either hanger or flank steak. If you see skirt steak, buy it, and cook it like flank.

SCIENCE DESK: Why Meat Should Rest

A FINAL BUT VERY IMPORTANT STEP WHEN COOKING flank steak—and all red meats—is allowing it to rest after it comes off the heat. As the proteins in the meat heat up during cooking they coagulate, which basically means they uncoil and then reconnect, or bond with each other, in a different configuration. When the proteins coagulate, they squeeze out part of the liquid that was trapped in their coiled structures and in the spaces between the individual molecules. The heat from the cooking source drives these freed liquids toward the center of the meat.

This process of coagulation explains why experienced chefs can tell how done a piece of meat is by pushing on it and judging the amount of resistance: The firmer the meat, the more done it is. But the coagulation process is apparently at least partly reversible, so as you allow the meat to rest and return to a lower temperature after cooking, some of the liquid is reabsorbed by the protein molecules as their capacity to hold moisture increases. As a result, if given a chance to rest, the meat will lose less juice when you cut into it, which in turn makes for much juicier and more tender meat.

This is common wisdom among cooks, but to be sure it was correct, we cooked two more flank steaks, sliced one up immediately after it came off the fire, and allowed the second to rest for 10 minutes before slicing it. Not only did the first steak exude almost 40 percent more juice than the second when sliced, it also looked grayer and was not as tender. In this case, it is crucial to follow the conventional wisdom: Give your steak a rest.

MARGARITAS

WHAT WE WANTED: Fresh-tasting margaritas with an emphasis on the citrus, not just the tequila.

America's obsession with margaritas has helped make the United States the world's leading consumer of tequila. Unfortunately, the typical margarita tends to be a slushy, headache-inducing concoction made with little more than ice, tequila, and artificially flavored corn syrup. At their best, though, margaritas are the perfect balance of tequila, orange liqueur, and fresh lime juice, shaken briskly with crushed ice and served on the rocks (with salt if preferred). We wanted to see if we could produce this ideal cocktail, balancing the distinctive flavor of tequila with a hint of orange and a bright burst of citrus.

As tequila is a margarita's most important ingredient, we started the testing there. We made margaritas with all types of tequila, using both superpremium 100 percent blue agave (agave is the plant from which tequila is distilled) as well as mixed tequilas, to which cane or corn syrup is often added.

Two types of tequila, known as silver (or white) and gold, are not aged; their young alcoholic flavor gave the margaritas we made a raw, harsh flavor. Margaritas made with the prized aged and very aged tequilas were extremely smooth, but their distinct tannic taste, produced as they age up to six years in oak casks, dominated the cocktail. Reposado, or "rested," tequila, made from 100 percent blue agave and aged for 12 months or less, was the favorite. Its slightly mellow flavor blended perfectly with the other ingredients.

Next we tested orange-flavored liqueurs. Both Grand Marnier and Cointreau were delicious, but many tasters thought their robust flavor too pronounced and "boozy" for a margarita. Triple Sec, an orange liqueur with a lower alcohol content, made a more delicate contribution.

Margaritas are traditionally made with lime juice, but some tasters thought the flavor too acidic. Those made with only lemon juice ended up tasting too much like lemonade. An equal mixture of both lime and lemon juice produced a margarita that was refreshing but too mild.

We turned to a technique we had used in the test kitchen to make lemonade. For that recipe, we found that mashing thinly sliced lemons extracted their full flavor. While this technique boosted the citrus flavor in the margaritas, the oil from the white pith was too bitter, giving the drink a medicinal flavor. Steeping just the grated zest of the lime and lemon in their juices for 24 hours deepened the citrus flavor without adding bitterness. (We later discovered that the steeping period could be reduced to four hours.) Adding sugar to the steeping mixture countered any remaining harshness from the citrus.

In testing the proportions of the three main ingredients, we found that tasters favored an equal portion of each, quite different from the tequila-heavy concoctions we had consumed in the past. Our last test was to try the margarita in a salt-rimmed glass. This was clearly a question of individual taste. So salt the glass or not, as you and your guests prefer.

WHAT WE LEARNED: For the ultimate margarita, mix premium tequila with fresh juice and zest. Use Triple Sec for a bright orange flavor that's not too alcoholic.

FRESH MARGARITAS makes about 1 quart, serving 4 to 6

The longer the zest and juice mixture is allowed to steep, the more developed the citrus flavors in the finished margaritas. We recommend steeping for the full 24 hours, although the margaritas will still be great if the mixture is steeped for only the minimum four hours. If you're in a rush and want to serve margaritas immediately, omit the zest and skip the steeping process altogether.

- 4 teaspoons grated zest plus ½ cup juice from 2 or 3 medium limes
- 4 teaspoons grated zest plus ½ cup juice from 2 or 3 medium lemons
- ¼ cup superfine sugar
  Pinch salt
- 2 cups crushed ice
- 1 cup 100 percent agave tequila, preferably reposado
- 1 cup Triple Sec

1. Combine lime zest and juice, lemon zest and juice, sugar, and salt in large liquid measuring cup; cover with plastic wrap and refrigerate until flavors meld, 4 to 24 hours.

2. Divide 1 cup crushed ice between 4 or 6 margarita or double old-fashioned glasses. Strain juice mixture into 1-quart pitcher or cocktail shaker. Add tequila, Triple Sec, and remaining crushed ice; stir or shake until thoroughly combined and chilled, 20 to 60 seconds. Strain into ice-filled glasses; serve immediately.

VARIATIONS

FRESH PINEAPPLE MARGARITAS

Peel and core 1 small ripe pineapple (about 3½ pounds); cut half of pineapple into rough 2-inch chunks (reserve remaining half for another use). Puree in workbowl of food processor fitted with steel blade until smooth and foamy, about 1 minute. Follow recipe for Fresh Margaritas, omitting zest and steeping process, reducing lemon and lime juices to ¼ cup each, and adding ½ cup pureed pineapple to juice mixture.

FRESH RASPBERRY MARGARITAS

To make strawberry margaritas, substitute an equal amount of hulled strawberries for the raspberries.

Follow recipe for Fresh Margaritas, omitting zest and steeping process and pureeing 1 cup fresh raspberries, lime and lemon juices, sugar, and salt in workbowl of food processor fitted with steel blade until smooth. Strain mixture into pitcher or cocktail shaker; continue with recipe, reducing Triple Sec to ½ cup and adding ½ cup Chambord (or desired raspberry liqueur) to juice and tequila mixture in pitcher.

EQUIPMENT CORNER: Zesters

WHAT'S THE BEST TOOL FOR REMOVING THE COLORED peel from limes, lemons, and oranges while leaving behind the bitter white pith? It depends on how you want your zest. Traditional zesters remove the peel in long, thin strips, which can be left as is (for garnish) or minced. Box graters and other similar tools yield tiny bits of moist zest.

Armed with bags of lemons and oranges, we set out to find the best tool for zesting. We assembled seven utensils. We not only wanted to determine which tool was the easiest to use but which produced zest without any pith and left the least amount of zest in the grater itself.

Traditional citrus zesters have short handles and stainless steel heads with beveled, sharp holes at the top. You must bear down with the tool and scrape away long strips of zest, turning the fruit as you go. Comfort and sharpness were the key issues when testing these models. The Oxo zester performed best—its ergonomic grip was not only soft but also short enough to nestle perfectly in testers' palms, allowing greater ease of movement. The sharp holes on this zester raced through the fruits cleanly and yielded long strips of oil-rich zest.

For grated zest, most cooks turn to four-sided box graters. This old kitchen standby usually has one side reserved for zesting, which consists of small holes with raised teeth. Another choice is a small paddle with small, raised holes. The newest grater/zester on the market is modeled after the traditional woodworking rasp, with tiny razor-sharp teeth set in a long, flat stainless steel base.

We quickly concluded that the box grater is a poor choice for zesting fruits. It mangled lemons and oranges, and most of the zest became trapped in the grater holes. We needed a toothbrush to remove the last stubborn bits of zest. The flat grater with raised teeth was only slightly easier to use. The rasplike Microplane (see photo, left) was the fastest and easiest grater/zester we tested. It created tiny fluffs of perfect zest, leaving pith and fruit intact.

An unusual butchering technique gets a 12-pound turkey out of the oven in less than two hours and delivers supercrisp skin and evenly cooked meat.

THANKSGIVING dinner

The only certain things in life are death, taxes, and turkey at Thanksgiving. Over the years, we have cooked hundreds of turkeys in the test kitchen to figure out how to bring the most flavorful, most beautiful bird to the holiday table.

Never ones to rest on our laurels, we are always looking for new and different ways to deal with the holiday turkey, always with improvement in mind. After a successful round of roasting chickens in a scorching hot 450-degree oven (the skin was the crispiest ever), we began to wonder if this method could be applied to turkey. After all, the goals are the same: dark, crisp skin; evenly cooked, moist meat; and quick cooking. We reasoned that if high-heat roasting was good enough for chicken, then it was good enough for turkey, too.

So we went into the kitchen, rolled up our sleeves, cranked up the oven, and started roasting turkeys. Several scorched turkeys later, and a panicked call from the boss to the test kitchen about the billows of smoke filling the air, we met with success. We had a turkey with crackling crisp skin and moist meat on the table with just two hours of work on Thanksgiving Day. We even figured out how to get the dressing and gravy done at the same time.

IN THIS CHAPTER

THE RECIPES

Crisp-Skin High-Roast Butterflied
    Turkey with Sausage Dressing
Golden Cornbread
Turkey Gravy

Basic Cranberry Sauce
Cranberry-Orange Sauce
Cranberry Sauce with Pears
    and Fresh Ginger

EQUIPMENT CORNER

Saucepans

SCIENCE DESK

How Brining Works

TASTING LAB

Boxed Stuffing

CRISP-SKIN HIGH-ROAST TURKEY

WHAT WE WANTED: A turkey in and out of the oven—and on the table with dressing and gravy—in less than 2 hours—given some prep time the day before.

We have cooked hundreds of turkey in the test kitchen, always with improvement in mind. In our latest effort, we put the emphasis on high roasting—a method that uses oven temperatures of at least 450 degrees. We had heard that high-roasting would produce a turkey with juicy meat and crisp skin in record time—less than two hours. This was clearly an opportunity we couldn't afford to pass up.

For our initial test, we placed the turkey (a 12-pound bird), breast-side up on a V-rack, placed the rack in a roasting pan, and roasted the turkey at 500 degrees, undisturbed, until the thigh meat registered around 175 degrees—in this case just under 2 hours. There was crisp skin as promised, but only a modicum of it. The recipe never called for rotating the turkey in the oven, so it was only the skin over the breast meat that was crisp. In addition, the breast meat had overcooked by the time the thighs had cooked. Even worse, the kitchen filled with black smoke caused by burnt pan drippings. Still, even with the outward failure of this initial attempt, we were encouraged by the short amount of time needed to roast the turkey.

Tackling the problem of the unevenly cooked meat first, we started the turkey breast down, then flipped the turkey from side to side, finally finishing breast-side up. This method yielded evenly cooked meat, but since each side of the turkey spent less time face up, the skin was not very crisp.

In their natural form, turkeys are not designed to roast evenly. The cathedral ceiling–shaped bone structure of the breast promotes faster cooking, while the legs lag behind. Because dark meat tastes best when cooked to a higher temperature than lean white meat (175 degrees for dark meat versus about 165 degrees for the breast), turkeys are not terribly well designed. You want the white meat to cook more slowly than the dark meat, not the other way around.

If we had any hope of getting the turkey in and out of the oven quickly and with crisp skin, we decided, a turkey redesign was in order. We butterflied the turkey—a technique in which the backbone is removed, then the bird is opened up and flattened. Logic stated that with the turkey flattened and all of the meat facing up at the same time, the turkey would cook more evenly, and the skin would have equal time to crisp. This method worked beautifully and had one additional benefit. Because the legs were now in contact with part of the breast, essentially shielding it, they prevented the white meat from overcooking. The thighs and the breast reached their target temperatures of 175 and 165 degrees, respectively, at the same time. Perfect!

Butterflying a chicken requires only a pair of good scissors to cut out the backbone. However, scissors are no match for the sturdier bone structure of the turkey. We found a good-quality chef's knife was necessary to cut along either side of the backbone. Even with a sharp blade, we still needed to apply some serious pressure to cut through the thicker bones, sometimes literally hacking down the backbone. Once the backbone was removed, we found that the sturdy rib cage would not flatten under the heel of a hand. We reached for a heavy-duty rolling pin, placed the turkey breast-side up, and whacked the breastbone until it flattened—aggressive culinary therapy, if you will.

We now had evenly cooked meat and crisp skin, but what to do about the profusion of smoke? Filling the roasting pan with water to keep the fat from hitting the bottom of the hot pan would work, but, instead of water, we turned to dressing. The dressing soaked up the drippings from the turkey—thereby eliminating the smoke while also picking up great flavor. For this test, we had been using our favorite cornbread dressing recipe, but we found a little

With the technical problems of high-roasting a turkey solved, we were now able to move on to flavor—or lack thereof. As is tradition here in the test kitchen, we turned to brining—a process in which the turkey is soaked in a salt/sugar/water solution (see the Science Desk on page 171). The salt in the solution makes its way into the meat and seasons it. The brine also gives the turkey needed moisture, which protects the meat from overcooking. But with this moisture comes soggy skin. Air-drying the brined turkey in the refrigerator the night before it was roasted allowed the moisture in the skin to evaporate, and once again the skin was crackling crisp. For those not inclined to brine, we also found that air-drying a kosher bird works well. Because it is salted during processing, a kosher turkey has a similar flavor to brined turkey.

Now we had great turkey and dressing, but what about the gravy? We had always made gravy using the precious pan drippings from the turkey, but in this recipe the dressing soaked up the drippings. Gravy made from a stock flavored only with giblets was weak tasting. We had to find a way to pump flavor into the gravy.

We butterflied yet another turkey, this time saving the backbone. We chopped it into small pieces and threw it into a roasting pan along with the neck and giblets and some celery, carrots, onion, and garlic. We roasted the bones and vegetables at 450 degrees until well browned. Then we placed them in a saucepan along with some chicken stock, white wine, and water and made a stock. After the stock cooled down, we removed the fat and reserved it. We used the reserved fat to make a roux—a flour and fat mixture that is used to thicken a sauce or gravy. This gravy was big on flavor, and by making the stock ahead of time, while the turkey was brining, we had less work to do on Thanksgiving day, when time is always at a premium.

tweaking was necessary. The dressing was greasy when left to soak up the drippings, so we lowered the fat in the recipe by reducing the amount of butter from 8 tablespoons to 2 and cutting the amount of half-and-half and sausage by half. We also found it necessary to reduce the amount of stock used in the original recipe; the dressing got the moisture it needed from the juices of the turkey. Now turkey and dressing were on the table in less than two hours.

All we needed now was a proper roasting pan to suit our two-story arrangement of butterflied bird and dressing. A broiler pan would have been ideal, since the slotted top would prevent the dressing from drying out and burning and would also keep the bird elevated enough so that it wasn't nesting in the dressing. But while the broiler pan top was the perfect size to hold the turkey, the bottom held only enough dressing for four—what about leftovers? After going through the kitchen's battalion of roasting pans to use with the broiler pan top, we resorted to using a disposable rectangular aluminum roasting pan. Big enough to hold plenty of dressing, sturdy enough to support the broiler pan top, and easy to clean up—just throw it away.

WHAT WE LEARNED: To get crisp skin and evenly cooked meat, butterfly the turkey and roast it at 450 degrees. To keep your kitchen from filling with smoke, line the roasting pan with dressing.

CRISP-SKIN HIGH-ROAST BUTTERFLIED TURKEY WITH SAUSAGE DRESSING

serves 10 to 12

If you prefer not to brine your turkey, we recommend a kosher bird. The dressing can be made with cornbread or white bread, but note that they are not used in equal amounts. The turkey is roasted in a 12 by 16-inch disposable roasting pan, sitting on a broiler pan top or a sturdy flat wire rack covered with foil. If using a wire rack, choose one that measures about 11 by 17 inches so that it will span the roasting pan and sit above the dressing in the pan. Cover with foil, cut slits in the foil for fat drainage, and spray with nonstick cooking spray. Serve turkey and dressing with gravy (see page 169).

turkey

- 2 cups kosher salt or 1 cup table salt
- 1 cup sugar
- 1 turkey (12 to 14 pounds gross weight), rinsed thoroughly; giblets, neck, and tailpiece removed and reserved for gravy; and turkey butterflied (see illustrations 1 through 5 on page 167)
- 1 tablespoon unsalted butter, melted

sausage dressing

- 12 cups cornbread (recipe follows) broken into 1-inch pieces (include crumbs), or 18 cups 1-inch challah or Italian bread cubes (from about 1½ loaves)
- 1¾ cups chicken stock or canned low-sodium chicken broth
- 1 cup half-and-half
- 2 large eggs, beaten lightly
- 12 ounces bulk pork sausage, broken into 1-inch pieces
- 3 medium onions, chopped fine (about 3 cups)
- 3 ribs celery, chopped fine (about 1½ cups)
- 2 tablespoons unsalted butter
- 2 tablespoons minced fresh thyme leaves
- 2 tablespoons minced fresh sage leaves
- 3 medium cloves garlic, minced
- 1½ teaspoons salt
- 2 teaspoons ground black pepper

1. TO BRINE TURKEY: Dissolve salt and sugar in 2 gallons cold water in large stockpot or clean bucket. Add turkey and refrigerate or set in very cool spot (about 40 degrees) for 8 hours.

2. TO PREPARE DRESSING: While the turkey brines, adjust one oven rack to upper-middle position and second rack to lower-middle position and heat oven to 250 degrees. Spread bread in even layers on 2 rimmed baking sheets and dry in oven 50 to 60 minutes for cornbread or 40 to 50 minutes for challah or Italian bread.

TECHNIQUE: Preparing the Turkey

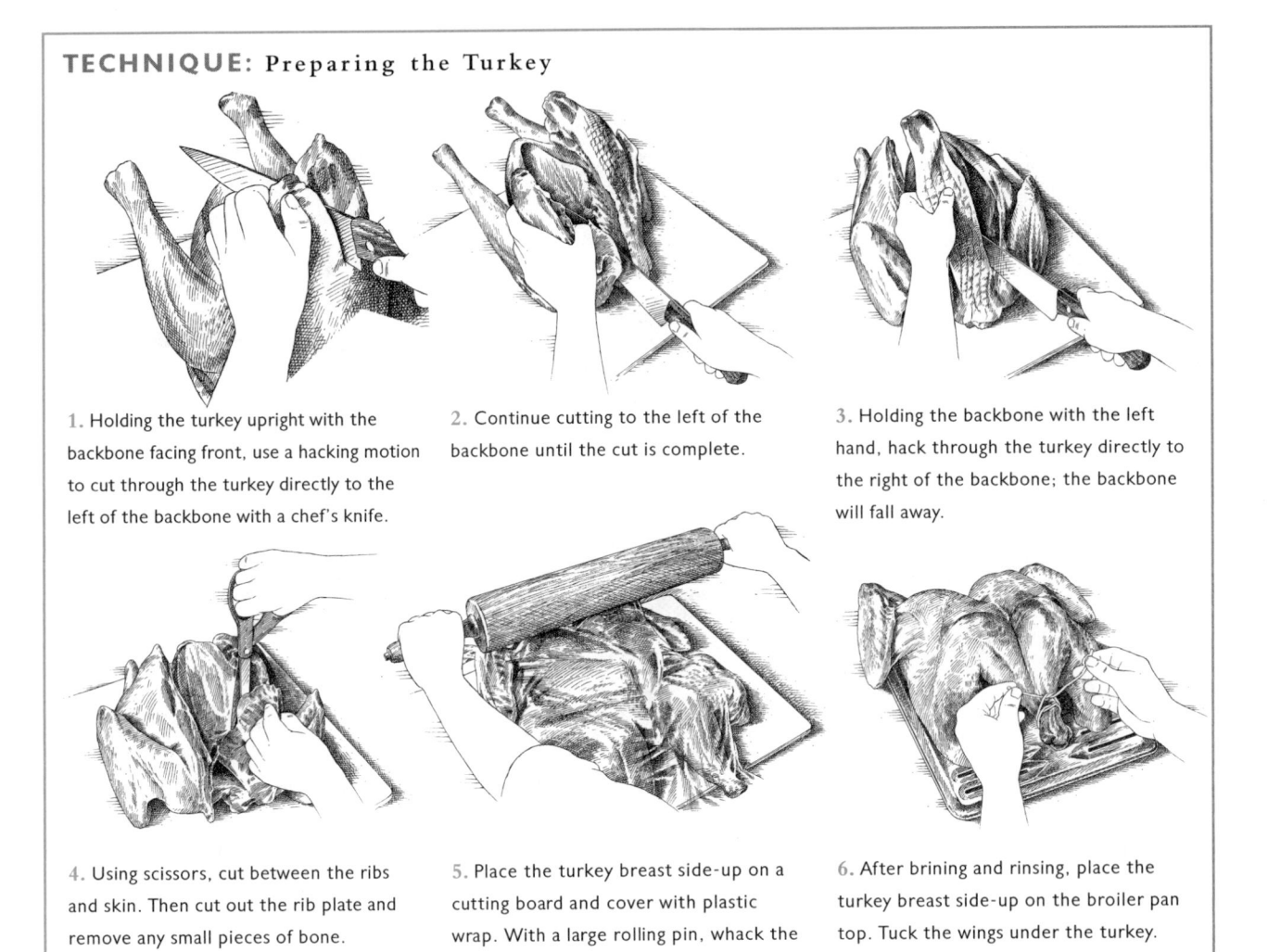

1. Holding the turkey upright with the backbone facing front, use a hacking motion to cut through the turkey directly to the left of the backbone with a chef's knife.

2. Continue cutting to the left of the backbone until the cut is complete.

3. Holding the backbone with the left hand, hack through the turkey directly to the right of the backbone; the backbone will fall away.

4. Using scissors, cut between the ribs and skin. Then cut out the rib plate and remove any small pieces of bone.

5. Place the turkey breast side-up on a cutting board and cover with plastic wrap. With a large rolling pin, whack the breastbone until it cracks and the turkey flattens.

6. After brining and rinsing, place the turkey breast side-up on the broiler pan top. Tuck the wings under the turkey. Push the legs up to rest between the thigh and breast. Tie the legs together.

3. Place bread in large bowl. Whisk together stock, half-and-half, and eggs in medium bowl; pour over bread and toss very gently to coat so that bread does not break into smaller pieces. Set aside.

4. Heat heavy-bottomed, 12-inch skillet over medium-high heat until hot, about 1½ minutes. Add sausage and cook, stirring occasionally, until sausage loses its raw color, 5 to 7 minutes. With slotted spoon, transfer sausage to medium bowl. Add about half the onions and celery to fat in skillet; sauté, stirring occasionally, over medium-high heat until softened, about 5 minutes. Transfer onion mixture to bowl with sausage. Return skillet to heat and add 2 tablespoons butter; when foam subsides, add remaining celery and onions and sauté, stirring occasionally, until softened, about 5 minutes. Stir in thyme, sage, and garlic; cook until fragrant, about 30 seconds; add salt and pepper. Add this mixture along with sausage and onion mixture to bread and stir gently to combine (try not to break bread into smaller pieces).

TECHNIQUE: Carving the Turkey

1. With a sharp carving knife, cut both leg quarters off the turkey.

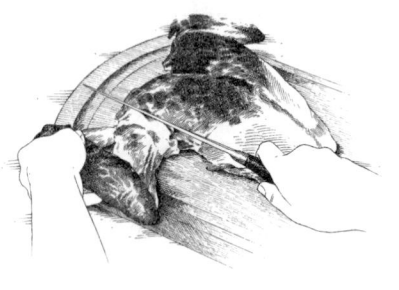

2. Cut both wing pieces off the breast section.

3. Slice straight down along the breastbone. Continue to slice down, with the knife hugging the rib bones, to remove the breast meat.

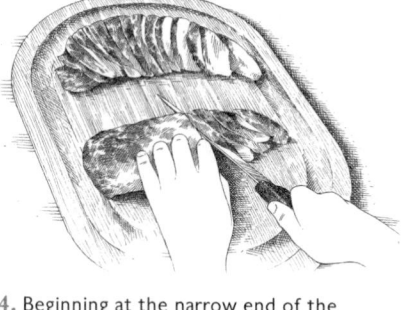

4. Beginning at the narrow end of the breast, slice the meat across the grain, about ¼ inch thick.

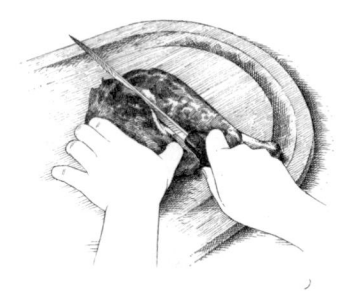

5. Pull the thigh and the drumstick apart and locate the joint. Cut through the joint, separating the two pieces.

6. Remove the largest pieces of meat from the thigh and slice the meat across the grain, about ¼ inch thick.

5. Spray disposable aluminum 12 by 16-inch roasting pan with nonstick cooking spray. Transfer dressing to roasting pan and spread in even layer. Cover pan with foil and refrigerate while preparing turkey.

6. TO PREPARE TURKEY FOR ROASTING: Remove turkey from brine and rinse well under cool running water. Following illustration 6 on page 167, position turkey on broiler pan top or foil-lined rack; thoroughly pat surface of turkey dry with paper towels. Place broiler pan top or rack with turkey on top of roasting pan with dressing; refrigerate, uncovered, 8 to 24 hours.

7. TO ROAST TURKEY WITH DRESSING: Adjust oven rack to lower-middle position and heat oven to 450 degrees. Remove broiler pan top with turkey and foil cover over roasting pan; replace broiler pan top with turkey. Brush turkey with 1 tablespoon melted butter. Place roasting pan with turkey on broiler pan top in oven and roast until turkey skin is crisp and deep brown and instant-read thermometer registers 165 degrees when inserted in thickest part of breast and 175 degrees in thickest part of thigh, 80 to 100 minutes, rotating pan from front to back after 40 minutes.

8. Transfer broiler pan top with turkey to cutting board, tent loosely with foil, and let rest 20 minutes. Meanwhile, adjust oven rack to upper-middle position, place roasting pan with dressing back in oven, and bake until golden brown, about 10 minutes. Cool dressing 5 minutes, then spoon into bowl or onto turkey serving platter. Carve turkey (see illustrations on page 168) and serve.

GOLDEN CORNBREAD makes about 16 cups
crumbled cornbread

You need about three-quarters of this recipe for the dressing; the rest is for nibbling.

- 4 large eggs
- 1⅓ cups buttermilk
- 1⅓ cups milk
- 2 cups yellow cornmeal, preferably stone-ground
- 2 cups (10 ounces) unbleached all-purpose flour
- 4 teaspoons baking powder
- 1 teaspoon baking soda
- 2 tablespoons sugar
- 1 teaspoon salt
- 4 tablespoons unsalted butter, melted, plus extra for greasing baking dish

1. Adjust oven rack to middle position and heat oven to 375 degrees. Grease 9 by 13-inch baking dish with butter.

2. Beat eggs in medium bowl; whisk in buttermilk and milk.

3. Whisk cornmeal, flour, baking powder, baking soda, sugar, and salt together in large bowl. Push dry ingredients up sides of bowl to make a well, then pour egg and milk mixture into well and stir with whisk until just combined; stir in melted butter.

4. Pour batter into greased baking dish. Bake until top is golden brown and edges have pulled away from sides of pan, 30 to 40 minutes.

5. Transfer baking dish to wire rack and cool to room temperature before using, about 1 hour.

TURKEY GRAVY makes about 1 quart

Because this gravy doesn't use drippings from the roasted turkey but instead uses the trimmings from butterflying the bird, the gravy can conveniently be made a day in advance (while the turkey brines and air-dries in the refrigerator) and then reheated before serving. When roasting the trimmings and vegetables, make sure to use a roasting pan that can go over the stovetop. The bottom of a broiler pan works well, too.

Reserved giblets (do not use liver), neck, tailpiece, and backbone and breast bones from turkey
- 1 medium carrot, cut into 1-inch pieces
- 1 rib celery, cut into 1-inch pieces
- 2 small onions, chopped coarse
- 6 cloves garlic, unpeeled
- 3½ cups chicken stock or canned low-sodium chicken broth
- 2 cups dry white wine
- 6 sprigs fresh thyme
- ¼ cup all-purpose flour
  Salt and ground black pepper

1. Heat oven to 450 degrees. Place turkey trimmings, carrot, celery, onions, and garlic in large flameproof roasting pan or broiler pan bottom. Spray lightly with vegetable oil spray and toss to combine. Roast, stirring every 10 minutes, until well-browned, 40 to 50 minutes.

2. Remove pan from oven, and place over burner(s) set at high heat; add chicken stock and bring to boil, scraping up browned bits on bottom of pan with wooden spoon.

3. Transfer contents of pan to large saucepan. Add wine, 3 cups water, and thyme; bring to boil over high heat. Reduce heat to low and simmer until reduced by half, about 1½ hours. Strain stock into large measuring cup or container. Cool to room temperature; cover with plastic wrap, and refrigerate until fat congeals on surface, about 2 hours.

4. Skim fat from stock using soup spoon; reserve fat. Pour stock through fine-mesh strainer to remove remaining bits of fat; discard bits in strainer. Bring stock to simmer in medium saucepan over medium-high heat.

5. In second medium saucepan, heat 4 tablespoons reserved turkey fat over medium-high heat until bubbling; whisk in flour and cook, whisking constantly, until combined and honey-colored, about 2 minutes. Continuing to whisk constantly, gradually add hot stock; bring to boil, then reduce heat to medium-low and simmer, stirring occasionally, until slightly thickened, about 5 minutes. Season to taste with salt and pepper. (Gravy can be refrigerated up to 3 days. After turkey comes out of oven, heat gravy in medium saucepan over medium heat until hot, about 8 minutes.)

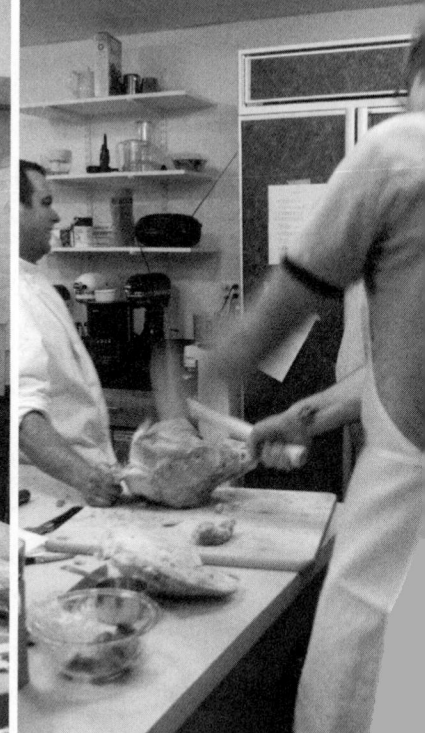

Our taste buds were right: Brined birds are juicier.

How does brining work? Brining promotes a change in the structure of the proteins in the muscle. The salt causes protein strands to become denatured, or unwound. This is the same process that occurs when proteins are exposed to heat, acid, or alcohol. When protein strands unwind, they get tangled up with one another, forming a matrix that traps water. Salt is commonly used to give processed meats a better texture. For example, hot dogs made without salt would be limp.

In most cases, we add sugar to the brine. Sugar has little if any effect on the texture of the meat, but it does add flavor and promotes better browning of the skin.

We usually list both kosher and regular table salt in recipes that call for brining. Because of the difference in the size of the crystals, cup for cup, table salt is about twice as concentrated as kosher salt.

TASTING LAB: Boxed Dressings

AFTER CHOPPING, MINCING, DICING, DRYING, AND CUBING our way through countless batches of homemade dressing, we wondered if there was an easier, less time-consuming way to make this dish. To answer this question, we held a blind taste test of seven leading brands of commercial dressing. We prepared each according to the package directions.

Not surprisingly, all of these commercial stuffings received disappointing scores. Most were too salty and greasy and much too bland. After reading ingredient labels, this is easy to understand. On all labels, wheat flour is listed first, followed by corn syrup, salt, and soybean oil.

Bell's Family Style Dressing was the best of the lot; tasters liked its "herby" and "sweet" flavor. Kellogg's Croquettes was a distant second, followed by Arnold Premium Sage & Onion and Pepperidge Farm Cubed Herb.

Our conclusion: The high amounts of sugar, salt, and fat in boxed dressings will not mask the absence of fresh ingredients like onions, celery, eggs, and stock. For dressing that tastes great, take the time to make homemade.

SCIENCE DESK: How Brining Works

WE FIND THAT SOAKING TURKEYS (AS WELL AS CHICKEN and even pork chops) in a saltwater solution before cooking best protects delicate white meat. Whether we are roasting a turkey or grilling chicken parts, we have consistently found that brining keeps the meat juicier. Brining also gives delicate (and sometimes mushy) poultry a meatier, firmer consistency and seasons the meat down to the bone. (We also find that brining adds moisture to pork and shrimp and improves their texture and flavor when grilled.)

To explain these sensory perceptions, we ran some tests. We started by weighing several 11-pound turkeys after they had been brined for 12 hours and found an average weight gain of almost ¾ pound. Even more impressive, we found that brined birds weighed 6 to 8 ounces more after roasting than a same-sized bird that had not been brined.

CRANBERRY SAUCE

WHAT WE WANTED: A well balanced sauce—neither too sweet or tart—with a soft gel-like texture and some whole berries.

Although cranberry jelly, molded in the shape of the can and sliced into neat disks, is one of the test kitchen's guilty pleasures, it's usually not our first choice for the holiday table. There, a soft, tart-sweet sauce with plenty of whole berries reigns. The best cranberry sauce has a clean, pure cranberry flavor, with enough sweetness to temper the assertively tart fruit but not so much that the sauce is cloying or candylike. The texture should be that of a soft gel, neither too liquidy nor too stiff, cushioning some softened but still intact berries.

Because simple cranberry sauce has only three ingredients—cranberries, sweetener, and liquid—the variables to test were relatively straightforward. Though many of the recipes we researched called for 1 pound of cranberries, we wanted to base ours on 12 ounces of berries simply because all the bags in stores are that size; we couldn't see the point of opening a second bag to use only a third of it.

Most cranberry sauce recipes use granulated sugar as a sweetener, but we also tried brown sugar, honey, maple syrup, and corn syrup. Granulated sugar was the tasters' favorite because it balanced the tartness of the berries with a direct sweetness, without adding a strong flavor profile of its own. The corn syrup tasted flat and bland, while the flavors of the maple syrup, brown sugar, and honey were too pronounced, compromising that of the berries. The amount of sugar called for in the recipes we turned up during our research ranged from ⅜ cup to 1½ cups for 12 ounces of berries. Tasters unanimously favored 1 cup of sugar.

The liquids used to make the sauce ran a wide gamut. We tried batches made with apple juice and cider, white and dark grape juice, orange juice, pineapple juice, cranberry juice cocktail, 7-Up, red wine, white wine, port, and champagne. Tasters agreed that none of these liquids—even the orange juice, which is traditional—offered a significant flavor advantage over plain water. In testing different amounts of water, we found that ¾ cup provided the ideal sauce-to-berry ratio once the sauce had reached serving temperature.

Tests of the various cooking times revealed that less is more. About five minutes over medium heat was all it took to achieve a supple, just-firm-enough set in the cooled sauce. Cranberries are high in pectin, a naturally occurring carbohydrate in many fruits. In the presence of sugar and acid (cranberries contain both), the large pectin molecules bond with each other to produce the characteristic jelled consistency. Since pectin molecules are released as the cells of the fruit break down during cooking, the longer the fruit cooks, the more pectin is released (and the more liquid is evaporated), and the stiffer the finished gel becomes. Cooking the sauce for 10 minutes, for instance, resulted in a gel you could slice with a knife. We also tested using a skillet instead of a saucepan and high heat rather than medium heat. We could see no advantage either way and decided to leave well enough alone.

The last round of tests focused on seasoning. Many recipes call simply for cranberries, water, and sugar, while others specify additions such as lemon juice, almond or vanilla extract, and salt. Lemon juice was much too tart, and both extracts left tasters cold, but we were amazed by the dramatic improvement a little salt could make. Just ¼ teaspoon of salt revealed heretofore unknown sweetness in the cranberries and heightened the flavor of the sauce overall, letting loose a full range of high and low flavor notes.

WHAT WE LEARNED: Keep it simple—just water, granulated sugar, and cranberries make the best sauce. Keep it short—simmering for more than five minutes results in a stiff, sliceable gel. And don't forget the salt.

BASIC CRANBERRY SAUCE   makes 2¼ cups

If you've got frozen cranberries, do not defrost them before use; just pick through them and add about 2 minutes to the simmering time.

- ¾   cup water
- 1   cup sugar
- ¼   teaspoon salt
- 1   (12-ounce) bag cranberries, picked through

Bring water, sugar, and salt to boil in medium nonreactive saucepan over high heat, stirring occasionally to dissolve sugar. Stir in cranberries; return to boil. Reduce heat to medium; simmer until saucy, slightly thickened, and about two-thirds of berries have popped open, about 5 minutes. Transfer to nonreactive bowl, cool to room temperature, and serve. (Can be covered and refrigerated up to 7 days; let stand at room temperature 30 minutes before serving.)

VARIATIONS

CRANBERRY-ORANGE SAUCE

Orange juice adds little flavor, but we found that zest and liqueur pack the orange kick we were looking for in this sauce.

Follow recipe for Basic Cranberry Sauce, heating 1 tablespoon grated orange zest with sugar mixture. Off heat; stir in 2 tablespoons orange liqueur (such as Triple Sec or Grand Marnier).

CRANBERRY SAUCE WITH PEARS AND FRESH GINGER

Peel, core, and cut 2 medium-sized firm, ripe pears into ½-inch chunks; set aside. Follow recipe for Basic Cranberry Sauce, heating 1 tablespoon grated fresh ginger and ¼ teaspoon ground cinnamon with sugar mixture and stirring pears into liquid along with cranberries.

EQUIPMENT CORNER: Saucepans

A MEDIUM SAUCEPAN (2 TO 2½ QUARTS) IS BEST FOR preparing cranberry sauce. You'll also use this pan to blanch small amounts of vegetables, prepare rice, or make pastry cream. To find out whether it's necessary to spend a lot of money on this pan, we tested seven leading brands. We sautéed minced onion in butter to judge sauté speed. We also tested the pans' ability to cook evenly by preparing rice in each vessel. To assess which pans could cook without the burning or scorching caused by inferior material or hot spots, we scalded milk in each saucepan and made pastry cream.

Our tests turned out a wide range of results. We found that really lightweight pans are prone to scorching and that heavy copper or enameled cast-iron saucepans are hard to maneuver because they weigh too much. We recommend a pan with some heft (two to three pounds is ideal for this size pan), but don't go overboard. Also look for pans with handles that won't become scorching hot. Hollowed-out stainless steel handles or even cheap plastic handles (a saucepan never goes into the oven, so there's no need to buy something ovenproof anyway) are better than solid metal handles, which became hot very quickly during our tests.

Our favorite saucepans were the All-Clad Stainless followed by Tramontina. Both had good conductivity, were easy to maneuver, and sautéed reasonably well. Both of these pans are made from stainless steel with a layer of aluminum sandwiched inside for increased heat conduction. On the All Clad pan, the aluminum layer runs across the bottom and up the entire side of the pan; on the Tramontina, the aluminum layer is only on the bottom. Expect to spend about $45 for the Tramontina pan and nearly $120 for All-Clad.

One final note. Although not an issue with cranberry sauce, many of the other jobs that a medium saucepan is suited for (making rice or oatmeal, heating milk for cocoa) involve ingredients that stick and leave a mess in the pan, even when the recipe comes out right. For this reason, you might want to consider buying a nonstick 2-quart saucepan.

CHRISTMAS dinner

CHAPTER 14

Christmas dinner is not the time to experiment with new recipes or techniques. What every cook needs is foolproof recipes for family favorites. Holiday cooks also need a streamlined menu with as little last-minute work as possible.

For us, prime rib with potatoes and green beans is the perfect Christmas dinner. It's festive (how often do you make prime rib at home?) but relatively easy to prepare. In fact, you can probably prepare this entire menu with just an hour or so of kitchen work on Christmas Day.

Of course, just because a menu is easy to prepare doesn't mean it's good. Prime rib that's overcooked isn't going to make anyone jolly. Each slice should be rosy from the center all the way to the crust.

Christmas dinner also needs great side dishes. Pommes Anna, an elegant French potato cake, is a great choice. Like so many classic French recipes, this one needed some updating for American kitchens.

And for cooks who want to pull out all the stops, you might start things off with Creamy Mushroom Soup (page 10) and conclude with our Bittersweet Chocolate Roulade (page 341).

Chris hurries from the prime
rib in the oven to the potatoes
on the stove.

PRIME RIB

WHAT WE WANTED: A foolproof method for roasting prime rib that delivers juicy, tender, rosy slices of meat.

A prime rib is a little like a turkey: You probably cook only one a year, usually for an important occasion such as Christmas. Although you know there are alternative cooking methods that might deliver a better roast, they're too risky. You don't want to be remembered as the cook who carved slices of almost raw standing rib or delayed dinner for hours waiting for the roast to finish cooking. Rather than chance it, you stick with the standard 350 degrees for X minutes per pound. A roast cooked this way, you decide, will at least not embarrass you. But a roast cooked this way won't be great either.

Other than using general terms like juicy and tender, we weren't quite sure how to define perfect prime rib when we started testing, so we had no preconceived ideas about what techniques or methods would deliver a superior roast. In addition to our normal cookbook research, we decided to interview a few of the thousands of chefs who cook prime rib every day. Between what we found in books and what we learned from these chefs, we came up with a dozen or so fairly different methods. Although there were minor issues, such as whether the roast needed to be tied or whether it should be roasted on a rack, one big question needed answering: At what temperature should prime rib be roasted?

We started with oven temperatures. Suggested roasting temperatures ranged from a tepid 250 degrees to a bold 425 degrees. Other recipes recommended an initial high-temperature sear (450 to 500 degrees), then reduced the oven temperature to a more moderate 350 degrees for actual roasting. Wanting to test the full range, we roasted prime ribs at temperatures ranging from 250 to 500 degrees.

All prime ribs roasted at oven temperatures exceeding 300 degrees looked pretty much the same. Each slice of carved beef was well-done around the exterior, medium toward the center, and a beautiful, pink medium-rare at the center. We might have been tempted to report that roasting temperature doesn't much matter if we hadn't tried cooking prime rib at oven temperatures under 300 degrees. The results surprised us, although it certainly wasn't love at first sight.

About halfway through the cooking time of the first roast tested at 250 degrees, we wrote in our notes, "Though the meat looks virtually raw, the internal temperature registers 110 degrees, and very little of its fat has rendered." But we changed our minds as soon as we carved the first slice. This roast was as beautiful on the inside as it was anemic on the outside. Unlike the roasts that cooked at higher temperatures, this one was rosy pink from the surface to the center—the juiciest and most tender of all the roasts we had cooked. This was restaurant prime rib at its best.

In addition to being evenly cooked, the prime rib roasted in a 250-degree oven had another thing going for it: Its internal temperature increased only a degree or two during its resting period. (Roasts are allowed to rest when they come out of the oven both to distribute the heat evenly and to allow the juices to reabsorb back into the outer layers of the meat. For more information on this phenomenon, see the Science Desk on page 158.) A roast cooked to 128 degrees, for example, moved only to 130 degrees after a 45-minute rest.

Not so with the roasts cooked at higher temperatures. Their internal temperatures increased much more dramatically out of the oven. As a matter of fact, we noticed a direct correlation between oven temperature and the increase in the temperature of the roast while resting. Prime ribs roasted at moderate temperatures (325 to 350 degrees) increased, on average, 14 degrees during resting. In other words, if pulled from the oven at a rare 126-degree internal temperature, these roasts moved up to a solid medium (140 degrees) by the end of the resting period. Meanwhile, the prime rib roasted at 425 degrees increased a whopping 24 degrees (from 119 to 143) during its rest. We considered a smaller increase in postcooking temperature a definite advantage. It let us pull the roast from the oven at the temperature we wanted instead of having to speculate as to how many degrees the temperature would climb during resting.

In addition to its more stable internal temperature, prime rib roasted at 250 degrees lost less weight during cooking than prime rib roasted at higher temperatures. A 6¾-pound roast cooked in a 250-degree oven weighed just over 6¼ pounds when it came out of the oven, a loss of less than half a pound. By contrast, similar roasts cooked in a 325-degree oven lost just more than a pound, while roasts cooked at 350 degrees lost 1½ pounds. The prime rib cooked at 425 degrees lost a shocking 2 pounds. Part of the weight loss is fat, but certainly a good portion is juice. This test confirmed our suspicions that the beef roasted at 250 degrees was indeed juicier than beef roasted at higher temperatures.

Because members of a trade group called National Cattlemen's Beef Association would not endorse an oven-roasting temperature below 300 degrees, we decided to check the safety of this low-heat method before getting too sold on it. After conversations with a number of food scientists across the country, we determined that low-temperature roasting is as safe a cooking method as higher-temperature roasting. And though the odds of finding bacteria inside a prime rib roast are close to nil, the only way to guarantee a bacteria-free slab of prime rib is to cook it to an internal temperature of 160 degrees, no matter

what cooking method is used, low temperature or high. Unfortunately, at 160 degrees, the meat is gray, tough, and unappetizing.

The only thing that bothered us about the slow-roasted prime rib was its raw-looking, fatty exterior. We solved this problem by searing the meat on top of the stove before low-roasting it, giving it a beautiful crusty brown exterior.

As we expected, our tests with various seasonings demonstrated that simpler is better. Good prime rib needs nothing other than salt and pepper. We did discover that aging the beef at home—keeping it uncovered on a rack over a pan in the refrigerator—will improve the flavor and texture of the meat. (For more information on aging, see the Science Desk on page 179.)

As nebulous as the meaning of "perfect prime rib" had been to us at the beginning of our tests, it became crystal clear the moment we carved off that first slice of low-roasted prime rib. We immediately recognized it as the beef you get at a great prime rib restaurant. As it turns out, many such restaurants slow-roast their meat. They use special ovens that roast the meat at 250 degrees until it reaches an internal temperature of 120 degrees. At that time, the oven heat is decreased to 140 degrees, causing the meat's internal temperature to increase to 130 degrees and remain there until ready to serve (up to 24 hours later). Unfortunately, few home cooks can use this method since most home oven thermostats do not go below 200 degrees. But by following our recipe, home cooks can very closely approximate the superb prime rib served in the country's best restaurants.

WHAT WE LEARNED: Roast prime rib in a 250-degree oven for meat that cooks evenly and yields rosy slices. To promote a brown crust, pan-sear the roast on top of the stove before it goes into the oven.

PRIME RIB serves 6 to 8

Even if you don't purchase the roast a week ahead of time as the instructions suggest, a day or two of aging in the refrigerator will help. (See the Science Desk on page 179 for more information on aging beef.)

> 1 (3-rib) standing rib roast (about 7 pounds),
> aged up to 1 week, set at room temperature for
> 1 hour, and tied with kitchen twine at both
> ends, twine running parallel to bone (see
> illustration below left)
> Salt and ground black pepper

1. Adjust oven rack to low position and heat oven to 250 degrees. Heat large roasting pan over two burners set at medium-high heat until hot, about 4 minutes. Place roast in hot pan and cook on all sides until nicely browned and about ½ cup fat has rendered, 6 to 8 minutes.

2. Remove roast from pan. Set wire rack in pan, then set roast on rack. Generously season with salt and pepper.

3. Place roast in oven and roast until meat registers 130 degrees (for medium-rare) on instant-read thermometer, 3 to 3½ hours. Remove roast from oven and tent with foil. Let stand 20 to 30 minutes to allow juices to redistribute themselves evenly throughout roast.

4. Remove twine and set roast on cutting board, rib bones at 90-degree angle to board. Carve (see illustrations below right), and serve immediately.

TASTING LAB: Prime Rib

BUTCHERS TEND TO CUT A RIB ROAST, WHICH CONSISTS of ribs 6 through 12 if left whole, into two distinct cuts. The more desirable of the two cuts consists of ribs 10 through 12. Since this portion of the roast is closer to the loin end, it is sometimes called the "loin end." Other butchers call it the "small end" or the "first cut." Whatever it is called, it is more desirable because it contains the large, single rib-eye muscle and is less fatty. A less desirable cut, which is still an excellent roast, consists of ribs 6 to 9, closer to the chuck end, and sometimes called the second cut. The closer to the chuck, the more multimuscled the roast becomes. Since muscles are surrounded by fat, this means a fattier roast. While some cooks may prefer this cut because the fat adds flavor, the more tender and more regularly formed loin end is considered the best.

TECHNIQUE: Tying Up Prime Rib

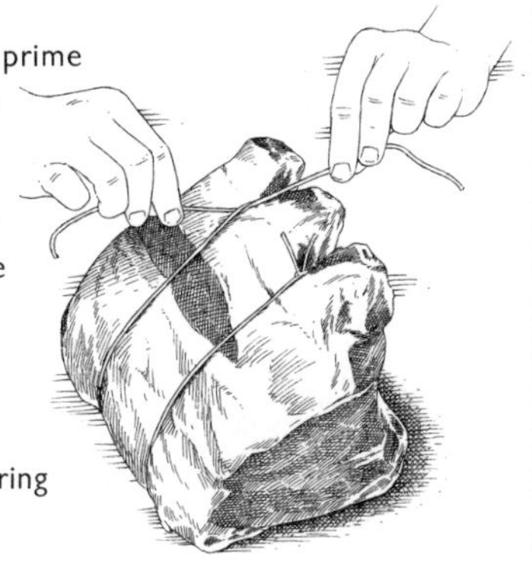

It is imperative to tie prime rib before roasting. If left untied, the outer layer of meat will pull away from the rib-eye muscle and overcook. To prevent this problem, tie the roast at both ends, running string parallel to the bone.

TECHNIQUE: Carving Prime Rib

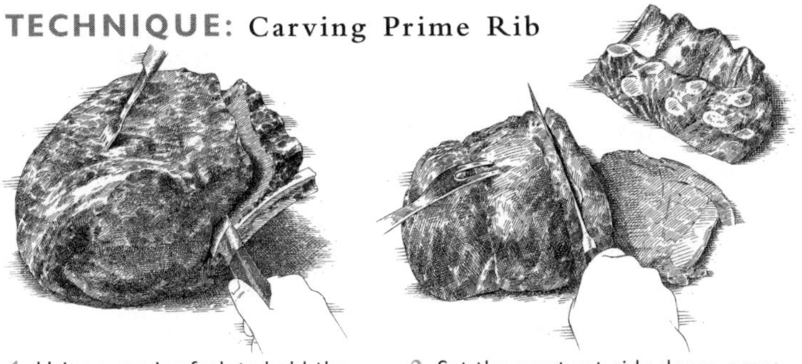

1. Using a carving fork to hold the roast in place, cut along the rib bones to sever the meat from the bones.

2. Set the roast cut-side down; carve the meat across the grain into thick slices.

SCIENCE DESK:
Why Aging Tenderizes Beef

MEAT IS AGED TO DEVELOP ITS FLAVOR AND IMPROVE ITS texture. This process depends on certain enzymes, whose function in a live animal is to digest proteins. (In the above photo, Doc is using hungry toy lizards to represent these enzymes.) After the animal is slaughtered, the cells that contain these enzymes start to break down, releasing the enzymes into the meat where they attack the cell proteins and break them down into amino acids, which have more flavor. The enzymes also break down the muscles, so the tissue becomes softer. This process can take from one to several weeks. (For the sake of safety, meat should not be aged for more than one week at home; beyond that time it must be done under carefully controlled conditions.)

Traditionally, butchers have hung carcasses in the meat locker to age their beef. Today, some beef is still aged on hooks (this process is called dry aging), but for the most part beef is wet-aged in vacuum-sealed packets. We wondered if it was worth it to the home cook to go the extra mile for dry-aged beef, so we ordered both a dry-aged and wet-aged prime rib roast from a restaurant supplier in Manhattan. The differences between the two roasts were clear-cut.

Like a good, young red wine, wet-aged beef tasted pleasant and fresh on its own. When compared with the dry-aged beef, though, we realized its flavors were less concentrated. The meat tasted washed out. The dry-aged beef, on the other hand, engaged the mouth. It was stronger, richer, and gamier-tasting, with a pleasant tang. The dry-aged and wet-aged beef were equally tender, but the dry-aged beef had an added buttery texture.

Unfortunately, most butchers don't dry-age beef anymore because hanging quarters of beef take up valuable refrigerator space. Dry-aged beef also dehydrates (loses weight) and requires trimming (loses more weight). That weight loss means less beef costs more money. Wet-aged beef loses virtually no weight during the aging process, and it comes prebutchered, packaged, and ready to sell. Because beef is expensive to begin with, most customers opt for the less expensive wet-aged beef. Why does dry aging work better than wet aging? The answer is simple: air. Encased in plastic, wet-aged beef is shut off from oxygen—the key to flavor development and concentration.

Because availability and price pose problems, you may simply want to age beef yourself. It's just a matter of making room in the refrigerator and remembering to buy the roast ahead of time, up to one week before you plan on roasting it. When you get the roast home, pat it dry and place it on a wire rack set over a paper towel–lined cake pan or plate. Set the racked roast in the refrigerator and let it age until you are ready to roast it, up to seven days. (Aging begins to have a dramatic effect on the roast after three or four days, but we also detected some improvement in flavor and texture after just one day of aging.) Before roasting, shave off any exterior meat that has completely dehydrated. Between the trimming and dehydration, a 7-pound roast will lose a pound or so during a week's aging.

TASTING LAB: Commercial Beef Broth

BEEF BROTH IS A TRADITIONAL EUROPEAN AND AMERICAN staple, a key ingredient in many classic sauces as well as the basis for popular beef soups. In the past several years, however, sales of beef broth have lagged. The most recent statistics for annual sales show that more than four times as many cans of chicken broth are sold than cans of beef broth.

When we tasted commercial beef broths, it became obvious why this situation has developed: Most beef broths simply do not deliver full-bodied, beefy flavor. There might be subtle beef suggestions, but after tasting nearly all of the selected broths—bouillon-based, canned, gourmet, and organic—there remained one nagging question: "Where's the beef?"

As things stand, U.S. regulations for beef broth do not require much beef. A commercial beef broth need contain only 1 part protein to 135 parts moisture, according to the U.S. Department of Agriculture's standards. That translates to less than about an ounce of meat (or about one-quarter of a hamburger) to 1 gallon of water. Most commercial products are very close to that limit, strictly because of

economics. Generally, manufactured beef broth derives its flavor from bare beef bones and a boost of various additives. A glance at the label on the side of any canned broth or boxed bouillon cubes will confirm this.

We wanted to talk to the manufacturers of beef broths to verify our impressions of the way they make their products, but calls to broth giants Hormel Foods and Campbell Soup Company were dead ends. Both declined to answer questions as to how their commercial beef broths are made. But beef bones plus additives would certainly explain why of the 12 commercial broths we tasted, none came even close to the full-bodied, beefy flavor of our homemade stock recipe—made with 6 pounds of meat. Nearly all of the commercial broths were thin and flavorless, with the exception of "off" or artificial flavors.

What seems to distinguish most supermarket broths from homemade, gourmet, or natural foods store broths is a riddling of flavor additives. Monosodium glutamate (MSG) can be found in nearly all supermarket beef broths. Disodium guanylate and disodium isonate, which are both yeast-based, hydrolyzed soy protein, are also typically added to commercial broths. Other yeast extracts also find their way into most of these broths. All approved by the U.S. Food and Drug Administration (FDA), these additives are intended to "enhance" flavor. As one FDA spokesperson explained, "You've got something that's kind of 'blah,' so to give it a little more taste they add these things."

Salt—and lots of it—also adds to the flavor of these broths. Most beef broth products contain about 35 percent of the daily allowance for sodium per serving. Salt is also added to help extract the needed protein from the bones.

The preferred product in our commercial broth tasting was a jarred beef base, Superior Touch Better Than Bouillon, but even this "winner" had an unflattering score of 4.6 on a scale of 0 to 10. Herb Ox Beef Bouillon Cubes lagged not too far behind. Forget about the more expensive gourmet and organic commercial broths, which not only failed to deliver beef flavor but also proved among the least palatable of the pack. Even if you get your hands on one of the "top finishers," we do not recommend that you use them in a recipe where the flavor of beef broth predominates, as it does in beef soup. They serve reasonably well when used as background flavor in a sauce or gravy and when heavily doctored up.

EQUIPMENT CORNER: Roasting Pans

THOUGH MOST COOKS HAUL OUT THEIR ROASTING PAN infrequently, when you need this large pan, nothing else will do. A roasting pan is a must for prime rib.

A roasting pan should promote deep, even browning of food. It should be easy to maneuver in and out of the oven. And it should be able to travel from oven to stovetop, so that you can deglaze the pan and loosen drippings.

Roasting pans can be made from stainless steel, enameled steel, nonstick-coated aluminum, or anodized aluminum, all of which we tested. We decided not to test pans lined with copper, which are prohibitively expensive; cast-iron pans, which when loaded with food are too heavy to lift; and pans made from Pyrex, ceramic, or stoneware, all of which seem better suited to lasagne and casseroles because they can't be used on top of the stove.

We tested eight roasting pans and preferred the materials we like in other cookware—stainless steel and anodized aluminum. These materials are heavy (though not prohibitively so) and produce good browning. Although nonstick coatings made cleanup easier, roasting racks slid around in these pans. For instance, when one test cook tilted a nonstick pan ever so slightly to remove it from the oven, a turkey and rack slid sharply to one side, which threw off her balance and nearly landed the hot turkey at her feet.

Roasting pans generally come in two different styles—upright handles and side handles (see photos, right). Upright handles tend to be square in shape, while side handles are generally oval loops. We found upright handles to be easier to grip. The problem with side handles is that their position, coupled with the large size of the pan, can cause you to bring your forearms perilously close to the hot oven walls. We tested one pan without handles, which was by far the most difficult to take out of the oven.

We tested pans ranging in length from 16 to 20 inches and in width from 11 to 14 inches. We preferred pans that measured about 16 inches long and 12 to 14 inches across. Larger pans made for an awkward fit in the oven, and, because of their large surface area, tended to burn pan drippings more easily.

In terms of weight, heavier pans performed better in all tests, especially on top of the stove. Lightweight pans buckled, and the meat browned quite spottily.

To summarize, heavy-duty pans made from stainless steel or anodized aluminum work best to brown foods, especially if the pan is to be used on top of the stove as well as in the oven, as is the case with our prime rib recipe. Expect to spend $150 on these top-flight pans.

ROASTING PANS
The handles on the roasting pan above are upright and easy to grasp. Side handles, like those on the roasting pan below, are more difficult to grasp than upright handles and seem more likely to cause burns.

POMMES ANNA

WHAT WE WANTED: A foolproof, simplified method for preparing this elegant potato cake that wouldn't sacrifice the buttery flavor and crisp texture that makes this dish so special.

Imagine thin potato slices layered meticulously in a skillet with nothing but butter, salt, pepper, and more butter, left to cook until the inverted dish reveals a potato cake with a lovely crisp, deep brown, glassine crust belying the soft, creamy potato layers within. This is pommes Anna, the queen of potato cookery.

Legend has it that Anna was a fashionable woman who lived during the reign of Napoleon III. Whoever Anna was, the creator of this dish was, to be sure, a chef with an inordinate amount of time on his hands, as the recipe requires painstaking procedures and the patience of Job. Given the amount of effort required to make just one dish of pommes Anna, it was particularly irritating when, in our preliminary recipe testing, those we made suffered a 50 percent rate of failure to release cleanly from the pan. It's no surprise, then, that pommes Anna is rarely seen on menus or home dinner tables and that recipes for it are sequestered in only the staunchest of French cookbooks.

We hoped to find a means of simplifying and foolproofing this classic. If we could do away with some of the maddening work and guarantee more than a crapshoot's chance of perfect unmolding, pommes Anna could find her way back onto the culinary map. . . and certainly onto the dining room table.

First we needed a pan for the perilous pommes. Of the four different cooking vessels we employed in tests—a cast-iron skillet, a copper pommes Anna pan, a heavy-bottomed skillet with a stainless steel cooking surface, and a heavy-bottomed nonstick skillet—only the nonstick effortlessly released the potatoes onto the serving platter. As reluctant as we were to make such specific equipment requisite for

pommes Anna, a nonstick skillet is essential to the dish's success. After all, once having expended the effort of slicing and arranging the potatoes, it is both enraging and mortifying to later witness them clinging stubbornly to the pan.

Most, if not all, recipes for pommes Anna begin with clarified butter. To make it, butter is melted, the foamy whey is spooned off the top, and the pure butterfat is poured or spooned off of the milky casein at the bottom. Since it lacks solids and proteins, clarified butter has a higher smoking point (and so is more resistant to burning) than whole butter, but it also lacks the full, buttery flavor that those solids and proteins provide. We have always been annoyed by clarified butter because of the time required to make it, the waste involved (typically, about 30 percent of the butter is lost with clarifying), and the loss of flavor. But pommes Anna, which spends a substantial amount of time cooking at moderately high temperatures, is always made with clarified butter. Our big coup, we thought, would be to circumvent its necessity, so we made a pommes Anna with whole butter to see if we couldn't prove false the centuries-old maxim that says clarified butter is a must. Sure enough, the surface of the potatoes was dotted with unappealing black flecks. Still, as a few tasters noticed, the whole butter gave the potatoes a richer, fuller flavor that we missed in the versions made with clarified butter.

We thought to replace the butter in the bottom of the skillet with oil, then drizzle melted whole butter between potato layers. This worked better than we could have hoped. Our newfangled pommes Anna had a lovely crisp brown crust rivaling that of any made with clarified butter.

Thinly sliced potatoes are a defining characteristic of pommes Anna, as is the overlapping arrangement of the slices in concentric circles. In the early stages of our testing, we preferred to slice the potatoes by hand (for no good reason), but as numbers increased, we took to a food processor fitted with a fine slicing disk that could get the job done

with effortless speed. If you own and are adept with a mandoline, it offers another quick means of slicing the potatoes.

Slicing wasn't the only obstacle presented by the potatoes. Because they will discolor if peeled and sliced and then kept waiting to be arranged in the skillet, they must be soaked in water, which in turn means that the slices must be dried before being layered. To avoid this incredible inconvenience, we opted to slice and arrange the potatoes in batches, making sure each group of slices was arranged in the skillet before slicing the next batch. This method prevented discoloration, but it was also awkward and inefficient. Someone suggested tossing the sliced potatoes in the melted butter to prevent them from discoloring (see the Science Desk on page 184.) We tried this, and though the butter did not prevent the discoloration, it did slow it down to the extent that all slices could be layered in the skillet before severe discoloration set in. That the butter no longer required drizzling between each layer was a bonus.

Most pommes Anna recipes have the cook start layering potato slices in the skillet as it heats on the stovetop. It may sound dangerous, but it isn't, really, and it saves much time. After all the slices are in, the skillet is transferred to a hot oven or left on the stovetop to complete cooking. After many tests, we determined that the potatoes—started in a cold skillet—require 30 minutes on the stovetop at medium-low heat, then—after a firm pressing with the bottom of a cake pan to compact the potatoes into a cohesive cake—25 minutes more in a 450-degree oven. The time on the stovetop gets the browning going on the bottom, and the oven time cooks through the potatoes' thickness while completing the bottom browning. Now, not only was a nonstick skillet necessary, but a nonstick ovenproof skillet was required to do the job.

The final step of pommes Anna is, of course, unmolding. If only it could be so easy as inverting a layer cake onto a cooling rack, but with a heavy, hot-handled skillet, the process is awkward and clumsy and can make an experienced cook feel like a bumbling one. Rather than trying to invert the potatoes directly onto a serving platter, where they cannot be unmolded in dead center because of the skillet's protruding handle, we lined the back of a baking sheet (a rimless cookie sheet will do) with lightly greased foil. We inverted the potatoes onto this surface, much as we would invert a cake onto a cooling rack, then slid them onto the serving platter. We found this technique a little less dangerous and much less complicated than going straight from pan to serving dish.

A last word on pommes Anna. Even simplified and streamlined, this recipe requires a good amount of patience, but it is no less a tour de force of culinary art and engineering than the classic rendition.

WHAT WE LEARNED: Skip the clarified butter and instead toss the sliced potatoes with melted butter. To keep the bottom layer from burning, coat the pan with oil. Use a nonstick skillet to prevent sticking and guarantee perfect release, and press down on the potatoes with a cake pan to compact them.

POMMES ANNA serves 6 to 8

Do not slice the potatoes until you are ready to start assembling. Remember to start timing when you begin arranging the potatoes in the skillet—no matter how quickly you arrange them, they will need 30 minutes on the stovetop to brown properly.

3 pounds russet, Yukon Gold, or white potatoes, peeled and sliced ¹⁄₁₆ to ⅛ inch thick
5 tablespoons unsalted butter, melted
¼ cup vegetable or peanut oil, plus additional for greasing baking sheet
   Salt and ground black pepper

1. Toss potato slices with melted butter in large bowl until potatoes are evenly coated. Adjust oven rack to lower-middle position and heat oven to 450 degrees.

2. Pour oil into 10-inch heavy-bottomed ovenproof non-stick skillet; swirl to coat pan bottom and set skillet over medium-low heat. Begin timing, and arrange potato slices in skillet, using nicest slices to form bottom layer. To start, place one slice in center of skillet. Overlap more slices in circle around center slice, then form another circle of overlapping slices to cover pan bottom. Sprinkle evenly with scant ¼ teaspoon salt and ground black pepper to taste. Arrange second layer of potatoes, working in opposite direction of first layer; sprinkle evenly with scant ¼ teaspoon salt and ground black pepper. Repeat, layering potatoes in opposite directions and sprinkling with salt and pepper, until no slices remain (broken or uneven slices can be pieced together to form single slice; potatoes will mound in center of skillet); continue to cook over medium-low heat until 30 minutes elapse from time you began arranging potatoes in skillet.

3. Using bottom of 9-inch cake pan, press potatoes down firmly to compact. Cover skillet and place in oven. Bake until potatoes begin to soften, about 15 minutes. Uncover and continue to bake until potatoes are tender, when

paring knife can be easily inserted in center and edge of potatoes near skillet is browned, about 10 minutes longer. Meanwhile, line rimless baking sheet or back of rimmed baking sheet with foil and coat very lightly with oil. Drain off excess fat from potatoes by pressing bottom of cake pan against potatoes while tilting skillet. (Be sure to use heavy potholders or oven mitts.)

4. Set foil-lined baking sheet on top of skillet. With hands protected by oven mitts or potholders, hold baking sheet in place with one hand and carefully invert skillet and baking sheet together. Lift skillet off potatoes. Carefully slide potatoes from baking sheet onto platter. Cut into wedges and serve immediately.

SCIENCE DESK:
Why Potatoes Turn Brown

AS MANY OF US FIND OUT THE HARD WAY, PEELED AND sliced potatoes take on a brick-red hue when left to sit out for several minutes before cooking. This was of particular concern in our pommes Anna recipe, because the peeled, sliced potatoes must wait to be layered in the skillet. We consulted spud expert Dr. Alfred Bushway, professor of food science at the University of Maine, to find out what causes potatoes to turn color. He explained that with slicing and peeling, potato cells are broken down and the enzyme polyphenol oxidase (PPO) is released. Two major substrates, chlorogenic acid and tyrosine, are also released.

The enzyme and substrates combine with oxygen, and they are then oxidized into a compound called ortho-quinone. The orthoquinone quickly polymerizes (a process in which many molecules link up to form a chain of more complex material with different physical properties) and creates the dark pink-red color that we see in the potatoes.

Tossing the potatoes with butter, as in the pommes Anna recipe, helps limit oxygen exposure and therefore retards discoloration. We had also noted that certain potatoes

discolor more rapidly than others. Bushway said that from cultivar to cultivar and over the storage season, potatoes vary in their enzyme and/or substrate concentrations and enzyme activity, so differences in discoloration rates can be expected. In our experience, russet potatoes seem to discolor most rapidly, so if you're a slow hand, opt for Yukon Golds or white potatoes for pommes Anna.

EQUIPMENT CORNER:
Vegetable Peelers

YOU MIGHT IMAGINE THAT ALL VEGETABLE PEELERS ARE pretty much the same. Not so. In our research, we turned up 25 peelers, many with quite novel features. The major differences were the fixture of the blade, either stationary or swiveling; the material of the blade, carbon stainless steel, stainless steel, or ceramic; and the orientation of the blade to the handle, either straight in line with the body or perpendicular to it. The last arrangement, with the blade perpendicular to the handle, is called a harp, or Y, peeler because the frame looks like the body of a harp or the letter Y. This type of peeler, which is popular in Europe, works with a pulling motion rather than the shucking motion of most American peelers.

To test the peelers, we recruited several cooks and asked them to peel carrots, potatoes, lemons, butternut squash, and celery root. In most cases, testers preferred the Oxo Good Grips peeler with a sharp stainless steel blade that swivels. Peelers with stationary blades are fine for peeling carrots, but they have trouble hugging the curves on potatoes. As for blade material, we found peelers made from stainless steel, carbon steel, and ceramic that were sharp and dull. We concluded that sharpness is a factor of quality control during the manufacturing process and not blade material.

The Y-shaped peelers tested well, although they removed more flesh along with the skin on potatoes, lemons, and carrots and therefore did not rate as well as the Oxo Good Grips. This liability turned into an asset with butternut squash, where these Y-shaped peelers took off the skin as well as the greenish-tinged flesh right below the skin in one pass. With the Oxo Good Grips, it was necessary to go over the peeled flesh once the skin had been removed. Among Y-shaped peelers, testers preferred the Kuhn Rikon. Because both the Oxo Good Grips and Kuhn Rikon peelers can be had for less than $10, we recommend that you purchase both.

BEST PEELERS
The Oxo Good Grips (left) is our favorite all-purpose peeler. The blade is sharp and great on curves. However, testers in the kitchen with very small hands did complain about the bulky handle. The Kuhn Rikon (right) is our favorite Y-shaped peeler. Because this type of peeler removes more skin than a conventional peeler, it's an especially good choice for peeling butternut squash or celery root.

GREEN BEANS

WHAT WE WANTED: A foolproof way of cooking beans ahead of time and then simply reheating and seasoning them just before serving.

Every cook who has prepared a big holiday meal knows the swell of frenzied activity in the final moments before serving. The last thing anyone wants to deal with at that point is preparing and cooking the requisite green bean side dish. That's why we wanted to identify the best way to cook green beans ahead, so that all they would need is a quick finish before serving. To do so, we had to determine the best cooking method and how long the beans could be held before they were finished and served.

Our test kitchen experiments on cooking methods included blanching, steaming, and braising the beans. We concluded that blanching, or boiling them briefly, was the way to go for two reasons. First, blanched beans cooked more evenly than steamed ones, and second, blanching made it easier to add salt to the beans as they cooked, thereby seasoning them more deeply.

For the finished, dressed beans to arrive at the table with a properly tender-crisp texture, we found that it was especially important not to overcook them. This meant halting their cooking abruptly and completely with a dunk in ice water, a process known as shocking. After that, we had to determine how long the beans could be refrigerated. To find out, we blanched, shocked, and dried a big batch of beans, stored them in the refrigerator, and sampled them twice a day to test for flavor and texture retention. None of the tasters noted any deterioration until the morning of the fourth day, so we concluded that it is fine to blanch the beans up to three days in advance of serving.

Just as flavorful ingredients contribute to the unique flavor and texture of each of the green bean dishes presented here, so too does the treatment of the butter. Butter adds a sweet, rich flavor and lush, refined mouthfeel, but it can bring even more to the party depending on how it is handled.

In the green beans with sautéed shallots and vermouth, the butter melts as it becomes incorporated into the sauce but is not cooked any further. Such gentle treatment preserves the butter's sweet, fresh flavor notes and works well with the delicate shallots. In the green beans with toasted hazelnuts and brown butter, on the other hand, the butter is cooked until its color deepens visibly. This causes the proteins in the butter to brown and take on a deep nutty flavor and more complex character. This stark transformation is accomplished in just 5 minutes over medium heat. Browned butter has the necessary richness and flavor to stand up to toasted hazelnuts.

As we developed these recipes, we reheated plenty of chilled beans and learned a thing or two about the process. Most important was to add a little bit of water—¼ cup will do—to the pan with the beans as they heat. This small amount of water will come to a boil quickly and evaporate almost completely, helping to heat the beans in just a minute or two. We found that tongs are the tool best suited to tossing the beans in the pan and arranging them on the platter.

WHAT WE LEARNED: For maximum flexibility and flavor, blanch beans in salted water, shock in ice water to stop the cooking process, then towel dry and refrigerate until needed. To serve, reheat beans with a little water and flavor with butter sauce.

BLANCHED GREEN BEANS enough for 4 to 6 servings

Blanched and cooled beans can be refrigerated in a zipper-lock plastic bag for up to 3 days. To blanch, dress, and serve the beans without holding them first, increase the blanching time to 5 to 6 minutes and don't bother shocking them in ice water. Instead, quickly arrange the warm, drained beans on a serving platter and top them with the sauce you've prepared as the beans blanch.

1   teaspoon salt
1   pound green beans, stem ends snapped off

Bring 2½ quarts water to boil in large saucepan over high heat; add salt and green beans, return to boil, and cook until beans are bright green and tender-crisp, 3 to 4 minutes. Drain beans in colander set in sink; transfer beans immediately to large heatproof bowl filled with ice water. When beans no longer feel warm to touch, drain in colander again and dry thoroughly with paper towels. Set aside until needed.

GREEN BEANS WITH SAUTÉED SHALLOTS AND VERMOUTH serves 4 to 6

4   tablespoons unsalted butter
4   large shallots (about 8 ounces), sliced thin
     (about 2 cups)
1   recipe Blanched Green Beans
     Salt and ground black pepper
2   tablespoons dry vermouth

1. Heat 2 tablespoons butter in small skillet over medium heat until foaming. Add shallots and cook, stirring frequently, until golden brown, fragrant, and just crisp around the edges, about 10 minutes. Set skillet aside, off heat.

2. Heat ¼ cup water and beans in 12-inch skillet over high heat; cook, tossing frequently, until warmed through, 1 to 2 minutes. Season with salt and pepper to taste and arrange neatly on warm serving platter.

3. Meanwhile, return skillet with shallots to high heat, stir in vermouth, and bring to simmer. Whisk in remaining 2 tablespoons butter, 1 tablespoon at a time; season with salt and pepper to taste. Top beans with shallots and sauce and serve immediately.

GREEN BEANS WITH TOASTED HAZELNUTS AND BROWN BUTTER serves 4 to 6

4   tablespoons unsalted butter
½   cup hazelnuts (about 2½ ounces), chopped fine
     and toasted in small skillet over medium heat
     until just fragrant, 3 to 4 minutes
     Salt and ground black pepper
1   recipe Blanched Green Beans

1. Heat butter in small, heavy-bottomed saucepan over medium heat and cook, swirling frequently, until nut brown and fragrant, 4 to 5 minutes. Add hazelnuts and cook, stirring constantly, until fragrant, about 1 minute. Season with salt and pepper to taste.

2. Meanwhile, heat ¼ cup water and beans in 12-inch skillet over high heat; cook, tossing frequently, until warmed through, 1 to 2 minutes. Season with salt and pepper to taste and arrange neatly on warm serving platter. Top beans with hazelnut butter and serve immediately.

WINTER supper

CHAPTER 15

In America's Test Kitchen, winter is the time for rich braises and stews. Braised short ribs are a favorite choice, not only because they are so delicious but also because short ribs are relatively inexpensive, appealing to our sense of Yankee frugality.

But cheap isn't necessarily good. Short ribs are full of fat—that's what gives them such great flavor. But all that fat can ruin the sauce. The challenge is to cook the short ribs until they are fall-off-the-bone tender while removing as much of the grease as possible.

What goes better with braised short ribs than mashed potatoes? Of course, any old mashed spuds won't do. They must be incredibly creamy, with a great potato flavor and plenty of buttery richness. We've worked out all the details so you can produce mashed potatoes worthy of a four-star restaurant. We've also perfected a foolproof method for roasting carrots that takes just 20 minutes and relies on just three ingredients.

We found that boiling whole potatoes in their skins prevents them from absorbing excess water and greatly improves the texture of mashed potatoes. To peel hot potatoes, spear them with a fork and remove the skin with a paring knife.

SHORT RIBS

WHAT WE WANTED: A cooking method that removes the grease from these fatty but flavorful ribs while braising them to perfect tenderness.

In the supermarket meat case, short ribs are often overlooked, seldom understood, rather intimidating hunks of meat and bone that are frequently turned a cold shoulder. But braise them, and they become yielding, tender, and succulent. Then douse them with a velvety sauce containing all the rich, bold flavors from the braise, and they are as satisfying as beef stew, but with much more panache. All of this, however, comes at a price: Short ribs are outrageously fatty. The challenge is to get them to give up their fat.

The first step in most braises is browning the meat. Browning adds color and flavor, but in the case of short ribs it also presents an opportunity to render some of the fat. We tried browning both on the stovetop and in the oven and quickly became a proponent of oven browning. As long as you own a roasting pan large enough to hold all of the ribs in a single layer, you can use the oven to brown them in just one batch. This eliminates the need to brown in multiple batches on the stove, which can create a greasy, splattery mess and result in burnt drippings in the bottom of the pot. In the oven, the ribs can brown for a good long time to maximize rendering.

Braising liquids required only a cursory investigation. Homemade beef stock was out of the question because just about no one makes it. Based on previous tastings in the test kitchen, we also discounted canned beef broth. Canned chicken broth, however, offered sufficient backbone and, when enriched by the flavor and body contributed by the short ribs themselves, made for a rich, robust sauce. We began using a combination of red wine, chicken broth, and water. We eventually eliminated water, but the sauce, despite the abundance of aromatics and herbs, remained strangely hollow and lacking. All along we had been using a cheap,

hardly potable wine. After stepping up to a good, solid one worthy of drinking, the sauce improved dramatically; it had the complexity and resonance that we were looking for.

If the braising liquid were to transform itself into the sauce we were after, it would need some thickening. After various experiments, we found that adding flour to the sautéed vegetables before pouring in the liquid resulted in a sauce that was lustrous and had the perfect consistency.

As they braise, the browned short ribs continue to release fat, which means that the braising liquid must be defatted before it is palatable. We found the easiest technique to be a two-day process, necessitating some forethought. Braise the ribs, let them cool in the liquid so that the meat does not dry out, remove them, strain the liquid, and then chill the ribs and the liquid separately. The next day, spoon the solidified fat off the liquid's surface, and heat the liquid and the ribs together.

WHAT WE LEARNED: Browning in the oven rather than on the stovetop is neater and more effective. A really good red wine is crucial to a rich-tasting braising liquid. Preparing the braise a day in advance makes for the easiest, most efficient way to defat the sauce.

SHORT RIBS BRAISED IN RED WINE WITH BACON, PARSNIPS, AND PEARL ONIONS

serves 6

If braising and serving the ribs on the same day, bypass cooling the ribs in the braising liquid; instead, remove them from the pot straight out of the oven, strain the liquid, then let it settle so that the fat separates to the top. With a wide shallow spoon, skim off as much fat as possible and continue with the recipe. Though this recipe and the one that follows calls for the widely available English-style short ribs, both recipes will also work with flanken-style short ribs. (We actually prefer flanken-style ribs, but they are more expensive and difficult to find.) We like to serve these short ribs with mashed potatoes (see page 195), but they also taste good over egg noodles. For information about roasting pans, see the Equipment Corner on page 181. For information about Dutch ovens, see the Equipment Corner on page 192.

short ribs

6	pounds bone-in English-style short ribs, trimmed of excess fat and silver skin, or bone-in flanken-style short ribs (see Tasting Lab on page 193)
	Salt and ground black pepper
3	cups dry full-bodied red wine
3	large onions, chopped medium
2	medium carrots, chopped medium
1	large celery stalk, chopped medium
9	medium cloves garlic, chopped (about 3 tablespoons)
¼	cup all-purpose flour
4	cups chicken stock or canned low-sodium chicken broth
1	(14.5 ounce) can diced tomatoes, drained
1½	tablespoons minced fresh rosemary leaves
1	tablespoon minced fresh thyme leaves
3	medium bay leaves
1	teaspoon tomato paste

bacon, pearl onion, and parsnip garnish

6	slices bacon (about 6 ounces), cut into ¼-inch pieces
8	ounces frozen pearl onions (do not thaw)
4	medium parsnips (about 10 ounces), peeled and cut diagonally into ¾-inch pieces
¼	teaspoon sugar
¼	teaspoon salt
6	tablespoons minced fresh parsley leaves

1. FOR THE SHORT RIBS: Adjust oven rack to lower-middle position and heat oven to 450 degrees. Arrange short ribs bone-side down in single layer in large flameproof roasting pan; season with salt and pepper. Roast until meat begins to brown, about 45 minutes; drain off all liquid and fat with bulb baster. Return pan to oven and continue to cook until meat is well browned, 15 to 20 minutes longer. (For flanken-style short ribs, arrange ribs in single layer in large roasting pan; season with salt and pepper. Roast until meat begins to brown, about 45 minutes; drain off all liquid and fat with bulb baster. Return pan to oven and continue to cook until browned, about 8 minutes; using tongs, flip each piece and cook until second side is browned, about 8 minutes longer.) Transfer ribs to large plate; set aside. Drain off fat to small bowl and reserve. Reduce oven temperature to 300 degrees. Place roasting pan on two stovetop burners set at medium heat; add wine and bring to simmer, scraping up browned bits with wooden spoon. Set roasting pan with wine aside.

2. Heat 2 tablespoons reserved fat in large Dutch oven over medium-high heat; add onions, carrots, and celery. Sauté, stirring occasionally, until vegetables soften, about 12 minutes. Add garlic and cook until fragrant, about 30 seconds. Stir in flour until combined, about 45 seconds. Stir in wine from roasting pan, chicken stock, tomatoes, rosemary, thyme, bay leaves, tomato paste, and salt and pepper to taste. Bring to boil and add short ribs, completely submerging meat in liquid; return to boil, cover, place in oven, and simmer until ribs are tender, about 2 to 2½ hours.

Transfer pot to wire rack and cool, partially covered, until warm, about 2 hours.

3. Transfer ribs from pot to large plate, removing excess vegetables that may cling to meat; discard loose bones that have fallen away from meat. Strain braising liquid into medium bowl, pressing out liquid from solids; discard solids. Cover ribs and liquid separately with plastic wrap and refrigerate overnight. (Can be refrigerated up to 3 days.)

4. FOR THE GARNISH AND TO FINISH DISH: In Dutch oven, cook bacon over medium heat until just crisp, 8 to 10 minutes; remove with slotted spoon to plate lined with paper towel. Add to Dutch oven pearl onions, parsnips, sugar, and salt; increase heat to high and sauté, stirring occasionally, until browned, about 5 minutes. Spoon off and discard solidified fat from reserved braising liquid. Add defatted liquid to Dutch oven and bring to simmer, stirring occasionally; adjust seasoning with salt and pepper. Submerge ribs in liquid; return to simmer. Reduce heat to medium and cook, partially covered, until ribs are heated through and vegetables are tender, about 5 minutes longer; gently stir in bacon. Divide ribs and sauce among individual bowls, sprinkle each with 1 tablespoon parsley, and serve.

VARIATION
PORTER-BRAISED SHORT RIBS WITH PRUNES, BRANDY, AND LEMON ESSENCE

Brandy-soaked prunes take the place of vegetables here, so this version is particularly suited to a mashed root vegetable or potato accompaniment. Use a dark, mildly assertive beer, not a light lager.

brandy, prune, and lemon essence garnish

½ cup brandy
8 ounces pitted prunes, each prune halved
2 teaspoons brown sugar
2 teaspoons grated zest from 1 lemon
6 tablespoons minced fresh parsley leaves

1. Follow recipe for Short Ribs Braised in Red Wine with Bacon, Parsnips, and Pearl Onions, substituting 3 cups porter beer for the red wine, eliminating rosemary, and substituting 2 tablespoons Dijon mustard and 2 teaspoons Worcestershire sauce for the tomato paste. Continue with recipe through step 3.

2. TO PREPARE GARNISH AND FINISH DISH: Bring brandy to boil in small saucepan; off heat, add prunes and let stand until plump and softened, about 15 minutes. Meanwhile, spoon off and discard solidified fat from braising liquid. Bring braising liquid to boil in Dutch oven over medium-high heat, stirring occasionally. Add prunes, brandy, and brown sugar; adjust seasoning with salt and pepper. Submerge ribs in liquid and return to simmer. Reduce heat to medium-low and cook until ribs are heated through, about 5 minutes longer; gently stir in lemon zest. Divide ribs and sauce among individual bowls, sprinkle each with 1 tablespoon parsley, and serve.

EQUIPMENT CORNER: Dutch Ovens

A DUTCH OVEN IS NOTHING MORE THAN A WIDE, DEEP pot with a cover. It was originally manufactured with "ears" on the side (small, round tabs used to pick up the pot) and a top that had a lip around the edge. The latter design element was important because a Dutch oven was heated through coals placed both underneath and on top of the pot. The lip kept the coals on the lid from falling off. One could bake biscuits, cobblers, beans, and stews in this pot. It was, in the full sense of the word, an oven. This useful pot supposedly came to be called "Dutch" because at some point the best cast iron came from Holland.

Now that everyone in America has an oven, the Dutch oven is no longer used to bake biscuits or cobblers. However, it is essential for dishes that start on top of the stove and finish in the oven. (For this reason, the handles on a Dutch oven must be ovenproof.) To make some recommendations about buying a modern Dutch oven, we tested 12 models.

We found that a Dutch oven should have a capacity of at least six quarts to be useful. Eight quarts is even better. As we cooked in the pots, we came to prefer wider, shallower Dutch ovens because it's easier to see and reach inside them, and they offer more bottom surface area to accommodate larger batches of meat for browning. This reduces the number of batches required to brown a given quantity of meat, and, with it, the chances of burning the flavorful pan drippings. Ideally, a Dutch oven should have a diameter twice as wide as its height.

We also preferred pots with a light-colored interior finish, such as stainless steel or enameled cast iron. It is easier to judge the caramelization of the drippings at a glance in these pots. Dark finishes can mask the color of the drippings, which may burn before you realize it. Our favorite pot is the 8-quart All-Clad Stainless Stockpot (despite the name, this pot is a Dutch oven). The 7-quart Le Creuset Round French Oven, which is made of enameled cast iron, also tested well. These pots are quite expensive, costing at least $150, even when on sale. A less expensive alternative is the seven-quart Lodge Dutch Oven, which is made from cast iron. This pot is extremely heavy (making it a bit hard to maneuver), it must be seasoned (wiped with oil) regularly, and the dark interior finish is not ideal, but it does brown food quite well and costs just $45.

TASTING LAB: Short Ribs

SHORT RIBS ARE JUST WHAT THEIR NAME SAYS THEY ARE— "short ribs" cut from any part along the length of the cow's ribs. They can come from the lower belly section or higher up toward the back, from the shoulder (or chuck) area, or the forward midsection.

When we started testing short ribs, we went to the local grocery store and bought out their supply. What we brought back to the test kitchen were 2- to 4-inch lengths of wide flat rib bone, to which a rectangular plate of fatty meat was attached (see photo below left). We also ordered short ribs from the butcher. Imagine our confusion when these turned out to be long, continuous pieces of meat, about ¾ inch thick, that had been cut across the ribs and grain and that included two or three segments of rib bone (see photo below right). The former, we learned, are sometimes called English-style short ribs, and the latter are called flanken-style ribs.

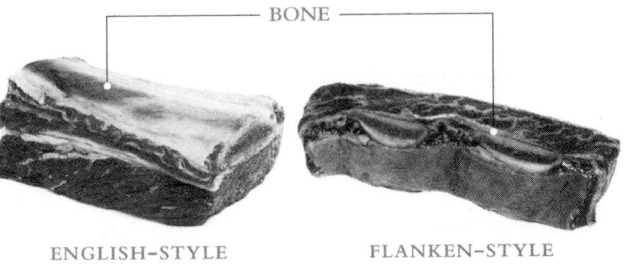

BONE

ENGLISH-STYLE   FLANKEN-STYLE

We began by braising both types of ribs. The ones from the butcher were favored by most tasters because the relatively thin, across-the-grain cut made the meat more pleasant to eat; the supermarket ribs were a bit stringier because they contained longer segments of "grain." Both types were equally tender and good, but considering the cost ($5.99 versus $2.99 per pound) and effort (special order) required to procure the butcher-cut specimens, we decided to go with the supermarket variety.

MASHED POTATOES

WHAT WE WANTED: Mashed potatoes that are perfectly smooth and creamy, with a great potato flavor and plenty of buttery richness.

Most of us who make mashed potatoes would never consider consulting a recipe. We customarily make them by adding chunks of butter and spurts of cream until our conscience—or a backseat cook—tells us to stop. Not surprisingly, we produce batches of mashed potatoes that are consistent only in their mediocrity.

Great stew deserves great spuds. The right mashed potatoes can transform the humblest stew or braise (like short ribs) into a meal fit for a king. For us, the consummate mashed potatoes are creamy, soft, and supple, yet with enough body to stand up to sauce from a stew. As for flavor, the sweet, earthy, humble potato comes first, then the buttery richness that keeps you coming back for more.

We determined that high-starch potatoes, such as russets, are best for mashing (see the Science Desk on page 197 for more information.) Next, we needed to figure out the best way to cook the potatoes. We started by peeling and cutting some potatoes into chunks to expedite their cooking while cooking others unpeeled and whole. Even when mashed with identical amounts of butter, half-and-half (recommended by a number of trustworthy cookbooks), and salt, the two batches were wildly different. The potatoes that had been peeled and cut made mashed potatoes that were thin in taste and texture and devoid of potato flavor, while those cooked whole and peeled after cooking yielded mashed potatoes that were rich, earthy, and sweet.

We talked to several food scientists, who explained that peeling and cutting the potatoes before simmering increases the surface area through which they lose soluble substances, such as starch, proteins, and flavor compounds, to the cooking water. The greater surface area also enables lots of water molecules to bind with the potatoes' starch

molecules. Combine these two effects and you've got bland, thin, watery mashed potatoes.

Next were the matters of butter and dairy. Working with 2 pounds of potatoes, which serves four to six, we stooped so low as to add only 2 tablespoons of butter. The potatoes ultimately deemed best in flavor by tasters contained 8 tablespoons. They were rich and full and splendid.

When considering dairy, we investigated both the kind and the quantity. Heavy cream made heavy mashed potatoes that were sodden and unpalatably rich, even when we scaled back the amount of butter. On the other hand, mashed potatoes made with whole milk were watery, wimpy, and washed out. When we tried adding more butter to compensate for the milk's lack of richness, the mixture turned into potato soup. Half-and-half, which we'd used in our original tests, was just what was needed, and 1 cup was just the right amount. The mashed potatoes now had a lovely light suppleness and a full, rich flavor that edged toward decadent.

The issues attending butter and dairy did not end there. We had heard that the order in which they are added to the potatoes can affect texture and that melted butter makes better mashed potatoes than softened butter. Determined to leave no spud unturned, we threw several more pounds into the pot. As it turns out, when the butter goes in before the dairy, the result is a silkier, creamier, smoother texture than when the dairy goes first; by comparison, the dairy-first potatoes were pasty and thick. Using melted rather than softened butter made the potatoes even more creamy, smooth, and light.

With our curiosity piqued by the significant textural differences effected by minor differences in procedure, we again contacted several food scientists, who explained that when the half-and-half is stirred into the potatoes before the butter, the water in it works with the starch in the potatoes to make the mashed potatoes gluey and heavy. When the butter is added before the half-and-half, the fat coats the starch molecules, inhibiting their interaction with the water in the half-and-half added later and thereby yielding silkier, creamier mashed potatoes. The benefit of using melted butter results from its liquid form, which enables it to coat the starch molecules quickly and easily. This buttery coating not only affects the interaction of the starch molecules with the half-and-half, it also affects the starch molecules' interaction with each other. All in all, it makes for smoother, more velvety mashed potatoes. (Melting the butter, as well as warming the half-and-half, also serves to keep the potatoes warm.)

There is more than one way to mash potatoes. In our testing, we had been using either a ricer or a food mill. We preferred the food mill because its large hopper accommodated half of the potatoes at a time. A ricer, which resembles an oversized garlic press, required processing in several batches. Both, however, produced smooth, light, fine-textured mashed potatoes.

A potato masher is the tool of choice for making chunky mashed potatoes, but it cannot produce smooth mashed potatoes on a par with those processed through a food mill or ricer. With a masher, potatoes mashed within an inch of their lives could not achieve anything better than a namby-pamby texture that was neither chunky nor perfectly smooth. Since the sentiment among our tasters was that mashed potatoes should be either smooth or coarse and craggy, a masher is best left to make the latter.

There are two styles of potato mashers—one is a disk with large holes in it, the other a curvy wire loop. We found the disk to be more efficient for reducing both mashing time and the number of lumps in the finished product.

WHAT WE LEARNED: To prevent the potatoes from absorbing too much water, boil them whole and unpeeled. Use a food mill or ricer for the smoothest texture imaginable. (A potato masher can be used if you prefer lumps.) Add melted butter before the half-and-half for the smoothest, creamiest texture.

MASHED POTATOES   serves 4 to 6

Russet potatoes make fluffier mashed potatoes, but Yukon Golds have an appealing buttery flavor and can be used. Mashed potatoes become gluey as they cool, so they are best served piping hot. If you must hold mashed potatoes, place them in a heatproof bowl, cover the bowl tightly with plastic wrap, and set the bowl over a pot of simmering water. The potatoes will remain hot and soft-textured for up to one hour. This recipe yields smooth mashed potatoes. If you don't mind lumps, use a potato masher, as directed in the variation.

2   pounds russet potatoes, scrubbed
8   tablespoons unsalted butter, melted
1   cup half-and-half, warmed
1½   teaspoons salt
     Ground black pepper

1. Place potatoes in large saucepan with cold water to cover by about 1 inch. Bring to boil over high heat, reduce heat to medium-low, and simmer until potatoes are just tender when pricked with thin-bladed knife, 20 to 30 minutes. Drain water from pan and remove potatoes.

2. Set food mill or ricer over now empty but still warm saucepan. Spear potato with dinner fork, then peel back skin with paring knife (see illustration 1 on page 196). Repeat with remaining potatoes. Working in batches, cut peeled potatoes into rough chunks and drop into hopper of food mill or ricer (see illustration 2 on page 196). Process or rice potatoes into saucepan.

3. Stir in butter with wooden spoon until incorporated. Gently whisk in half-and-half, salt, and pepper to taste. Serve immediately.

VARIATIONS

GARLIC MASHED POTATOES

Toasted garlic contributes the truest, purest garlic flavor imaginable to mashed potatoes. Best of all, the garlic can be peeled after toasting, when the skins will slip right off. Just make sure to keep the heat low and to let the garlic stand off heat until fully softened.

Toast 22 small to medium-large garlic cloves (about ⅔ cup), skins left on, in a small covered skillet over lowest possible heat, shaking pan frequently, until cloves are dark spotty brown and slightly softened, about 22 minutes. Remove pan from heat and let stand, covered, until cloves are fully softened, 15 to 20 minutes. Peel cloves and, with paring knife, cut off woody root end. Follow recipe for Mashed Potatoes, dropping peeled garlic cloves into food mill or ricer with peeled potatoes.

LUMPY MASHED POTATOES
We prefer silky, smooth mashed potatoes and therefore recommend using a food mill or ricer. If you prefer chunky mashed potatoes, use a potato masher instead.

Follow recipe for Mashed Potatoes, dropping peeled potato chunks back in warm saucepan and mashing with potato masher until fairly smooth. Proceed as directed, reducing half-and-half to ¾ cup.

MASHED POTATOES WITH PARMESAN AND LEMON
Follow recipe for Mashed Potatoes, stirring in 1 cup grated Parmesan cheese and minced or grated zest from 1 lemon along with half-and-half, salt, and pepper.

MASHED POTATOES WITH ROOT VEGETABLES
Most root vegetables are more watery than potatoes, so you will need less than the full cup of half-and-half.

Follow recipe for Mashed Potatoes, replacing 1 pound of potatoes with 1 pound of parsnips, rutabagas, celery root, carrots, or turnips that have been peeled and cut into 1½-inch to 2-inch chunks. Add half-and-half ¼ cup at a time until desired consistency is obtained.

BUTTERMILK MASHED POTATOES
Buttermilk gives mashed potatoes a pleasing tang and rich texture, even when less butter is used. If you are interested in mashed potatoes with less fat, this is your best option.

Follow recipe for Mashed Potatoes, reducing butter to 1 tablespoon and replacing half-and-half with 1 cup warmed buttermilk.

TECHNIQUE: Making Mashed Potatoes

1. Hold the drained potato with a dinner fork and peel off the skin with a paring knife.

2. Cut the peeled potato into rough chunks, and drop the chunks into the food mill.

SCIENCE DESK: Starch in Potatoes

POTATOES ARE COMPOSED MOSTLY OF STARCH AND water. The starch is in the form of granules, which in turn are contained in starch cells. The higher the starch content of the potato, the fuller the cells. In high-starch potatoes (russets are a good example), the cells are completely full— they look like plump little beach balls. In medium-starch (Yukon Golds) and low-starch potatoes (Red Bliss), the cells are more like underinflated beach balls. The space between these less-than-full cells is taken up mostly by water.

In our tests, we found that the full starch cells of high-starch potatoes are most likely to maintain their integrity and stay separate when mashed, giving the potatoes a delightfully fluffy texture. In addition, the low water content of these potatoes allows them to absorb milk, cream, and/or butter without becoming wet or gummy. Starch cells in lower-starch potatoes, on the other hand, tend to clump when cooked and break more easily, allowing the starch to dissolve into whatever liquid is present. The broken cells and dissolved starch tend to make sticky, gummy mashed potatoes.

However, the high moisture content of red potatoes makes them an excellent choice for dishes such as potato salad, where you want the potatoes to hold their shape. Because they contain a fair amount of moisture, they don't absorb much water as they boil. In contrast, low-moisture russets suck up water when boiled and fall apart. The resulting potato salad is starchy and sloppy-looking.

EQUIPMENT CORNER: Food Mills

A FOOD MILL IS NO LONGER A FIXTURE IN AMERICAN kitchens, but it is a terrific tool to have on hand. Think of it as part food processor, refining soft foods to a puree, and part sieve, separating waste such as peels, seeds, cores, and fiber from the puree as you go. And it accomplishes all of this with the simple turn of a crank, which rotates a gently angled, curved blade. The blade catches the food and forces it down through the holes of a perforated disk at the bottom of the mill. The separation of unwanted material from the puree is the food mill's raison d'être, but another benefit is that it does not aerate the food as it purees, as do food processors and blenders, so you are able to avoid an overly whipped, lightened texture. (In the case of potatoes, a food processor or blender would create a gummy texture.)

Since you can spend as little as $15 and as much as $100 on a food mill (some really huge mills cost as much as $200), we wondered if some were better than others. So we gathered six different models (including an electric one) and used them to make mashed potatoes and applesauce. Honestly, there was very little difference among the purees—they were all fine, smooth, and free of unwanted material. Thus, we evaluated the mills more on design factors, such as how easy it was to turn the crank, how efficiently the food was processed, and whether the mills offered adjustments in the texture of the puree produced.

The best mills in the group were the stainless steel Cuisipro, the VEV Vigano, and the white plastic Moulinex. Each was easy to crank and efficient and all came with fine, medium, and coarse disks. The top performer was the Cuisipro, but at $80, it was also the most expensive. The $15 Moulinex did nearly as well, so it became the pick of the pack for its combination of low price and high performance. The plastic is surely not as strong as the Cuisipro's stainless steel, but for occasional use, it was just fine.

Both the Foley and the Norpro mills were noticeably less efficient; their blades pushed the food around instead of forcing it through the perforated disk. In addition, neither one offered additional disks for different textures. There was just one medium disk, fixed in place. But the real loser was the Kenwood Passi Electric food mill. Though it was easier than hand-cranking, the power button did not have an "on" position, so you had to hold it in place. And it took forever to process the food. Also, the blade could not be cranked in the reverse direction (as it could on all of the manual models), so there was no way to loosen the food when it got stuck.

ROASTED CARROTS

WHAT WE WANTED: Perfectly caramelized carrots that are smooth and tender inside.

Roasted carrots' sublime nature lies in their rustic charm. Simple, sweet, and pure, their perfectly caramelized outer layer gently gives way to a smooth, tender interior—unless they are undercooked and have a crisp, bitter center or, on the opposite end of the spectrum, are subjected to such intense heat that they become wan, limp, and utterly unpalatable. Our ideal roasted carrot recipe, we decided, would be one that let us throw a couple of ingredients together, toss the carrots into the oven, and let them roast until they were done—a simple and painless side dish.

We started with the basic question of what type of carrot to use. We tested bunch carrots (those with greens still attached), bagged carrots, and bagged baby carrots. The bagged whole carrots were too toothy, fibrous, and bitter. Baby and bunch carrots were the best—sweet and tender. While the flavor and presentation of bunch carrots edged out the bagged babies (bunch carrots were breathtaking when roasted whole with just a nub of green stem left attached), the baby carrots needed no peeling, trimming, or chopping. They were effortless and easy, just what we had in mind.

Still, without a little help from a fatty cohort, we knew that the glossy, bronzed carrots we envisioned would not be possible. So we tossed batches of carrots with vegetable oil, olive oil, extra-virgin olive oil, butter, and clarified butter and roasted them. We were surprised to discover that our favorite was plain olive oil; it neither masked the carrots' sweetness, as did extra-virgin olive and vegetable oils, nor changed their texture, as did the butter.

We next examined possible roasting methods, times, and temperatures. We tried covering the broiler pan with foil to help keep the carrots moist and hasten the roasting,

but when we pulled these carrots out from their sealed bed, they had become reminiscent of cafeteria carrots: slightly bitter, pale, and soggy. Carrots covered for only part of the roasting time fared little better. The best batch was the most straightforward: roasted at 475 degrees, uncovered, for 20 minutes, until the carrots were brown and caramel colored.

We proceeded to roast carrots in different sorts of pans to see which would give us the best color and the easiest cleanup. After pitting broiler-pan bottoms against cookie sheets and roasting pans against Pyrex glass dishes and non-stick aluminum pans, we found the broiler-pan bottom to be the best for browning the carrots without burning them.

During this testing, we came to wonder just what a baby carrot was. Bagged baby carrots are made by taking long, thin carrots (usually carrot varieties grown for their high sugar and beta carotene content, which makes them sweet and bright in color) and forcing them through a carrot-trimming machine that peels the carrots and cuts them down to their ubiquitous baby size.

Real baby carrots are varieties of carrots that are miniature in size when mature; contrary to popular belief, they are not carrots of the standard length that are picked early. Unfortunately, real baby carrots are available only through specialty produce purveyors that sell to restaurants and other professional kitchens. If you are lucky enough to spy true, greens-still-attached, tapered baby carrots in your grocery store or farmer's market, buy them in the cooler months and roast according to our recipe. Baby carrots harvested in the warmer spring and summer months tend to be less sweet and have more of a metallic, turpentine-like flavor.

WHAT WE LEARNED: With a broiler pan and a hot oven, you can produce perfectly cooked, caramelized roasted carrots in just 20 minutes.

BASIC ROASTED CARROTS serves 8 as a side dish

Inspect your bag of baby carrots carefully for pockets of water. Carrots taken from the top of the supermarket's carrot pile are often waterlogged. This not only makes carrots mealy, it also dashes any hopes of caramelization in the oven.

- 2 pounds baby carrots (two 16-ounce bags)
- 2 tablespoons olive oil
- ½ teaspoon salt

Adjust oven rack to middle position and heat oven to 475 degrees. Toss carrots, oil, and salt in broiler-pan bottom. Spread into single layer and roast for 12 minutes. Shake pan to toss carrots; continue roasting about 8 minutes longer, shaking pan twice more, until carrots are browned and tender.

VARIATIONS

ROASTED MAPLE CARROTS WITH BROWNED BUTTER

Follow recipe for Basic Roasted Carrots, decreasing oil to 1½ teaspoons. After carrots have roasted 10 minutes, heat 1 tablespoon butter in small saucepan over medium heat, swirling occasionally, and simmer until deep gold, about 1 minute. Off heat, stir in 1 tablespoon maple syrup and drizzle mixture over carrots after 12 minutes of roasting; shake pan to coat, and continue roasting according to recipe.

ROASTED CARROTS WITH GINGER-ORANGE GLAZE

Follow recipe for Basic Roasted Carrots. After carrots have roasted 10 minutes, bring 1 heaping tablespoon orange marmalade, 1 tablespoon water, and ½ teaspoon grated fresh ginger to simmer in small saucepan over medium-high heat. Drizzle mixture over carrots after 12 minutes of roasting; shake pan to coat, and continue roasting according to recipe.

GREEN-TOPPED ROASTED CARROTS

Long, slender roasted carrots (no thicker than ½ inch) with little green stems still attached make a stunning table presentation. If you like, you can apply the instructions below to the preceding variations.

Follow recipe for Basic Roasted Carrots, replacing baby carrots with 2 pounds slender bunch carrots, trimmed of all but ½ inch of green stems. Increase total roasting time by 5 to 7 minutes.

ROASTED CARROTS, POTATOES, AND SHALLOTS

Give the potatoes a head start so they will be done at the same time as the carrots and shallots.

- 1 pound baby red potatoes, cut in half lengthwise
- 2 tablespoons olive oil
- 1 teaspoon salt
- 1 pound baby carrots (one 16-ounce bag)
- 6 shallots (about 6 ounces), peeled and cut in half lengthwise

1. Heat oven to 425 degrees. Place potatoes in broiler-pan bottom, add 1 tablespoon olive oil and ½ teaspoon salt; toss to coat. Arrange potato halves so cut sides face down, cover pan with aluminum foil, and roast 20 minutes.

2. Remove foil. Add carrots, shallots, remaining 1 tablespoon olive oil, and ½ teaspoon salt to potatoes. Toss to mix all ingredients together (it's OK if potatoes are not facing down), spread in single layer, and increase oven temperature to 475 degrees. Roast for 12 minutes. Shake pan to toss vegetables; continue roasting about 8 minutes longer, shaking pan twice more, until carrots are browned and tender.

After just 30 seconds of kneading,
the dough for our cream biscuits
is ready to be patted into a circle,
cut into rounds, and baked.

HAM, BISCUITS, & greens

CHAPTER 16

Southern food has a special place in the test kitchen.
For many of us, this is comfort food. A favorite meal is ham, biscuits, and greens. But we aren't content with just any old ham, biscuits, and greens.

We ventured into new territory when one of our staff members suggested soaking fresh ham in cola. After figuring out how to brine, season, roast, and glaze a fresh ham, we created our own version of cola ham. Many cooks in the test kitchen say it's the best pork roast they ever tasted.

Ham needs biscuits. But if not handled properly, biscuits can turn out flat and tough. Part of the problem is the fat, which must be at the ideal temperature to be worked evenly into the flour. Many cooks have hot hands or overwork the dough, and the results are disappointing. To avoid this problem, we developed a cream biscuit—without any butter or shortening—that's nearly foolproof.

What's a southern meal without a mess o' greens? But if the greens are soupy, tired, and bland, what's the point? We wanted to make greens as good as the rest of the meal. Our recipes for great greens are easy and quick.

IN THIS CHAPTER

THE RECIPES
Roast Fresh Ham
Coca-Cola Ham
Cider and Brown Sugar Glaze
Spicy Pineapple-Ginger Glaze
Orange, Cinnamon, and Star
    Anise Glaze
Coca-Cola Glaze with Lime
    and Jalapeño

Cream Biscuits
Cream Biscuits with Fresh Herbs
Cheddar Biscuits

Sautéed Tender Greens
Sautéed Tender Greens
    with Raisins and Almonds
Quick-Cooked Tough Greens
Quick-Cooked Tough Greens
    with Prosciutto
Quick-Cooked Tough Greens
    with Red Bell Pepper
Quick-Cooked Tough Greens
    with Black Olives and Lemon
Quick-Cooked Tough Greens
    with Bacon and Onion

EQUIPMENT CORNER
Digital Scales

TASTING LAB
All-Purpose Flour

ROAST FRESH HAM

WHAT WE WANTED: A new centerpiece roast to serve as an alternative to the more traditional turkey or leg of lamb.

Although this roast is called a ham, it gains much of its undeniable appeal from the fact that it's not really a ham at all—or at least not what most of us understand the term to mean. It's not cured in the fashion of a Smithfield ham or salted and air-dried like prosciutto. It's not pressed or molded like a canned ham, and it's not smoked like a country ham. In fact, the only reason this cut of pork is called a ham is because it comes from the pig's hind leg.

Even before we began roasting, we had decided that a full fresh ham, weighing in at about 20 pounds, was too much for all but the very largest feast. So we decided to use one of the two cuts into which the leg is usually divided— the sirloin, which comes from the top of the leg, or the shank, from the bottom of the leg (see page 205). We also decided that we wanted our ham skin-on (we couldn't see giving up the opportunity for cracklings). Fortunately, this is how these roasts are typically sold.

From our experiences with other large roasts, we knew that the big problem would be making sure the roast cooked all the way through while the meat stayed tender and moist. In our first set of tests, then, we wanted to assess not only the relative merits of sirloin and shank but also the best oven temperature and cooking time.

Early on in this process, we determined that the roast needed to be cooked to a lower final internal temperature than some experts recommend. We found that we preferred the roast pulled from the oven at 145 to 150 degrees—at this point, the meat is cooked to about medium and retains a slight blush. While the roast rests, its residual heat brings the temperature up to approximately 155 to 160 degrees.

That determined, we started testing different oven temperatures. First to come out of the oven was a ham from the sirloin end of the leg that we had roasted at a high temperature, 400 degrees, for its entire stay in the oven. Carving this ham was akin to whittling wood: Olympics-worthy agility with the carving knife was required to get around the aitchbone (part of the hip), the cracklings were more suited for tap shoes than consumption, and the meat was dry, dry, dry. We moved on to roasting a shank-end ham at a low heat the whole way through. This ham tasted like a wrung-out washcloth, with no cracklings in sight. What we did appreciate was the straightforward bone composition of the shank end, which simplified carving and convinced us to use this end of the fresh ham for the remainder of our tests.

Next we roasted a shank-end ham by starting it at a low temperature (325 degrees) and finishing it at a higher one (400 degrees), hoping to end up with both moist meat and crispy cracklings. To our dismay, this ham was also rather dry, which we attributed to the ham's long stay in the oven, made necessary by the low cooking temperature. What's more, the brief hike in the temperature at the end of cooking didn't help to crisp the skin.

Again, we figured we ought to try the opposite: starting the ham at a high temperature to give the meat a head start and get the skin on its way to crisping, then turning down the heat for the remainder of the roasting time to cook the meat through. Although meat cooked according to this method was slightly chalky and dry, the skin was close to our goal, crispy enough to shatter between our teeth yet tender enough to stave off a trip to the dentist. We decided that this would be our master roasting method.

Hoping to solve the dry meat dilemma, we brined a shank-end ham, immersing it in a solution of saltwater and spices to tenderize and flavor it. More than slightly biased from the positive results we achieved in past brining experiments with turkey, chicken, shellfish, and other cuts of pork, we expected brining to make the meat incredibly juicy. The salt in a brine causes the protein structure in meat to unravel and trap water in its fibers; brining also encourages the unwound proteins to gel, forming a barrier that helps seal in moisture. Together, these effects allow the cook to increase the roasting temperature, thus speeding the roasting process without fear of drying out the meat. Our estimations proved accurate: The brined shank emerged from the oven succulent and flavorful, with meat tender enough to fall apart in your mouth.

Just when we thought the ham couldn't possibly get any better, we decided to try roasting one shank face-down on a rack set in a roasting pan rather than letting it sit directly in the pan. This adjustment kept the cut end from becoming tough and leathery from direct contact with the hot pan. Rack roasting also allowed the heat to circulate around the ham constantly, promoting faster and more even cooking.

With our timing and temperature firmly in place, we turned to tweaking the flavor of the roast and obtaining the type of cracklings we had heard of but never really tasted. Not content with the infusion of flavor from the brine, we turned to spice rubs to further develop the flavor of the roast. Fresh thyme, sage, rosemary, garlic, brown sugar, cloves, dried mustard, juniper berries, peppercorns, and salt were all given an equal opportunity to complement the pork. We liked the combination of sage's earthy sweetness and garlic's pungent bite as well as the edge of fresh parsley, peppercorns, and kosher salt. Since our composed rub didn't lean strongly in the direction of any one particular spice, we were left with a wide-open field of glazing options.

While some recipes we tried called for simply basting the roast in its own drippings, we veered in the direction of sugary glazes, opting for sugar's ability to crisp, caramelize, and sweeten the skin. Starting the ham at 500 degrees negated glazing it at the outset: The sugary glaze would definitely char black before the roast had been in the oven very long. We decided to let the roast cook unglazed at 500 degrees for the first 20 minutes. We then turned the oven temperature down to 350 degrees and began to brush the roast liberally with glaze. We continued to do so in 45-minute intervals, which amounted to three bastings during the

roasting period. This ham was the one: flavorful meat with sweetened, crunchy skin.

More than one person in the test kitchen proclaimed this ham was the best roast pork they'd ever eaten. Rich and tender, with an underlying hint of sweetness, the meat had the power to quiet a room full of vocal, opinionated cooks and editors. Perhaps even better was the sweet, slightly salty, crisp, and crunchy skin that intensifies to a deep crimson by the time the roast is done. It was attacked with precision and proprietary swiftness during our trials in the test kitchen. Unbelievably succulent, tender, and uncomplicated, this culinary gem will leave you wondering how you could have gotten along so far without it.

WHAT WE LEARNED: Use the shank end, brine the meat, rub it with herbs and garlic, then roast in a hot oven for 20 minutes before lowering the temperature and applying a sweet glaze.

ROAST FRESH HAM serves 8 to 10

Fresh ham comes from the pig's hind leg. Because a whole leg is quite large, it is usually cut into two sections. The sirloin, or butt, end is harder to carve than our favorite, the shank end. If you don't have room in your refrigerator, brine the ham in an insulated cooler or a small plastic garbage can; add five or six freezer packs to the brine to keep it well cooled.

roast

1   bone-in fresh half ham with skin, 6 to 8 pounds, preferably shank end, rinsed

brine

4   cups kosher salt or 2 cups table salt
3   cups packed dark or light brown sugar
2   heads garlic, cloves separated, lightly crushed and peeled
10 bay leaves
½   cup black peppercorns, crushed

garlic and herb rub

1   cup lightly packed sage leaves from 1 large bunch
½   cup parsley leaves from 1 bunch
8   medium cloves garlic, peeled
1   tablespoon kosher salt or 1½ teaspoons table salt
½   tablespoon ground black pepper
¼   cup olive oil

glaze

1   recipe glaze (recipes follow)

1. FOR THE ROAST: Carefully slice through skin and fat with serrated knife, making 1-inch diamond pattern. Be careful not to cut into meat.

2. FOR THE BRINE: In large (about 16-quart) bucket or stockpot, dissolve salt and brown sugar in 1 gallon hot tap water. Add garlic, bay leaves, crushed pepper, and 1 gallon cold water. Submerge ham in brine and refrigerate 8 to 24 hours.

3. Set large disposable roasting pan on baking sheet for extra support; place flat wire rack in roasting pan. Remove ham from brine; rinse under cold water and dry thoroughly with paper towels. Place ham, wide cut-side down, on rack. (If using sirloin end, place ham skin-side up.) Let ham stand, uncovered, at room temperature 1 hour.

4. FOR THE RUB: Meanwhile, adjust oven rack to lowest position and heat oven to 500 degrees. In workbowl of food processor fitted with steel blade, process sage, parsley, garlic, salt, pepper, and oil until mixture forms smooth paste, about 30 seconds. Rub all sides of ham with paste.

5. Roast ham at 500 degrees for 20 minutes. Reduce oven temperature to 350 degrees and continue to roast, brushing ham with glaze every 45 minutes, until center of ham registers 145 to 150 degrees on instant-read thermometer, about 2½ hours longer. Tent ham loosely with foil and let stand until center of ham registers 155 to 160 degrees on thermometer, 30 to 40 minutes. Carve, following illustrations on page 205, and serve.

VARIATION
COCA-COLA HAM serves 8 to 10

Although cooking with Coke may seem unconventional, you haven't lived until you've tried cola pork. Cola pork was born when a member of our staff mentioned the southern tradition of Coca-Cola glaze and joked that we should try brining the meat in it. After giving this joke fair consideration, we dumped 6 liters of Coca-Cola Classic into a bucket, added kosher salt, and let the ham soak overnight. The next day we cooked it according to our recipe. The outcome was the talk of the kitchen. It was juicy; it was unusual; it was fantastic. The Coke had added its own unique flavor to the ham while tenderizing the meat even more than our regular brine. The meat was falling off the bone and unbelievably tender.

Follow recipe for Roast Fresh Ham, substituting 6 liters Coke Classic for both hot and cold water in brine, omitting sugar, and reducing salt to 3 cups kosher salt or 1½ cups table salt. Proceed as directed, rubbing ham with garlic and herb mixture and using Coca-Cola Glaze with Lime and Jalapeño.

GLAZES

CIDER AND BROWN SUGAR GLAZE

makes about 1⅓ cups, enough to glaze ham

1   cup apple cider
2   cups packed dark or light brown sugar
5   whole cloves

Bring cider, brown sugar, and cloves to boil in small nonreactive saucepan over high heat; reduce heat to medium-low and simmer until syrupy and reduced to about 1⅓ cups, 5 to 7 minutes. (Glaze will thicken as it cools between bastings; cook over medium heat about 1 minute, stirring once or twice, before using.)

SPICY PINEAPPLE-GINGER GLAZE   makes about 1⅓ cups, enough to glaze ham

1   cup pineapple juice
2   cups packed dark or light brown sugar
1   (1-inch) piece fresh ginger, grated (about 1 tablespoon)
1   tablespoon red pepper flakes

Bring pineapple juice, brown sugar, ginger, and red pepper flakes to boil in small nonreactive saucepan over high heat; reduce heat to medium-low and simmer until syrupy and reduced to about 1⅓ cups, 5 to 7 minutes. (Glaze will thicken as it cools between bastings; cook over medium heat about 1 minute, stirring once or twice, before using.)

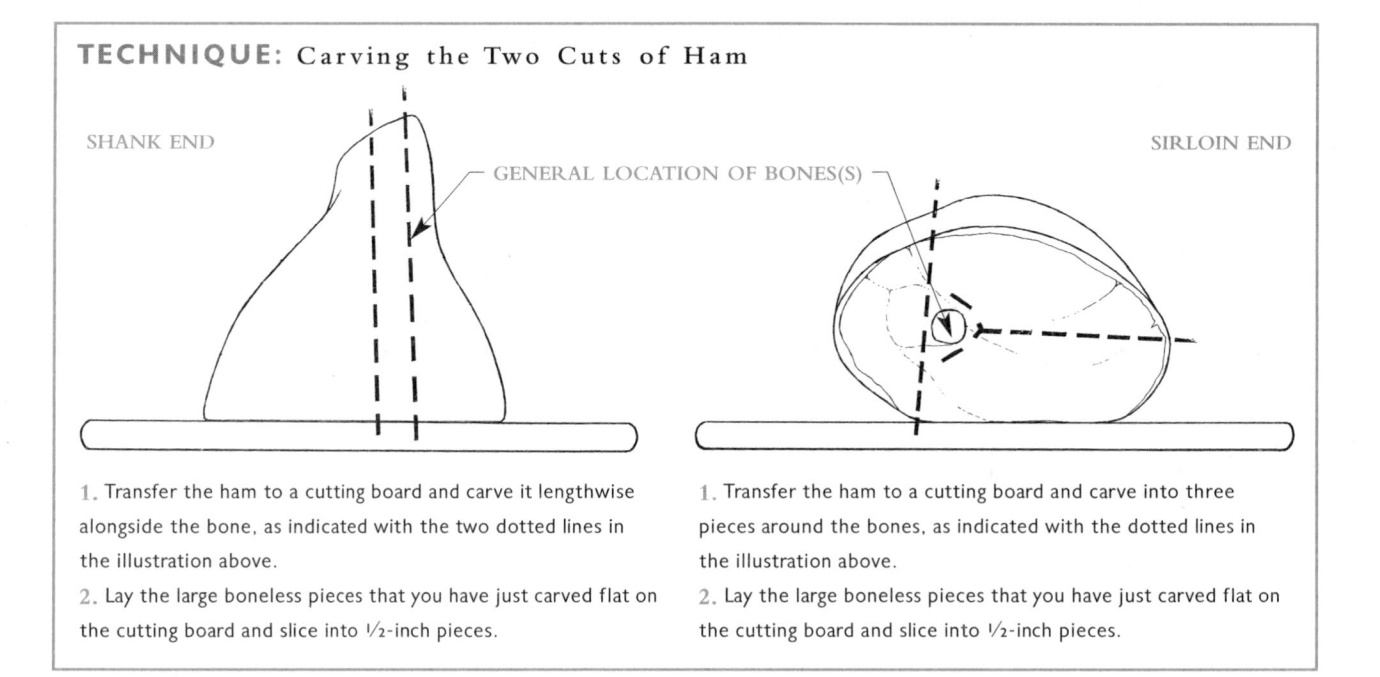

TECHNIQUE: Carving the Two Cuts of Ham

SHANK END   GENERAL LOCATION OF BONES(S)   SIRLOIN END

1. Transfer the ham to a cutting board and carve it lengthwise alongside the bone, as indicated with the two dotted lines in the illustration above.
2. Lay the large boneless pieces that you have just carved flat on the cutting board and slice into ½-inch pieces.

1. Transfer the ham to a cutting board and carve into three pieces around the bones, as indicated with the dotted lines in the illustration above.
2. Lay the large boneless pieces that you have just carved flat on the cutting board and slice into ½-inch pieces.

ORANGE, CINNAMON, AND STAR ANISE
GLAZE makes about 1⅓ cups, enough to glaze ham

    1   cup juice plus 1 tablespoon grated zest from
        2 large oranges
    2   cups packed dark or light brown sugar
    4   pods star anise
    1   (3-inch) cinnamon stick

Bring orange juice, brown sugar, star anise, and cinnamon to boil in small nonreactive saucepan over high heat; reduce heat to medium-low and simmer until syrupy and reduced to about 1⅓ cups, 5 to 7 minutes. (Glaze will thicken as it cools between bastings; cook over medium heat about 1 minute, stirring once or twice, before using.)

COCA-COLA GLAZE WITH LIME AND
JALAPEÑO makes about 1⅓ cups, enough to glaze ham

    1   cup Coke Classic
    ¼   cup juice from 2 limes
    2   cups packed dark or light brown sugar
    2   medium jalapeño chiles, cut crosswise into
        ¼-inch-thick slices

Bring Coke Classic, lime juice, brown sugar, and jalapeños to boil in small nonreactive saucepan over high heat; reduce heat to medium-low and simmer until syrupy and reduced to about 1⅓ cups, 5 to 7 minutes. (Glaze will thicken as it cools between bastings; heat over medium heat about 1 minute, stirring once or twice, before using.)

CREAM BISCUITS

WHAT WE WANTED: Great homemade biscuits without the bother of cutting fat into the flour.

Many cooks are intimidated by biscuits. They are not comfortable with the process of cutting butter into flour. We wondered if there was such a thing as a great recipe for homemade biscuits that would not require cutting fat into flour. In effect, could we take the guesswork out of making biscuits to create a foolproof recipe?

We began with a basic recipe calling for 2 cups flour, 2 teaspoons baking powder, 1 tablespoon sugar, and ½ teaspoon salt. Now we had to figure out what to add to this mixture instead of butter or vegetable shortening to make a dough. We decided to try plain yogurt, sour cream, milk, milk combined with melted butter, and whipped heavy cream, an idea borrowed from a scone recipe.

The biscuits made with yogurt and sour cream were a bit sodden in texture, those with the milk and milk/butter combination were tough and lifeless, and the whipped cream biscuit was too light, more confection than biscuit. This last approach also required another step—whipping the cream—which seemed like too much trouble for a simple recipe. So we tried using plain heavy cream, without whipping, and this biscuit was the best of the lot. (Cream biscuits are not our invention. James Beard includes such a recipe in his seminal work *American Cookery* [Little, Brown, 1972]).

Next, we decided to do a blind tasting, pitting the cream biscuits against our favorite buttermilk biscuit recipe, which requires cutting butter into the flour. The result? Both biscuits had their partisans. The cream biscuits were lighter and more tender. They were also richer tasting. The buttermilk biscuits were flakier and had the distinctive tang that many tasters associate with good biscuits. Although neither biscuit was sweet, the buttermilk version seemed more savory.

At this point, we decided that cream biscuits were a worthy (and easier) alternative to traditional buttermilk biscuits. Still, we were running into a problem with the shape of the biscuits—they spread far too much during baking. We have always followed the conventional advice about not overworking the dough. In our experience, the best biscuits are generally made from dough that is handled lightly. This is certainly true of buttermilk biscuits.

But cream biscuits, being less sturdy than those made with butter, become soft and "melt" during baking. In this case, we thought, a little handling might not be such a bad thing. So we baked up two batches: The first dough we patted out gingerly; the second dough we kneaded for 30 seconds until it was smooth and uniform in appearance. The results were remarkable. The more heavily worked dough produced much higher, fluffier biscuits than the lightly handled dough, which looked short and bedraggled.

Although we find it easy enough to quickly roll out this dough and then cut it into rounds with a biscuit cutter, you can simply shape the dough with your hands or push it into the bottom of an 8-inch cake pan. The dough can then be flipped onto the work surface and cut into wedges.

As for dough thickness, ¾ inch provided a remarkably high rise, more appealing than biscuits that started out ½ inch thick. We also discovered that it was best to add just enough cream to hold the dough together. A wet dough did not hold its shape as well during baking.

Our final ingredient tests included sugar—tasters felt that 1 tablespoon was a bit much, so we dropped it to 2 teaspoons—and baking powder, which we found we could reduce to 1 teaspoon with no decrease in rise. For oven temperature, we tried 375, 400, and 425 degrees, and found the latter best for browning.

WHAT WE LEARNED: Cream is the best choice for turning flour, baking powder, salt, and sugar into light, tender biscuits. Knead the dough slightly to produce higher, fluffier biscuits.

CREAM BISCUITS makes eight 2½-inch biscuits
Bake the biscuits immediately after cutting them; letting them stand for any length of time can decrease the leavening power and thereby prevent the biscuits from rising properly in the oven.

> 2   cups (10 ounces) unbleached all-purpose flour
> 2   teaspoons sugar
> 1   teaspoon baking powder
> ½   teaspoon salt
> 1½ cups heavy cream

1. Adjust oven rack to upper-middle position and heat oven to 425 degrees. Line baking sheet with parchment paper.

2. Whisk together flour, sugar, baking powder, and salt in medium bowl. Add 1¼ cups cream and stir with wooden spoon until dough forms, about 30 seconds. Transfer dough from bowl to countertop, leaving all dry, floury bits behind in

bowl. In 1 tablespoon increments, add up to ¼ cup cream to dry bits in bowl, mixing with wooden spoon after each addition, until moistened. Add these moistened bits to rest of dough and knead by hand just until smooth, about 30 seconds.

3. Following illustrations on page 209, cut biscuits into rounds or wedges. Place rounds or wedges on parchment-lined baking sheet and bake until golden brown, about 15 minutes. Serve immediately.

VARIATIONS
CREAM BISCUITS WITH FRESH HERBS
Use the herb of your choice in this variation.

Follow recipe for Cream Biscuits, whisking 2 tablespoons minced fresh herbs into flour along with sugar, baking powder, and salt.

CHEDDAR BISCUITS
Follow recipe for Cream Biscuits, stirring ½ cup (2 ounces) sharp cheddar cheese cut into ¼-inch pieces into flour along with sugar, baking powder, and salt. Increase baking time to 18 minutes.

TASTING LAB: All-Purpose Flour

WE WANTED TO KNOW IF THERE WAS A SINGLE ALL-PURPOSE flour that would be best for those who keep only one kind of flour in the pantry. So we stocked our test kitchen shelves with nine brands of all-purpose flour and started a bake-off that eventually stretched over some six months. We ended up preparing two kinds of cookies, pie pastry, biscuits, cake, muffins, and bread with each brand of flour, often making several batches of each item.

When milling all-purpose flour, a flour company must make a number of choices that will influence the way its product performs in recipes. For starters, there is the essence of the flour, the wheat itself. All-purpose flour is typically made from hard red winter wheat, soft red winter wheat, or a combination of the two. Of the flours we used in the taste tests, five were made from hard winter wheat, one was made from soft wheat, and three were a mix of soft and hard.

Perhaps the primary difference between these types of wheat—and, consequently, the flours made from them—is the variation in protein content. Hard winter wheat is about 10 to 13 percent protein, soft wheat about 8 to 10 percent. Mixtures of the two wheats are somewhere in between. You can actually feel this difference with your fingers; the hard wheat flours tend to have a subtle granular feel, while soft wheat flours feel fine but starchy, much like cornstarch.

High-protein flours are generally recommended for yeasted products and other baked goods that require a lot of structural support. The reason is that the higher the protein level in a flour, the greater the potential for the formation of gluten. The sheets that gluten forms in dough are elastic enough to move with the gas released by yeast yet sturdy enough to prevent that gas from escaping, so the dough doesn't deflate. Lower-protein flours, on the other hand, are recommended for chemically leavened baked goods. This is because baking powder and baking soda are quick leaveners. They lack the endurance of yeast, which can force the naturally resistant gluten sheets to expand. Gluten can overpower quick leaveners, causing the final baked product to fall flat.

A second important difference in flours is whether they are bleached or not. Technically, every all-purpose flour is bleached. Carotenoid pigments in wheat lend a faint yellowish tint to freshly milled flour. But in a matter of about 12 weeks, these pigments oxidize, undergoing the same chemical process that turns a sliced apple brown. In this case, yellowish flour changes to a whiter hue (though not stark white). Early in this century, as the natural bleaching process came to be understood, scientists identified methods to chemically expedite and intensify it. Typically, all-purpose flours are bleached with either benzoyl peroxide or chlorine gas. The latter not only bleaches the flour but also alters the flour proteins, making them less inclined to form strong gluten. Today consumers prefer chemically bleached flour

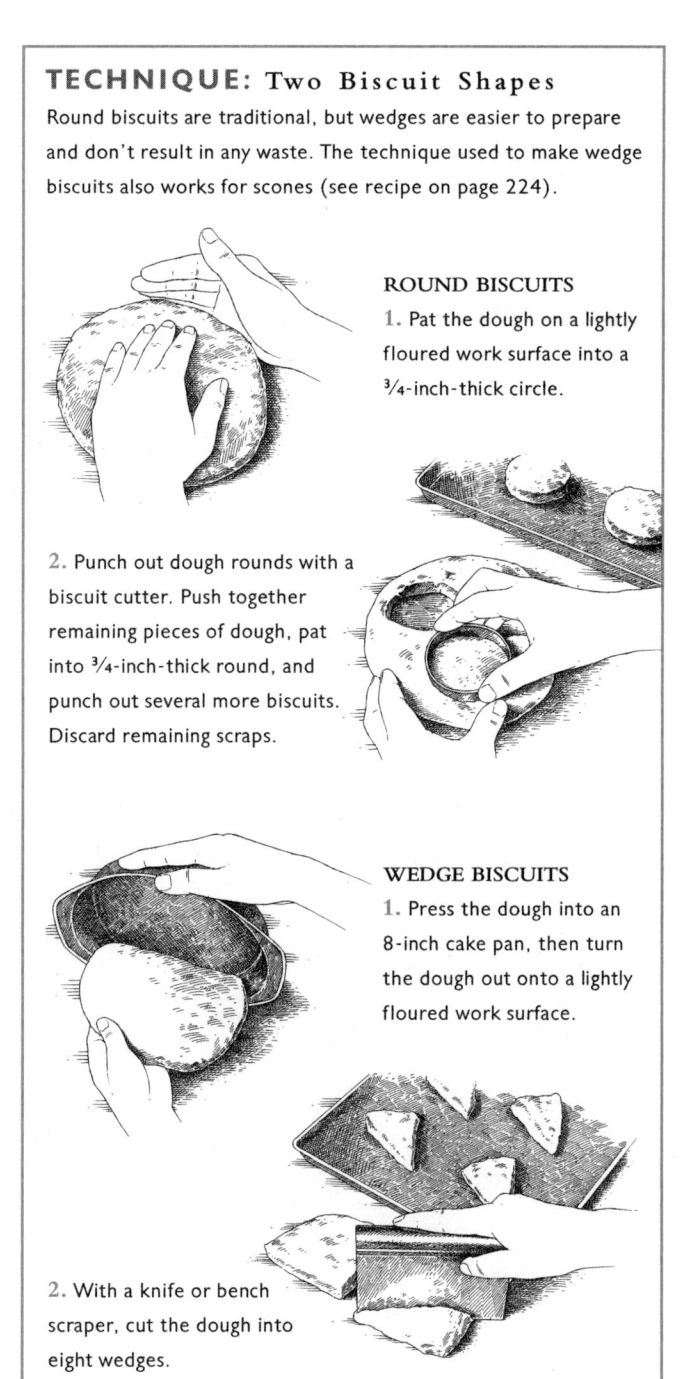

TECHNIQUE: Two Biscuit Shapes

Round biscuits are traditional, but wedges are easier to prepare and don't result in any waste. The technique used to make wedge biscuits also works for scones (see recipe on page 224).

ROUND BISCUITS

1. Pat the dough on a lightly floured work surface into a ¾-inch-thick circle.

2. Punch out dough rounds with a biscuit cutter. Push together remaining pieces of dough, pat into ¾-inch-thick round, and punch out several more biscuits. Discard remaining scraps.

WEDGE BISCUITS

1. Press the dough into an 8-inch cake pan, then turn the dough out onto a lightly floured work surface.

2. With a knife or bench scraper, cut the dough into eight wedges.

over unbleached because they associate the whiter color with higher quality. In our tests, some of the baked goods made with bleached flour were such a pure white that they actually looked startlingly unnatural and "commercial" versus homemade.

Of all the product taste tests we have run, these flour tastings were undoubtedly the most difficult. The differences in flavor between the various versions of the selected recipes were usually extremely subtle. For example, tasting nine different plain muffins in which the only ingredient difference was the brand of flour required shrewd discrimination on the tasters' part. The most obvious differences were often in appearance.

That is not to say, however, that the tests were inconclusive. As difficult as it was for tasters to pick up differences, they were remarkably consistent in their observations. The performance of each of the flours tested, however, was not so consistent. All of the flours baked up well enough in most of the recipes. And some baked up better than that—at times. Failure also occurred, sometimes without apparent reason.

As an overall category, the four bleached flours in our tests in fact did not perform as well as the unbleached flours and were regularly criticized for tasting flat or carrying "off" flavors, often described as metallic. These characteristics, however, were more difficult to detect in recipes that contained a high proportion of ingredients other than flour. Coincidentally, our cake tests and chocolate chip cookie tests (both sugary recipes) were the two tests in which off flavors carried by the bleached flour went undetected or were considered faint.

Despite the variations and subtleties, however, the good news is that we did end up with two flours we can recommend wholeheartedly. Both King Arthur and Pillsbury unbleached flours regularly made for highly recommended baked goods, producing a more consistent range of preferred products than the other seven flours in the taste tests. If you are going to have only one flour in the house, our advice is to choose one of these two.

No matter the type or brand, we measure all flour by the dip-and-sweep method. Dip a metal or plastic dry measure into

a bag of flour so that the cup is overflowing with flour. Then use a knife or icing spatula to level off the flour, sweeping the excess back into the bag. Short of weighing flour (which is what professional bakers do), this measuring method is your best guarantee of using the right amount of flour. Spooning the flour into the measuring cup aerates it, and you might end up with as much as 25 percent less flour by weight.

EQUIPMENT CORNER: Digital Scales

EVERY SERIOUS COOK NEEDS AN ACCURATE SCALE FOR weighing fruits, vegetables, and meats. When making bread, a scale is even more critical. Professional bakers know that measuring flour by volume can be problematic. A cup of flour can weigh between 4 and 6 ounces, depending on the type of flour, the humidity, whether or not the flour has been sifted, and the way the flour has been put into the cup. Weight is a much more accurate way to measure flour.

There are two basic types of kitchen scales. Mechanical scales operate on a spring and lever system. When an item is placed on the scale, internal springs are compressed. The springs are attached to levers, which move a needle on the scale's display (a ruler with lines and numbers printed on a piece of paper and glued to the scale). The more the springs are compressed, the farther the needle moves along the ruler.

Electronic, or digital, scales have two plates that are suspended at a fixed distance. The bottom plate is stationary, the top plate is not. When food is placed on the platform attached to the top plate, the distance between the plates changes slightly. The movement of the top plate (no more than one thousandth of an inch) causes a change in the flow of electricity through the scale's circuitry. This change is translated into a weight and expressed in numbers displayed on the face of the scale.

We tested 10 electronic scales and 9 mechanical scales. As a group, the electronic scales were vastly preferred. Their digital displays are much easier to read than the measures on most mechanical scales, where the lines on the ruler are so closely spaced it's impossible to nail down the precise weight within half an ounce. Also, many mechanical scales could weigh items only within a limited range—usually between 1 ounce and 5 pounds. What's the point of owning a scale that can't weigh a large chicken or roast? Most electronic scales can handle items that weigh as much as 10 pounds and as little as ¼ ounce. Among the electronic scales we tested, we found that several features make the difference between a good electronic scale and a great one.

Readability is a must. The displayed numbers should be large. Also, the displayed numbers should be steeply angled and as far from the weighing platform as possible. If the display is too close to the platform, the numbers can hide beneath the rim of a dinner plate or cake pan.

An automatic shut-off feature will save battery life, but this feature can be annoying, especially if the shut-off cycle kicks in at under two minutes. A scale that shuts off automatically after five minutes or more is easier to use.

A large weighing platform (that detaches for easy cleaning) is another plus. Last, we preferred electronic scales that display weight increments in decimals rather than fractions. The former are more accurate and easier to work with when scaling a recipe up or down.

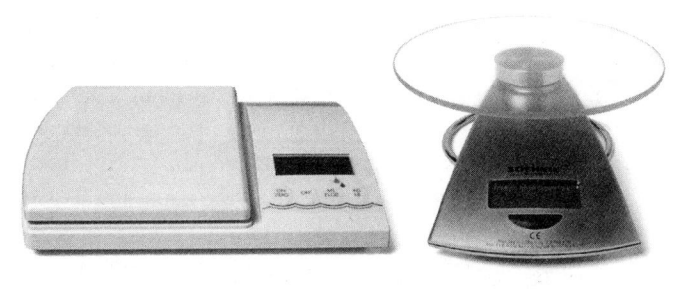

BEST SCALES
Despite the high price tag and minor quirks, the Soehnle Cyber Electronic (right) was the runaway winner in our testing. It has a detachable glass measuring platform that is especially easy to clean. The Salter Electronic Aquatronic (left) is half the price, but food can become trapped between the weighing platform and base.

GREENS

WHAT WE WANTED: Southern-style greens that are tender but not limp. The cooking method should preserve their great color and flavor.

Many cooks think that all leafy greens can be treated alike, even though some are delicate enough for salads while others seem as tough as shoe leather. After cleaning, stemming, and cooking more than 100 pounds of leafy greens, we found that they fell into two categories, each of which should be handled quite differently.

Spinach, beet greens, and Swiss chard are tender and rich in moisture. They require no additional liquid during cooking. They taste of the earth and minerals but are still rather delicate. Kale as well as mustard, turnip, and collard greens are tougher and require the addition of some liquid as they cook. Their flavor is much more assertive, even peppery in some cases, and can be overwhelming.

We tested boiling, steaming, and sautéing tender greens. Boiling produced the most brilliantly colored greens, but they were also very mushy and bland. The water cooked out all of their flavor and texture. While steamed greens were less mushy, the generally unsatisfactory results of steaming showed us these tender greens did not need any liquid at all. Damp greens that were tossed in a hot oil (which could be flavored with aromatics and spices) wilted in just two or three minutes in a covered pan. Once wilted, we found it best to remove the lid so the liquid in the pan would evaporate.

This method has the advantage of flavoring the greens as they cook. Our basic recipe cooks greens in olive oil flavored with garlic, but the choices are endless. Use Asian sesame oil and add ginger along with the garlic. Or use vegetable oil and cook ginger, garlic, chiles, and curry powder before adding the damp greens.

Tougher greens don't have enough moisture to be wilted in a hot pan; they scorch before they wilt. Steaming these greens produces a better texture but does nothing to tame their bitter flavor. Tough greens benefit from cooking in some water, which washes away some of their harsh notes.

We tested boiling 2 pounds of greens in an abundant quantity of salted water and what might be called shallow-blanching in just 2 quarts of salted water. We found that cooking the greens in lots of water diluted their flavor too much. Shallow blanching removed enough bitterness to make these assertive greens palatable, but not so much as to rob them of their character. Blanched greens should be drained and then briefly cooked with seasonings.

Our preferred method is to heat some olive oil, garlic, and hot red pepper flakes, add the blanched and drained greens, and then stir to coat the greens with seasonings. Tough greens have a tendency to dry out—even after blanching—so we found it best to add a little chicken stock to the pan and cook the greens, covered, just until well seasoned. To change seasonings, use a different oil or add other ingredients—such as diced ham, olives, peppers, or ginger—to the oil before tossing the blanched greens into the pan.

WHAT WE LEARNED: Leafy greens can be divided into two categories—tender and tough—and each must be cooked differently. Tender greens like spinach should be wilted in a hot pan with seasonings. Tough greens like collards should be blanched in a minimum of water, drained, then sautéed with seasonings.

SAUTÉED TENDER GREENS   serves 4

To stem spinach and beet greens, simply pinch off the leaves where they meet the stems. A thick stalks runs through each Swiss chard leaf, so it must be handled differently; see top illustration at right. A large, deep Dutch oven or even a soup kettle is best for this recipe.

3   tablespoons extra-virgin olive oil
2   medium cloves garlic, minced
2   pounds damp tender greens, such as spinach,
     beet greens, or Swiss chard, stemmed, washed
     in several changes of cold water, and coarsely
     chopped
     Salt and ground black pepper
     Lemon wedges (optional)

1. Heat oil and garlic in Dutch oven or other deep pot and cook until garlic sizzles and turns golden, about 1 minute. Add wet greens, cover, and cook over medium-high heat, stirring occasionally, until greens completely wilt, about 2 to 3 minutes.

2. Uncover and season with salt and pepper to taste. Cook over high heat until liquid evaporates, 2 to 3 minutes. Serve immediately, with lemon wedges if desired.

VARIATION
SAUTÉED TENDER GREENS WITH RAISINS AND ALMONDS

This Italian recipe works surprisingly well with our roast ham. If you prefer, replace the almonds with an equal amount of toasted pine nuts.

Follow recipe for Sautéed Tender Greens, adding ¼ teaspoon hot red pepper flakes with garlic, ⅓ cup golden raisins with spinach, ½ teaspoon minced lemon zest with salt and pepper, and 3 tablespoons toasted slivered almonds just before serving.

TECHNIQUE: Preparing Leafy Greens

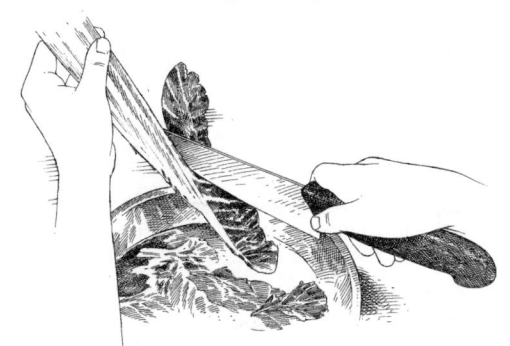

A. To prepare Swiss chard, kale, collards, and mustard greens, hold each leaf at the base of the stem over a bowl filled with water and use a sharp knife to slash the leafy portion from either side of the thick stem.

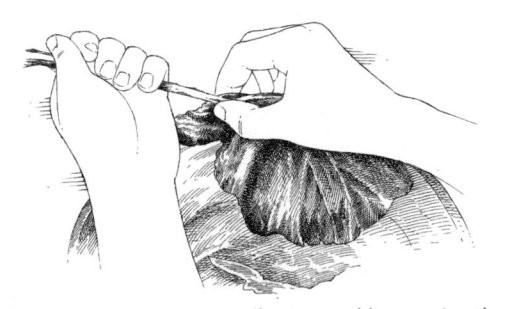

B1. Turnip greens are most easily stemmed by grasping the leaf between your thumb and index finger at the base of the stem and stripping it off by hand.

B2. When using this method with turnip greens, the very tip of the stem will break off along with the leaves. The tip is tender enough to cook along with them.

QUICK-COOKED TOUGH GREENS serves 4

See the box on page 213 for tips on stemming kale, collards, mustard greens, and turnip greens. Shallow-blanched greens should be shocked in cold water to stop the cooking process, drained, and then braised. Shocked and drained greens can be held for up to an hour before being braised.

- Salt
- 2 pounds assertive greens, such as kale, collards, mustard, or turnip, stemmed, washed in several changes of cold water, and coarsely chopped
- 2 large cloves garlic, sliced thin
- ¼ teaspoon hot red pepper flakes
- 3 tablespoons extra-virgin olive oil
- ⅓–½ cup homemade chicken stock or canned low-sodium chicken broth
- Lemon wedges (optional)

1. Bring 2 quarts water to boil in soup kettle or other large pot. Add 1½ teaspoons salt and greens and stir until wilted. Cover and cook until greens are just tender, about 7 minutes. Drain in colander. Rinse kettle with cold water to cool, then refill with cold water. Pour greens into cold water to stop cooking process. Gather handful of greens, lift out of water, and squeeze until only droplets fall from them. Repeat with remaining greens.

2. Heat garlic, red pepper flakes, and oil in large sauté pan over medium heat until garlic starts to sizzle, about 1 minute. Add greens and stir to coat with oil. Add ⅓ cup stock, cover, and cook over medium-high heat, adding more stock if necessary, until greens are tender and juicy and most of stock has been absorbed, about 5 minutes. Adjust seasonings, adding salt and red pepper flakes to taste. Serve immediately, with lemon wedges if desired.

VARIATIONS

QUICK-COOKED TOUGH GREENS WITH PROSCIUTTO

Follow recipe for Quick-Cooked Tough Greens, adding 1 ounce thin-sliced prosciutto that has been cut into thin strips along with garlic and red pepper flakes. Proceed as directed, stirring in ¼ teaspoon grated lemon zest just before serving.

QUICK-COOKED TOUGH GREENS WITH RED BELL PEPPER

Follow recipe for Quick-Cooked Tough Greens through step 1. Sauté ½ thinly sliced red bell pepper in oil until softened, about 4 minutes. Add garlic and red pepper flakes and proceed as directed.

QUICK-COOKED TOUGH GREENS WITH BLACK OLIVES AND LEMON

Follow recipe for Quick-Cooked Tough Greens, adding ⅓ cup pitted and chopped black olives, such as kalamatas, after garlic starts to sizzle. Add greens and proceed as directed, stirring in ¼ teaspoon grated lemon zest just before serving.

QUICK-COOKED TOUGH GREENS WITH BACON AND ONION

Follow recipe for Quick-Cooked Tough Greens through step 1. Fry 2 bacon slices, cut crosswise into thin strips, in large sauté pan over medium heat until crisp, 4 to 5 minutes. Remove bacon with slotted spoon and set aside on small plate. If necessary, add vegetable oil to bacon drippings to yield 2 tablespoons of fat. Add 1 small onion, minced, and sauté until softened, about 4 minutes. Add 2 minced garlic cloves and cook until fragrant, about 1 minute. Add greens and proceed as directed, sprinkling bacon bits and 2 teaspoons cider vinegar over greens just before serving.

A light cream and sugar glaze applied before baking gives scones an attractive sheen and burst of crunchy sweetness.

MUFFINS &scones

CHAPTER 17

Muffins and scones are both quick breads, leavened chemically with baking powder and/or baking soda rather than yeast. Few baking projects deliver such satisfying rewards in so little time. You can enjoy homemade blueberry muffins or scones in less than an hour, including baking and cooling time.

Just because these muffin and scone recipes are fast, it doesn't mean that they are foolproof. When quick breads go wrong, they really go wrong. If not handled properly, quick breads can turn out dry and tough. There's a reason why the English refer to some scones as rock cakes.

We think the ideal muffin is tender and delicate, like a butter cake. Too often, though, muffins are gargantuan and tough. Scones can suffer similar indignities. They should be tender and buttery, not coarse and craggy.

To solve these problems, we turned the test kitchen into the neighborhood bakeshop. The smells of freshly baked blueberry muffins and cream scones filled the air from morning until nightfall. Our final recipes are simple but memorable.

IN THIS CHAPTER

THE RECIPES
Blueberry Muffins
Cinnamon Sugar–Dipped
    Blueberry Muffins
Ginger- or Lemon-Glazed
    Blueberry Muffins

Cream Scones
Glazed Scones
Cakey Scones
Oatmeal-Raisin Scones
Ginger Scones

EQUIPMENT CORNER
Muffin Tins

TASTING LAB
Butter

BLUEBERRY MUFFINS

WHAT WE WANTED: Rich, moist, and dainty muffins, not the big, bland, coarse muffins so popular today.

The *Oxford Companion to Food* defines American muffins as "small, squat, round cakes," yet today's deli muffins are, by comparison, big and buxom, inflated by chemical leavening and tattooed with everything from chocolate chips to sunflower seeds. We wanted a blueberry muffin with a daintier stature, a moist, delicate little cake that would support the blueberries both physically, and, if we may say so, spiritually (in terms of flavor).

Despite the easy promise of a gingham-lined basket of warm, cuddly blueberry muffins, much can go wrong from kitchen to table. We made a half-dozen recipes, producing muffins that ranged from rough and tough to dense, sweet, and heavy to the typical lackluster coffee shop cake with too few blueberries and too little flavor. It was clear that blueberry muffins came in no one style, flavor, or size, so we asked tasters to state which basic style of muffin they fancied: round tea cake or craggy biscuit. Of the 15 tasters, all but one said tea cake.

Since minor fluctuations in ingredients occasioned seismic differences in the resulting muffins, we thought it best to hold fast to a recipe whose proportions landed in between the two extremes in the original tests. That meant we would be working with 1 stick of butter, 1 cup sugar, 2 cups flour, and ½ cup milk. It was not a perfect recipe but would be a serviceable springboard for future testing.

The two principal methods available to the muffin baker are mixing and creaming. The former is a one-two-three-done courtship in which dry ingredients go in one bowl, liquid in another, and then join up under a light touch. The second method, called creaming, is standard procedure for butter cakes. Everyone knows the drill: You beat butter with sugar until light and fluffy, add eggs one at a time, and then stir in dry ingredients and milk or cream alternately.

But creaming is a nuisance when you want to whip up muffins for breakfast. It's a nuisance to soften butter and haul out a mixer. In side-by-side tests using the control recipe above, we got a firsthand taste of both methods. Had we been merely licking batter off our fingers, there would have been no contest. The creamed version was like a cake batter you could suck through a straw. But the two baked muffins were nearly identical. Though the mixed muffin was slightly squatter than its creamed companion, its texture was not inferior. We were pretty sure this was a technique we could work with—or around.

For flour we remained true to unbleached all-purpose. Cake flour produced a batter that was too light to hold the blueberries aloft. Bleached flour lacked the flavor spectrum of unbleached. We set off next in pursuit of the perfect amount of butter to turn out a moister, richer muffin, more like the tea cake our tasters had preferred. Increasing the butter in the control recipe simply weighed down the crumb without making the muffins any more moist. We also increased the liquid (we tested both milk and buttermilk) and added extra egg yolks. Neither approach brought improvement. When we substituted yogurt for milk, the muffins had the springiness of an old camp mattress.

Knowing that sour cream is often used in quick breads such as muffins, we decided to give it a try. At the same time, we wondered if the egg white protein from two eggs might be too much of the wrong type of liquid—adding structure rather than tenderness. Our new recipe, then, called for 1 egg, 1 cup sour cream, no milk, and only half a stick of butter. It was a great success—the muffin was tender and rich, and the sour cream played up to the blueberries' flavor. An additional ¼ cup sour cream made even nicer muffins.

Through additional testing, we discovered that this rather heavy batter required a full tablespoon of baking powder to rise and shine, but tasters noted no off chemical flavor. (When too much chemical leavener is used, the baked good puckery, flavorless fresh berries. In addition, the tiny wild berries distributed themselves in the batter nicely, like well-mannered guests, whereas the cultivated berries took the muffin by storm, leaving huge pockets of sour fruit pulp. So impressed were we by the superiority of the wild berries that we resolved to offer them top billing in the recipe. (You shouldn't have to be vacationing in Maine to make a decent blueberry muffin.) We came across one last trick. Frozen blueberries tend to be bleeders—and gummy when tossed with flour—so we discovered that they must remain completely frozen until stirred into the batter. The maximum amount of berries our batter could support was 1½ cups.

These were perfect workaday muffins, but we wanted to give them a chance to play dress-up, to be more like little cakes. With that in mind we considered a couple of options. A big fan of pebbly streusel topping dusted with confectioners' sugar, we picked up the recipe from our Dutch apple pie topping and pared it down to meet the demands of a dozen muffins. The streusel weighed heavily on the muffins and diminished their lift. Even after raising the oven temperature to 375 degrees (up from 350 degrees) and increasing baking time by five minutes, this topping was too heavy and too dry.

Our next topping idea came from Marion Cunningham's *Breakfast Book* (Knopf, 1987) in which she rolls whole baked muffins in melted butter and then dries them in cinnamon-sugar. The concept was a winning one. The melted butter seeped into the muffin's crown, the sugar stuck, and the muffin was transformed into a tender sugar-tufted pillow.

We also made a simple syrup glaze with lemon juice. Brushed on the muffin tops it made a nice adhesive for the granulated sugar (which we mixed with either finely grated lemon zest or fresh ginger). Finally, muffins to take to the ball.

often suffers from a bitter, soapy flavor.) Next, we refined the mixing method. Hoping to get more lift into the picture, we whisked the egg and sugar together by hand until the sugar began to dissolve, whisked in the melted butter, then the sour cream, and poured them into the dry ingredients. This method of mixing promised to deliver more air—and lift—to the egg, sugar, and butter. We folded everything together using the gentlest strokes possible. (We found that these muffins, like most others, become tough when overmixed.) This modified technique produced lovely muffins with a nice rise and beautifully domed crowns.

Until now, the major player in this muffin had been not only off-stage but out of season as well. Our winter testing left us with a choice between pricey fresh blueberries the size of marbles and tiny frozen wild berries. The flavor and sweetness of the frozen berries gave them a big edge over the

WHAT WE LEARNED: **You don't need to cream the butter and sugar together. Simply mix the dry ingredients in one bowl, the wet in another, and then combine. Sour cream makes muffins rich and tender, while frozen wild blueberries taste great and are just the right size for muffins.**

BLUEBERRY MUFFINS makes 12 muffins

When making the batter, be sure to whisk vigorously in step 2, then fold carefully in step 3. There should not be large pockets of flour in the finished batter, but small occasional sprays may remain.

2	cups (10 ounces) unbleached all-purpose flour
1	tablespoon baking powder
½	teaspoon salt
1	large egg
1	cup (7 ounces) sugar
4	tablespoons unsalted butter, melted and cooled slightly
1¼	cups (10 ounces) sour cream
1½	cups frozen blueberries, preferably wild

1. Adjust oven rack to middle position and heat oven to 350 degrees. Spray standard muffin tin with nonstick vegetable cooking spray.

2. Whisk flour, baking powder, and salt in medium bowl until combined. Whisk egg in second medium bowl until well-combined and light-colored, about 20 seconds. Add sugar and whisk vigorously until thick and homogenous, about 30 seconds; add melted butter in 2 or 3 additions, whisking to combine after each addition. Add sour cream in 2 additions, whisking just to combine.

3. Add frozen berries to dry ingredients and gently toss just to combine. Add sour cream mixture and fold with rubber spatula until batter comes together and berries are evenly distributed, 25 to 30 seconds. (Small spots of flour may remain and batter will be thick. Do not overmix.)

4. Use ice cream scoop or large spoon to drop batter into greased muffin tin. Bake until light golden brown and toothpick or skewer inserted into center of muffin comes out clean, 25 to 30 minutes, rotating pan from front to back halfway through baking time. Invert muffins onto wire rack,

TECHNIQUE: Portioning Batter

Use an ice cream scoop to portion batter into a muffin tin.

stand muffins upright, and cool 5 minutes. Serve as is or use one of the toppings below.

VARIATIONS

CINNAMON SUGAR–DIPPED BLUEBERRY MUFFINS

While muffins are cooling, mix ½ cup sugar and ½ teaspoon ground cinnamon in small bowl and melt 4 tablespoons butter in small saucepan. After baked muffins have cooled 5 minutes, and working one at a time, dip top of each muffin in melted butter and then cinnamon sugar. Set muffins upright on wire rack; serve.

GINGER- OR LEMON-GLAZED BLUEBERRY MUFFINS

While muffins are baking, mix 1 teaspoon grated fresh ginger or grated lemon zest and ½ cup sugar in small bowl. Bring ¼ cup lemon juice and ¼ cup sugar to simmer in small saucepan over medium heat; simmer until mixture is thick and syrupy and reduced to about 4 tablespoons. After baked muffins have cooled 5 minutes, brush tops with glaze, then, working one at a time, dip tops of muffins in lemon sugar or ginger sugar. Set muffins upright on wire rack; serve.

EQUIPMENT CORNER: Muffin Tins

THE MAJORITY OF MUFFIN TINS ON THE MARKET ARE MADE of coated aluminum and are lightweight. We purchased two tins of this type as well as two heavy-gauge "professional" aluminum tins and one "air-cushioned" aluminum tin. Three had a nonstick coating.

We baked up two different varieties of muffins to test the two things that really matter—browning and sticking. We wanted the muffins to brown uniformly and to be easily plucked from the tin. Corn muffins were ideal for the browning test, blueberry for the sticking test—no one wants a sweet, sticky berry left in the tin rather than the muffin.

Browning ended up being the deciding factor in these tests. Sticking was not an issue as long as the tins were sprayed with cooking oil. The best tins browned the muffins evenly, the worst browned them on the top but left them pallid and underbaked on the bottom. As we had observed in other bakeware tests, darker coated metals, which absorb heat, do the best job of browning baked goods. The air-cushioned tin produced pale muffins that were also small (the cushioning made for a smaller cup capacity, about ⅓ cup rather than the standard ½ cup).

We found the heavier-gauged aluminum tins to have no advantage—they are much more expensive than other tins, weigh twice as much, and do not produce superior muffins. Their heft may make them durable, but unless you bake commercially, the lightweight models will last a lifetime. The $5 Ekco Baker's Secret tin took top honors, besting tins that cost five times as much.

TASTING LAB: Butter

BUTTER IS A KEY INGREDIENT IN MUFFINS AND SCONES, and there's no reason you can't slather more butter over both when they come warm from the oven. For this purpose (and so many others), we wondered if the brand of butter makes a difference. To answer this question, we embarked on a two-month odyssey, testing eight brands of butter in six different applications. We tasted the butters plain (both at room temperature and melted), in pie crust, in yellow cake, in butter-cream frosting, and in sautéed turkey cutlets.

All butter must consist of at least 80 percent milk fat, according to U.S. Department of Agriculture standards. Most commercial butters do not exceed this. European butters and Hotel Bar's Plugrá are exceptions, with anywhere from 82 to 88 percent milk fat. All butters contain about 2 percent milk solids, and the remainder is water.

The results of our extensive testing were somewhat surprising. Although the two high-fat butters in the tasting (Plugrá and Celles Sur Belle, a French brand sold in many gourmet stores) performed well in most tests, they were not runaway winners. In fact, most tasters felt that all the cakes, pie crusts, and sautéed turkey cutlets tasted pretty much the same, no matter which brand of butter was used. Even tasted plain the results were fairly close.

One test did reveal some discernible differences. In a rich buttercream frosting made with softened butter, confectioners' sugar, and a little milk, the Plugrá was head and shoulders above the others for both a pleasant, delicate butter flavor and an airy texture. The other high-fat butter, Celles Sur Belle, scored well but was not judged to have as light a texture as the Plugrá. In this one instance, the butter is such an important ingredient and the recipe is so simple that a higher-fat butter created a noticeable difference in both flavor and texture.

Overall, however, we recommend that you pay more attention to the condition in which you buy the butter and the conditions under which you store it than to the particular brand. Throughout the testing, we ran across sticks of butter that were rancid or stale-tasting. We attributed these problems to improper shipping or poor storage at the market, not the manufacturer. We recommend that you purchase butter from a store that has a high turnover of products.

Butter can also spoil in your refrigerator, turning rancid from the oxidation of fatty acids. Exposure to air or light is particularly damaging, which explains why Land O'Lakes takes the precaution of wrapping its unsalted butter in foil. We find that the best way to store butter is sealed in an airtight plastic bag in your freezer, pulling out sticks as you need them. Butter will keep in the freezer for several months and in the refrigerator for no more than two to three weeks.

The fat in butter is vulnerable not only to oxidation but also to picking up odors. While butter is particularly susceptible at warmer temperatures, it can take on odors even when chilled or frozen. For this reason, we advise against storing butter in your refrigerator's butter compartment, which tends to be warmer because it's inside the door. To find out how much of a difference this made, we stored one stick of butter in its original wrapper in the butter compartment and one in the center of the refrigerator. After one week, the butter in the compartment had begun to pick up off flavors, while the one stored in the center still tasted fresh.

One final note about butter. We use unsalted butter in our test kitchen. We like its sweet, delicate flavor and prefer to add our own salt to recipes. We find that the quality of salted butter is often inferior and that each manufacturer adds a different amount of salt, which makes recipe writing difficult. While you can certainly get away with using salted butter in some savory recipes (as long as you adjust the total amount of salt in the recipe), we strongly recommend using unsalted butter when baking.

TASTING LAB: Store-Bought Muffins

1. STICKY SURFACE   2. MASHED BERRIES   3. ARTIFICIAL BERRIES   4. COARSE TEXURE   5. FLAT TOP

A lot can go wrong with blueberry muffins. Some problematic muffins we encountered in our testing, from left to right: (1) Cottony grocery-store muffins often have sticky, clammy tops. (2) Muffins made with mashed berries taste fine but look all wrong. (3) A quick packaged mix with artificial berries baked up into little hockey pucks. (4) This deli muffin is dry and coarse, with mushy, marble-sized blueberries. (5) If the muffin cups are overfilled with batter, the baked muffins will have flat tops.

SCONES

WHAT WE WANTED: Light, tender scones with a buttery flavor and gentle sweetness.

Scones, the quintessential tea cake of the British Isles, are delicate, fluffy biscuits, which may come as a surprise to Americans—the clunky mounds of oven-baked sweetened dough called rock cakes by the English are often called scones in our restaurants and coffee shops. Unlike rock cakes, in which dough is dropped from a spoon onto a baking sheet, traditional scones are quickly rolled or patted out and cut into rounds or wedges.

We started our testing by focusing on the flour. We made a composite recipe with bread flour, with all-purpose flour, and with cake flour. The differences in outcome were astonishing. The scones made with bread flour were heavy and tough. The scones made with all-purpose flour were lighter and much more flavorful. Cake flour produced scones that were doughy in the center, with a raw taste and poor texture. Subsequent tests revealed that a low-protein all-purpose flour, such as Gold Medal or Pillsbury, is better than a high-protein flour, such as King Arthur. (Lower-protein flours produce more tender baked goods.)

After trying scones made with butter and with lard, we decided we preferred the rich flavor of butter. (If we made scones commercially we might reconsider because day-old scones made with lard hold up better. The preservative effects of different fats, along with lower cost, may be why store-bought scones are often made with margarine or other hydrogenated fats.) We found that 5 tablespoons butter (a rather modest amount) to 2 cups flour was just right. More butter and the scones almost melted in the oven. Less butter and they baked up dry and tough.

The choice of liquid can also profoundly affect the flavor of a scone. We tested various liquids and found that cream made the best scones—tender and light. Scones made with milk were bland and dry. Buttermilk gave the scones plenty of flavor, but they were too flaky and biscuit-like. Scones made with cream were more moist and flavorful than any others.

We tried adding an egg and found that it made the scones cakey, more American-style than British. Because many tasters liked the scones made with egg and because egg helps the scones hold onto moisture and remain fresher longer, we decided to use one in a variation called Cakey Scones.

In traditional recipes, one to two tablespoons of sugar is enough to sweeten an entire batch of scones. American scones tend to be far sweeter than the British versions, which are usually sweetened with toppings such as jam. Americans seem to eat their scones like muffins, without anything more than a smear of butter, so the sweetness is baked in. We prefer the British approach but decided to increase the sugar slightly to 3 tablespoons.

Finally, scones are often glazed to enhance their appearance and add sweetness. We tried brushing the dough with a beaten egg as well as with heavy cream just before baking. Scones brushed with egg can become too dark in the oven. We preferred the more delicate look of scones brushed with cream and then dusted with a little granulated sugar.

Scones can be mixed by hand or with a food processor. (The processor is used to cut fat into flour; minimal hand mixing is required afterward.) We found the food processor to be more reliable than our hands, which would sometimes overheat the butter and cause it to soften. Once the dough comes together, we prefer to pat it into a cake pan, gently turn it out onto a floured surface, and then cut the dough into eight wedges. We found this method to be easier and more reliable than using a rolling pin.

WHAT WE LEARNED: All-purpose flour is a better choice than cake flour, cream adds richness and moisture, and butter is a must, but you don't need as much as you might think. For a texture that's more cakey than biscuit-like, add an egg.

CREAM SCONES makes 8

The easiest and most reliable approach to mixing the butter into the dry ingredients is to use a food processor fitted with a steel blade. Resist the urge to eat the scones hot out of the oven. Letting them cool for at least 10 minutes firms them up and improves their texture.

      2   cups (10 ounces) unbleached all-purpose flour,
          preferably a low-protein brand such as
          Gold Medal or Pillsbury
      1   tablespoon baking powder
      3   tablespoons sugar
     ½   teaspoon salt
      5   tablespoons chilled unsalted butter, cut into
          ¼-inch cubes
     ½   cup currants
      1   cup heavy cream

1. Adjust oven rack to middle position and heat oven to 425 degrees.

2. Place flour, baking powder, sugar, and salt in large bowl or workbowl of food processor fitted with steel blade. Whisk together or pulse six times.

3. *If making by hand,* use two knives, a pastry blender, or your fingertips and quickly cut in butter until mixture resembles coarse meal, with a few slightly larger butter lumps. Stir in currants. *If using food processor,* remove cover and distribute butter evenly over dry ingredients. Cover and pulse 12 times, each pulse lasting 1 second. Add currants and pulse one more time. Transfer dough to large bowl.

4. Stir in heavy cream with rubber spatula or fork until dough begins to form, about 30 seconds.

5. Transfer dough and all dry, floury bits to countertop and knead dough by hand just until it comes together into a rough, slightly sticky ball, 5 to 10 seconds. Following illustrations for Wedge Biscuits on page 209, cut scones into 8 wedges. Place wedges on ungreased baking sheet. (Baking sheet can be wrapped in plastic and refrigerated for up to 2 hours.)

6. Bake until scone tops are light brown, 12 to 15 minutes. Cool on wire rack for at least 10 minutes. Serve warm or at room temperature.

VARIATIONS

GLAZED SCONES
A light cream and sugar glaze gives scones an attractive sheen and sweeter flavor. If baking scones immediately after making the dough, brush the dough just before cutting it into wedges.

Follow recipe for Cream Scones, brushing tops of scones with 1 tablespoon heavy cream and then sprinkling with 1 tablespoon sugar just before baking them.

CAKEY SCONES
An egg changes the texture and color of the scones and helps them stay fresher longer, up to 2 days in an airtight container.

Follow recipe for Cream Scones, reducing butter to 4 tablespoons and cream to ¾ cup. Add 1 large egg, lightly beaten, to dough along with cream.

OATMEAL-RAISIN SCONES
Mix this dough in the food processor; the metal blade breaks down the coarse oats and incorporates them into the dough.

Follow recipe for Cream Scones, making dough in food processor and substituting 1 cup rolled oats for ½ cup all-purpose flour. Increase sugar to 4 tablespoons and butter to 6 tablespoons. Replace currants with ¾ cup raisins.

GINGER SCONES
Follow recipe for Cream Scones, substituting ½ cup chopped crystallized ginger for currants.

Breakfast Strata with Spinach and Gruyère page 262

Short Ribs Braised in Red Wine with Bacon, Parsnips, and Pearl Onions page 191

Cream Biscuits page 208

Garlic Mashed Potatoes page 195

Roast Fresh Ham page 204

Lemon-Glazed Blueberry Muffins page 220

Raspberry Squares page 270

Classic Apple Pie page 303

Kiwi, Raspberry, and Blueberry Tart page 284

Chocolate Cream Pie page 290

Free-Form Apple Tartlets page 307

Lattice-Top Fresh Peach Pie **page 313**

236

Rhubarb Fool page 333

237

Panna Cotta **page 328** with Raspberry Coulis **page 329**

Bittersweet Chocolate Roulade **page 341**

BACON, EGGS, &
home fries

Bacon, eggs, and potatoes are the classic components of an all-American breakfast. When the bacon is crisp, the omelet tender, and the home fries perfectly browned, this combination can be divine. But as anyone who eats in diners knows, this meal can fall far short of this ideal.

Every diner in America serves home fries, but the potatoes are rarely memorable. Home fries seem to fall into two categories—burnt and dry versus soft and mushy. Is it possible to brown the exterior of home fries while getting the interior tender and moist?

Bacon should be easy to cook—just heat until browned—but why is it so often brittle in some spots, raw in others? Is the microwave the solution to this problem, or does it make matters worse? We cooked up pounds and pounds of bacon to figure out a foolproof method.

A cheese omelet is a simple yet special way to enjoy eggs. But for a dish that requires nothing more than eggs, cheese, butter, salt, and pepper, lots can go wrong. The cheese sometimes leaks out of the omelet or, worse still, doesn't melt. The eggs can overcook and become tough. This dish requires perfect execution—but how to go about it?

Bridget is ready for Chris to roll a cheese omelet onto her plate. (She returns the favor on page 247.)

HOME FRIES

WHAT WE WANTED: Cubes of potatoes that would be deep golden brown and crisp on the outside and tender on the inside.

When we began trying to uncover the secret of the ultimate home fries, we went right to the source—to diners. But soon we learned that the problems with this dish are often the same, no matter where they are cooked and consumed. Frequently, the potatoes are not crisp, they are greasy, and the flavorings are either too bland or too spicy.

Our first step was to define home fries—individual pieces of potato cooked in fat in a frying pan on top of the stove and mixed with caramelized onions. We also knew what they should look and taste like: They should have a deep golden brown crust and a tender interior with a full potato flavor. The potatoes should not be greasy but instead feel crisp and moist in your mouth.

Although there are dozens of varieties, potatoes can be divided into three major categories based on their relative starch content. Experience has taught us that high-starch potatoes (like russets) make the best baked potatoes and French fries, while low-starch potatoes (all red-skinned and new potatoes) are the top choice for boiling, making salads, and roasting. Medium-starch potatoes (like all-purpose and Yukon Gold) can be roasted, baked, or mashed. Because the cooking method and the type of potato used are so intimately interconnected, we decided it made sense to try each cooking method with all three types of potatoes.

We knew the potatoes would end up in a skillet with fat, but would it be necessary to precook them, as our research suggested? We began testing with the simplest approach: dice them raw and cook them in a hot skillet with fat. But in test after test, no matter how small we cut them, it proved challenging to cook raw potatoes all the way through and obtain a crisp brown crust at the same time. Low temperatures helped cook the inside, but the outside didn't crisp. High temperatures crisped the outside, but the potatoes had to be taken off the heat so early to prevent scorching that the insides were left raw. We decided to precook the potatoes before trying them in a skillet.

Because a common approach to home fries is to use leftover baked potatoes, we baked some of each type, stored them in the refrigerator overnight, then diced them and put them in a skillet with fat. These tests were disappointing. None of the resulting home fries had a great potato flavor. They all tasted like leftovers, and their texture was somewhat gummy. The exterior of the red potatoes was not crisp, although they looked very good, and the starchier russet potatoes fell apart.

Next we tried starting with freshly boiled potatoes. Potatoes that were boiled until tender broke down in the skillet, and the inside was overcooked by the time the exterior was crisp. So we tried dicing and then braising the potatoes, figuring we could cook them through in a covered pan with some water and fat, remove the cover, let the water evaporate, and then crisp up the potatoes in the remaining fat. Although this sounded like a good idea, the potatoes stuck horribly to the skillet.

Finally, we considered a technique we found in Lydie Marshall's book *Passion for Potatoes* (HarperPerennial, 1992). Marshall instructs the cook to cover diced raw potatoes with water, bring the water to a boil, then immediately drain the potatoes well and sauté them. This treatment allows the potatoes to cook briefly without absorbing too much water, which is what makes them susceptible to overcooking and breaking down.

We tested this technique with russets, Red Bliss potatoes, and Yukon Golds. Eureka! It worked better with all three varieties of potato than any of the other methods we had tried. The Yukon Golds, though, were the clear favorite. Each individual piece of potato had a crisp exterior, and the inner flesh was tender, moist, and rich in potato flavor. The appearance of each was superior as well, the golden yellow color of the flesh complementing the crispy brown exterior. The russets were drier and not as full flavored but were preferred over the Red Bliss by all tasters. These potatoes were somewhat mushy and tasted disappointingly bland.

We decided to test another medium-starch potato. All-purpose potatoes also browned well and were tender and moist on the inside, but they lacked the rich buttery potato flavor and yellow color of the Yukon Golds, which remained the favorite.

Having discovered the ideal cooking method and the preferred potato variety, we moved on to the best way to cut the potatoes. We found sliced potatoes much harder to cook than diced ones. A pound of sliced potatoes stacks up three or four layers deep in a large skillet. The result is uneven cooking, with some slices burning and others remaining undercooked. Countless tests had convinced us that one of the keys to success

in cooking home fries is to cook the potatoes in a single layer. When a pound of potatoes is diced, one cut side of each potato piece can have contact with the skillet at all times. We tested dices of various size and found the ½-inch cube to be ideal: easy to turn and to eat, characterized by that pleasing combination of crispy outside and soft fleshy inside.

Deciding whether or not to peel the potatoes was easy. All tasters preferred the texture and flavor contributed by the skin. Leaving it on also saves time and effort.

Thus far we had determined that letting the potatoes sit undisturbed in hot fat to brown each side was critical to a crisp exterior. We found it best to let the potatoes brown undisturbed for four to five minutes before the first turn, then to turn them a total of three or four times. Three tablespoons turned out to be the ideal amount of fat for 1 pound of potatoes. When sampling potatoes cooked in different frying mediums, we found that a combination of butter and oil offered the best of both worlds, providing a buttery flavor with a decreased risk of burning (butter burns more easily than vegetable oils). Refined corn and peanut oils, with their nutty overtones, were our first choice.

Soft, sweet, and moist, onions are the perfect counterpoint to crispy potatoes, but we had to determine the best way to include them. Tests showed the easiest and most efficient way also produced the best results: Dice the onions and cook them before cooking the potatoes. More flavor can be added with help from parsley, red or green bell peppers (sautéed with the onion), or cayenne pepper, as you wish. Whatever your choice, these are going to be home fries worth staying home for.

WHAT WE LEARNED: Yukon Golds are the best-looking, best-tasting potatoes for home fries. To keep them from turning mushy when cooked, precook briefly in water, then fry. When frying, use butter for flavor and oil to lower the risk of burning.

DINER-STYLE HOME FRIES   serves 2 to 3

If you need to double this recipe, cook two batches of home fries separately. While making the second batch, keep the first batch hot and crisp by spreading the fries on a baking sheet placed in a 300-degree oven. The paprika adds a warm, deep color, but it can be omitted. An alternative is to toss in 1 tablespoon minced parsley just before serving the potatoes.

2½   tablespoons corn or peanut oil
1   medium onion, chopped small
1   pound (2 medium) Yukon Gold or all-purpose
      potatoes, scrubbed and cut into ½-inch cubes
1¼   teaspoon salt
1   tablespoon unsalted butter
1   teaspoon paprika
      Ground black pepper

1. Heat 1 tablespoon oil in 12-inch heavy-bottomed skillet over medium-high heat until hot but not smoking. Add onion and sauté, stirring frequently, until browned, 8 to 10 minutes. Transfer onion to small bowl and set aside.

2. Meanwhile, place diced potatoes in large saucepan, cover with ½ inch water, add 1 teaspoon salt, and place over high heat. As soon as water begins to boil, about 6 minutes, drain potatoes thoroughly in colander.

3. Heat butter and remaining 1½ tablespoons oil in now-empty skillet over medium-high heat until butter foams. Add potatoes and shake skillet to evenly distribute potatoes in single layer; make sure that one side of each piece is touching surface of skillet. Cook without stirring until one side of potatoes is golden brown on bottom, about 4 to 5 minutes, then carefully turn potatoes with wooden or heat-proof plastic spatula. Spread potatoes in single layer in skillet again and repeat process until potatoes are tender and browned on most sides, turning three or four times, 10 to 15 minutes longer. Add onions, paprika, remaining ¼ teaspoon salt, and pepper to taste; stir to blend and serve immediately.

EQUIPMENT CORNER: Colanders

A COLANDER IS ESSENTIALLY A PERFORATED BOWL designed to allow liquid to drain through the holes. It has many uses: draining potatoes, pasta, and more. In our initial survey of models, we were not surprised to find colanders made from a range of materials: plastic, enameled steel, stainless steel, anodized aluminum, and wire mesh (which is like a screen). What did surprise us was the range of prices. Who would have thought that you could drop almost $115 on a simple colander, especially in light of the price tag on the least expensive contestant, just $3.99? This made the idea of a test even more tantalizing.

As is our fashion in the test kitchen, we put the colanders through a battery of tests to obtain an objective assessment of their performance. We drained pounds and pounds of cooked spaghetti, orzo, and frozen baby peas in each one. Early in testing, we splashed scalding water and hot pasta out of a tiny 3-quart model by pouring it too fast from the cooking pot, so we eliminated that size from the running. The 5- and 7-quart models (10 altogether) performed on par, so we included both in our tests.

Most colanders on the market come with one of two types of bases, either a circular metal ring attached to the bottom, on which the bowl sits pedestal-style, or individual feet soldered to the bottom of the bowl. No matter which

BEST COLANDER
The Endurance Colander/Strainer has a meshlike perforated bowl that traps even the smallest bits of food.

type it is, the base should be unfailingly stable, to prevent spills. Our research and reading on colanders consistently noted the superiority of the ring over the feet, claiming that a colander on feet is less stable because it touches the ground in only three or four spots. That sounded like a reasonable theory to us until we tested the two models in the group with feet.

These colanders (the Endurance Stainless Steel Footed Colander and the Norpro Expanding Over-the-Sink Colander with Stand) were perfectly stable. During none of the tests did either one tip and spill its contents. (The Norpro can also be suspended between the sides of a sink by extending two metal arms. On our test kitchen sinks, this feature worked just fine, but on some sink designs this colander may be less stable.) In fact, the Endurance remained upright even when we accidentally bumped it with a heavy stockpot. Similarly, and as we expected, the eight colanders with ring bases also enjoyed total stability.

We also expected that the size, placement, and pattern of the drainage holes would be key for quick, efficient draining. Seven of our 10 colanders had the look we expected, that of a metal or plastic bowl with perforations arranged in straight lines, starbursts, or circles; the remaining three had more unusual designs. True to its name, the Endurance Colander/Strainer was a hybrid with a metal bowl that was

so thoroughly perforated it almost looked like wire mesh. Two other colanders, the Harold Imports and the Norpro expandable colander, were made from wire mesh, like a strainer. These three colanders had more holes than their more traditional counterparts, and each one performed very well, draining quickly and completely, with no pooling of water and no food—even the wily orzo—slipping through the holes. In truth, though, all of the other colanders also met—or came darn close to meeting—these standards. The traditional colanders with larger holes did allow some orzo to slip through (anywhere from just a few pieces for the Rösle to almost three-quarters of a cup for the Silverstone), but only the Silverstone allowed so much orzo through that it merited a downgrade in the ratings.

When all was said and drained, every colander in the group got the job done, be it the $4 Hoan plastic model or the gleaming $115 Rösle stainless steel model. To make a recommendation, then, we have to be a bit more subjective than usual. So here it is: Based on this testing and our gut feeling, the colander we'd most like to bring home is the Endurance Colander/Strainer. It's reasonably priced at $25, it's solid and comfortable to wield, it drains like a pro and keeps all its contents in check, and many editors here considered it to be an unusually handsome specimen of a colander. When it comes to this basic kitchen utensil, extra money is not well spent.

BACON

WHAT WE WANTED: Crisp, evenly cooked bacon with a minimum of mess and hassle.

Many home cooks now use the microwave to cook bacon, while others still fry bacon in a skillet. In restaurants, many chefs "fry" bacon in the oven. We decided to try each of these methods to find out which worked best.

For each cooking technique, we varied temperature, timing, and material, cooking both a typical store-bought bacon and a thick-cut mail-order bacon. The finished strips were compared in terms of flavor, texture, and appearance, while the techniques were compared for consistency, safety, and ease.

While the microwave would seem to have the apparent advantage of ease—stick the pieces in and forget about them—it turned out that this was not the case. Strips were still raw at 90 seconds; at two minutes they were medium-well-done in most spots, but still uneven; but by two minutes and 30 seconds the strips were hard and flat and definitely over-cooked. The finished product didn't warrant the investment of time it would take to figure out the perfect number of seconds. Microwaved bacon is not crisp, it is an unappetizing pink/gray in color even when well-done, and it lacks flavor.

The skillet made for a significantly better product. The bacon flavors were much more pronounced than in the nuked version, the finished color of the meat was a more appealing brick red, and the meat had a pleasing crispness. There were, however, a number of drawbacks to pan-frying. In addition to the functional problems of grease splatter and the number of 11-inch strips you can fit into a 12-inch round pan, there were problems of consistency and convenience. Because all of the heat comes from below the meat, the strips brown on one side before the other. Moreover, even when using a cast-iron pan, as we did, heat is not distributed perfectly evenly across the bottom of the pan. This means that to get consistently cooked strips of bacon you have to turn them over and rotate them in the pan. In addition, when more strips are added to an already-hot pan, they tend to wrinkle up, making for raw or burnt spots in the finished product.

The best results from stovetop cooking came when we lowered the heat from medium to medium-low, just hot enough to sizzle. The lower temperature allowed the strips to render their grease more slowly, with a lot less curling and spitting out of the pan. Of course, this added to cooking time, and it did not alleviate the need for vigilance.

Oven-frying seemed to combine the advantages of microwaving and pan-frying while eliminating most of the disadvantages. We tried cooking three strips in a preheated 400-degree oven on a 9 by 12-inch rimmed baking sheet that would contain the grease. Bacon was medium-well-done after 9 to 10 minutes and crispy after 11 to 12 minutes. The texture was more like a seared piece of meat than a brittle cracker, the color was that nice brick red, and all of the flavors were just as bright and clear as when pan-fried. Oven-frying also provided a greater margin of error when it came to timing than either of the other methods, and, surprisingly, it was just about as easy as microwaving, adding only the steps of preheating the oven and draining the cooked bacon on paper towels. Finally, the oven-fried strips of bacon were more consistently cooked throughout, showing no raw spots and requiring no turning.

Our last test was to try 12 strips of bacon—a pretty full tray—in a preheated oven. This test was also quite successful. The pieces cooked consistently, the only difference being between those in the back and those in the front of the oven; we corrected for this by rotating the tray once from front to back during cooking. That was about the limit of our contact with the hot grease.

WHAT WE LEARNED: For crisp, evenly cooked bacon that requires almost no attention, the oven is definitely the way to go.

OVEN-FRIED BACON *serves 4 to 6*

Use a large, rimmed baking sheet that is shallow enough to promote browning, yet tall enough (at least ¾ inch in height) to contain the rendered bacon fat. If cooking more than one tray of bacon, exchange their oven positions once about halfway through the cooking process.

12   slices bacon, thin- or thick-cut

Adjust oven rack to middle position and heat oven to 400 degrees. Arrange bacon slices in baking sheet or other shallow baking pan. Roast until fat begins to render, 5 to 6 minutes; rotate pan front to back. Continue roasting until bacon is crisp and brown, 5 to 6 minutes longer for thin-sliced bacon, 8 to 10 minutes for thick-cut. Transfer with tongs to paper towel–lined plate, drain, and serve.

TASTING LAB: Orange Juice

CAN ANYTHING RIVAL THE JUICE YOU SQUEEZE AT HOME? To find out, we gathered 34 tasters to evaluate 10 brands of supermarket orange juice as well as juice we squeezed in the test kitchen and juice fresh-squeezed at the supermarket.

Our top choice had been squeezed the day before at a local supermarket, closely followed by the juice we squeezed ourselves. Cartons of chilled not-from-concentrate juices took third and seventh places, with three brands of frozen concentrate squeezed in the middle. Chilled juices made from concentrate landed at the bottom of the rankings.

How could juice squeezed the day before at a supermarket beat out juice squeezed minutes before the tasting? And how could frozen concentrate beat out more expensive chilled juices from concentrate?

The produce manager at the store where we bought fresh-squeezed juice told us he blends oranges to produce good-tasting juice. This can be a real advantage, especially when compared with juice squeezed at home from one kind of orange. Any loss in freshness can be offset by the more complex and balanced flavor of a blended fresh juice, as was the case in our tasting.

Although no one was surprised that the two fresh juices took top honors, the strong showing of the frozen concentrates was a shock. It seems that frozen concentrate doesn't deserve its dowdy, old-fashioned reputation.

Why does juice made at home from frozen concentrate taste better than prepackaged chilled juice made from concentrate? Heat is the biggest enemy of orange juice. Frozen concentrates and chilled juices not made from concentrate are both pasteurized once at around 195 degrees to eliminate microorganisms and neutralize enzymes that will shorten shelf life. Chilled juices made from concentrate are pasteurized twice, once when the concentrate is made and again when the juice is reconstituted and packaged. This accounts for the lack of fresh-squeezed flavor in chilled juices made from concentrate.

CHEESE OMELET

WHAT WE WANTED: A foolproof method for cooking a cheese omelet with a tender, supple mouthfeel, a creamy interior filled with completely melted cheese, and no leaks.

Cheese omelets are fraught with problems. First and foremost is the issue of how to achieve perfect texture. Just a few seconds too long in the pan can turn an omelet from light, soft, and creamy to dark, tough, and rubbery. But you can't skimp too much on cooking time, either, because the cheese must melt completely before the omelet leaves the pan. And, speaking of cheese, we wanted to know if there was a way to make sure that none of that delicious filling would creep out of its egg casing during cooking.

Some initial tests convinced us about some basics. A good-quality, nonstick skillet with gently sloped sides is the superior implement for the production of a great omelet. We found that beating the eggs thoroughly ensures uniform texture for the exterior and interior of the omelet, a quality that is particularly important for filled omelets. We also concluded that the texture of an omelet is improved by stirring the eggs once they are in the pan; eggs cooked without stirring produced an uneven, loose omelet. Further testing confirmed that heavy cream, half-and-half, milk, and water all diffused the delicate flavor of the eggs and should not be added. Finally, we agreed that butter added rich flavor.

Now that we had the basics in hand, we set out to refine our technique. We began cooking three-egg cheddar omelets for anyone who came within range of the stove. Tasters liked best the omelets filled with 3 tablespoons of cheese. But with this large amount of cheese, we found that our trusty 8-inch skillet was no longer big enough. When we opted for a 10-inch skillet, the eggs spread out to a thinner shell that was much easier to wrap around the cheese.

We also discovered that merely folding or rolling the eggs around the cheese was insufficient to contain it. The cheese inevitably found a way out. The perfect method turned out to be the classic French style, in which a pan is titled and jerked to shape the omelet.

Even after making several omelets with this method, we noticed that they were all a little too well-done and brown. We played around with the idea of reducing the heat after the eggs set up, but we found it impractical to have to readjust the heat, especially on an electric stove. Eventually, we realized that every stove has one universal temperature setting: no heat. We started the omelet with the same technique that we had been using, but this time we turned the flame off completely, hoping that the residual heat in the pan would be sufficient to finish cooking the omelet.

Oddly enough, even with the flame off, the omelet colored a little too much. Next we tried taking the pan off the heat completely. This time the omelet was perfect. As it turns out, once the cheese has been added, the pan retains enough residual heat to continue cooking the omelet. This new method produced perfectly colored, blond omelets, no matter the stove, no matter the cook.

The on-burner, off-burner technique had one drawback. The cheese, which had melted perfectly until this point, now melted only partially. We hoped this could be remedied with a finer grating of cheese. We threw the box grater back in the drawer and pulled out the fine grater we often use for Parmesan. This time the cheese melted throughout.

It was now time to see which cheeses worked best in the omelet. Only the harder cheeses (Pecorino Romano, Asiago, Parmesan) failed to melt completely within the small window of time open to them. Many other cheeses worked well. The only rule of thumb is to use a cheese that can be grated.

WHAT WE LEARNED: Use a nonstick 10-inch pan, tilt and jerk the pan to enclose the cheese, and then finish cooking the omelet off heat to prevent toughening.

CHEESE OMELET serves 1

Making perfect omelets takes some practice, so don't be disappointed if your first effort fails to meet your expectations. For those times when a plain cheese omelet just won't do, we developed a few more substantial variations. Limit the amount of filling to a maximum of ¼ cup—anything more and the omelet will burst open. Just about any ingredient must be sautéed beforehand; the less-than-a-minute cooking time of the eggs is not sufficient to properly cook the filling. Be sure to prepare the filling before you begin making the omelet.

- 3 large eggs
  Salt and ground black pepper
- ½ tablespoon unsalted butter, plus melted butter for brushing on finished omelet
- 3 tablespoons very finely grated Gruyère, cheddar, Monterey Jack, or other cheese of your choice
- 1 recipe filling, optional (recipes follow)

1. Beat eggs and salt and pepper to taste with fork in small bowl until thoroughly combined.

2. Heat butter in 10-inch nonstick skillet over medium-high heat; when foaming subsides and butter just begins to color, pour in eggs. Cook until edges begin to set, 2 to 3 seconds, then, with rubber spatula, stir in circular motion until slightly thickened, about 10 seconds. Use spatula to pull cooked edges in toward center, then tilt pan to one side so that uncooked egg runs to edge of pan. Repeat until omelet is just set but still moist on surface, about 20 to 25 seconds. Sprinkle cheese and filling, if using, down center of omelet, perpendicular to handle of skillet.

3. Remove skillet from burner. Use rubber spatula to fold lower third (nearest you) of omelet to center; press gently with spatula to secure seams, maintaining fold.

4. Run spatula between outer edge of omelet and pan to loosen. Jerk pan sharply toward you a few times to slide omelet up far side of pan. Jerk pan again so that 2 inches of unfolded edge folds over itself, or use spatula to fold edge over. Invert omelet onto plate. Tidy edges with spatula, brush with melted butter, and serve.

SAUTÉED MUSHROOM FILLING WITH THYME makes about ½ cup, enough to fill 2 omelets

This filling is particularly good when paired with Gruyère.

Heat 1 tablespoon butter in medium skillet over medium heat until foaming; add 1 small shallot, minced (about 1 tablespoon), and cook until softened and just beginning to color, about 2 minutes. Add 2 medium white mushrooms (about 2 ounces), cleaned and sliced ¼ inch thick. Cook, stirring occasionally, until softened and lightly browned, about 3 minutes. Off heat, stir in 1 teaspoon fresh minced thyme leaves and salt and pepper to taste; transfer mixture to small bowl and set aside until ready to use.

SAUTÉED RED BELL PEPPER FILLING WITH MUSHROOM AND ONION makes about ½ cup, enough to fill 2 omelets

Monterey Jack is our choice of cheese for this filling.

Heat 1 tablespoon butter in medium skillet over medium heat until foaming; add ½ small onion, chopped fine, and cook, stirring occasionally, until softened but not browned, about 2 minutes. Add 1 medium white mushroom (about 1 ounce), cleaned and sliced ¼ inch thick. Cook, stirring occasionally, until softened and beginning to brown, about 2 minutes. Add ¼ red bell pepper (about 2 ounces), seeds discarded, cut into ½-inch dice; cook, stirring occasionally, until softened, about 2 minutes. Off heat, stir in 1 teaspoon minced fresh parsley leaves and salt and pepper to taste; transfer mixture to small bowl and set aside until ready to use.

After tasting nine brands of
maple syrup on as many waffles,
it's time to clean up.

FRENCH TOAST,
waffles, &
breakfast strata

Most people we know are passionate about breakfast, especially weekend breakfasts, when there's time for something other than a bowl of cold cereal or a slice of dry toast and juice. Because we get to eat a real breakfast so infrequently, we have high expectations when it comes to these classic dishes.

Soggy, overly eggy French toast simply won't do. Neither will rubbery, bland waffles. If you are going to spend the time making French toast and waffles, they better be good.

In addition to the right recipes, you need to think about equipment. Waffles require a good waffle iron, but they all look pretty much the same—how do you pick the best model? Some chefs swear by griddles for preparing French toast; can a skillet work just as well? We've tested these items and also rated the number one breakfast condiment—maple syrup. With the right tools and ingredients on hand, you can make a great breakfast, no matter how bleary-eyed you might be.

Sometimes it's nice to take a break from tradition. A breakfast strata—a savory bread pudding made with stale bread, cheese, eggs, and milk—is a good change of pace. All the ingredients are familiar, but the presentation and concept are fresh. Best of all, a strata is best assembled a day in advance, so you can sleep in on Sunday morning, pop the casserole dish in the oven when you wake up, and have a great breakfast on the table by the time you've read the morning paper.

IN THIS CHAPTER

THE RECIPES

French Toast for Challah or
    Sandwich Bread
French Toast for Firm European-
    Style Bread

Buttermilk Waffles
Almost-as-Good-as Buttermilk
    Waffles

Breakfast Strata with Spinach,
    Shallots, and Gruyère
Breakfast Strata with Sausage,
    Mushrooms, and Monterey Jack
Breakfast Strata with Potatoes,
    Rosemary, and Fontina

EQUIPMENT CORNER

Griddles
Refrigerators
Waffle Irons

SCIENCE DESK

Why Commercial Baking Powder
    Doesn't Work in Waffles

TASTING LAB

Maple Syrup

FRENCH TOAST

WHAT WE WANTED: French toast that's crisp on the outside and custardy on the inside. The toast shouldn't be too eggy, either.

F rench toast (or *pain perdu*, "lost bread") started out as a simple way to use up old bread by dipping it in a beaten egg and frying it. Many recipes today deviate little from this basic technique, calling for a couple of eggs and a touch of milk. What they produce, however, is a toast that tastes mostly of fried egg and that, depending on the amount of liquid, is either overly soggy or still dry in the middle.

We wanted something quite different: bread that was crisp and buttery on the outside, soft and custardlike inside. We wanted to taste a balance of flavors rather than just egg. We wanted our French toast to be sweet enough to eat with only a sprinkling of confectioners' sugar, but not so sweet that we couldn't top it with syrup or macerated fruit if we chose to.

We started testing with a simple formula: 2 eggs beaten with ½ cup milk to soak four slices of ¾-inch-thick, day-old French bread. From this starting point, we wanted to settle first on which bread works best for French toast, but that proved to be the hardest part of the testing. At first, it seemed simple. One-inch-thick slices of any sort of bread were too thick; they either soaked up too much liquid and didn't cook through, or they stayed dry in the middle with shorter soaking. So we stuck with ¾-inch slices and tried different kinds of bread: baguettes, supermarket breads, challah, brioche, and a dense white bread.

At the end of these tests, we thought we had the answer. Challah was clearly best, adding a lot of flavor and richness, staying generally crisp outside and somewhat moist inside—not perfect, but likely to improve with changes in the liquid component. Baguette slices and slices of a high-quality Italian bread, so long as they weren't more than a day old, came in second. Hard-to-find brioche was only acceptable.

Brioche can vary widely in quality, and the open-textured version we had failed to take up the liquid evenly. Dense white bread simply tasted like fried bread, so it rated near the bottom. Presliced sandwich bread was acceptable in a pinch, although just barely. Worst, though, was the supermarket bakery version of French or Italian bread. Spongy and flabby, this bread simply fell apart when we took it out of the liquid. For the moment, the bread issue seemed resolved. So, using challah for testing, we moved on to the liquids.

Because we didn't want our French toast to be too eggy, we first tried dropping one egg from the test recipe. That decision showed an immediate improvement, yielding a finished product that was crispier outside but still soft inside. To be sure that fewer eggs made for a better result, we tried going the opposite way, using 3 eggs to ½ cup milk. That confirmed it: More egg seemed to create a barrier on the outside of the bread, causing the interior to stay dry while the outside tasted like fried egg.

The next logical step seemed to be to increase the milk, given that a higher proportion of milk to egg had worked so far. A jump to 1 cup milk made the bread too wet inside, but it was better than ½ cup. Three-quarters cup

milk proved to be ideal, as the toast stayed custardlike inside and fairly crisp outside.

When we tried half-and-half instead, we could not discern enough difference in taste to warrant the additional grams of fat. Cream was certainly good, but after we added other flavorings to the basic recipe, we returned to milk, as the cream became too rich. A test with buttermilk, which we generally love, was awful, with a sharp, almost metallic edge.

Throughout our tests with egg and dairy, our basic recipe had tasted flat. We were looking forward to the final tests, when we would add other ingredients. We first tried salt, which gave the recipe a big boost: just ¼ teaspoon and the toast finally had some flavor. We added sugar next, which also made a great difference. At this point, 1 tablespoon seemed like a good amount for toast that would be covered with syrup; after making the recipe adjustments described below, though, we found that 2 tablespoons proved best. Finally, we added vanilla. Few recipes call for it, but 2 teaspoons really pulled things together, balancing the flavors.

At this point, we were ready to develop some variations on our basic recipe. We tried cinnamon, almond extract, and various liqueurs in place of the vanilla. The cinnamon and almond were nice alternatives, but the liqueurs were wholly unsuccessful.

After all this, we had a French toast that was better than any we could remember, yet still not ideal. It was fairly crisp, but not exactly what we were after: an almost deep-fried crispness. We knew the sugar helped, but there had to be something else. More butter in the skillet (until now we'd been using 1½ tablespoons for 4 pieces of bread) only made the challah greasier, and a heat level higher than medium to medium-high simply burned the toast. When one editor mentioned a French toast version she'd once had in which the bread was dipped in pancake batter, plus a recipe that called for a pinch of flour, it got us thinking about what flour could do. Ultimately, what it did was solve the puzzle.

At first we liked 1 tablespoon flour to help get the exterior extracrisp and not greasy, but in later tests we noticed that this made the toast somewhat soggy inside; yet when we went up to 2 tablespoons, the bread became tough. So we started trying more flour—but with butter added to keep the bread from toughening. After a few more tests, we finally had fabulous French toast: A batter with ⅓ cup flour balanced by 2 tablespoons melted butter gets the outside of the challah evenly crisped and brown and lets just enough moisture through to the interior to keep it custardlike but not heavy.

A few other tests answered some final questions. We tried cooking in all kinds of skillets and ended up liking cast iron best, with a regular (not nonstick) skillet a close second. Using medium heat with 1 tablespoon butter worked well with these skillets; nonstick skillets made the bread too greasy, even with less butter and other heat settings.

Unfortunately, our perfect French toast recipe worked wonders with challah but failed with chewy French and Italian breads. While we strongly recommend using challah if you can, we know it's less likely to be the day-old bread people have on hand. So we worked out a separate recipe for French and Italian breads, but we recommend it with a caveat: If you're using soft supermarket-style French bread or sliced white sandwich bread, go with the challah recipe.

With a chewier, drier French or Italian loaf, however, the high amount of flour in the batter used for challah prevented needed moisture from soaking into the bread. Also, the exterior had a harder time crisping because the rougher surface of this somewhat open-textured bread didn't make good contact with the pan. To get the interior moist, we tried dropping some of the flour; to get the exterior crisped, we again tried a two-egg recipe. Neither trick worked. In the end, more tests showed that the recipe needed even more milk for a custardlike interior and just 1 tablespoon of flour to aid in crisping; with this little flour, the batter needed no butter.

WHAT WE LEARNED: **Different breads require different kinds of custard. Challah makes the best French toast, but crusty French or Italian bread can be used as well as sandwich bread in a pinch. Use plenty of milk to keep the French toast from tasting too eggy; add flour to crisp the exterior of the toast and melted butter to keep the interior tender.**

FRENCH TOAST FOR CHALLAH OR SANDWICH BREAD
makes 4 or 5 slices from challah or 6 to 8 slices from sandwich bread

Though thick-sliced challah is best for French toast, you can substitute high-quality, presliced sandwich bread. Flipping challah is easiest with tongs, but a spatula works best with sandwich bread. To speed the cooking of large quantities of French toast, heat two or more skillets to brown a few batches at once. To vary the flavor of the batter, try adding ¾ teaspoon ground cinnamon or ½ teaspoon ground nutmeg with the dry ingredients, or try substituting almond extract for the vanilla extract.

- 1 large egg
- 2 tablespoons unsalted butter, melted, plus extra for frying
- ¾ cup milk
- 2 teaspoons vanilla extract
- 2 tablespoons sugar
- ⅓ cup all-purpose flour
- ¼ teaspoon salt
- 4–5 slices day-old challah, cut ¾ inch thick, or 6 to 8 slices day-old sandwich bread

1. Heat 10- to 12-inch skillet (preferably cast iron) over medium heat for 5 minutes. Meanwhile, beat egg lightly in shallow pan or pie plate; whisk in butter, then milk and vanilla, and finally sugar, flour, and salt, continuing to whisk until smooth. Soak bread without oversaturating, about 40 seconds per side for challah or 30 seconds per side for sandwich bread. Pick up bread and allow excess batter to drip off; repeat with remaining slices.

2. Swirl 1 tablespoon butter in hot skillet. Transfer prepared bread to skillet; cook until golden brown, about 1 minute 45 seconds on first side and 1 minute on second side. Serve immediately. Continue, adding 1 tablespoon butter to skillet for each new batch.

FRENCH TOAST FOR FIRM EUROPEAN-STYLE BREAD
makes 4 or 8 slices, depending on the loaf

This recipe has less flour, allowing the batter to penetrate more easily into drier, chewier French or Italian loaves.

- 1 large egg
- 1 cup milk
- 2 teaspoons vanilla extract
- 2 tablespoons sugar
- 1 tablespoon all-purpose flour
- ¼ teaspoon salt
- 4–8 slices firm, day-old European-style bread, such as French or Italian, ¾ inch thick
  Unsalted butter to grease skillet (about 1 tablespoon per batch)

1. Heat 10- to 12-inch skillet (preferably cast iron) over medium heat for 5 minutes. Meanwhile, beat egg lightly in shallow pan or pie plate; whisk in milk and vanilla, and then sugar, flour, and salt, continuing to whisk until smooth. Soak bread without oversaturating, about 30 seconds per side. Pick up bread and allow excess batter to drip off; repeat with remaining slices.

2. Swirl 1 tablespoon butter in hot skillet. Transfer prepared bread to skillet; cook until golden brown, about 2 minutes on first side and 1 minute and 15 seconds on the second. Serve immediately. Continue, adding 1 tablespoon butter to skillet for each new batch.

EQUIPMENT CORNER: Griddles

YOU JUST CAN'T MAKE A LOT OF FRENCH TOAST AT THE same time in a skillet, so we decided to test griddles, which have a much larger surface area, to see what they could do.

First we checked out four nonstick electric griddles. We preheated each to 400 degrees, gave it a coating of butter, and added as many batter-dipped bread slices as would comfortably fit. All four electric griddles accommodated between seven and nine slices of challah French toast, versus only two in the cast-iron skillet, but none was able to produce the crustiness we were after. Some browned a little more evenly than others, but even the best of them had cool spots around the edges or corners, perhaps because a single heating coil runs beneath the cooking surface.

We next tested a stove-top cast-iron griddle that spans two burners. We heated it up over medium heat, coated the surface with butter, and placed six slices of bread on top to cook. As we expected, the slices that rested on the center surface of the griddle, with no burner underneath, failed to brown at all. Hence, we were able to successfully make only four slices of French toast. These four slices, however, did have the crispy crust that we were looking for.

After all this testing, we concluded that our hands-down preference for making French toast was still the cast-iron skillet, even if it means making slices continuously as people eat them.

EQUIPMENT CORNER: Refrigerators

ALTHOUGH WE DON'T OFTEN THINK ABOUT IT, EVERY refrigerator has hot and cold spots. Together they create a complex food storage matrix inside a basic three-shelf refrigerator. You can make the temperature flux in your refrigerator work to your advantage by learning where these hot and cold spots are located.

We spoke with several refrigeration experts about hot and cold spots, and the information we gathered was consistent. To verify this data in the real world, we hooked up a test kitchen refrigerator to a piece of equipment called a chart scan data recorder. The recorder was connected to a laptop computer as well as several temperature monitors placed in strategic locations on the shelves and drawers inside the refrigerator. The refrigerator was then closed and left undisturbed for 24 hours while the interior temperatures were monitored and recorded.

Keeping in mind that a refrigerator goes through many cooling cycles throughout a 24-hour period (that is, at times the temperature may be well above or below 34 degrees Fahrenheit, the optimal temperature for a home refrigerator), our results provided some interesting information. For example, the butter compartment was not the warmest spot in the fridge, as we had expected, although it wasn't very cold either. Instead, the middle shelf on the door and front portion of the bottom cabinet shelf registered the highest readings—all the way up to 43 degrees. Not a place where you would want to store your milk or eggs, both of which should be kept below 40 degrees.

The meat compartment remained the coolest area of the refrigerator (on average, 33 degrees), making it perfect for storing what it is supposed to store: meat. Other cool spots included the back of the top, middle, and bottom shelves, as well as the bottom compartment on the refrigerator drawer. The crisper drawer was moderate-to-cool, making it an ideal place to keep vegetables, which should stay well above the 32-degree mark.

WAFFLES

WHAT WE WANTED: A waffle with a crisp, well-browned exterior and a moist, fluffy interior. It should be like a rich, just-cooked soufflé encased in a flavorful crust.

After testing more than 15 recipes, we realized that our ideal waffle requires a thick batter, so the outside can become crisp while the inside remains custardy. We also learned that a good waffle must be quickly cooked; slow cooking evens out the cooking rate, causing the center to overcook by the time the exterior is crisp and brown.

Many waffle batters are too thin, usually because the proportion of milk to flour—at 1 cup each—is too high. Such thin batter results in disappointing, gummy-textured waffles with dry, unappealing interiors. We found that ⅞ cup buttermilk, or ¾ cup regular milk, to 1 cup flour is a far better proportion.

Most recipes omit buttermilk entirely or, at best, list it as an option. Yet we found that buttermilk is absolutely crucial. Why? Because buttermilk, when teamed up with baking soda, creates a much thicker batter than the alternative, regular milk paired with baking powder. We eventually found a way to make good waffles with regular milk (reduce the amount of liquid and use homemade baking powder for a thicker batter), but buttermilk waffles will always taste better.

Although many recipes for buttermilk waffles call for baking powder, it's not necessary. All that's required is baking soda, which reacts with the acid in the buttermilk to give the batter lift. Baking powder is essentially baking soda plus cream of tartar, an acidic ingredient. Baking powder is useful when the batter itself contains no other source of acid. We eliminated the baking powder from our working recipe and found not only that it wasn't necessary but that it wasn't all that helpful; these waffles cooked up crispier. Out of curiosity, we also tried to make a waffle with buttermilk and baking powder, eliminating the baking soda. The waffle was inedible. (See the Science Desk on page 258 for more information on how baking powder and soda work.)

Some waffle recipes call for separating the egg and then whipping the white and folding it into the mixed batter. We made waffles this way and found that folding in beaten egg whites improves things. The batter is glossier, and the waffle is fluffier inside. If you cut through a cooked waffle made with beaten egg whites, you can actually see pockets of air trapped inside. The same examination of a whole-egg waffle revealed a flatter, more consistent texture.

Look at a number of waffle recipes and you'll see a wide range of recommendations as to how to combine ingredients. But most have this in common: They add all of the liquid ingredients at once. This practice necessitates overmixing and usually results in clumps of unmoistened flour. When we used a whisk to combine the ingredients until they were smooth, the batter was thin and the waffle tough.

The objective is to moisten the flour thoroughly, not to create a smooth batter, and for this there is no question that a gentle hand is crucial. This is the technique that worked best for us: Pour the liquid ingredients into the dry ingredients very slowly, mixing gently with a rubber spatula. When most of the liquid has been added, the batter becomes thicker; switch to a folding motion, similar to that used in folding egg whites, to finally combine and moisten the batter. Then continue folding as you add the beaten egg white.

When you bake waffles, remember that darker waffles are better than lighter ones. The browning reaction promotes the development of flavor. Waffles should be cooked until medium-brown, not lightly tanned. Toasty brown waffles will also stay crispier longer than manila-colored waffles, which are likely to become soggy by the time they get to the table.

WHAT WE LEARNED: More flour than liquid creates a thick batter that makes waffles crisp on the outside and moist on the inside. Buttermilk provides the best flavor, and whipping the egg white makes waffles lighter.

BUTTERMILK WAFFLES makes 3 to 4, depending on size of waffle iron

The secret to great waffles is a thick batter, so don't expect a pourable batter. The optional dash of cornmeal adds a pleasant crunch to the finished waffle. This recipe can be doubled or tripled. Make toaster waffles out of leftover batter—undercook the waffles a bit, cool them on a wire rack, wrap them in plastic wrap, and freeze. Pop them in the toaster for a quick breakfast.

    1   cup (5 ounces) unbleached all-purpose flour
    1   tablespoon cornmeal (optional)
    ½   teaspoon salt
    ¼   teaspoon baking soda
    1   large egg, separated
    ⅞   cup buttermilk
    2   tablespoons unsalted butter, melted and cooled

1. Heat waffle iron. Whisk dry ingredients together in medium bowl. Whisk yolk with buttermilk and butter.

2. Beat egg white until it just holds a 2-inch peak.

3. Add liquid ingredients to dry ingredients in thin, steady stream while mixing gently with rubber spatula. (Do not add liquid faster than you can incorporate it into batter.) Toward end of mixing, use folding motion to incorporate ingredients. Gently fold egg white into batter.

4. Spread appropriate amount of batter onto waffle iron. Following manufacturer's instructions, cook waffle until golden brown, 2 to 5 minutes. Serve immediately. (In a pinch, you can keep waffles warm on wire rack in 200-degree oven for up to 5 minutes.)

VARIATION

ALMOST-AS-GOOD-AS BUTTERMILK WAFFLES makes 3 or 4

If you're out of buttermilk, try this variation with milk. By making your own baking powder (using baking soda and cream of tartar; see the Science Desk on page 258) and by cutting back on the quantity of milk, you can make a thick, quite respectable batter. The result is a waffle with a crisp crust and moist interior.

Follow recipe for Buttermilk Waffles, adding ½ teaspoon cream of tartar to dry ingredients and substituting scant ¾ cup milk for buttermilk.

EQUIPMENT CORNER: Waffle Irons

NO MATTER HOW FOOLPROOF THE RECIPE, ALL WAFFLES will be rubbery and flaccid if cooked in the wrong waffle iron. To find out which waffle irons work the best, we gathered six traditional (not Belgian) waffle makers, with prices ranging from $20 to $50. We narrowed our selection to include only round models, as they account for 60 percent of waffle iron sales.

The differences in brands were dramatic. The top-rated models turned out crisp, well-browned waffles in just three minutes. The worst models produced rubbery or hard waffles that took nearly twice as long to cook.

What makes the difference? The critical issue is how hot the waffle iron can get. We tested each waffle maker with an infrared thermometer, measuring the temperature of each quadrant and then averaging the results for each machine. The models producing the rubbery waffles had an average temperature of 330 degrees, while the highly rated models averaged 380 degrees. That difference is enough to sear and crisp the exterior without drying out the interior. The weaker models didn't have enough heat to set up the contrasting textures—crisp on the outside, creamy in the middle—that we wanted.

All models tested had lights indicating when the iron was ready to use, but many of these lights were inconveniently placed and difficult to see. Only a few models also had a "done" light, indicating when the waffles were fully cooked. This feature effectively eliminated all guesswork—

simply set the degree of doneness, and voilà, a perfectly browned, crisp waffle.

Our favorite waffle irons were the Farberware Millennium Deluxe ($30) and the Cuisinart Classic Round ($50). The Villaware Perfect Waffler ($40) also received high marks, but testers soon wearied of the piercing chirp this model emitted when the waffles were done.

SCIENCE DESK: Why Commercial Baking Powder Doesn't Work in Waffles

BAKING POWDER IS MADE FROM TWO MAJOR ELEMENTS: an acid (such as cream of tartar) and baking soda. A batter made with regular milk, for example, instead of with an acidic ingredient such as yogurt or buttermilk, will not rise without the help of the acid in baking powder. Baking powder is used in place of baking soda when there is no natural acidity in the batter.

When baking soda comes in contact with a moist, acidic environment, carbon dioxide gas is produced, which in turn provides "rise." This chemical reaction is quite pronounced in a buttermilk batter—buttermilk contains lactic acid, which reacts strongly with the soda, generating a thick, spongy batter in seconds.

The reaction between regular milk and baking powder isn't as strong, so the batter remains thin. This is partially because most baking powder is "double acting"—that is, it produces a rise once at room temperature, when added to the batter, and once in the oven, when the temperature climbs above 120 degrees. Baking powder is designed to create gas slowly, so that a cake, for example, will have plenty of time to rise in the oven before the bubbles dissipate and the cake sets.

In our tests, it was clear that most of the rise with baking powder occurs at oven temperature. Since waffles are cooked so quickly, baking powder is not ideally suited to this type of batter; the amount of "room-temperature" acid it can provide is insufficient. With waffles you want a lot of room-temperature reaction, and therefore it's best, when using regular milk instead of buttermilk, to make your own recipe for baking powder, using cream of tartar (which works at room temperature) and baking soda.

TASTING LAB: Maple Syrup

WHAT ARE WAFFLES OR FRENCH TOAST (OR PANCAKES FOR that matter) without maple syrup? We wondered how the consumer should buy maple syrup. By grade? By source (is Vermont syrup really better than the rest)? We also wondered if any of the pancake syrups—those supermarkets staples made with a tiny percentage of maple syrup—were demonstratively better than their peers.

In general, a maple syrup's grade is determined by the period during which it was made (the sugaring season lasts from February to early April). Technically, the grades of maple syrup are measured by the amount of light that can pass through the syrup. Straight from the tree, maple sap is clear, consisting of about 98 percent water and 2 percent sugar. To make maple syrup, the water has to be boiled off to a concentration of 66 percent sugar. (This means boiling off about 39 gallons of water to get one gallon of syrup.)

Early in the season, maple syrups tend to be near-transparent because the sugar molecules in the boiled-down sap are able to reflect much light. As temperatures warm outside, wild yeasts in the sap begin feeding on and breaking down the sugar. As a result, light can be absorbed. So as the season progresses, the syrup darkens.

This breakdown of sugar also affects flavor. If maple sap is concentrated without boiling (by freeze-drying, for example), the syrup will taste sweet but otherwise have little flavor. The flavor we perceive as "maple" is actually the result of chemical reactions that occur when the sap is boiled. One of the two primary flavor notes is derived from the compounds that form when sugar molecules break down. The process is similar to caramelization. This may explain why the darker syrups produced later in the season have more of the caramel notes distinct to maple syrup. The second flavor

price was established more than 100 years ago, when "sugaring" was about just that—turning maple syrup into sugar. The lighter syrup made a finer sugar that could be sold at a higher cost, which simply never changed. Today Grade A light syrups are primarily used to make maple sugar candies.

The season's second syrup is Grade A medium amber. This has a warmer caramel color with a medium-strength flavor. It is generally touted as the syrup for pancakes. Right on the heels of medium amber is Grade A dark amber, which is slightly deeper in color and has a more pronounced flavor.

After the ambers falls Grade B, the darkest and typically least expensive of the syrups on the market. It is traditionally considered cooking grade because of its strength of flavor. Only Vermont makes Grade B syrup for consumer table use. Other states make a similar syrup but sell it only in bulk to the food industry because it is deemed too strong and too dark. Some natural foods stores carry it in bulk.

Last, there is a Grade C, characterized by strong, almost molasses-like flavor. It is sold only to the food industry.

Of the nine samples in our tasting, tasters decided that if they had the choice, they would reach for the Vermont "B" syrup to drizzle on their pancakes. Most tasters were won over by the depth of flavor and the dark rum color of the syrup. Many wrote comments such as "tastes real." And, unlike many of the syrups, which lost their distinction when poured on a waffle, this one's bold characteristics held up.

The close runner-up in our tasting was a Grade A dark amber. Overall, tasters preferred the dark amber syrups to the medium ambers, which failed to spark tasters' interest, apparently because they were not bold enough. Not surprisingly, then, tasters flat-out rejected the one "Fancy" grade syrup we included in the tasting. None of our results indicated syrup made from one region or state is superior to another, and industry experts agree that it is difficult, if not impossible, to determine by taste where a syrup is made.

Because pancake syrups far outsell real maple syrups, we decided to do an additional tasting of the three top-selling national pancake syrups. The high scorer was Aunt Jemima, which is made of high fructose corn syrup.

note is vanilla, which is produced from compounds in the sap that the tree uses to make wood.

While vanilla and caramel are essential maple flavor elements, the full flavor of maple is far more complex. One producer's syrup can vary from a neighbor's because of differences in the soil, the tree chemistry, or the method of heating the sap.

The season's earliest sap flow produces Grade A light, or "Fancy," as it is called in Vermont. Honey gold and near-transparent, it has a pronounced sweetness and a delicate vanilla flavor. Grade A light can be the most expensive syrup and is not typically found in supermarkets. While it takes no more energy to produce than the other grades, its higher

BREAKFAST STRATA

WHAT WE WANTED: A hearty breakfast casserole with bread, eggs, milk, and cheese—basically a savory bread pudding—that is puffed and golden.

What's quicker than quiche, sturdier than soufflé, and combines the best qualities of both? The answer is strata, a layered casserole that, in its most basic form, comprises bread, eggs, cheese, and milk or cream. Layered among them are flavorful fillings that provide both substance and character, and the result is essentially a golden brown, puffed, hearty, savory bread pudding. Strata is easy to prepare, can be made ahead, and feeds a crowd for breakfast or brunch.

But strata is not without its issues. First, it is easy to go overboard with too much of a good thing. Many of the stratas we sampled in the test kitchen to kick off the recipe development process were simply too rich for breakfast, with a belly-busting overabundance of custard. Strata is breakfast food, so it should fill you up without making you feel sick or lazy for the rest of the day. The bread should neither call attention to itself nor get lost among the other ingredients. And then there are the fillings. In our experience, strata often suffers from largesse, with recipes adding as many fillings as they can possibly squeeze in. This everything-but-the-kitchen-sink approach leads to wet, sagging, overwrought stratas, like one we sampled early on that included mustard, garlic, nutmeg, marinated artichoke hearts, raw green peppers, cherry tomatoes, ham, Parmesan, fontina, and goat cheese. Such overindulgence not only sends unlucky diners scrambling for Maalox but also turns a simple, workhorse dish into a parody of itself. A good strata should have a restrained filling with a couple of components chosen to accent the bread, custard, and cheese.

In essence, then, we wanted to scale strata back, keeping it just rich enough and choosing fillings that would add to the picture without stealing the show. We also wanted a cohesive casserole rather than a bunch of stray ingredients baked together in a pan. All the principal aspects of the dish—custard, bread, and fillings, and how and when they were assembled and cooked—were open to inspection.

Bread is the foundation of strata. Though sliced white sandwich bread was the type specified in most recipes, we also saw calls for Italian, French, sourdough, multigrain, rye, pumpernickel, challah, focaccia, and even hamburger and hot dog buns. We tried them all, and tasters preferred supermarket Italian and French breads for their strong crumb and neutral flavor. Since tasters had no objection to the crust, we left it in place. Also, while many recipes specify cubes of bread, we preferred slices because they added to the layered effect of the casserole. The slices were best at about ½-inch thick, as thicker slices remained too chewy and really thin ones just melted away. We also learned that the texture of stale bread (or fresh bread dried briefly in the oven) was preferable to that of fresh and that we appreciated the richness and flavor added by a little butter on the slices.

The tender custard that binds the bread was our other major target. In a battery of custard tests, tasters' preferences were divided between mixtures with equal parts dairy and egg and those with twice as much dairy as egg. The solution was to meet in the middle, adding just a little extra dairy to the 50/50 mixture. Along the way, we also tested different dairy products. Recipes commonly call for low-fat or whole milk or half-and-half and sometimes even heavy cream (usually in combination with another dairy liquid). We tried each one of these alone and in every conceivable combination, and most tasters preferred half-and-half on its own. The last adjustment we made to the custard was its overall quantity, which for many tasters was too little, making for a dry strata. Increasing the ratio of custard to bread made the strata more moist and cohesive.

Though our basic strata was very good, it's the flavorings and fillings that catapult it to glory. As a basic flavoring, sautéed shallots won over onions and garlic. We had a surprise in store when we tested another flavoring common to strata recipes, namely, white wine. It showed promise, lightening the flavor of the whole dish. But it also imparted a boozy flavor that was out of place. We corrected this problem by reducing the wine to cook off the alcohol and concentrate the flavor. This eliminated the alcoholic overtones, and the reduced wine brightened the flavor of the whole dish considerably.

One last observation we can offer about the most basic seasonings, salt and pepper: A heavy hand is best. Strata required a generous dose of each, and seasoning both custard and filling individually and liberally was the most effective way to bring all the flavors into focus.

Even with the right basic ingredients in the right proportions, test after test proved that high-moisture fillings such as sausage and raw vegetables ruined the strata's texture. Their moisture leached into the casserole, leaving it wet enough to literally slosh and ooze when cut. To correct this problem, we took to sautéing all filling ingredients until they looked dry in the pan. This step saved the day by evaporating moisture that would otherwise end up in the strata. Whatever your filling choice, this critical step will make the difference between a moist, tender dish and one that's more like a sopping-wet sponge mop.

One of strata's charms is that it can—in fact, most recipes claim it should—be assembled well ahead of time. We tested stratas that had been assembled and rested overnight for four hours, for one hour, and one that had not been rested at all. Only the fresh-made strata, which was noticeably less cohesive than the rested versions, failed to make the cut. Otherwise, there wasn't much difference between them in texture. So you can give it the rest that fits your schedule best, anywhere from one hour to overnight.

A test kitchen colleague suggested weighing down the assembled strata during its rest, and this step had a dramatic effect. Without exception, the weighted stratas had a perfectly even, custardy texture throughout. In stratas rested without the weight, we were apt to encounter a bite of bread that had not been fully penetrated with custard.

In the oven, we found that a wide, shallow baking dish allowed the strata to bake much more evenly than the deep soufflé dish recommended in many recipes. Lowering the baking temperature from the widely recommended 350 degrees to 325 was another tactic we adopted to even out the cooking.

Cooking the strata until the top was crisp and golden brown was a common recommendation, but we found that this usually overcooked the interior, leaving it too firm, even a bit rubbery. Instead, we found it best to remove the strata from the oven when the top was just beginning to brown and the center was barely puffed and still slightly loose when the pan was jiggled gently. Though we wondered if the strata was cooked through, with just a five-minute rest it not only cooled enough to eat without burning our throats on the way down, but the center finished cooking from residual heat, reaching the perfectly set, supple texture we prized.

WHAT WE LEARNED: Use stale Italian or French bread, make the custard with half-and-half and eggs, and sauté all filling ingredients to remove excess water. For a cohesive texture, assemble the strata in advance and weight the top while it rests before baking.

BREAKFAST STRATA WITH SPINACH
AND GRUYÈRE   Makes one 8 by 8-inch strata, serving 6

To weigh down the assembled strata, use two 1-pound boxes of brown or powdered sugar, laid side by side over the plastic-covered surface. To double this recipe or those that follow, use a 9 by 13-inch baking dish greased with only 1½ tablespoons butter and increase baking times as suggested in each recipe.

8–10   (½-inch thick) slices supermarket French or
      Italian bread (6–7 ounces)
   5   tablespoons unsalted butter, softened
   4   medium shallots, minced (about ½ cup)
   1   (10-ounce) package frozen chopped spinach,
      thawed and squeezed dry
      Salt and ground black pepper
  ½   cup medium-dry white wine, such as
      Sauvignon Blanc
   6   ounces Gruyère cheese, grated (about 1½ cups)
   6   large eggs
1¾   cups half-and-half

1. Adjust oven rack to middle position and heat oven to 225 degrees. Arrange bread in single layer on large baking sheet and bake until dry and crisp, about 40 minutes, turning slices over halfway through drying time. (Alternatively, leave slices out overnight to dry.) When cooled, butter slices on one side with 2 tablespoons butter; set aside.

2. Heat 2 tablespoons butter in medium nonstick skillet over medium heat. Sauté shallots until fragrant and translucent, about 3 minutes; add spinach and salt and pepper to taste and cook, stirring occasionally, until combined, about 2 minutes. Transfer to medium bowl; set aside. Add wine to skillet, increase heat to medium-high, and simmer until reduced to ¼ cup, 2 to 3 minutes; set aside.

3. Butter 8-inch square baking dish with remaining 1 tablespoon butter; arrange half of buttered bread slices, buttered-side up, in single layer in dish. Sprinkle half of spinach

mixture, then ½ cup grated cheese evenly over bread slices. Arrange remaining bread slices in single layer over cheese; sprinkle remaining spinach mixture and another ½ cup cheese evenly over bread. Whisk eggs in medium bowl until combined; whisk in reduced wine, half-and-half, 1 teaspoon salt, and pepper to taste. Pour egg mixture evenly over bread layers; cover surface flush with plastic wrap, weigh down (see note), and refrigerate at least 1 hour or up to overnight.

4. Remove dish from refrigerator and let stand at room temperature 20 minutes. Meanwhile, adjust oven rack to middle position and heat oven to 325 degrees. Uncover strata and sprinkle remaining ½ cup cheese evenly over surface; bake until both edges and center are puffed and edges have pulled away slightly from sides of dish, 50 to 55 minutes (or about 60 minutes for doubled recipe). Cool on wire rack 5 minutes; serve.

VARIATIONS
BREAKFAST STRATA WITH SAUSAGE,
MUSHROOMS, AND MONTEREY JACK

8–10   (½-inch thick) slices supermarket French
      or Italian bread (6–7 ounces)
   3   tablespoons unsalted butter, softened
   8   ounces bulk breakfast sausage, crumbled
   3   medium shallots, minced (about ⅓ cup)
   8   ounces white button mushrooms, cleaned
      and quartered
      Salt and ground black pepper
  ½   cup medium-dry white wine, such as
      Sauvignon Blanc
   6   ounces Monterey Jack cheese, grated
      (about 1½ cups)
   6   large eggs
1¾   cups half-and-half
   2   tablespoons minced fresh parsley leaves

Follow recipe for Breakfast Strata with Spinach and Gruyère through step 1. Fry sausage in medium nonstick skillet over medium heat, breaking sausage apart with wooden spoon, until it loses raw color and begins to brown, about 4 minutes; add shallots and cook, stirring frequently, until softened and translucent, about 1 minute longer. Add mushrooms to skillet, and cook until mushrooms no longer release liquid, about 6 minutes; transfer to medium bowl and season to taste with salt and pepper. Reduce wine as directed in step 2; continue with recipe from step 3, adding parsley to egg mixture along with salt and pepper and substituting sausage mixture for spinach. (For doubled recipe, increase baking time to about 1 hour 20 minutes.)

BREAKFAST STRATA WITH POTATOES, ROSEMARY, AND FONTINA

8–10 (½-inch thick) slices supermarket French or
      Italian bread (6–7 ounces)
   5 tablespoons unsalted butter, softened
      Salt and ground black pepper
  12 ounces new potatoes (about 2 medium), cut
      into ½-inch cubes
   3 medium shallots, minced (about ⅓ cup)
   2 medium cloves garlic, minced or pressed
      through garlic press
 1½ teaspoons minced fresh rosemary leaves
  ½ cup medium-dry white wine, such as
      Sauvignon Blanc
   6 ounces fontina cheese, grated (about 1½ cups)
   6 large eggs
 1¾ cups half-and-half
   2 tablespoons minced fresh parsley leaves

Follow recipe for Breakfast Strata with Spinach and Gruyère through step 1. Bring 1 quart water to boil in medium saucepan over medium-high heat; add 1 teaspoon salt and boil potatoes until just tender when pierced with tip of paring knife, about 4 minutes; drain potatoes. Heat 2 tablespoons butter in medium nonstick skillet over medium heat and cook potatoes until just beginning to brown, about 10 minutes. Add

shallots and cook, stirring frequently, until softened and translucent, about 1 minute longer; add garlic and rosemary and cook until fragrant, about 2 minutes longer. Transfer mixture to medium bowl; season to taste with salt and pepper and set aside. Reduce wine as directed in step 2; continue with recipe from step 3, adding parsley to egg mixture along with salt and pepper and substituting potato mixture for spinach. (For doubled recipe, increase baking time to about 1 hour 10 minutes.)

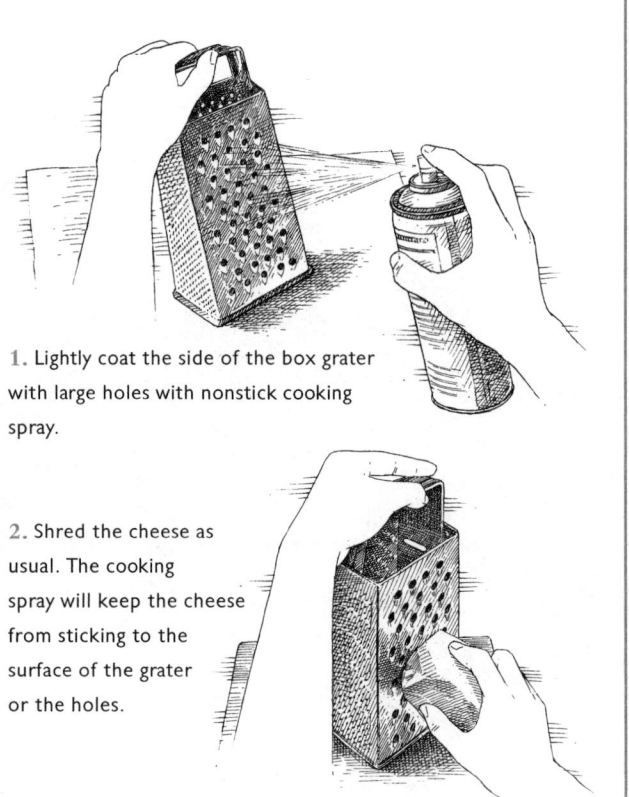

TECHNIQUE: Shredding Soft Cheese

Semi-soft cheeses such as Monterey Jack, cheddar, or mozzarella can stick to a box grater and cause a real mess. Here's how to keep the holes on the grater from becoming clogged.

1. Lightly coat the side of the box grater with large holes with nonstick cooking spray.

2. Shred the cheese as usual. The cooking spray will keep the cheese from sticking to the surface of the grater or the holes.

Lining a baking pan with foil makes removal of baked raspberry squares a breeze—just lift out the entire block and slide it onto a cutting board.

BAR cookies

CHAPTER 20

Everyone loves bar cookies—especially the cook, because there's no need to form individual balls of dough. But baking dough in a pan, rather than in balls on a cookie sheet, can cause problems.

Many cooks wait until the tester poked into the center of a pan of brownies comes out dry before removing them from the oven. That's a big mistake. Dusty, dry brownies have almost no chocolate flavor and need a lot of milk to go down easily. We like our brownies fudgy and chewy, with a big hit of chocolate. After making 50 batches, we finally hit upon the right recipe.

Few cookies are more comforting than a raspberry crumble bar with oats and nuts. But this is one of those desserts that usually sounds better than it tastes. After making plenty of dull bars, the test kitchen discovered the secret to this homey dessert: give part of the dough a headstart in the oven and then add the preserves and topping. This way the bottom crust bakes up crisp, not soggy, and offers a great contrast to the filling and streusel topping.

BROWNIES

WHAT WE WANTED: Brownies with a moist, velvety texture, a hint of chew, and deep chocolate flavor.

Americans are passionate about brownies. Some are passionate about eating them, about a brownie's rich, chocolatey decadence. Others are passionate about a recipe, scrawled on a stained index card bequeathed to them by their mother, guaranteeing everyone they meet that this family heirloom produces the best brownie of all.

We've sampled good brownies, but rarely have we ever encountered the brownie to beat all others. And yet somehow we know exactly how the perfect brownie ought to taste and look. Those light cakey versions are not for us. We imagine a moist, dark, luscious interior with a firm, smooth, velvety texture that your teeth glide through easily, meeting just a little resistance in chewing. Our perfect brownie must pack an intense chocolate punch and have deep, resonant chocolate flavor, but it must fall just short of overwhelming the palate. It must not be so sweet as to make your teeth ache, and it must certainly have a thin, shiny, papery crust and edges that crisp during baking, offering a contrast with the brownie's moist center.

Our baking sense told us that the taste and texture of the brownie we sought lay in a delicate balance of the five ingredients basic to all brownie recipes: chocolate, flour, sugar, butter, and eggs. After gathering a number of recipes that promised to deliver a fudgy brownie, we made a select six that confirmed our expectations. The varying proportions of these five ingredients produced batches of brownies that were soft and pasty; dry and cakey; or chewy, like a Tootsie Roll. Chocolate flavor was divergent, too, ranging from intense but one-dimensional jolts to weak, muted passings on the palate. Our next step was to cobble together a composite recipe that would incorporate the best traits of these six recipes. It would serve as the foundation for all of our testing.

The two essential qualities we were looking for in these brownies were a chewy, fudgy texture and a rich chocolate flavor. We went to work on flavor first. After making the six initial test recipes, we knew that unsweetened chocolate was a good source of assertive chocolate flavor. Semisweet and bittersweet chocolates don't have as much chocolate punch because of the large amount of sugar they contain. But this is also why they are smoother and milder. One of our favorite recipes from the initial test yielded a brownie with exceptional chocolate flavor. This recipe combined unsweetened and bittersweet chocolates, so to the composite recipe we tried adding varying amounts of the two chocolates. (Semisweet and bittersweet chocolates are not identical but can be exchanged for one another in many recipes; we'll refer to semisweet from here on because it's what we used when testing the recipes.)

Too much unsweetened chocolate and the brownies were sour and acrid, too much semisweet chocolate and they were one-dimensional and boring. We found that 5 ounces of semisweet and 2 ounces of unsweetened created just the right flavor balance. Next we thought to add some cocoa powder, which typically adds flavor but no harshness.

We were pleased with this combination. The unsweetened chocolate laid a solid, intense chocolate foundation, the semisweet provided a mellow, even, sweet flavor, and the cocoa smoothed any rough edges and added depth and complexity. We tried both Dutch-processed cocoa and natural cocoa and found them to work equally well.

We then fiddled with the type and quantity of sugar needed to sweeten the brownies, given the amount and types of chocolate and cocoa they contained. In addition to white sugar, we tried brown sugar to see if it might add flavor, but it didn't. We also tried a bit of corn syrup, thinking it might add moistness and chew, but it only made the brownies wet and gummy and the crust dull. Satisfied that white sugar was the best sweetener for the job, we tested varying amounts. We knew we didn't want overly sweet brownies. Too little sugar, though, left the brownies with a chocolate flavor that was dull, muted, and flat, much like mashed potatoes without salt. Just the right degree of sweetness was provided by 1¼ cups sugar.

Satisfied with the flavor of the brownies, we moved on to refining the texture, starting with flour. Our composite recipe contained ¾ cup flour, but wanting to exhaust all reasonable quantities, we baked brownies with as little as ¼ cup and up to 1¼ cups, increasing the quantity in ¼ cup increments. The batch with the least amount of flour was like goopy, sticky, chocolate-flavored Spackle, so pasty it cemented your mouth shut. The one with 1¼ cups flour had good chew, but it verged on dry, and the chocolate flavor was light and muted. One cup was perfect. The chocolate flavor remained deep and rich, and the texture was fudgy, smooth, and dense, the moist crumb putting up a gentle resistance when chewed.

Butter was up next. Melting butter, rather than creaming it with sugar and eggs, makes for a dense, fudgy texture. Creaming produces an aerated batter, which bakes into lighter, cakier brownies. Had we questioned this baker's axiom after the initial test, in which all of the six recipes employ the melted butter technique, any doubts would have been dispelled. But now the question of how much butter remained.

Semisweet chocolate contains more fat than unsweetened chocolate, yet many recipes that call exclusively for one type of chocolate frequently call for the same amount of butter (some 16 tablespoons) per cup of flour. As it stood, our working recipe used semisweet and unsweetened chocolate, cocoa, 1 cup flour, and 10 tablespoons butter. The texture of the brownies this recipe produced was moist and dense, albeit a bit sodden and pasty. Improvement came with less butter. Minus 2 tablespoons, the brownies shed their soggy, sodden quality but still remained moist and velvety.

With butter and flour set, we went to work on eggs. We tried as few as two and as many as six. Two eggs left the brownies dry and gritty and compromised the chocolate flavor. With four or more eggs, the brownies baked into cakey rubber erasers with an unattractive, high-domed, dull matte crust. Three was the magic number—the brownies were moist and smooth, with great flavor and delicate chew.

We finalized the recipe by making adjustments to vanilla and salt and then began to examine other factors that might have an impact on the brownies. First we tried baking in a water bath, a technique used for delicate custards, reasoning that gentle heat might somehow improve texture. Not so. We got a grainy, sticky, puddinglike brownie.

We experimented with midrange oven temperatures. Three-hundred-fifty degrees did the job and did it relatively quickly, in about 35 minutes (many brownies bake for nearly an hour). As is the case with most other brownies, if baked too long, these brownies run the risk of drying out; they must be pulled from the oven when a toothpick inserted into the center comes out with some sticky crumbs clinging to it.

After making more than 50 batches, we really appreciated an aspect of brownies quite beside their rich flavor and texture—with only a couple of bowls, a whisk, and a spatula, the batter can be mixed and in the oven in 10 minutes.

WHAT WE LEARNED: **Use three kinds of chocolate—unsweetened, semisweet, and cocoa powder—for the most complex, richest flavor. Don't go overboard with the butter, and use three eggs for good chew.**

CHEWY, FUDGY TRIPLE-CHOCOLATE BROWNIES   makes sixty-four 1-inch brownies

Either Dutch-processed or natural cocoa works well in this recipe. These brownies are very rich, so we prefer to cut them into small squares for serving.

  5   ounces semisweet or bittersweet chocolate, chopped
  2   ounces unsweetened chocolate, chopped
  8   tablespoons (1 stick) unsalted butter, cut into quarters
  3   tablespoons cocoa powder
  3   large eggs
  1¼ cups (8.75 ounces) sugar
  2   teaspoons vanilla extract
  ½   teaspoon salt
  1   cup (5 ounces) unbleached all-purpose flour

1. Adjust oven rack to lower-middle position and heat oven to 350 degrees. Spray 8-inch-square baking pan with non-stick cooking spray. Fold two 16-inch pieces of foil lengthwise to measure 7 inches wide. Fit one sheet in bottom of greased pan, pushing it into corners and up sides of pan (overhang will help in removal of baked brownies). Fit second sheet in pan in same manner, perpendicular to first sheet. Spray foil with nonstick cooking spray.

2. In medium heatproof bowl set over pan of almost-simmering water, melt chocolates and butter, stirring occasionally until mixture is smooth. Whisk in cocoa until smooth. Set aside to cool slightly.

3. Whisk together eggs, sugar, vanilla, and salt in medium bowl until combined, about 15 seconds. Whisk warm chocolate mixture into egg mixture; then stir in flour with wooden spoon until just combined. Pour mixture into prepared pan, spread into corners, and level surface with rubber spatula; bake until slightly puffed and toothpick inserted in center comes out with small amount of sticky crumbs clinging to it, 35 to 40 minutes. Cool on wire rack to room temperature, about 2 hours, then remove brownies from pan using foil handles. Cut into 1-inch squares and serve. (Do not cut brownies until ready to serve; brownies can be wrapped in plastic and refrigerated up to 5 days.)

VARIATION
TRIPLE-CHOCOLATE ESPRESSO BROWNIES

Follow recipe for Chewy, Fudgy Triple-Chocolate Brownies, whisking in 1½ tablespoons instant espresso or coffee powder along with cocoa in step 2.

SCIENCE DESK:
Chocolate Flavor Diffusion

ONE OF THE MORE INTERESTING IDEAS WE HEARD ABOUT the dos and don'ts of working with chocolate desserts was proposed to us by famed New York chef Jean-Georges Vongerichten, who stated that the less one cooks chocolate, the better it tastes. We decided to check this out with Tom Lehmann, director of bakery assistance at the American Institute of Baking. He agreed.

Chocolate, Lehmann explained, is a very delicate substance, full of highly sensitive, volatile compounds that give chocolate much of its flavor. When chocolate is heated, the liquids in it turn to steam and carry away these volatile compounds. That's what makes the kitchen smell so good when brownies are in the oven. The bad news is that these volatile compounds are no longer in the brownies—which is where you really want them to be. Exposure to heat, therefore, has no benefits; it simply makes chocolate more bitter and less complex tasting.

So, what are the lessons to be learned about baking with chocolate? First, underbaking is always better than overbaking. Dry chocolate desserts will have much less flavor and tend to be bitter. Second, use as much fat as possible. Fat increases the retention of volatile compounds. That's why low-fat chocolate desserts usually taste like sugar but not chocolate.

RASPBERRY SQUARES

WHAT WE WANTED: A buttery, tender, golden brown crust and crumb topping with just the right amount of sweet/tart raspberry preserves in the middle.

Raspberry squares are one of the best, and easiest, bar cookies to prepare. With raspberry squares, the filling is ready-made (it comes straight from a jar of raspberry preserves). And these homey bars have textural interest created by the layering of filling on crust.

A short pastry (such as that used in raspberry squares) has a tender, almost sandy crumb that it gets by way of the right combination of flour, fat, sugar, and salt—with an emphasis on the fat and the flour. In a short pastry (think of shortbread), a generous amount of fat is required to coat the particles of flour, the purpose of this coating being to restrict the flour's access to liquid. Flour contains proteins that when combined with water form gluten—a substance that is desirable in bread, where you want chew, but not in a raspberry square, where you want tenderness.

In the many recipes for all manner of "short" bar cookies we looked at, the amount of butter ranged from ½ cup to 1 cup for about 2½ cups of flour. We found that a whole cup of butter made the raspberry squares greasy, whereas ½ cup left them on the dry side; ¾ cup butter was just right.

The sugar in many of the recipes also ranged from ½ cup to 1 cup, with some calling for white sugar, some for brown, some for a mix of the two. Here, too, we went for the midway, deciding on equal amounts of white and light brown sugar, which made for a deeper flavor than white alone, and on a total of ⅔ cup, which was sweet enough to be pleasing but not cloying.

We were attracted by the idea of adding some oats or nuts, which would make a more subtle contribution to flavor while also adding some textural interest. The oats, with their bulk and absorbency, would have to displace some of the flour. After trying various proportions we found

that we liked the combination of 1¼ cups oats to 1½ cups flour. We played around with the nuts and found ourselves preferring a pairing of sweet almonds with nutty pecans (although either also works on its own).

We were now pretty pleased with our crust except for one nagging problem: It was rather pale, not golden brown. We wanted that golden brown color not only for appearance' sake but for flavor; we knew that a deeply colored crust would have a more developed, nutty flavor.

The procedure we had been following to prepare the squares for baking was recommended in a number of recipes. It involved lining the bottom of the pan with most of the dough, spreading the preserves on top, and then covering the preserves with the rest of the dough. One or two recipes had recommended baking the bottom crust alone first to brown it and firm it up, but we had rejected this option as being a bit fussy. Now we tried this procedure and were happy to learn that it effectively colored—and flavored—the crust.

WHAT WE LEARNED: For a flavorful, golden brown bottom crust, prebake it before layering with raspberry preserves and top crust. Add oats and nuts to the crust for textural interest and complementary flavors.

RASPBERRY SQUARES makes 25 squares

Lining the pan with foil makes removal of the squares for cutting very easy (just lift out the entire block and place it on a cutting board to cut). For a nice presentation, trim ¼ inch off the outer rim of the uncut baked block. The outside edges of all cut squares will then be neat.

1½	cups (7.5 ounces) unbleached all-purpose flour
1¼	cups quick-cooking oats
⅓	cup (2.3 ounces) granulated sugar
⅓	cup packed light brown sugar
¼	teaspoon baking soda
¼	teaspoon salt
½	cup finely chopped pecans or almonds, or a combination
12	tablespoons (1½ sticks) unsalted butter, cut into 12 pieces and softened but still cool
1	cup raspberry preserves

1. Adjust oven rack to lower-middle position and heat oven to 350 degrees. Spray 9-inch-square baking pan with nonstick cooking spray. Fold two 16-inch pieces of foil lengthwise to measure 8 inches wide. Fit one sheet in bottom of greased pan, pushing it into corners and up sides of pan (overhang will help in removal of baked squares). Fit second sheet in pan in same manner, perpendicular to first sheet. Spray foil with nonstick cooking spray.

2. In bowl of standing mixer, mix flour, oats, sugars, baking soda, salt, and nuts at low speed until combined, about 30 seconds. With mixer running at low speed, add butter pieces; continue to beat until mixture is well-blended and resembles wet sand, about 2 minutes.

3. Transfer ⅔ of mixture to prepared pan and use hands to press crumbs evenly into bottom. Bake until starting to brown, about 20 minutes. Using rubber spatula, spread preserves evenly over hot bottom crust; sprinkle remaining oat/nut mixture evenly over preserves. Bake until preserves bubble around edges and top is golden brown, about 30 minutes, rotating pan from front to back halfway through baking time. Cool on wire rack to room temperature, about 1½ hours, then remove from pan using foil handles. Cut into 1¼- to 1½-inch squares and serve.

TASTING LAB: Raspberry Preserves

JELLY, JAM, PRESERVES, FRUIT SPREAD—WHAT'S THE difference, and is any one of these products better than the other for baking or spreading on toast? We put eight leading brands to a taste test to find out. But before we give you the results, some definitions are in order.

A jelly is a clear, bright mixture made from fruit juice, sugar, and often pectin or acid. No less than 45 pounds of fruit must be used for each 55 pounds of sugar.

A jam is a thick mixture of fruit and sugar that is cooked until the pieces of fruit are very soft and almost formless. It is also made with 45 pounds of fruit combined with 55 pounds of sugar. Preserves are almost identical to jams, but preserves may contain large chunks of fruit or whole fruit.

Fruit spreads, which have become common grocery store stock over the last 10 years, do not fall under the labeling standards applied to jellies and jams—hence the generic name, fruit spreads. These products are usually made with concentrated grape and/or pear juice or low-calorie sweeteners, which replace all or part of the sugar.

TECHNIQUE:
Packing Brown Sugar

When a recipe calls for some quantity of packed brown sugar, fill the correct dry measure with the sugar and use the next smallest cup to pack it.

Although tasters preferred preserves and jams to jellies (they liked bits of fruit), they were most concerned with flavor. Too many brands were overly sweet—so sweet it was hard to taste the raspberries. The top two brands were Trappist Jam and Smucker's Preserves. Interestingly, both of these products are made with corn syrup, yet tasters felt these brands had the strongest raspberry flavor.

Tasters were not wild about fruit spreads. Although fruit spreads are less sweet than traditional jams and jellies, tasters felt that the concentrated fruit juices obscured the flavor of the raspberries. The result was a generic "fruit roll-up flavor."

EQUIPMENT CORNER: Coffee Makers

IN THE TEST KITCHEN WE LOVE A GOOD CUP OF COFFEE to wash down brownies or raspberry squares. But what's the best means of brewing it? To find out, we assembled a group of appliances representing the major methods used to brew coffee: a percolator, an expensive automatic-drip machine with thermos, an inexpensive automatic-drip machine with burner plate, a manual plastic drip cone that fits over a glass carafe, a flip pot (also known as a Napoletana), a plunger pot (also called a French press), and a vacuum coffee maker. We rated each set-up based on the temperature, flavor, and body of the coffee it produced, as well as on ease of use.

We quickly dismissed several methods based on the poor quality of the coffee or the hassle involved in getting the device to work. A flip pot can brew only one or two cups of coffee at a time, takes 20 minutes to work, seems excessively dangerous (you must flip the burning hot metal pot), and makes gritty, slightly burnt coffee.

A plunger pot is easier to use, but tasters felt that too much sediment passed through the mesh filter that separates the spent grounds from the coffee, even when coarsely ground beans were used.

The percolator performed as expected. It worked quickly and delivered very hot coffee, but tasters complained about weak flavor. That's because the water doesn't spend much time in contact with the coffee—it's too busy being recycled through the inner tubing in this device.

Our two automatic-drip machines were easy to use, but the coffee tasted bitter, especially when we tried to make a full pot. According to experts we spoke with, the water and grounds should stay in contact for four to six minutes. Beyond the six-minute mark, the grounds start to release bitter compounds that will harm the flavor of the coffee. We found that automatic drip machines can turn out two or three cups of coffee within the proper time frame but that it often takes 10 minutes to yield six cups.

The model tested with the burner had an added problem—coffee that was so-so right after brewing quickly developed a horrible burnt flavor. The drip machine with the thermos did not have this problem.

Two brewing methods stand out as superior, at least in terms of quality. Coffee brewed in a vacuum pot has much to offer—properly hot temperature, a rich flavor that captures the nuances in expensive beans without any bitterness, and a full body without sediment. The real problem here is convenience. This showy device relies on a vacuum created between two glass bowls. Although not hard to use, the glass bowls are wobbly and liable to break. As an intriguing finale to an occasional meal, this conversation piece makes sense, but not every day at six in the morning.

Our favorite coffee brewing method is the manual drip. The convenience factor is second only to an automatic drip. Grind and measure the coffee into the filter-lined cone, then add water just off a boil in batches. You can't leave the kitchen, but the coffee tastes great without the bitterness associated with an automatic drip machine. That's because the plastic cones on manual drip models are larger than the cones inside automatic drip machines, so the water runs through the grounds more quickly.

If you let the coffee drip into an insulated thermos (prewarmed by rinsing it with hot tap water) rather than a glass carafe, the coffee will stay hot and fresh-tasting for hours. Best of all, you can pick up a plastic cone for $5 and a thermos for $25.

Brushing a fruit tart with hot jelly can move the berries and disrupt a perfect design. To glaze a tart and keep the design intact, use a pastry brush to dab, drizzle, and flick the hot jelly onto the fruit.

TWO FRENCH tarts

Just as pies are a true expression of fine American cooking, tarts represent the very best in French pastry. The crust should be tender, buttery, and crumbly—almost like a good butter cookie. The fillings are usually rich and creamy, so a little goes a long way.

A lemon tart, filled with nothing more than lemon curd, is perhaps the simplest French tart for the home cook to prepare. When made right, this tart is light, refreshing, and altogether delicious. But when things go wrong—as they often do—the filling can be thick, eggy, harsh, or gluey.

Glistening in the windows and glass cases of pâtisseries, fresh fruit tarts are things of beauty. But these fruit tarts are tarts indeed. They draw you in with their beguiling looks—but venture beneath the surface and you are quickly disappointed with their substance. Most often, the pastry cream filling is an institutional pudding with either a goopy, overstarched texture or a stiff, rubbery demeanor. Even when the pastry cream filling is well made, it typically infuses the crust with a different malaise: If the tart has been sitting pretty long enough (and you can bet it has), the crust has gotten soggy. Or, in the worst case, juices have begun to seep out of the fruit to form a sticky puddle in which the tart wallows.

These simple, elegant tarts demand the finest ingredients. They are also best made at home, where care can be taken in their preparation and timing can be controlled. Our tarts will put even the finest pâtisseries to shame.

IN THIS CHAPTER

THE RECIPES
Sweet Tart Pastry (Pâte Sucrée)

Lemon Tart

Fresh Fruit Tart with Pastry Cream

EQUIPMENT CORNER
Rolling Pins
Tart Pans

SCIENCE DESK
Eggs and Acid

TASTING LAB
Lemon Zest, Oils, and Extracts

SWEET TART PASTRY

WHAT WE WANTED: Tart dough can be finicky and hard to roll out. We wanted to produce a crisp, flavorful pastry dough using the fastest and most foolproof method available.

Over the years we have come to value the virtues of a traditional pie dough as much as those of its European cousin, pâte sucrée (literally, "sugar dough"). But many American pie bakers have yet to discover the virtues of sweet pastry dough. What is it, and how does it differ from regular pie dough? Does it deserve a place at our table? The answer is, emphatically, yes.

While a regular pie dough is tender and flaky, a sweet tart dough is tender and crisp. Fine-textured, buttery rich, and crumbly, it is often described as cookielike. In fact, cookies are actually descendants of sweet pastry dough—a dough deemed so delicious by the French that it was considered worth eating on its own. There are also differences in the dough's relationship to the filling. Rather than encasing a deep hearty filling, a tart shell shares the stage with its filling. Traditional tart fillings—caramel, marzipan, pastry cream, or even jam, often adorned with glazed fresh fruits or nuts—would seem excessive if housed in a deeper pie. But these intense flavors and textures are perfect in thin layers balanced by a crisp, thin pastry.

We have eaten our share of thick, tough, and flavorless tart doughs. Many American recipes for these doughs call for too little butter or sugar, thus compromising texture, but more often poor technique is to blame.

Though you can make sweet pastry as you would cookie dough, by creaming the butter and sugar together, then adding flour and finally egg, we found this technique too time-consuming. Like pie pastries, most sweet pastry recipes direct the cook to cut butter into flour by hand or food processor and then add liquid. Knowing cold butter and minimal handling to be critical to the success of this method, we headed straight for the food processor. Pulsing very cold butter with dry ingredients to obtain a fine, pebbly consistency took all of 15 seconds.

The addition of liquid was a trickier matter. We were reluctant to use a food processor, feeling it gave us less control. But the alternative, tossing the pebbly dough onto a countertop and fluffing the liquid in by hand, followed by a *fraisage* (flattening the dough in short strokes with the heel of the hand to incorporate ingredients) seemed tiresome and unnecessary. Though the manual method for adding liquid produced a marginally more delicate, tender dough, we found that in fact the difference was barely discernible— and only in side-by-side comparisons. Addition of liquid ingredients with the food processor took about 25 seconds. Armed with this quick, no-fuss technique, we wanted to tweak the major players in the dough to tease out the most tender, tastiest pastry imaginable.

The first ingredients to come under scrutiny were the butter and sugar. The higher the proportion of butter in a pâte sucrée, the more delicate its crumb. We experimented with the amount and found 10 tablespoons (5 ounces) to be the maximum allowable for ease of handling. More butter simply made the dough too soft and did not improve its flavor or texture. As for the sugar, the traditional half cup did not seem overly sweet, and any less than that produced a dough lacking in flavor and tenderness. Most recipes recommend the use of superfine sugar (thought to be important for dissolving in a dough with so little liquid), but because few people (if any) have it in their pantry, we tried confectioners' sugar, an ingredient most people have on hand. We found that ¾ cup confectioners' sugar gave us a crisper dough than the one made with granulated sugar.

Next up for examination were the liquid ingredients. Though most recipes call for a whole egg, some call for a combination of egg yolk and cream. (As in any cookie dough, the egg lends structure to a dough that would otherwise be completely crumbly.) Testing these side by side, we discovered that the yolk and cream combination (1 yolk and 2 tablespoons of cream) created a lovely crust with a degree of flakiness, a quality we value over the slightly firmer dough produced when using a whole egg alone.

The last major player to be manipulated was the flour. Perfectly happy with our tests using all-purpose, we nevertheless performed a couple of tests using half all-purpose and half pastry flour, as well as half all-purpose and half cake flour. Our reasoning was this: Low-protein flours, such as pastry and cake flours (equal in protein percentage at about 8 percent, compared with all-purpose at about 11 percent) tend to retard gluten development, thus yielding a more tender dough. We were surprised to learn that in composition pastry and cake flours are identical; cake flour is simply bleached. (Bleaching improves the rise of high-sugar batters, like those used in cakes; pastry flour is used in pie doughs, where rise isn't so important.) To be honest, we liked the dough made with half pastry flour. It was a bit more tender and delicate than that made entirely with all-purpose and no more difficult to work with. But the improvement was not impressive enough to cause us to recommend the pastry flour, particularly since it's often not that easy to find. The dough made with half cake flour had a pleasing texture as well, but a less-pleasing flavor; bleaching can impart a slightly metallic taste to flour.

In the end, the proportions we were using made too much dough for a 9-inch tart pan. While many recipes calling for 1½ cups flour declared a yield of dough for one 9- or 11-inch tart, we scaled our proportions back to fit the pan.

Sweet pastry dough typically requires at least an hour of refrigerated resting time for the liquid ingredients to hydrate the dough fully and make it more manageable. In fact, a two-hour rest was even better. The butter gives the dough a nice plasticity if the dough is cold enough and makes rolling relatively easy. We knew it would be a challenge to roll out the dough directly on the counter. Best results were obtained with minimal flouring and by rolling the dough out between double layers of wide parchment paper or plastic wrap without letting it become warm. Though many recipes suggest

that a sweet pastry dough can simply be pressed into a pan, our tests did not support this recommendation. The patchwork technique made the crucial "even thickness" all but unattainable, and the imperfectly fused pieces did not have the same structural integrity as a correctly fitted, single sheath of dough. The patched crust tended to crumble along the fault lines as it was unmolded or cut.

A half hour in the freezer "set" the dough nicely to prepare it for "blind baking" (baking the shell without any filling). A baking sheet placed directly beneath the tart shell (to conduct heat evenly to the crust bottom) browned the tart beautifully. Because of the crust's delicate nature, the metal weights used to blind-bake the tart are best left in place until the crust's edges are distinctly brown, about 30 minutes, at which point the weights can be removed and the top side of the crust allowed to brown.

WHAT WE LEARNED: Make the dough in the food processor and roll it out between sheets of parchment or plastic to prevent excess flouring or sticking. Use confectioners' sugar for extra crispness and a combination of egg yolk and heavy cream for extra flakiness.

SWEET TART PASTRY (PÂTE SUCRÉE) makes one
9- to 9½-inch tart shell

If the dough becomes soft and sticky while rolling, rechill it until it becomes easier to work with. Better to rechill than to add too much flour, which will damage the delicate, crisp texture of the dough. We find a tapered French rolling pin to be the most precise instrument for rolling tart pastry. Bake the tart shell in a 9- to 9½-inch tart pan with a removable bottom and fluted sides about 1 to 1⅛ inches high.

    1   large egg yolk
    1   tablespoon heavy cream
    ½   teaspoon vanilla extract
    1¼ cups (6.25 ounces) unbleached all-purpose flour
    ⅔   cup (3 ounces) confectioners' sugar
    ¼   teaspoon salt
    8   tablespoons (1 stick) very cold unsalted butter,
        cut into ½-inch cubes

1. Whisk together yolk, cream, and vanilla in small bowl; set aside. Pulse to combine flour, sugar, and salt in bowl of food processor fitted with steel blade. Scatter butter pieces over flour mixture; pulse to cut butter into flour until mixture resembles coarse meal, about fifteen 1-second pulses. With machine running, add egg mixture and process until dough just comes together, about 25 seconds. Turn dough onto sheet of plastic wrap and press into 6-inch disk. Wrap in plastic and refrigerate at least 1 hour or up to 48 hours.

2. Remove dough from refrigerator (if refrigerated longer than 1 hour, let stand at room temperature until malleable). Unwrap and roll out between lightly floured large sheets of parchment paper or plastic wrap to 13-inch round. (If dough is soft and sticky, slip onto baking sheet and refrigerate until workable, 20 to 30 minutes.) Transfer dough to tart pan by rolling dough loosely around rolling pin and unrolling over 9- to 9½-inch tart pan with removable bottom. Working around circumference of pan, ease dough into pan corners by gently lifting dough with one hand while pressing dough into corners with other hand. Press dough into fluted sides of pan. (If some edges are too thin, reinforce sides by folding excess dough back on itself.) Run rolling pin over top of tart pan to remove excess dough. Set dough-lined tart pan on large plate and freeze 30 minutes. (The dough-lined tart pan can be sealed in a gallon-sized zipper-lock plastic bag and frozen up to 1 month.)

3. Meanwhile, adjust oven rack to middle position and heat oven to 375 degrees. Set dough-lined tart pan on baking sheet, press 12-inch square of foil inside frozen tart shell and over edge, and fill with metal or ceramic pie weights. Bake for 30 minutes, rotating halfway through baking time. Remove from oven and carefully remove foil and weights by gathering edges of foil and pulling up and out. Continue to bake until deep golden brown, 5 to 8 minutes longer. Set baking sheet with tart shell on wire rack.

EQUIPMENT CORNER: Rolling Pins

WE PURCHASED TWO WOODEN PINS WITHOUT HANDLES—one with tapered ends, and one that was straight. Three other wooden pins had standard dowel-type handles with ball bearings and represented three different sizes: The largest weighed in at 3½ pounds and was 15 inches long, another was a quite small 1½ pounds and 10½ inches long, and the last was in between these two, at 2½ pounds and 11½ inches long. We purchased three novelty pins—one marble, one nonstick coated aluminum, and one wooden model with ergonomic comfort grips. The grips on this last model were made of molded plastic and had the feel of a steering wheel, with thumbs on top and wrists straight. Prices ranged from $6.99 to $35.99.

We decided to test the pins on three kinds of dough: a standard pie dough, a delicate sugar cookie dough, and a resilient yeasted coffee cake dough. We were particularly interested in the versatility of these pins—whether they could perform equally well in all tasks. No one wants more than one pin in the kitchen. For all three doughs, we were looking for a fast, easy roll—one that allowed us to feel the dough and did not require application of too much pressure.

Almost immediately a favorite and a least favorite became evident. The tapered wood pin without handles ($6.99) took first place. Testers could easily turn and pivot the tapered pin and apply pressure as needed across the dough. In addition, this pin measured 20 inches long, making it suitable for any task. Many of the other wooden pins were too short (some just 10 or 11 inches in length) and could not be used to roll out large pieces of dough.

The marble pin ($8.99) was a bit heavy over delicate sugar cookie dough, but this pin could be refrigerated before handling buttery doughs, which was a plus. It landed in second place. The ergonomic pin ($35.99) landed near the bottom of the ratings, as did the nonstick model ($9.99), which was much too light and most definitely not stickfree.

EQUIPMENT CORNER: Tart Pans

TART PANS WITH REMOVABLE BOTTOMS ARE AVAILABLE IN three types of finishes. The traditional tinned steel tart pan is silver and reflective. Then there is the nonstick version coated with a brown finish inside and out. The third type, a black steel tart pan (also sometimes called blue steel), is quite difficult to find, at least in this country.

A tinned steel pan is what we used throughout recipe development of the fruit tart—without incident. So we wondered what a nonstick tart pan—at 2½ times the cost—could possibly improve upon. The answer is nothing, really. Tart pastry is brimming with butter and is not likely to stick to flypaper, so a nonstick tart pan is superfluous. And despite its darker finish, it browned the pastry at the same rate as the tinned steel pan.

The black steel pan was another matter. Colored to absorb heat and encourage browning, it did just that, actually taking the pastry a bit past even our preference for very deeply browned. This pan would be fine for baking a filled tart (the filling slows down the baking), but for unfilled pastry—like the lemon tart and fruit tart in this chapter—it was a bit impetuous. If you own one and are using it to prebake tart pastry, try lowering your oven temperature by about 25 degrees.

BEST TART PAN
Unlike a black steel pan, a tinned steel pan won't cause over-browning. And because tart dough has so much butter, we found there's no point spending extra money for a nonstick finish.

LEMON TART

WHAT WE WANTED: A lemon tart with a silken texture, the perfect balance of tart and sweet, and a taste that isn't too "eggy."

With its minimal interplay of ingredients and straightforward style, the lemon tart achieves a near-transcendent simplicity of form and content. Light, refreshing, and beautiful, when it's good, it is very, very good—but when it's bad, you wish you'd ordered the check instead. Despite its apparent simplicity, there is much that can go wrong with a lemon tart. It can slip over the edge of sweet into cloying; its tartness can grab at your throat; it can be gluey or eggy or, even worse, metallic-tasting. Its crust can be too hard, too soft, too thick, or too sweet. If by chance you bring more than one of these flaws to bear on a single tart, the results are horrific.

There is more than one way to fill a tart, of course. We considered briefly but dismissed the notion of an unbaked lemon filling—a lemon pastry cream or a lemon charlotte. In each case, the filling (the former containing milk and thickened with eggs and flour, the latter containing cream and thickened with eggs and gelatin) is spooned into a baked tart shell and chilled. Not only did we find the flavor of these fillings too muted and their texture too billowy, but we realized that we wanted a proper lemon tart, one in which the filling is baked with the shell. That meant only one thing: lemon curd, and a thin, bracing layer of it at that.

Originally an old English recipe that was to be eaten like a jam and called lemon cheese, lemon curd is a stirred fruit custard made of eggs, lemon juice, sugar, and, usually, butter. Cooked over low heat and stirred continuously, the mixture thickens by means of protein coagulation. The dessert owes its bright flavor not to lemon juice but to oils released by finely grated peel, the equivalent of a lemon twist in a vodka martini. Butter further refines a lemon curd's flavor and texture. The result is a spoonable custard that can be spread on scones or used as a base for desserts. When baked, its color deepens and it "sets up," remaining supple and creamy yet firm enough to be sliceable. It is intense, heady stuff, nicely modulated—if you must—by a cloud of whipped cream.

Several variables warranted exploration. Most straightforward was the ratio of sugar to lemon juice. We wanted just enough sugar to offset the acid. More complex was the proportion of eggs. Egg yolks contain both cholesterol and lecithin, which act as emulsifiers and create a satiny texture. Whole eggs contain albumin as well, the protein in the egg white that is responsible for "setting" a custard. What, we wondered, would produce the best texture—whole eggs, the egg yolks alone, a combination of egg yolks and whole eggs, or maybe even whole eggs plus egg whites? Temperature is the critical factor in coaxing a custard to thicken without curdling, and the slower the journey, the more forgiving the process. Cook the eggs too quickly and you won't know when to pull back. The heat within will have gathered force and taken the curd to the breaking point even if you've pulled the pan off the stove. Chemical reactions, too, accelerate at higher temperatures. Then what, exactly, is the correct temperature for cooking this stirred custard? Would a double boiler be necessary to produce a fine curd, or could we simply proceed with care (and proper equipment) over direct heat? As for the butter, should it be added at the outset of cooking or stirred in at the end?

We began by following the usual test kitchen protocol of preparing a number of classic recipes. For an 8- or 9-inch tart we estimated that we would need about 3 cups of filling. The traditional lemon curds all contained between 1 and 1½ cups sugar, but the amount of lemon juice varied widely, between ½ and 1½ cups. There was also quite a bit of play between whole eggs and yolks, with the average falling between 8 and 10 eggs total. Though the recipes were divided on the matter of using direct heat versus a double still-liquid curd proved superior to whisking the butter in after stovetop cooking. Though the latter curd looked glossy and beautiful before it was baked, the butter aerated the filling, causing it to rise in the oven and overrun the shell's borders.

Holding the proportions of the above ingredients constant, we made a number of lemon curds testing various combinations of whole eggs and yolks. Somewhat surprisingly, the curds that tasted great in a spoon were not always the ones that tasted best baked. The curd made with whole eggs alone had a light texture in the spoon and a gorgeous sheen, but it had a muted color and a texture most tasters described as "mayonnaise-like" when baked. The curd made with whole eggs and whites had a smooth, translucent surface but firmed up too much, while the curd made with an equal ratio of whole eggs to yolks was faulted for being cloyingly rich. In the end, most tasters preferred a curd made principally with yolks and only a couple of whole eggs for structure. Creamy and dense with a vibrant color, it did not become gelatinous when baked, as did those curds made with all whole eggs, but it did set up enough to slice. Its flavor also lingered and teased. This made sense, because fats carry flavors and hold them on the palate. Egg yolks are high in fat.

But the most interesting discovery was still to come. Remembering a lemon mousse we had made, we wanted to see what a softening splash of cream might do to the curd. Adding cream before cooking the curd on the stovetop gave it a cheesy flavor. But 3 tablespoons of cold, raw cream stirred in just before baking proved a winning touch. It cooled the just-cooked curd, blunted its acidity, and lightened its final baked texture to a celestial creaminess. If you don't get around to baking a crust, buy some fresh berries and grab a spoon.

WHAT WE LEARNED: For the creamiest texture and most vibrant color, make lemon curd with mostly egg yolks and add two whole eggs for structure. Cook butter with lemon, sugar, and eggs, then stir a little chilled cream into the finished curd for superb creaminess.

boiler, most were quite cavalier about cooking time, with visual descriptions of the desired final texture ranging from "thick" to "very thick" to "like whipped cream." Only two mentioned cooking temperatures: 160 and 180 degrees, a rather wide range when dealing with eggs. Some recipes added butter at the beginning of the cooking time; others preferred to whisk it in later.

During these early experiments, certain proportions emerged easily. The balance of sweetness and tartness we sought came in at roughly 2 parts sugar to 1 part lemon juice. Four full tablespoons of finely grated lemon zest (strained out after cooking, along with any hardened bits of egg whites) packed enough lemon punch without having to linger in the final custard, where it would become bitter or usurp the silky texture. A pinch of salt brightened the flavor. Four tablespoons of butter were perfect, smoothing taste and refining texture. Adding cold butter chunks to the

LEMON TART serves 8 to 10

Once the lemon curd ingredients have been combined, cook the curd immediately; otherwise it will have a grainy finished texture. To prevent the curd from acquiring a metallic taste, make absolutely sure that all utensils coming into contact with it—bowls, whisk, saucepan, and strainer—are made of nonreactive stainless steel or glass. Since the tart pan has a removable bottom, it is more easily maneuvered when set on a cookie sheet. If your prebaked tart shell has already cooled, place it in the oven just before you start the curd and heat it until warm, about 5 minutes. Serve the tart with lightly whipped cream (see page 294), which is the perfect accompaniment to the rich, intensely lemon filling.

1   fully baked tart shell, 9 to 9½ inches (see page 276), warm
7   large egg yolks, plus 2 large eggs
1   cup plus 2 tablespoons (7.9 ounces) sugar
⅔   cup juice from 4 to 5 medium lemons, plus ¼ cup finely grated zest
    Pinch salt
4   tablespoons unsalted butter, cut into 4 pieces
3   tablespoons heavy cream

1. Adjust oven rack to upper-middle position and heat oven to 375 degrees. Place tart pan with shell on cookie sheet.

2. In medium nonreactive bowl, whisk together yolks and whole eggs until combined, about 5 seconds. Add sugar and whisk until just combined, about 5 seconds. Add lemon juice, zest, and salt; whisk until combined, about 5 seconds. Transfer mixture to medium nonreactive saucepan, add butter pieces, and cook over medium-low heat, stirring constantly with wooden spoon, until curd thickens to thin saucelike consistency and registers 170 degrees on an instant-read thermometer, about 5 minutes. Immediately pour curd through single-mesh stainless steel strainer set over clean nonreactive bowl. Stir in heavy cream; pour curd into warm tart shell immediately.

3. Bake until filling is shiny and opaque and the center 3 inches jiggle slightly when shaken, 10 to 15 minutes. Cool on wire rack to room temperature, about 45 minutes. Remove outer metal ring, slide thin metal spatula between bottom crust and tart pan bottom to release, then slip tart onto cardboard round or serving plate. Cut into wedges and serve.

SCIENCE DESK: Eggs and Acid

WHEN WE BEGAN TESTING LEMON TART RECIPES, WE wondered how such a high proportion of eggs in the presence of a relatively small amount of liquid could produce the creamy, silken texture of lemon curd, while the same proportion of eggs and cream, for example, would simply scramble.

We suspected that it had something to do with acid content. So we did a little experiment. We placed one egg in each of three separate pans over medium heat and added 2 tablespoons rice vinegar to one pan, 2 tablespoons lemon juice to the second pan, and the same amount of water to the third pan. The egg stirred with vinegar cooked quickly and remained pale yellow and very creamy. The egg stirred with lemon juice turned a more lemony yellow, took longer to cook, and, though it also remained creamy, formed a more solid gel than the egg cooked with vinegar. The egg stirred with water took almost twice as long to cook as the first egg and contained distinctly coagulated bits of bright yellow egg—just like scrambled eggs.

Egg proteins are tangled bundles of amino acids. Each bundle carries a similar electrical charge, which causes them to repel each other. Applying heat causes the bundles to unravel, at which point they are inclined to pull together and form a clump. In the process of clumping, the amino acid molecules squeeze out any liquid that comes between them. This is known as curdling.

Introducing an acid to the egg proteins can increase their electrical charges. Consequently, when the proteins are heated and unwind they are even more strongly repelled from one another and are inclined to interact more with the liquid. The effect is to create a layer of liquid between the ribbons of protein, like a sandwich. This creates what we know as a gel, the effect that we pleasantly experienced with our lemon curd ("curd" is a misnomer in this case). The vinegar created a similar but different effect because different acids have different degrees of ability to change the charge on the proteins. Thus the lemon juice, while encouraging an egg to cook and form a solid, keeps the solid moist and creamy.

TASTING LAB:
Lemon Zest, Oils, and Extracts

WHEN MAKING A LEMON TART OR ANY DESSERT WITH lemon, is there an acceptable substitute for lemon zest? There are lemon oils and lemon extracts on the market, but can they pinch-hit for the real thing? To find out, we tested grated zest, two lemon oils, and two lemon extracts (one natural, one imitation) in four different applications—lemon soufflé, lemon curd, lemon pound cake, and lemon butter-cream frosting.

Tasters had no trouble picking out the desserts made with real lemon zest. Zest provided a wider range of lemon flavor, from bitter to sweet, which made desserts more complex tasting and more interesting. With zest, the front of the tongue immediately picks up the sharp bite of lemon, which then mellows in the back of the mouth.

In general, tasters found that the extracts were the worst choices, producing dull desserts. The extracts also gave delicate desserts, such as lemon curd and lemon soufflé, a harsh alcoholic flavor. Imitation extract was particularly alcoholic and devoid of lemon flavor.

Oils produced good lemon flavor, but it was monochromatic. The oils lacked the highs and lows of zest. Of the two oils tested, Boyajian Pure Lemon Oil was the hands-down favorite. This oil is pressed from fresh lemons and boasts lemon flavors without any mysterious undertones.

FRESH FRUIT TART WITH PASTRY CREAM

WHAT WE WANTED: Our own pâtisserie creation that, unlike most bakery tarts, tastes as good as it looks.

The perfect fresh fruit tart has components working in concert to produce complementary textures and flavors. Its crust is buttery and sweet, crisp and sugar-cookie-like, not flaky like a pie pastry. The pastry cream filling is creamy and lithe, just sweet enough to counter the tartness of fresh fruits and just firm enough to support their weight. A finish of jellied glaze makes the fruits sparkle and keeps them from drying out. With each forkful, you experience the buttery crumbling of crust, the chill of cool, rich, silky pastry cream, and the juicy explosion of lusty ripe fruit.

The pastry for a fresh fruit tart is called pâte sucrée, or sweet pastry (see page 276). The tart shell is baked empty (aka prebaked, blind-baked, or baked *au blanc*) until it reaches a deep golden hue. It is then cooled completely, filled with pastry cream, topped with fruit, glazed, et voilà.

Pastry cream is cooked in a saucepan on the stovetop like a homemade pudding. Making it is not necessarily difficult, but making it just right, we knew, would mean finding the perfect balance of ingredients—milk (or cream), eggs, sugar, and starch (usually either cornstarch or flour). We gathered and then prepared a number of recipes for pastry cream and even included a couple of atypical fruit tart fillings—whipped cream and crème anglaise (stirred custard), both stabilized with gelatin. These anomalies were quickly and unanimously rejected by tasters for being uninteresting and Jell-O-like, respectively. We also included basic pastry creams stabilized with gelatin and lightened with egg whites or whipped cream (both often called crème chiboust in the French pastry vernacular), but these more labor-intensive preparations turned out not to be worth the effort. It was evident from this tasting that a simple, basic pastry cream was the one to pursue.

With the information gleaned from this first round, we were able to formulate a working recipe from which we could test components systematically. We sought to determine which was preferable: milk, half-and-half, or heavy cream. Milk was lean on flavor, and cream was superfluous in its fat. Half-and-half was the dairy of choice; the pastry cream made with it was silky in texture and agreeably, not overly, rich. To fill a 9- to 9½-inch tart shell, we needed 2 cups, sweetened with only ½ cup of sugar.

Egg yolks—and sometimes whole eggs—help thicken and enrich pastry cream. A whole egg pastry cream was too light and flimsy. An all-yolk cream was richer, fuller flavored, and altogether more serious. Three yolks were too few to do the job, four (a very common proportion of yolks to dairy) were fine, but with five yolks the pastry cream was sensational—it was like smooth, edible silk, with a remarkable glossy translucency much like that of mayonnaise.

Thickener was up next. We made four batches of pastry cream, using 3 or 4 tablespoons of cornstarch or flour in each one. Four tablespoons of either starch made gummy, chewy, gluey messes of the pastry creams. Three tablespoons was the correct amount; any less would have resulted in soup. In equal amounts, cornstarch and flour were extremely close in flavor and texture, but cornstarch inched out in front with a slightly lighter, more ethereal texture and a cleaner and purer flavor; flour had a trace of graininess and gumminess. That a cornstarch pastry cream is marginally easier to cook than one made with flour was a bonus. Once a cornstarch cream reaches a boil, it is done. A pastry cream with flour must remain on the heat for a few minutes to allow the raw flour flavor to cook off and the cream to reach maximum viscosity.

Most pastry cream recipes finish with a whisking of butter into the just-made cream. As fine-grained sandpaper removes the smallest burrs and gives wood a velveteen finish, butter, we found, rounds out the flavor of pastry cream and endows it with a smooth, silken texture. We found that a relatively generous amount of butter (4 tablespoons) also helped the chilled cream behave better when it came time to slice; it resisted sliding and slipping much more than it had without the extra butter. When the tart was well chilled, the pastry cream held its own.

As for timing, we found it best to prepare the pastry cream before beginning the pastry shell. In fact, it can be made a day or two in advance. This gives the cream adequate time to chill, and we did find a fruit tart with filling that is cool on the tongue much more thrilling to eat. And since it is best to fill the pastry fairly close to serving time lest it become soggy, the cream must be cold when it goes into the shell and is topped with fruit.

Small, soft, self-contained fruits—in other words, berries—are ideal atop fresh fruit tarts. Raspberries, blackberries, and blueberries require no paring and no slicing. That means no breaking of fruit skin to release juices that can ruin a tart. Strawberries are certainly acceptable. They do need to be hulled, and sliced strawberries can make an attractive display if arranged, glazed, and served swiftly. While fruits like mangoes and papayas, with their juicy, soft, creamy textures, might seem inviting, they aren't good candidates for a tart because they quickly send their juices flowing. What's more, their irregular and awkward shapes can be difficult to slice and arrange attractively. Kiwis, however, work well and are gorgeous complements to the berry reds and blues. But use kiwis sparingly, as they, too, can water things down. We do not wash berries that are destined to grace a fruit tart. They need to be utterly dry and completely bruise- and blemish-free. Any excess water can cause the tart to weep, which ultimately results in a soggy bottom.

In the test kitchen, the tarts that met with the most flattery were the simple ones that showed restraint, not the overdesigned ones with lots of fanfare. If you are not inclined to create your own design, follow one of those suggested on page 285. If you are so inclined, bear in mind that one goal is to arrange the fruit in a tight design so that very little to none of the ivory-toned pastry cream peeks out of the spaces between the fruit. Also, the nicest designs are those in which the tallest points are at the center of the tart, with a gradual and graceful descent to the edges.

The finishing touch on a fruit tart is the glaze. For tarts that are covered only with berries of red and blue hues, garnet-colored red currant jelly is perfect. For tarts covered with kiwi and other fair-colored fruits (for instance, golden raspberries), apricot jam is the norm because of its neutral tones, but we took to using apple jelly because it eliminated the need to strain out chunks of fruit and then reheat.

Fresh fruit tarts are often displayed with a shellacked armor of glaze painted on the fruit. After glazing dozens of tarts, we can vouch that sticky brush bristles can ensnare and dislodge bits of fruit, wrecking a design. Instead, we adopted a technique of dabbing/drizzling/flicking the glaze on the tart with a pastry brush. The result is not a smooth, even coat but something more dazzling—a sheath of droplets that catch light and glisten like dewdrops. The caveat is that the glaze must have the correct consistency. Too thin and the glaze will run off the fruit and pool in valleys; too thick and it falls from the brush in heavy globules. We found it helpful to bring the jelly to a boil, stirring it occasionally to ensure that it melts entirely, then use it straight off the stove.

WHAT WE LEARNED: Make a basic pastry cream thickened with egg yolks and cornstarch. Add butter to the finished cream for flavor and improved consistency. Chill the pastry cream before spreading it in a cooled tart shell, top with whole berries, and then drizzle and dab with hot jelly glaze.

FRESH FRUIT TART WITH PASTRY CREAM

serves 8 to 10

Remove the chalazae with your fingers (see right). The pastry cream can be made a day or two in advance, but do not fill the prebaked tart shell until just before serving. Once filled, the tart should be topped with fruit, glazed, and served within half an hour or so.

pastry cream

2	cups half-and-half
½	cup (3.5 ounces) sugar
	Pinch salt
5	large egg yolks, chalazae removed (see box, above right)
3	tablespoons cornstarch
4	tablespoons cold unsalted butter, cut into 4 pieces
1½	teaspoons vanilla extract
1	fully baked tart shell, 9 to 9½ inches (see page 276), cooled to room temperature

fruit and glaze

	Fruit, unwashed (see Three Fruit Tart Designs on page 285)
½	cup red currant or apple jelly (see Three Fruit Tart Designs on page 285)

1. FOR THE PASTRY CREAM: Heat half-and-half, 6 tablespoons sugar, and salt in medium heavy-bottomed saucepan over medium heat until simmering, stirring occasionally to dissolve sugar.

2. Meanwhile, whisk egg yolks in medium bowl until thoroughly combined. Whisk in remaining 2 tablespoons sugar and whisk until sugar has begun to dissolve and mixture is creamy, about 15 seconds. Whisk in cornstarch until combined and mixture is pale yellow and thick, about 30 seconds.

TECHNIQUE: Removing the Chalazae

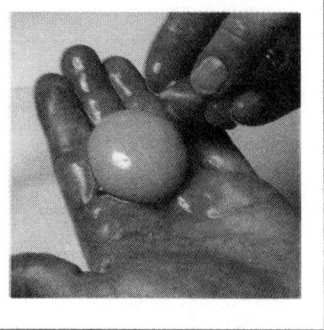

The cordlike strands of egg white protein attached to the yolk, called the chalazae, will harden when cooked. Removing them when separating the yolks and whites precludes the need to strain the pastry cream after cooking.

3. When half-and-half mixture reaches full simmer, gradually whisk simmering half-and-half into yolk mixture to temper. Return mixture to saucepan, scraping bowl with rubber spatula; return to simmer over medium heat, whisking constantly, until 3 or 4 bubbles burst on surface and mixture is thickened and glossy, about 30 seconds. Off heat, whisk in butter and vanilla. Transfer mixture to medium bowl, press plastic wrap directly on surface, and refrigerate until cold and set, at least 3 hours or up to 2 days.

4. TO ASSEMBLE AND GLAZE THE TART: Spread cold pastry cream over bottom of tart shell, using offset spatula or large spoon. (Can press plastic wrap directly on surface of pastry cream and refrigerate up to 30 minutes.) Arrange fruit on top of pastry cream, following a design on page 285.

5. Bring jelly to boil in small saucepan over medium-high heat, stirring occasionally to smooth out lumps. When boiling and completely melted, apply by dabbing and flicking onto fruit with pastry brush; add 1 teaspoon water and return jelly to boil if it becomes too thick to drizzle. (Tart can be refrigerated, uncovered, up to 30 minutes.) Remove outer metal ring of tart pan, slide thin metal spatula between bottom of crust and tart pan bottom to release, then slip tart onto cardboard round or serving platter; serve.

KIWI, RASPBERRY, AND BLUEBERRY TART:

Peel 2 large kiwis, halve lengthwise, and cut into half-moon slices about ⅜ inch thick. Arrange them cut-side down in an overlapping circle propped up against the inside edge of the pastry. Sort two ½ pints raspberries by height, and arrange them in three tight rings just inside the kiwi, using the tallest berries to form the inner ring. Mound ½ pint blueberries in the center. Use apple jelly to glaze this tart.

STRAWBERRY TART:

Brush dirt from 3 quarts ripe strawberries of medium, uniform size; slice off the tops. Sort the berries by height and place the tallest strawberry in the center of the tart. Arrange the nicest and most evenly shaped berries in tight rings around the center, placing them in order of descending height to the edge of the pastry. Quarter the remaining berries lengthwise and use them to fill gaps between the whole berries (see tips below). Use red currant jelly to glaze this tart.

MIXED BERRY TART:

Sort ½ pint blueberries, ½ pint blackberries, and two ½ pints raspberries, discarding any blemished fruit. Place all berries in a large plastic bag, then very gently shake the bag to combine them. Empty the berries on top of the tart, distributing them in an even layer. Then, using your fingers, adjust the berries as necessary so that they cover the entire surface and the colors are evenly distributed. Use red currant jelly to glaze this tart.

TECHNIQUE: Tips for Perfect Tarts

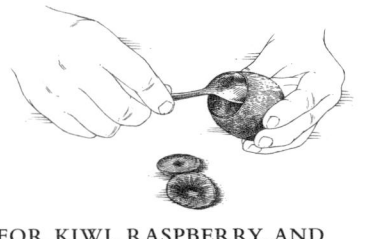

FOR KIWI, RASPBERRY, AND BLUEBERRY TART: To peel kiwi, cut off the ends, then slip a wide, shallow spoon between skin and flesh. Rotate the kiwi while pushing the spoon into the fruit, freeing it from the skin.

FOR STRAWBERRY TART: To fill gaps between the whole berries, begin at the center of the tart and place berries cut in quarters between them, pointed side up and skin-side out, leaning the quartered berries toward the center.

FOR MIXED BERRY TART: Place the berries in a large plastic bag. Hold the bag closed with one hand, and use the other to gently jostle the berries about to combine them.

DINER pies

CHAPTER 22

Those cream-topped pies in the revolving case at the diner always look better than they taste. Given what is required of these pies (they must look great for days on end), it's no surprise that these institutional creations are generally made with too much thickener and too few quality ingredients. But when prepared at home, where they can be enjoyed the day they are made, these pies can be a revelation.

Chocolate cream pie has almost universal appeal. Who doesn't like chocolate pastry cream and whipped cream delivered in a chocolate cookie crust? The key is to create a filling that is soft and creamy yet stiff enough to be cut cleanly. It's not as easy as it sounds. Use too much starch and the filling is thick and stodgy. Don't add enough egg yolks or starch and the filling literally runs all over the plate.

Key lime pie presents similar issues. This American classic begins with sweetened condensed milk. Many recipes don't require baking, but when made this way we found the filling to be loose and slurpy. After suffering through a dozen failed pies, we discovered that 15 minutes in the oven transforms the filling, making it sliceable and more flavorful.

Julia shows Chris how whisking lime zest with egg yolks tints the yolks a lovely shade of green and dispenses with the need for food coloring when making Key lime pie.

CHOCOLATE CREAM PIE

WHAT WE WANTED: A filling of voluptuous creaminess that would also be sliceworthy, with a well-balanced chocolate flavor somewhere between milkshake and melted candy bar.

Despite its grand flourishes and snowcapped peaks, a chocolate cream pie is essentially pastry cream whose substance has been given form. Comprising very basic ingredients—milk or cream, eggs, sugar, flour or cornstarch, butter, vanilla, and chocolate—it is cooked on the stovetop in a matter of minutes, chilled in a baked pie shell for a couple of hours, then topped with whipped cream. This pie, while looking superb, can be gluey or gummy, too sweet, even acrid.

A pastry cream, while in essence a quick, simple production, will form tapioca-like lumps of varying diameter in the presence of sloppiness or inattention. Sequencing is pretty standard: While the milk or cream is brought to a boil with most of the sugar, a small portion of the sugar is held back, combined with the starch, and mixed thoroughly with the yolks. This yolk mixture is then tempered, or warmed with a fraction of the simmering milk or cream, allowing the starch molecules to expand gently. The warmed emulsion is reintroduced to the simmering milk or cream, and the whole is brought rapidly to a boil under constant stirring or whisking. Despite the fact that it contains eggs, a pastry cream can and must boil if the starch molecules are to expand and thicken.

We began by assessing a classic pastry cream recipe— 4 egg yolks, ½ cup sugar, 3 tablespoons cornstarch, 2 cups milk, 1 teaspoon vanilla extract, and 2 tablespoons butter— realizing that the proportions might require substantial modification for a chocolate filling. We wanted first to settle on the ingredient base and ran some comparative tests, most of which left us true to our original candidates. Egg yolks, for example, produced a cream of unsurpassed texture and flavor, far superior to one made with whole eggs. Cornstarch tasted lighter and cleaner than flour. Cold butter stirred into the finished cream effected tremendous improvements in texture and flavor, making the pastry cream supple and lush. One ingredient was to change. Half-and-half provided enhanced mouthfeel and textural support for the chocolate; it was markedly better than milk or cream.

Through multiple trials and tweakings we developed a basic recipe that contained all of the ingredients mentioned above, along with more half-and-half to increase overall volume. It also called for higher proportions of egg yolks (6) and butter (6 tablespoons) than a standard pastry cream. Testing had convinced us that the texture of a chocolate cream filling benefits immeasurably when fats are used as thickeners and basic starch is minimized. Butter, egg yolks, and half-and-half render a silky texture and provide most of the requisite thickening with greater finesse than cornstarch.

We had three chocolate options: semisweet (or bittersweet, which is quite similar), unsweetened, or a mixture of the two. Tasters felt that fillings made exclusively with semisweet or bittersweet chocolate lacked depth of flavor, while those made with unsweetened chocolate alone hit a sour note. Without exception, tasters wanted the filling to land on the dark, intense bittersweet side and the cream topping to be sweet and pure.

The roundest, most upfront chocolate flavor, with lingering intensity at the finish, came in the form of 6 ounces semisweet and 1 ounce unsweetened chocolate. The apparently negligible amount of unsweetened chocolate contributed hugely to the flavor. Unsweetened chocolate, which does not undergo the kneading, grinding, and smoothing process known as conching, retains all of its strong and sometimes bitter flavors that translate well in small amounts.

This was not the only advantage of using a small amount of unsweetened chocolate. Because it further thickened the cream (see the Science Desk on page 291), we were able to reduce the cornstarch from 3 tablespoons to 2.

Next we moved on to compare fancy imported chocolates with domestic grocery store brands. The first test, pitting the widely available Baker's unsweetened chocolate against several unsweetened chocolates with European pedigrees, confirmed our fears that the supermarket stuff would be no match for its European competition. (Of the imported chocolates, all tasters preferred Callebaut.) Even at 1 ounce, the Baker's chocolate contributed an "off" flavor and rubberiness of texture that everyone noticed. But the next round of testing brought unexpected good news: Hershey's Special Dark chocolate was a consistent winner in the semisweet category, beating out not only a premium American semisweet entry but also its European competitors—and you can buy it in a drugstore! Hershey's unsweetened chocolate, while not as refined in flavor and texture as Callebaut unsweetened, placed a respectable second to Callebaut and was miles ahead of Baker's.

Because the filling is three standing inches of pure chocolate, a texture less than faultlessly smooth will deliver an experience less than ethereal. Temperature, timing, and technique are important.

On occasions when we didn't combine the eggs adequately with the sugar and starch (which meant mixing almost until the yolks ribboned) or when we left the emulsion to sit around awaiting the simmering half-and-half, the sugar began to break down the yolks and made the finished texture of the cream grainy. For the pastry cream to attain a flawless texture, the half-and-half in the pan was best left at a simmer—rather than pulled off the stove—while the yolks were tempered. This way the introduction of the warmed yolks barely registered on the half-and-half, which quickly came up to a boil and was finished.

As for the crust, tasters swooned over a crumb crust made with chocolate cookie crumbs to the exclusion of all others. While easier to make than rolled pastry dough and arguably better suited to chilled pudding fillings, crumb crusts are not altogether seamless enterprises. Sandy and insubstantial at one extreme, tough and intractable at the other, they can be a serving nightmare. While no one expects a slice of cream pie to hold up like a slab of marble, it isn't expected to collapse on a bed of grit or lacerate a cornea with airborne shrapnel, either. It's got to slice.

The standard cookie used to make a chocolate crumb crust is Nabisco Famous Chocolate Wafers, but we didn't care for the flavor of these crusts unbaked and found them somewhat tough (if sliceable) baked. After trying without much success to soften the crust with a percentage of fresh white bread crumbs, we made a leap of faith to Oreo cookies pulverized straight up with their filling. We hoped that the creaminess of the centers would lend flavor and softness to the finished crust. The Oreo flavor came through loud and clear, and the creamy centers, along with a bit of butter, prevented the baked crumbs from becoming tough. No additional sugar or even salt was required.

Why did Oreos work so well? Oreo centers are sweetened hydrogenated shortening, like the Crisco icing on an inexpensive wedding cake. Hydrogenation refers to a process in which hydrogen gas is forced under pressure into the molecules of a vegetable oil, expanding, or "saturating," them into a semisolid state. Harold McGee, in *On Food and Cooking* (Scribner, 1984), terms this "a modern oil that is conveniently pre-creamed"—in other words, whipped. It is this quality in an Oreo filling that gives Oreo crumb crusts their edge over crusts made with plain chocolate cookies and melted butter. The fat in a hydrogenated shortening encases millions of air pockets. When the fat melts during baking, the air pockets remain, creating small empty spaces between the crumbs, thereby making the crust register as light and agreeably crisp—not hard—to the teeth.

Ten minutes in a 350 degree-oven set the crust nicely; higher temperatures burned the cocoa. The crisp salty-sweet chocolate crumbs gave the rich filling voice and definition. Cloaked with whipped cream, this piece moves as one.

WHAT WE LEARNED: Use a combination of bittersweet and unsweetened chocolate for best flavor and texture, and grind Oreos for a crust that's light, crisp, and sliceable.

CHOCOLATE CREAM PIE serves 8 to 10

For the best chocolate flavor and texture, we recommend either Callebaut semisweet and unsweetened chocolates or Hershey's Special Dark and Hershey's unsweetened chocolates. Do not combine the yolks and sugar in advance of making the filling—the sugar will begin to break down the yolks, and the finished cream will be pitted.

chocolate cookie crumb crust

16	Oreo cookies (with filling), broken into rough pieces, about 2½ cups
2	tablespoons unsalted butter, melted and cooled

chocolate cream filling

2½	cups half-and-half
	Pinch salt
⅓	cup (2.3 ounces) sugar
2	tablespoons cornstarch
6	large egg yolks, room temperature, chalazae removed (see photo on page 284)
6	tablespoons cold unsalted butter, cut into 6 pieces
6	ounces semisweet or bittersweet chocolate, finely chopped
1	ounce unsweetened chocolate, finely chopped
1	teaspoon vanilla extract
3	cups Whipped Cream (page 294), whipped to soft peaks

1. FOR THE CRUST: Adjust oven rack to middle position and heat oven to 350 degrees. In bowl of food processor fitted with steel blade, process cookies with fifteen 1-second pulses, then let machine run until crumbs are uniformly fine, about 15 seconds. (Alternatively, place cookies in large zipper-lock plastic bag and crush with rolling pin.) Transfer crumbs to medium bowl, drizzle with butter, and use fingers to combine until butter is evenly distributed.

2. Pour crumbs into 9-inch Pyrex pie plate. Press crumbs evenly onto bottom and up sides of pie plate. Once crumbs are in place, line pan flush with large square of plastic wrap, and use spoon to smooth crumbs into curves and sides of pan. Refrigerate lined pie plate 20 minutes to firm crumbs, then bake until crumbs are fragrant and set, about 10 minutes. Cool on wire rack while preparing filling.

3. FOR THE FILLING: Bring half-and-half, salt, and about 3 tablespoons sugar to simmer in medium saucepan over medium-high heat, stirring occasionally with wooden spoon to dissolve sugar. Stir together remaining sugar and

cornstarch in small bowl. Whisk yolks thoroughly in medium bowl until slightly thickened, about 30 seconds. Sprinkle cornstarch mixture over yolks and whisk, scraping down sides of bowl, if necessary, until mixture is glossy and sugar has begun to dissolve, about 1 minute. When half-and-half reaches full simmer, drizzle about ½ cup hot half-and-half over yolks, whisking constantly to temper; then whisk egg yolk mixture into simmering half-and-half (mixture should thicken in about 30 seconds). Return to simmer, whisking constantly, until 3 or 4 bubbles burst on surface and mixture is thickened and glossy, about 15 seconds longer.

4. Off heat, whisk in butter until incorporated; add chocolates and whisk until melted, scraping pan bottom with rubber spatula to fully incorporate. Stir in vanilla, then immediately pour filling into baked and cooled crust. Press plastic wrap directly on surface of filling and refrigerate pie until filling is cold and firm, about 3 hours.

5. Just before serving, spread or pipe whipped cream over chilled pie filling. Cut pie into wedges and serve.

SCIENCE DESK: Chocolate as Thickener

EVERYONE KNOWS THAT BITTERSWEET AND UNSWEETENED chocolates have different flavors and levels of sweetness. But their dissimilarities do not end there. As we developed our chocolate cream pie recipe, we discovered that ounce-for-ounce, unsweetened chocolate has more thickening power. We were aware of chocolate's starchy properties (cocoa solids are rich in starches), but we were not prepared for the dramatic differences in texture revealed in side-by-side pie fillings made with each type. Though both fillings had roughly the same amount of cocoa solids by volume, the unsweetened chocolate filling was significantly stiffer and had a viscous, gummy quality. Its counterpart made only with bittersweet chocolate had a smooth and creamy texture.

While many cookbook substitutions fail to take into account the higher starch concentration of unsweetened chocolate, cooks should be mindful of its thickening power. Comparable amounts of bittersweet or semisweet chocolate and unsweetened chocolate plus sugar will not produce identical results. While a direct swap might work well enough in fudgy brownies, it could wreak havoc on a delicate custard or airy cake.

So why did we decide to include unsweetened chocolate in our filling if it can produce such unappealing results? The chocolate's intensity is essential to the filling's character. By using just a single ounce of unsweetened chocolate in our recipe, we were able to attain the perfect balance of nuanced chocolate flavor and pleasing, velvety texture. What's more, as mentioned in our story on developing the recipe for the pie (page 288), the thickening power of even this small amount of unsweetened chocolate helped us keep a cap on the cornstarch, which can detract from a custard's silky texture when added in copious amounts.

EQUIPMENT CORNER: Whisks

THERE IS A BOUNTY OF WHISKS ON THE MARKET—FLAT round, balloon, and coiled. We wanted to see if the average cook needed more than one whisk and, if so, which ones.

We purchased 15 whisks representative of the flat, round, balloon, and coiled varieties. Some models were made of nonstick plastic. Others were silicone-coated. One even had a small round wire cage containing a ceramic ball. The whisks ranged in size from 8 to 12 inches and in price from $5.95 to $21.95. We tested their performance in three classic tasks: making a béchamel sauce (a classic sauce made from butter, flour, and milk), beating egg whites, and whipping cream. All three jobs require constant movement from the whisk.

For the béchamel, we wanted a whisk that would work well in a smaller saucepan, that would keep the roux from burning, and that would emulsify the butter and flour into the milk without lumps. For egg whites and cream, we wanted a whisk that would create a tight foam with minimum effort and forearm cramping. We were also looking for whisks that created the least mess—no splashes of hot milk or dollops of cream and egg white.

Early into the testing, we discovered that, indeed, different whisks are better for different tasks—but only two different whisks are worth owning. A balloon whisk is perfect for air incorporation but too large for sauces and emulsification. Conversely, a flat whisk is ideal for sauces and emulsification but not very good at air incorporation.

The winning whisk for the béchamel was a flat silicone-coated model from Williams-Sonoma ($9). It was both quiet and effective, with the tines conforming to the pan sides perfectly. The least effective flat whisk was the Calphalon flat plastic nonstick whisk. It was cumbersome and had too few tines that were also too large.

Although intrigued by the concept, we were not impressed overall by the unusual coiled models. One had a very uncomfortable handle and required pressure to flatten the coiled head, while the other had a very short handle set at an awkward angle.

The winning balloon whisk was a standard, larger (12-inch) model. It was comfortable in the hand and was large enough to incorporate air quickly and efficiently. Our two least favorite models were the Calphalon nonstick plastic, which was large and messy, and the Williams-Sonoma with the caged ceramic ball, which flung bits of cream out of the bowl and onto our aprons and counters.

WHIPPED CREAM

WHAT WE WANTED: Perfectly whipped and lightly sweetened cream that could be spooned over a pie, cobbler, or pudding.

Whipped cream often makes the difference between a good dessert and a great one. But if you are going to the trouble to whip cream, it better be good. You certainly don't want overwhipped cream that's curdled and lumpy. Likewise, achingly sweet cream, or cream marred by the presence of gritty granules of sugar, is not acceptable. For our testing, we wanted to examine the ingredients (the type of cream, the type of sugar) and the best whipping technique.

Ultrapasteurized heavy cream is the standard choice in most dairy cases, although you may occasionally see pasteurized heavy cream or organic heavy cream, which is usually pasteurized rather than ultrapasteurized. We whipped several cartons of each cream and found that pasteurized organic heavy cream was the favorite in the test kitchen. It delivers the sweetest cream flavor, and although it pours the thinnest, it whips up to double its volume.

Regular pasteurized heavy cream is thicker and has a richer mouthfeel, owing no doubt to additives intended to bulk up the texture. However, it was not as sweet and did not whip quite as well as the organic cream.

The ultrapasteurized heavy cream made the worst whipped cream in our testing. While it is the thickest by far out of the container, its volume increased by just 50 percent when whipped. Several experts explained that the high temperatures required for ultrapasteurization destroy some of the proteins and enzymes that promote whipping. The higher heat (which prolongs shelf life) also leaves the cream with a slightly cooked taste. We found that pasteurized cream, which is subject to less heat but has a shorter shelf life, delivers better flavor and volume every time and is worth seeking out. A supermarket or natural foods store that carries organic milk will probably sell organic cream, and we think this is your best bet. If you must use ultrapasteurized cream, the whipping time should be increased by 10 to 20 seconds, and you certainly should not expect the cream to double in volume.

Many sources suggest sweetening cream with confectioners' sugar to ensure that the sugar dissolves. In our tests, regular granulated sugar dissolved just fine as long as it was added before beating, not after. When making a highly sweetened whipped cream topping (with more than 3 tablespoons sugar per cup of heavy cream), it is best to use fine confectioners' sugar to prevent the possibility of grittiness. But we find that cream whipped with this much sugar is unbearably sweet for most uses.

Vanilla extract is a common addition to whipped cream, adding complexity and rounding out the flavors. We found that ½ teaspoon of extract is the right amount for 1½ cups cream.

With our ingredients set, we turned our attention to technique. Most sources indicate that chilled cream will beat more easily and to greater heights than warm cream. We found this to be the case. In fact, for maximum volume we recommend chilling the bowl and beaters as well.

Most recipes for whipping cream are quite vague about mixing speed. We obtained the best results when we started the cream and sugar on low speed, raised the speed to medium, and then finished at high speed. The whole process should take about 1½ minutes. We found that gradually increasing the speed of the mixer allows the cream to hold more air. Cream whipped at high speed from the outset was less stable and not as voluminous.

WHAT WE LEARNED: For best flavor and volume, use pasteurized rather than ultrapasteurized cream. Granulated sugar, when used in moderate amounts, will dissolve just fine if added before whipping. Finally, whip slowly at first, increasing the speed as you go, to obtain soft, billowy peaks.

WHIPPED CREAM   makes about 3 cups

When you think the cream is almost properly whipped, you may want to switch from an electric mixer to a whisk for greater control. Cream can go from properly whipped to overwhipped in a matter of seconds. If cream becomes granular and curdled-looking, you've beaten it too long and must start over with a new batch of cream. This recipe can be halved if needed.

- 1½   cups heavy cream, chilled, preferably pasteurized or pasteurized organic
- 1½   tablespoons granulated sugar
- ½   teaspoon vanilla extract

1. Chill deep bowl and beaters of electric mixer in freezer for at least 20 minutes. (If freezer is too crowded to fit bowl, place beaters in bowl, fill bowl with ice water, and chill on counter. When bowl and beaters are well chilled, dump out water and dry thoroughly.)

2. Add cream, sugar, and vanilla to chilled bowl. Beat on low speed until small bubbles form, about 30 seconds. Increase speed to medium and continue beating until beaters leave a trail, about 30 seconds. Increase speed to high and continue beating until cream is smooth, thick, and nearly doubled in volume, about 20 seconds for soft peaks or about 30 seconds for stiff peaks (see illustrations at right). If necessary, finish beating with whisk to adjust consistency. Serve immediately or spoon into fine sieve or strainer set over measuring cup and refrigerate for up to 8 hours.

SCIENCE DESK:
Temperature and Whipped Cream

WHY DO SO MANY WHIPPED CREAM RECIPES, INCLUDING ours, call for chilled cream as well as chilled beaters and bowl? Whipped cream is a foam stabilized by fat. The foam is nothing more than air bubbles beaten into the cream by the beaters. When things work right, the fat globules are dispersed evenly among the air bubbles and they stick to together, thus supporting the foam.

However, the fat globules must be at the right temperature if they are to stick together. If they are too warm, they won't stick together and the foam collapses. When the cream is cold, the fat globules are stickier.

Keep it cold and cream should whip perfectly. But don't overwhip the cream. If you whip too long, the cream can curdle and separate. That's because prolonged beating has warmed the cream. If the cream gets too warm, the fat globules start to separate and your whipped cream curdles.

TECHNIQUE: Whipping Cream to Soft or Stiff Peaks

SOFT PEAKS
Cream whipped to soft peaks will droop slightly from the ends of the beaters or whisk.

STIFF PEAKS
Cream whipped to stiff peaks will cling tightly to the ends of the beaters or whisk and will hold its shape.

KEY LIME PIE

WHAT WE WANTED: A filling with real lime flavor that would be creamy but firm enough to slice easily.

The standard recipe for Key lime pie is incredibly short and simple: beat 4 egg yolks, add a 14-ounce can of sweetened condensed milk, and then stir in ½ cup lime juice and a tablespoon of grated lime zest. Pour it all into a graham cracker crust and chill it until firm, about two hours. Top the pie with sweetened whipped cream and serve.

It would be lovely if this recipe worked, but we found that it doesn't, at least not to our total satisfaction. Although the filling does set firm enough to yield clean-cut slices, it has a loose, "slurpy" consistency. We tried to fix the consistency by beating the yolks until thick, as some recipes direct, but this did not help. Nor did it help to dribble in the lime juice rather than adding it all at once, as other recipes suggest. We also made the filling with only two yolks and with no yolks at all (such "eggless" versions of the recipe do exist), but this yielded even thinner fillings.

Still, the time spent mixing Key lime pie fillings in various ways was not a total loss. While in the heat of experimenting, we inadvertently threw the lime zest into a bowl in which we had already placed the egg yolks. When we whisked up the yolks, they turned green, and the whole filling ended up tinted a lovely shade of pale lime. What a great way to dispense with food coloring.

Having found the mix-and-chill method wanting, we decided to try baking the pie, as some recipes suggest. We used the same ingredients as we had before and simply baked the pie until the filling stiffened slightly, about 15 minutes in a moderate oven. The difference between the baked pie (which was really a custard) and the unbaked pie (which had merely been a clabber) was remarkable. (See the Science Desk on page 297 for more information on how Key lime pie thickens.) The baked filling was thick, creamy, and unctuous, reminiscent of cream pie. It also tasted more pungent

and complex than the raw fillings had, perhaps because the heat of the oven released the flavorful oils in the lime zest.

Up until this point, we had been working with regular supermarket limes (called Persian limes), but we wondered if Key limes would make a better pie. True Key limes, or *Citrus aurantifolia,* have not been a significant commercial crop in this country since storms destroyed the Florida groves early in this century. However, a few growers have recently begun to revive the crop, and Key limes occasionally show up in supermarkets.

We'd love to say that Key lime juice made all the difference in the world, but it didn't. We found that it tasted pretty much the same as the juice of supermarket limes. Key limes are also a nuisance to zest and squeeze. They are thin-skinned, full of seeds, and generally little bigger than walnuts. Whereas you need only three or four Persian limes to make a Key lime pie, you need up to a dozen Key limes. So despite the name of the pie, we actually find the juice of Persian limes preferable as an ingredient.

WHAT WE LEARNED: Whisk the lime zest and yolks together to release oils from the zest and give the filling a lovely green color. Don't just pour the filling into the pie shell and serve. Baking makes the filling reminiscent of cream pie—thick, creamy, and unctuous. The heat of the oven releases the flavorful oils in the lime zest and makes the filling taste better, too.

KEY LIME PIE serves 8 to 10

Despite this pie's name, we found that tasters could not tell the difference between pies made with regular supermarket limes (called Persian limes) and true Key limes. Since Persian limes are easier to find and juice, we recommend them.

lime filling

4	teaspoons grated zest plus ½ cup strained juice from 3 or 4 limes
4	large egg yolks
1	(14-ounce) can sweetened condensed milk

graham cracker crust

11	full-size graham crackers, processed to fine crumbs (1¼ cups)
3	tablespoons granulated sugar
5	tablespoons unsalted butter, melted
1½	cups Whipped Cream (page 294), made without vanilla and whipped to stiff peaks
½	lime, sliced paper thin and dipped in sugar (optional)

1. FOR THE FILLING: Whisk zest and yolks in medium bowl until tinted light green, about 2 minutes. Beat in milk, then juice; set aside at room temperature to thicken.

2. FOR THE CRUST: Adjust oven rack to center position and heat oven to 325 degrees. Mix crumbs and sugar in medium bowl. Add butter; stir with fork until well blended. Scrape mixture into 9-inch pie pan. Press crumbs evenly onto bottom and up sides of pie plate. Once crumbs are in place, line pan flush with large square of plastic wrap, and use spoon to smooth crumbs into curves and sides of pan. Refrigerate lined pie plate 20 minutes to firm crumbs. Bake until lightly browned and fragrant, about 15 minutes. Transfer pan to wire rack; cool to room temperature, about 20 minutes.

3. Pour lime filling into crust; bake until center is set yet wiggly when jiggled, 15 to 17 minutes. Return pie to wire rack; cool to room temperature. Refrigerate until well chilled, at least 3 hours. (Can be covered with lightly oiled or oil-sprayed plastic wrap laid directly on filling and refrigerated up to 1 day.)

4. Decoratively pipe whipped cream over filling or spread evenly with rubber spatula. Garnish with optional sugared lime slices and serve.

SCIENCE DESK: How Key Lime Pie Thickens

THE EXTRAORDINARILY HIGH ACID CONTENT OF LIMES and the unique properties of sweetened condensed milk are responsible for the fact that lime pie filling will thicken without cooking.

The acid in the lime juice does its work by causing the proteins in both the egg yolks and the condensed milk to coil up and bond together. This effect is similar to that of heat. The same process can be observed in the Latin American dish ceviche, in which raw fish is "cooked" simply by being pickled in lime juice.

But this process does not work well with just any kind of milk; it requires both the sweetness and the thickness of sweetened condensed milk. This canned product is made by boiling the moisture out of fresh milk and then adding sugar. Because the milk has been evaporated, or condensed, it is thick enough to stiffen into a sliceable filling when "cooked" by the lime juice. The sugar, meanwhile, plays the crucial role of separating, or "greasing," the protein strands so that they do not bond too tightly. If they did, the result would be a grainy or curdled filling rather than a smooth and creamy one. Of course, a liquidy, curdly filling is exactly what would result if fresh milk were used instead of canned. Fresh milk lacks the crucial added sugar and is also much thinner.

We also discovered that cream is not a viable substitute for sweetened condensed milk. It does not curdle the way milk does because its fat, like the sugar in condensed milk, buffers the effects of the lime juice. Cream is roughly 50 percent liquid, however, and thus it will only thicken, not stiffen, when clabbered.

Apple pies ready for their 15 minutes of fame before the cameras.

APPLE pies

CHAPTER 23

Making good pie crust can be a simple procedure, but almost everyone who has tried can tell horror stories of crusts that turned out hard, soggy, flavorless, oversalted, underbaked, crumbly, or unworkable. Advice is easy to come by: One expert says that butter is the secret to perfect crust; others swear by vegetable shortening, lard, even canola oil. Some omit salt, some omit sugar, some insist that working the dough by hand is essential, some use cake flour or pastry flour in addition to all-purpose flour, some freeze the dough, some do away with the rolling pin . . . and so on.

To test these propositions, we made hundreds of doughs, with all types of ingredients, and in all types of devices. The resulting recipe, American Pie Dough, is the culmination of years of kitchen work and testing.

Of course, you need to fill pie dough with something. We've chosen apples (a similar dough can be used to make peach pie; see the recipe on page 313) and present two versions—the classic pie with a double crust as well as a more rustic free-form tart that bakes on a cookie sheet, not in a pie plate.

AMERICAN PIE DOUGH

WHAT WE WANTED: A great-tasting, flaky dough that is easy to roll out and handle.

Simple as it can be, pie crust—essentially a combination of flour, water, and fat—raises numerous questions: What are the ideal proportions of the main ingredients? What else should be added for character? What methods should be used to combine these ingredients?

The most controversial ingredient in pastry is fat. We've found that all-butter crusts have good taste, but they are not as flaky and fine-textured as those made with shortening. All-shortening crusts have great texture but lack flavor; oil-based crusts are flat and entirely unappealing; and those made with lard are heavy and strongly flavored. After experimenting with a variety of combinations, we ultimately settled on a proportion of 3 parts butter to 2 parts shortening as optimal for both flavor and texture.

Vegetable shortenings such as Crisco are made from vegetable oil that has been hydrogenated, a process in which hydrogen gas is pumped into the molecules of a vegetable oil to incorporate air and to raise its melting point above room temperature. Crisco is about 10 percent gas and does a good job of lightening and tenderizing. (The way the butter is incorporated into the flour also contributes to flakiness. See the Science Desk on page 304 for details.)

Pie crusts are usually made with all-purpose flour. No matter what we've tried—substituting cornstarch for part of the all-purpose flour (a cookie-baking trick that increases tenderness), adding 1/4 teaspoon baking powder to increase rise and flakiness, and mixing cake flour or pastry flour with the all-purpose flour (again, to increase tenderness)—we always come back to plain old all-purpose flour. We also tackled the proportions of salt and sugar, which were much easier to resolve. After testing amounts ranging from 1/4 teaspoon to as much as 2 tablespoons, we settled on 1 teaspoon salt and 2 tablespoons sugar for a double-crust pie, amounts that enhance the flavor of the dough without shouting out their presence.

We experimented with buttermilk, milk, and cider vinegar. No liquid additions improved our basic recipe, so we recommend that you stick with ice water.

Pie dough can be made by hand, but we've found that the food processor is faster and easier and does the best job of cutting the fat into the flour. Proper mixing is important. If you undermix, the crust will shrink when baked and became hard and crackly. If you overprocess, you'll get a crumbly, cookie-like dough. The shortening should be pulsed with the flour until the mixture is sandy; butter is then pulsed in until the mixture looks like coarse crumbs, with butter bits no larger than the size of a pea.

Once the flour and fat have been combined, ice water is mixed in. We've come to favor a rubber spatula and a folding motion to mix in the water, which exposes all of the dough to moisture without overworking it, something that can happen if the dough is left in the food processor and the water is pulsed in. Using a spatula to incorporate water makes it possible to minimize the amount of water used (less water means a more tender dough) and reduces the likelihood of overworking the dough. Still, we've also learned that it doesn't pay to be too stingy with the water. If there isn't enough, the dough will be crumbly and hard to roll.

Finally, we found that pie dough need not be difficult to roll out if you remember two basic guidelines: Make sure the dough is well chilled before rolling, and add a minimum of flour to the work surface. Flour added during rolling will cause the dough to toughen. If the dough seems too soft to roll, it's best to refrigerate it rather than adding more flour.

WHAT WE LEARNED: Use a mixture of butter for flavor and shortening for flakiness. Cut the fat into the flour in the food processor, but turn the dough into a bowl and incorporate the water with a spatula.

AMERICAN PIE DOUGH for one double-crust 9-inch pie

2½ cups (12.5 ounces) unbleached all-purpose flour
1 teaspoon salt
2 tablespoons sugar
8 tablespoons all-vegetable shortening, chilled
12 tablespoons unsalted butter, chilled, cut into ¼-inch pieces
6–8 tablespoons ice water

1. Pulse flour, salt, and sugar in food processor fitted with steel blade until combined. Add shortening and process until mixture has texture of coarse sand, about 10 seconds. Scatter butter pieces over flour mixture; cut butter into flour until mixture is pale yellow and resembles coarse crumbs, with butter bits no larger than small peas, about ten 1-second pulses. Turn mixture into medium bowl.

2. Sprinkle 6 tablespoons ice water over mixture. With blade of rubber spatula, use folding motion to mix. Press down on dough with broad side of spatula until dough sticks together, adding up to 2 tablespoons more ice water if it will not come together. Divide dough into two balls and flatten each into 4-inch-wide disk. Wrap each in plastic and refrigerate at least 1 hour or up to 2 days before rolling.

VARIATIONS

AMERICAN PIE DOUGH FOR LATTICE-TOP PIE

This crust has a firmer texture than the basic recipe, making it easier to work with when creating a lattice top for peach pie (see page 313).

Follow recipe for American Pie Dough, increasing flour to 3 cups (15 ounces), reducing shortening to 7 tablespoons, reducing butter to 10 tablespoons, and increasing ice water to 10 tablespoons. Divide dough into two pieces, one slightly larger than the other. (If possible, weigh pieces. They should register 16 ounces and 14 ounces.) Flatten larger piece into a rough 5-inch square and smaller piece into a 4-inch disk; wrap separately in plastic and chill as directed.

AMERICAN PIE DOUGH FOR FREE-FORM TART

For a rustic free-form tart, we don't mind if the pastry isn't as flaky, so we use butter alone, with no shortening. This dough is also a bit sweeter than our standard recipe.

Follow recipe for American Pie Dough, reducing flour to 1¼ cups (6.25 ounces) and salt to ½ teaspoon. Omit shortening, reduce butter to 10 tablespoons, and reduce ice water to 3 to 4 tablespoons. Do not divide dough. Flatten into single disk; wrap and chill as directed.

EQUIPMENT CORNER: Pie Plates

WE TESTED THREE TYPES OF PIE PLATE—GLASS, CERAMIC, and metal—and found that a Pyrex glass pie plate did the best job of browning the crust, both when filled and baked blind (the bottom crust baked alone, filled with pie weights to hold its shape). Several metal pie plates also browned quite well, but the glass pie plate has a number of advantages.

Because you can see through a Pyrex plate, it's easy to judge just how brown the bottom crust has become during baking. With a metal pie plate, it's easy to pull the pie out of the oven too soon, when the bottom crust is still quite pale. A second feature we like about the traditional Pyrex plate is the wide rim, which makes the plate easier to take in and out of the oven and also supports fluted edges better than thin rims. Finally, you can store a pie filled with acidic fruit and not worry about metal giving the fruit an off flavor.

Pyrex pie plates do heat up more quickly than metal, so pies may be done a bit sooner than you think, especially if you are following a recipe that was tested in a metal plate. All the times in our recipes are based on baking in a glass pie plate; if baking in metal you may need to add two to three minutes for empty crusts and five minutes for filled pies.

APPLE PIE

WHAT WE WANTED: A classic pie that really tastes like apples, with a modicum of juice and a tender crust.

Cooks who slather the apples in their pies with butter, cinnamon, and sugar do themselves and the apples a disservice; we set out to make a pie in which the apples shine through. We started by examining the choice of apples for the filling. We tested the nine best-selling apples, figuring that we wanted a recipe that would work with apples commonly available in supermarkets throughout the year.

We determined that Granny Smith and McIntosh both have excellent qualities; the former is tart with good texture, and the latter has excellent flavor. But each also has its drawbacks. A pie made with Grannies alone was too sour and a bit dull in flavor, while an all-McIntosh pie was too soft, more like applesauce in a crust than apple pie. A pie made with both varieties, however, was outstanding. The Grannies hold up well during cooking, and the Macs add flavor. The mushy texture of the Macs becomes a virtue in this setting, providing a nice base for the harder Grannies and soaking up some of the juice.

We also tested a dozen not-so-common apple varieties, the kinds you may see in local markets during the fall, especially if you live near apple orchards. We found that Macoun, Royal Gala, Empire, Winesap, Rhode Island Greening, and Cortland apples all make excellent pies. Unlike Granny Smiths, these well-balanced apples work well on their own without thickeners or the addition of McIntosh.

We have always used butter in our pies. In fact, we used to use up to 6 tablespoons in a deep-dish pie, cutting this back to a more modest 2 tablespoons over the years. But when we taste-tested pies with and without butter, the leaner pies won hands down. Butter simply dulls the fresh taste of apples, so now we do without it altogether. Lemon juice, however, is absolutely crucial to a good apple pie, heightening the flavor of the apples rather than dulling or masking it. In the end, we settled on 1 tablespoon of lemon juice and 1 teaspoon of zest.

To our thinking, many recipes call for too much thickener (usually flour), and the result is a lifeless filling. A bit of tart, thin juice gives the pie a breath of the orchard, whereas a thick, syrupy texture is dull. In the end, we prefer to thicken the filling for our apple pie very lightly, with just 2 tablespoons flour.

Many cookbooks claim that letting apples sit in a bowl with the sugar, lemon juice, and spices, otherwise known as macerating, is key in developing flavors and juice. We found, however, that this simply caused the apples to dry out, making them rubbery and unpleasant. In addition, the apples themselves lose flavor, having exuded all of their fruitiness into the juice. So macerating, a common step in apple pie making, was clearly out.

In many apple pies, the top crust sets up quickly, leaving an air space between it and the apples, which reduce in volume as they cook. With our crust recipe, however, this is not an issue. Sufficient shortening is cut into the flour so that the crust sinks down onto the apples as they cook. We did notice, however, that this high ratio of shortening produces a very flaky crust, one that is not easily cut into perfect slices. In addition, because there is still a fair amount of juice, which we find essential for good flavor, the filling may spread slightly once the pie is cut into individual slices.

WHAT WE LEARNED: If relying on supermarket apples, use a blend of Granny Smiths for tartness and firmness and McIntosh for flavor and thickening ability. Butter dulls the flavor of the apples (the crust has plenty, anyway), while lemon juice brightens their flavor. Use just a whisper of flour to thicken the filling.

CLASSIC APPLE PIE serves 8

When all of the apples have been sliced, you should have a total of about 8 cups. The pie is best eaten when cooled to room temperature, or even the next day.

  1   recipe American Pie Dough (page 301)
1½ pounds Granny Smith apples (about
      3 medium)
  2   pounds McIntosh apples (about
      4 large)
  1   tablespoon juice and 1 teaspoon zest
      from 1 lemon
 ¾ cup (5.25 ounces) plus 1 tablespoon sugar
  2   tablespoons all-purpose flour
 ¼ teaspoon salt
 ¼ teaspoon ground nutmeg
 ¼ teaspoon ground cinnamon
 ⅛ teaspoon ground allspice
  1   egg white, beaten lightly

1. Adjust oven rack to lowest position and heat rimmed baking sheet and oven to 500 degrees. Remove one piece of dough from refrigerator (if refrigerated longer than 1 hour, let stand at room temperature until malleable).

2. Roll dough on lightly floured work surface or between two large sheets of plastic wrap to 12-inch disk. Transfer dough to pie plate by rolling dough around rolling pin and unrolling over 9½-inch pie plate or by folding dough in quarters, then placing dough point in center of pie plate and unfolding. Working around circumference of pie plate, ease dough into pan corners by gently lifting dough edges with one hand while pressing around pan bottom with other hand. Leave dough that overhangs lip of pie plate in place; refrigerate dough-lined pie plate.

3. Peel, core, and cut apples in half, and in half again widthwise; cut quarters into ¼-inch slices and toss with lemon juice and zest. In a medium bowl, mix ¾ cup sugar, flour, salt, and spices. Toss dry ingredients with apples. Turn fruit mixture, including juices, into chilled pie shell and mound slightly in center.

4. Roll out second piece of dough to 12-inch disk and place over filling. Trim top and bottom edges to ½ inch beyond pan lip. Tuck this rim of dough underneath itself so that folded edge is flush with pan lip. Flute edging or press with fork tines to seal. Cut four slits on dough top. If pie dough is very soft, place in freezer for 10 minutes. Brush egg white onto top of crust and sprinkle evenly with remaining 1 tablespoon sugar.

5. Place pie on baking sheet and lower oven temperature to 425 degrees. Bake until top crust is golden, about 25 minutes. Rotate pie and reduce oven temperature to 375 degrees; continue baking until juices bubble and crust is deep golden brown, 30 to 35 minutes longer.

6. Transfer pie to wire rack; cool to room temperature, at least 4 hours.

APPLE PIE WITH CRYSTALLIZED GINGER

Follow recipe for Classic Apple Pie, adding 3 tablespoons chopped crystallized ginger to apple mixture.

APPLE PIE WITH DRIED FRUIT

Macerate 1 cup raisins, dried sweet cherries, or dried cranberries in lemon juice plus 1 tablespoon applejack, brandy, or cognac. Follow recipe for Classic Apple Pie, adding macerated dried fruit and liquid to apple mixture.

APPLE PIE WITH FRESH CRANBERRIES

Follow recipe for Classic Apple Pie, increasing sugar to 1 cup (7 ounces) and adding 1 cup fresh or frozen cranberries to apple mixture.

SCIENCE DESK:
What Makes Pastry Flaky?

WHY IS IT THAT SOME COOKS PRODUCE PIE CRUSTS THAT are consistently tender and flaky, while others repeatedly deliver tough, cookie-like crusts? Part of the answer has to do with butter, and the degree to which it is incorporated in the dough. While shortening makes a big contribution to the flakiness, our pie crust also benefits from relatively large pieces of butter. As the butter melts during baking, evaporation produces steam. The steam creates pockets in the dough, which help to make it flaky.

When a dough is overprocessed and the butter is dispersed too evenly, it coats the flour and prevents it from absorbing liquid; the same thing happens when a dough is made with oil. The result is a crumbly dough rather than a flaky one. Underprocessing, however, will create a tough dough, because the fat has failed to coat the flour enough.

EQUIPMENT CORNER: Paring Knives

AS WE SLICED OUR WAY THROUGH MORE THAN 100 pounds of apples en route to developing these apple pie recipes, the easiest way to peel, core, and slice apples became a hotly debated subject. We began to wonder about all those kitchen gadgets designed to help with some or all phases of apple preparation. Glancing through some catalogs, we came across apple corers, corer/slicers, and a fancy crank-operated gizmo that peels, cores, and slices in a single motion. In addition, we found small paring knives with special curved blades, called bird's beak knives, specifically designed for peeling round fruits. We decided to give them all a try.

Most corers have a diameter between ¾ inch and ⅞ inch (ours was ¾ inch), which is too small to consistently remove all of the seeds and the seed cavity. We had the same

Brae-
burn

Golden
Del.

Pink
Lady

Fu

problem with the corer/slicers, plus the slices were thicker than we wanted. Crank-operated apple-paring machines were something of an improvement, but they didn't wow us. This tool works best with very hard, fresh fruit. Some of our Macs were less than perfectly firm, and the peeling blade slid right over the skin, failing to do its job. When the peeling blade did work well on a firm Granny Smith, it showered us with apple juice as it peeled.

We then went back to the tried-and-true method, using a paring knife. We tested the straight-edged paring knife against the curved blade of the bird's beak model, but none of the testers found the bird's beak to be significantly easier to use or more effective.

But which paring knife is best? Prices range from a modest $5 plus change to a grand $50, which invites the obvious question for a home cook: Is the most expensive knife really 10 times better than the cheapest model? To find, out we put seven all-purpose paring knives through a series of kitchen tests, including peeling and slicing shallots, peeling and slicing apples and turnips, coring tomatoes, peeling and mincing fresh ginger, and slicing lemons and limes.

The way the knives were made (by forging or stamping) wasn't much of a factor in our ratings of paring knives. By definition, a paring knife is used for light tasks where weight and balance are not terribly important (it doesn't take huge effort to peel an apple). The way the handle felt in testers' hands was much more important. Most testers preferred medium-sized, ergonomically designed plastic handles. Slim wooden handles were harder to grasp. Testers also preferred paring knives with flexible blades, which make it easier to work in tight spots. Peeling turnips or sectioning oranges is much easier done with a flexible than a stiff blade. Stiffer blades are slightly better at mincing and slicing, but these are secondary tasks for paring knives. Among the knives tested, expensive forged knives from Wüsthof and Henckels performed well, as did an inexpensive stamped knife made by Forschner.

FREE-FORM APPLE TART

WHAT WE WANTED: Something simpler than apple pie, with a tender, sturdy crust, moist filling, and rich apple flavor.

A free-form apple tart (called a crostata in Italy or a galette in France) is made in the shape of a flat disk. The dough is rolled out into a circle, the filling is piled in the center, and the dough is then gathered up along the edges to form a border around the filling. Because a free-form tart has only a single crust that does not have to be fitted into a pie plate, it's easier to make a tart than a pie. Even so, a number of things can go wrong.

Because a tart has no top crust to seal in moisture, the apple filling can dry out during baking. Another consideration is the type of dough used to form the tart. It must be sturdy enough to contain the filling while also providing a complementary texture and flavor.

We started with the filling. Obviously, the variety of apple used would be key. And the method used to prepare the apples would affect their taste and texture. Should they be sliced thick or thin when placed in the tart? Should they be precooked or raw?

To answer these questions, we gathered some of the most commonly available apple varieties: Granny Smith, Gala, McIntosh, Braeburn, Fuji, and Red and Golden Delicious. We tested each type in a tart. In every case but one the apples cooked up tough, dry, and leathery. The exception was the McIntosh, which baked to the other extreme; they were so moist that they turned to mush.

Of the varieties tested, we found that Granny Smiths, Galas, and McIntosh had the most distinct flavor after being baked. It looked like the solution that had worked in our Classic Apple Pie recipe (to combine Grannies with Macs) would here, too. We tested Macs with both Granny Smiths and Galas and, sure enough, tasters preferred the Granny-Mac combo. The apple filling had good apple flavor and a decent texture, but it was still a bit dry.

Next we attempted to cook the apples before placing them in the tart, hoping this would make the filling more moist. We sautéed the apples, reduced their cooking juices, and added the liquid to the tart. This was not a success. The apples turned mushy, and the pure apple flavor we had wanted to preserve was lost during precooking.

We returned to our original method—layering raw apple slices into the tart—but this time sliced them thinner and increased the oven temperature. These thinner slices were more moist, but still not perfect. A colleague suggested that we sprinkle the apples with sugar as they cooked. This turned out to be a great idea; the sugar prevented the apples from drying out in the oven and the filling was moist but not runny. When sugar is sprinkled on top of fruit during baking, it combines with some of the moisture the fruit has released and forms a syrup. This syrup doesn't give up water easily and thus keeps the filling moist.

With the filling done, we focused on the crust. Our basic pie dough had been working fine, but we wondered if we might make some improvements. Several test cooks felt that an all-butter crust would be appropriate because flakiness is not such an issue here. We made two tarts, one with an all-butter crust, the other with a butter-and-shortening crust. Tasters appreciated the richer flavor of the all-butter crust. Everyone agreed that the dough could be a tad sweeter.

Our free-form tart was perfect, but several test cooks wanted individual tartlets. With a few minor modifications, we were able to produce six tartlets with minimal extra effort. Since tartlets are so much easier to serve than a single tart (no cutting or messy slices), we made them the master recipe. The single tart is offered as a variation.

WHAT WE LEARNED: Use a combination of Granny Smith and McIntosh apples for best flavor and texture. Slice the apples thin, don't bother precooking them, but do sugar the apples during baking to keep them moist.

FREE-FORM APPLE TARTLETS serves 6

When all of the apples have been sliced, you should have a total of about 6 cups. Use a rimmed baking sheet to catch any juices released during baking. Serve the warm tartlets with a scoop of ice cream or lightly sweetened whipped cream (see page 294).

1	recipe American Pie Dough for Free-Form Tart (page 301)
1¼	pounds Granny Smith apples (about 3 small)
1¼	pounds McIntosh apples (about 3 medium)
2	tablespoons juice from 1 lemon
¼	cup (1.75 ounces) plus 2 tablespoons sugar
¼	teaspoon ground cinnamon
2	large egg whites, beaten lightly

1. Remove dough from refrigerator (if refrigerated longer than 1 hour, let stand at room temperature until malleable). Cut dough into 6 equal pieces and flatten into 3-inch disks. Working one at a time, roll out disks between two sheets of lightly floured parchment paper into circles about 6 inches in diameter. Peel off top sheets of parchment and discard; trim bottom sheets of parchment to rectangles about 2 inches larger than dough. Stack rectangles with parchment on plate; cover plate with plastic wrap and refrigerate while preparing fruit.

2. Peel, core, and cut apples into ¼-inch-thick slices and toss with lemon juice, ¼ cup sugar, and cinnamon in large bowl.

3. Remove dough from refrigerator and arrange parchment-lined dough rounds in single layer on work surface. Following illustrations 1 and 2 on page 308, arrange about 1 cup apple slices, thick edges out, in circular mound on each dough round, leaving 1-inch border of dough. Fold dough border up and over filling, pleating dough to fit snugly around apples. With cupped hands, gently press dough toward filling, reinforcing shape and compacting apples (see illustration 3 on page 308). Using parchment

lining for support, slide 3 tartlets onto each of 2 rimmed baking sheets. Chill formed tartlets on pans for 30 minutes.

4. Adjust one oven rack to highest position and other rack to lowest position; heat oven to 400 degrees. Slide pans with tartlets into oven and bake until pale golden brown, about 15 minutes. Brush crusts with beaten egg whites and sprinkle apples with remaining 2 tablespoons sugar. Return pans with tartlets to oven, switching positions, and bake until crusts are deep golden brown and apples are tender, about 15 minutes. Remove pans from oven and cool tartlets on pans for 5 minutes. Using wide metal spatula, remove tartlets from parchment and transfer to cooling rack. Serve tartlets warm.

FREE-FORM APPLE TART

This one tart, with its large mound of apples, must bake longer and at a lower temperature than individual tartlets. This tart is formed in the same way as the individual tartlets (see illustrations at right), but on a larger scale.

1. Remove dough from refrigerator (if refrigerated longer than 1 hour, let stand at room temperature until malleable). Roll dough between two large sheets of lightly floured parchment paper to 15-inch disk. Peel off top sheet and, using parchment lining for support, slide dough onto rimmed baking sheet; cover with plastic wrap and refrigerate while preparing fruit.

2. Peel, core, and cut apples into ¼-inch-thick slices and toss with lemon juice, ¼ cup sugar, and cinnamon in large bowl.

3. Remove dough from refrigerator and arrange apple slices, thick edges out, in circular mound, leaving 3-inch border of dough. Fold dough border up and over filling, pleating dough to fit snugly around apples. With cupped hands, gently press dough toward filling, reinforcing shape and compacting apples. Chill formed tart on pan for 30 minutes.

4. Adjust oven rack to lower-middle position and heat oven to 375 degrees. Slide pan with tart into oven and bake until pale golden brown, about 30 minutes. Brush crust with beaten egg whites and sprinkle apples with remaining 2 tablespoons sugar. Return pan with tart to oven and bake until crust is deep golden brown and apples are tender, about 30 minutes. Remove pan from oven and cool tart on pan for 10 minutes. Loosen parchment where it may have stuck to pan, then, using parchment lining, slide tart onto cooling rack. Place a large, round plate on top of tart, invert tart, peel off parchment, and re-invert tart onto serving platter. Serve tart warm.

TECHNIQUE: Making Tartlets

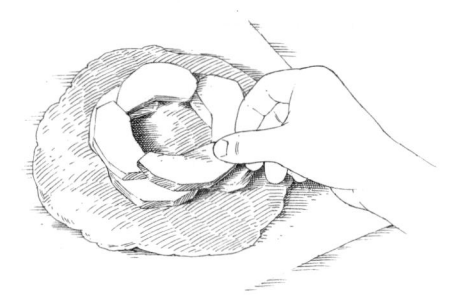

1. Arrange apple slices in an even circle over the dough, leaving free a 1-inch perimeter of dough for a pleated edge.

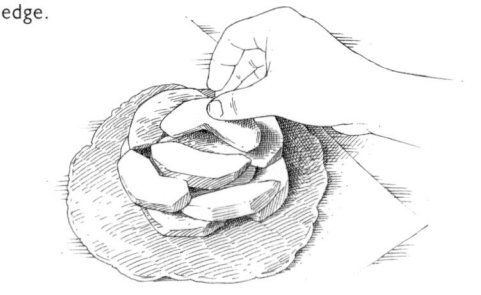

2. Fill in the center with additional slices, lending support to the circular wall of apples.

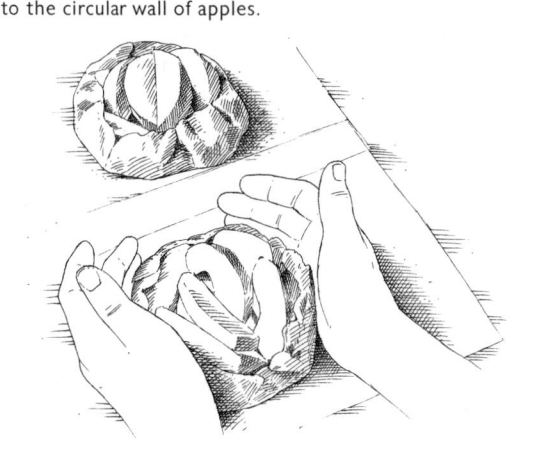

3. Fold the outer lip of the dough snugly inward over the apples and cup with your hands to compress and shape.

PEACH PIE &
CHAPTER 24 *cherry cobbler*

Nothing quite says summer like a slice of peach pie or a bowl of cherry cobbler. Add a scoop of vanilla ice cream and you've got two of the best desserts imaginable.

But peach pie and cherry cobbler can disappoint. Who hasn't made a peach pie with runny, watery filling and soggy, pale crust? Cherry cobbler can be even trickier. At least with peaches, you know that any fruit that smells and tastes good will make a decent pie. But with cherries, the home cook has no such luck. Sweet Bing cherries become insipid when baked. Sour cherries are a must. But where do you get sour cherries? The season seems to last about three weeks in many parts of the country. Is there an acceptable jarred or canned alternative to fresh fruit?

To answer these questions, we made cherry cobblers in the dead of winter. We talked to experts who had traveled behind the Iron Curtain in the 1980s searching for new cherry cultivars. We also made enough lattice tops for peach pies to cover a garden shed. We're happy to report that our efforts paid off handsomely.

Peach pie so good it
flies out of the plate.

PEACH PIE

WHAT WE WANTED: A filling that would be juicy but not soupy, a well-browned bottom crust, and an easy-to-make lattice top.

Our occasional disappointment with peach pies in the past has taught us to wait for peach season and then buy only intoxicatingly fragrant fruit, peaches ripe enough when squeezed to make you swoon. But even ripe peaches vary in juiciness from season to season and from peach to peach, making it difficult to know just how much thickener or sweetener a pie will need. Because fresh peaches are so welcome, we are inclined to forgive them if the pie they make is soupy or overly sweet or has a bottom crust that didn't bake properly.

But we wanted to remove the guesswork from this anthem to summer. We wanted to create a filling that was juicy but not swimming in liquid, its flavors neither muscled out by spices nor overwhelmed by thickeners. The crust would be buttery, flaky, and well browned on the bottom with a handsome, peekaboo lattice on the top.

Our standard recipe for pie dough is ultrarich, made with butter for flavor and shortening for flakiness (see American Pie Dough on page 301). But when we used this recipe for our first tests with peaches and a lattice-weave top crust, we were confronted with melting lattice strips. We realized that the crust on this particular pie would demand certain adjustments. We needed a sturdier dough, which meant less fat and more flour.

Our second challenge was to find a thickener that would leave the fruit's color and flavor uncompromised. Our favorite thickener for juicy fruit pies is tapioca. But past experience has taught us that tapioca works only in double-crust pies. Sure enough, when we used tapioca in our peach pie, undissolved beads of tapioca could be seen through the pie's open latticework design. We felt we could lessen the problem by pulverizing the tapioca, but that seemed like an unnecessary bother for a simple pie.

Past tests demonstrated that flour and cornstarch made their presence too obvious. Then we found an old recipe that suggested potato starch. We conducted side-by-side tests with flour, cornstarch, pulverized Minute tapioca, and potato starch. Flour and cornstarch fared no better than expected. The ground tapioca performed admirably, having no lumps. But the potato starch scored big. Its clarity outshone flour but was less cosmetically glossy than cornstarch; its thickening qualities rivaled tapioca, but there was no need for pulverizing.

Next we turned our attention to the peaches themselves. After attempting to shave a ripe peach with a vegetable peeler, we resorted to traditional blanching and found that two full minutes in boiling water were necessary to humble even the ripest of peaches. A quick dip in an ice bath stabilized the temperature of the fruit and got the peels moving.

Experimenting with different sugars, we were surprised to discover that both light and dark brown sugar bullied the peaches, while white sugar complemented them. As in most fruit pies, lemon juice brightened the flavor of the peaches. It also kept the peach slices from browning before they went into the pan. A whisper of ground cinnamon and nutmeg and a dash of salt added a note of complexity.

Trying different oven rack levels and temperatures to satisfy the browning requirements of both the top and bottom crust brought us back to our apple pie recipe (page 303), which recommends a low rack, initial high heat (425 degrees), and moderately high heat (375 degrees) to finish. We found that a glass pie dish and preheated sheet pan gave us a pleasantly firm and browned bottom crust. A quick pre-baking spritz of the lattice top with water and a sprinkle of sugar brought this pie home.

WHAT WE LEARNED: Reduce the fat in the dough for a well-structured lattice top. Use potato starch to thicken the peach filling, and season the filling gently.

LATTICE-TOP FRESH PEACH PIE serves 8

If your peaches are larger than tennis balls, you will probably need 5 or 6; if they're smaller, you will need 7 or 8. Cling and freestone peaches look identical; try to buy freestones, because the flesh will fall away from the pits easily. Use the higher amount of potato starch if the peaches are very juicy, less if they are not terribly juicy. If you don't have or can't find potato starch, substitute an equal amount of pulverized Minute tapioca ground for about 1 minute in a food processor or spice grinder. Serve the pie with vanilla ice cream or whipped cream (page 294).

1	recipe American Pie Dough for Lattice-Top Pie (page 301)
6–7	ripe, medium-sized peaches (about 7 cups when sliced)
1	tablespoon juice from 1 lemon
1	cup (7 ounces) plus 1 tablespoon sugar
	Pinch ground cinnamon
	Pinch ground nutmeg
	Pinch salt
3–5	tablespoons potato starch (see note)

1. Remove dough from refrigerator (if refrigerated longer than 1 hour, let stand at room temperature until malleable). Roll larger dough piece to 11 by 15-inch rectangle, about ⅛ inch thick; transfer dough rectangle to baking sheet lined with parchment paper. With pizza wheel, fluted pastry wheel, or paring knife, trim to even out long sides of rectangle, then cut rectangle lengthwise into eight strips, 1¼ inches wide by 15 inches long. Freeze strips on cookie sheet until firm, about 30 minutes.

2. Roll smaller dough piece on lightly floured work surface or between two large sheets of plastic wrap to 12-inch disk. Transfer dough to pie plate by rolling dough around rolling pin and unrolling over 9-inch pie plate or by folding dough in quarters, then placing dough point in center of pie plate

and unfolding. Working around circumference of pie plate, ease dough into pan corners by gently lifting dough edges with one hand while pressing around pan bottom with other hand. Leave dough that overhangs lip of pie plate in place; refrigerate dough-lined pie plate.

3. Remove dough strips from freezer; if too stiff to be workable, let stand at room temperature until malleable and softened slightly but still very cold. Following illustrations 1 through 3 on page 314, form lattice top and place in freezer until firm, about 15 minutes.

4. Meanwhile, adjust oven rack to lowest position, place rimmed baking sheet on rack, and heat oven to 500 degrees. Bring 3 quarts water to boil in large saucepan and fill large bowl with 2 quarts cold water and 2 trays ice cubes. With paring knife, score small X at base of each peach. Lower peaches into boiling water with slotted skimmer or spoon. Cover and blanch until their skins loosen, about 2 minutes. Use slotted skimmer to transfer peaches to ice water and let stand to stop cooking, about 1 minute. Cool peaches, then, starting from scored X, peel each peach, halve and pit it, and cut into ⅜-inch slices.

5. Toss peach slices, lemon juice, 1 cup sugar, cinnamon, nutmeg, salt, and potato starch in medium bowl.

6. Turn peach mixture into dough-lined pie plate. Remove lattice from freezer and place on top of filled pie. Trim lattice strips and crimp pie edges (see illustration 4 on page 314). Lightly brush or spray lattice top with 1 tablespoon water and sprinkle with remaining 1 tablespoon sugar.

7. Lower oven temperature to 425 degrees. Place pie on baking sheet and bake until crust is set and begins to brown, 25 to 30 minutes. Rotate pie and reduce oven temperature to 375 degrees; continue baking until crust is deep golden brown and juices bubble, 25 to 30 minutes longer. Cool pie on wire rack for at least 2 hours before serving.

SCIENCE DESK: How Starches Work

IN ITS NATURAL STATE, STARCH EXISTS IN THE FORM OF essentially insoluble granules. These granules only begin to absorb water with the introduction of energy in the form of heat. As the water seeps into the granules, they swell and begin to bump into one another, so that the mixture thickens. As the mixture is heated further (past 150 degrees), the starch granules begin to leak two kinds of starch molecules—amylose and amylopectin—into the liquid. These molecules, particularly the long amylose chains, form a web that traps the swollen granules, thickening the liquid even further. Amylopectin has a more limited thickening power.

When making cherry cobbler, which has a lot of juice, you want to use a starch high in amylose, such as cornstarch, that will thicken the abundant cherry juices and wine. Peaches, which give off a lot less juice than cherries, don't need such a strong starch. Here a starch higher in amylopectin, such as potato starch, is the better bet. Potato starch thickens the peach juices lightly. High-amylose cornstarch overthickens peach juices, making them gummy.

TECHNIQUE: Making a Lattice Top

1. Lay out 4 strips of dough on parchment paper. Fold the first and third strips back, then place a long strip of dough slightly to the right of the center, as shown.

2. Unfold the first and third strips over the perpendicular strips and fold the second and fourth strips back. Add a second perpendicular strip of dough. Now unfold the second and fourth strips.

3. Repeat this process with two more perpendicular strips (you will have a total of eight strips, four running in each direction). Freeze the lattice until firm, about 15 minutes.

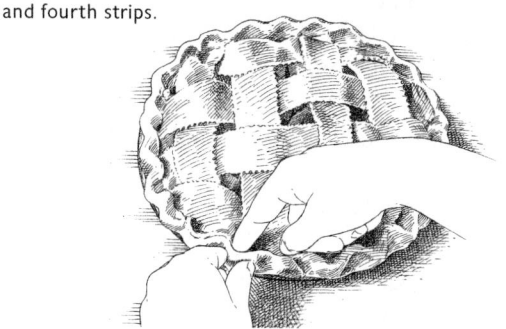

4. Place the lattice on top of the filled pie. Trim off the excess lattice ends, fold the rim of the shell up over the lattice strips, and crimp.

CHERRY COBBLER

WHAT WE WANTED: Real cherry flavor paired with a tender, feather-light, deeply browned biscuit topping.

No more than a fleet of tender biscuits on a sea of sweet fruit, good cobblers hold their own against fancy fruit desserts. But unlike fancy fruit desserts, cobblers come together in a couple of quick steps and can be dished up hot, ready to hit the dance floor with a scoop of vanilla ice cream. Picking fresh sour cherries one summer in Vermont and cooking them up into a compote for crêpes acquainted us with their virtues. Sour cherries have sufficient acidity to cook up well and become truly expressive with a touch of sugar and some heat. (Sweet eating cherries, like Bings, lose their flavor when cooked.) Until then, the only sour, or baking, cherries we had known of were the canned variety. And however plump and lacquered their depiction on the label, those that slid from under a lattice were so pale, so limp and exhausted, that their flavor barely registered. But we knew sour cherries would feel at home in a cobbler—if we could find some good ones.

Though sour cherries are grown in relatively large quantities in Michigan, here in the Northeast our grocery shelves are bereft of sour cherry products, save the crayon-red canned gravy with lumps called "pie filling." So we were grateful to find two different kinds of jarred sour cherries at our local Trader Joe's during the off season (all 11 months of it). In addition, the Cherry Marketing Institute of Michigan provided us with variously processed sour cherries—frozen, canned, and dried. Since it would be months before we could try making cobbler with fresh cherries, we began our tests with processed.

Early tests in which we prepared quick fruit fillings elicited unenthusiastic comments from tasters. While frozen Michigan sour cherries maintained their color well, flavor was left largely to the imagination. Both canned and jarred sour cherries from Michigan were flaccid and developed an anemic pallor when cooked. Adding a handful of dried cherries did little to heighten their impact. Only Trader Joe's jarred Morello cherries drew a crowd. Deep ruby red, plump, meaty, and tart, they delivered bracing flavor and a great chew right out of the jar.

This experience prompted us to do a little research. Sour cherries, we learned, are classified in two groups, amarelles and griottes. The former have lighter flesh—tan on the inside—and clear juices; the latter are dark—even black—with deep red juice. The best known examples of each group are Montmorency (an amarelle) and Morello (a griotte). Most tart cherries grown in the United States are Montmorency. Those from Eastern Europe are Morello. We decided to base our recipe on jarred Morellos.

A cobbler should be juicy, but not swimming in juice, and it should taste like the fruit whose name it bears. Jarred and canned cherries come awash in juices, which we would use to produce the sauce. Since jarred and canned cherries have already been processed, they are already cooked. The less heat they're exposed to thereafter, the better. Straining off the juice, we dumped the drained contents of four 24-ounce jars of Morellos into a 9 by 13-inch baking dish, then thickened and sweetened 3 cups of the juice. The resulting flavor was a bit flat. We replaced 1 cup of the cherry juice with red wine and added a cinnamon stick, a pinch of salt, and a whiff of almond extract. Much better. Red wine and sour cherries have a natural affinity; the cinnamon stick added a fragrant woody depth; and, as with all fruits, salt performed its usual minor miracle. The almond extract brought the entire flavor experience up a couple of notches. For thickener we resolved to go with cornstarch. It could be mixed in with the sugar and brought directly to a simmer with the reserved cherry juices, then poured over the waiting cherries and baked. Lightly thickened fruit is best; a cobbler shouldn't be thick enough to spread on toast.

We also had some requirements for the cobbles. We

wanted them feather-light but deeply browned and crisp. This said a number of things to us. The first was no eggs. Eggs would make our biscuits too heavy and substantial. (After working for years with the test kitchen's scone recipe, a light and tender English biscuit that uses no eggs, we felt supported in that expectation.) The second thing it said was buttermilk. Buttermilk biscuits are famously light and tender. We baked several biscuit variations to confirm these notions, settling on all-purpose flour, a moderate amount of butter, small amounts of baking powder and soda, a touch of sugar (plus more on top for crunch), a wave of buttermilk, and a nice hot oven. Dispensing with rolling altogether, we simply dropped the biscuits onto the fruit. The biscuits had a buttery lightness, a mild tang, and a crunchy, sugary top.

Not quite satisfied with their pale bellies touching the fruit, we undertook to bake the biscuits for 15 minutes on a baking sheet while the filling was coming together on the stove. We then wedded them to the fruit for only 10 minutes in the oven. By then the fruit (already hot from the cooked sauce) was bubbling around the biscuits, which were deeply browned on top and baked through underneath. Heaven in about a half-hour.

Jarred Morellos made a fine cobbler. But we wanted more, and, finally, summer came. Searching for fresh cherries, we made an exciting discovery: Morello cherries had made their way to the United States.

In 1984, well before unrestricted travel and commerce in Eastern Bloc countries became commonplace, Dr. Amy Iezzoni, professor of horticulture at Michigan State University, traveled extensively throughout Hungary to locate a vigorous sour cherry cultivar she could bring home to Michigan. Having spent years hybridizing local sour cherry seedlings, Hungarian breeders were prepared to release new cultivars with improved characteristics.

Iezzoni returned home with a dazzling Morello cultivar, which she named Balaton (after a lake in its native environs). She enlisted it in her breeding program, currently the only sour cherry breeding program in the United States. Under her care, the Balaton has thrived in its new climate.

Unlike the fragile and perishable Montmorency (a 400-year-old cultivar that has not been subject to crossbreeding to make it more vigorous), Balaton cherries are robust enough once harvested to endure shipping well. They are not only larger and plumper than Montmorency cherries, but their dark juices are also beautiful and mysterious.

With this knowledge and some fresh cherries, we got to work in the test kitchen. To test available varieties, we used both Morellos and the more delicate Montmorency cherries.

And how were the fresh cobblers? Both varieties of fresh cherries graced the recipe, yielding cobblers with plump, gorgeous, deeply flavorful fruit. The Montmorency cherries bore a candy apple red and a flavor resonant with almond accents; the fresh Morellos were transcendent, with a smooth richness and complex flavor notes. If you can get your hands on fresh sour cherries during their brief season in July, buy them and start baking. And take heart. When the brief sour-cherry season is over, jarred Morello cherries will create a cobbler that is almost as wonderful.

WHAT WE LEARNED: Jarred Morello cherries are the best year-round choice for a cobbler. Spike the cherry juices with red wine and cinnamon and thicken with cornstarch. For really crisp biscuits, bake them separately for 15 minutes, then slide the biscuits over the warm cherry filling and bake just 10 minutes longer.

SOUR CHERRY COBBLER   serves 12

Use the smaller amount of sugar in the filling if you prefer your fruit desserts on the tart side and the larger amount if you like them sweet. Serve with vanilla ice cream or lightly sweetened whipped cream (page 294).

biscuit topping

2	cups (10 ounces) unbleached all-purpose flour
6	tablespoons (2.6 ounces) sugar plus additional 2 tablespoons for sprinkling
½	teaspoon baking powder
½	teaspoon baking soda
½	teaspoon salt
6	tablespoons cold unsalted butter, cut into ½-inch cubes
1	cup buttermilk

cherry filling

4	(24-ounce) jars Morello cherries, drained (about 8 cups drained cherries), 2 cups juice reserved
¾–1	cup (5.25 to 7 ounces) sugar
3	tablespoons plus 1 teaspoon cornstarch
	Pinch salt
1	cup dry red wine
1	(3-inch) stick cinnamon
¼	teaspoon almond extract

1. Adjust rack to middle position and heat oven to 425 degrees. Line baking sheet with parchment paper.

2. In workbowl of food processor fitted with steel blade, pulse flour, 6 tablespoons sugar, baking powder, baking soda, and salt to combine. Scatter butter pieces over and process until mixture resembles coarse meal, about fifteen 1-second pulses. Transfer to medium bowl; add buttermilk and toss with rubber spatula to combine. Using a 1½- to 1¾-inch spring-loaded ice cream scoop, scoop 12 biscuits onto baking sheet, spacing them 1½ to 2 inches apart. Sprinkle biscuits evenly with 2 tablespoons sugar and bake until

lightly browned on tops and bottoms, about 15 minutes. (Do not turn off oven.)

3. Meanwhile, spread drained cherries in even layer in 9 by 13-inch glass baking dish. Stir sugar, cornstarch, and salt together in medium nonreactive saucepan. Whisk in reserved cherry juice and wine, and add cinnamon stick; set saucepan over medium-high heat, and cook, whisking frequently, until mixture simmers and thickens, about 5 minutes. Discard cinnamon stick, stir in almond extract, and pour hot liquid over cherries in baking dish.

4. Arrange hot biscuits in 3 rows of 4 over warm filling. Bake cobbler until filling is bubbling and biscuits are deep golden brown, about 10 minutes. Cool on wire rack 10 minutes; serve.

VARIATION

FRESH SOUR CHERRY COBBLER

Morello or Montmorency cherries can be used in this cobbler made with fresh sour cherries. Do not use sweet Bing cherries. If the cherries do not release enough juice after macerating for 30 minutes, cranberry juice makes up the difference.

cherry filling

1¼	cups (8.75 ounces) sugar
3	tablespoons plus 1 teaspoon cornstarch
	Pinch salt
4	pounds fresh sour cherries, pitted (about 8 cups), juices reserved
1	cup dry red wine
	Cranberry juice (if needed)
1	(3-inch) cinnamon stick
¼	teaspoon almond extract
1	recipe biscuit topping (see left)

1. Stir together sugar, cornstarch, and salt in large bowl; add cherries and toss well to combine. Pour wine over cherries;

let stand 30 minutes. Drain cherries in colander set over medium bowl. Combine drained and reserved juices (from pitting cherries); you should have 3 cups. If not, add enough cranberry juice to equal 3 cups.

2. While cherries macerate, prepare and bake biscuit topping.

3. Spread drained cherries in even layer in 9 by 13-inch glass baking dish. Bring liquid and cinnamon stick to simmer in medium nonreactive saucepan over medium-high heat, whisking frequently, until mixture thickens, about 5 minutes. Discard cinnamon stick, stir in almond extract, and pour hot liquid over cherries in baking dish.

4. Arrange hot biscuits in 3 rows of 4 over warm filling. Bake cobbler until filling is bubbling and biscuits are deep golden brown, about 10 minutes. Cool on wire rack 10 minutes; serve.

TASTING LAB: Vanilla Ice Cream

IS THERE A BETTER WAY TO CROWN A BOWL OF WARM cherry cobbler than with a scoop of vanilla ice cream? With so many brands on the market, we wondered which would serve our cobbler best. To find out, we gathered 20 tasters to sample eight leading national brands of vanilla ice cream, made in what's known as the French, or custard, style, with egg yolks.

Many ice cream manufacturers add stabilizers—most often carrageenan gum or guar gum—to prevent "heat shock," an industry term for the degradation in texture caused by the partial melting and refreezing that takes place when ice cream is subjected to extreme temperature changes during transit to the supermarket or when an ice cream case goes through its self-defrosting cycle. Gum additives stabilize ice cream by trapping water in the frozen mass and slowing down the growth of ice crystals during melting and refreezing.

We thought that the presence of stabilizers might affect the test results. To our surprise, this was not the case. The top two brands in our tasting, Edy's Dreamery and Double Rainbow, use stabilizers.

We also expected the nature of the ice creams' vanilla flavor—artificial or real—to affect the outcome of the test. Again we were a bit surprised with the results. Blue Bell was the only brand in the tasting that contained artificial vanilla flavor, and it rated smack-dab in the middle, thus negating any link between natural flavor and superior flavor. In fact, tasters took greater issue with several brands made with real vanilla extract—including Häagen-Dazs, Ben & Jerry's, and Edy's Grand—for tasting "artificial" and "boozy." To help explain this odd result, we contacted Bruce Tharp, an independent ice cream consultant based in Wayne, Pennsylvania. He explained that the perceived artificial and alcohol flavors are often caused by the quantity of vanilla extract added to the ice cream. That is, the more extract, the more likely one is to taste the alcohol. Although it's impossible to confirm this theory (manufacturers won't release their recipes to the public), it was clear that the absence of stabilizers and use of natural flavorings were not reliable indicators of quality.

Next up was the issue of butterfat, which contributes to smooth texture, rich flavor, and structure. By law, an ice cream can't be called an ice cream unless its prefrozen mix contains a minimum of 10 percent butterfat. Of the ice creams we tasted, butterfat content ranged from 10 to 16 percent and, in general, the higher the butterfat content, the higher the ice cream rated. Our two top-rated ice creams had butterfat contents of 14.5 percent (Edy's Dreamery) and 15 percent (Double Rainbow). The two lowest rated brands had butterfat contents of 10 to 12 percent and 13 percent.

All commercial ice cream makers also add air to the mix. Oddly enough, this helps to provide structure by dividing and distributing air cells evenly throughout the frozen mass. Without it, the ice cream would look more like an ice cube. The air that is thus incorporated into ice cream is called overrun.

While the top two ice creams had low overruns of 21

and 26 percent, our third favorite had a whopping overrun of 93.5 percent. Furthermore, the two last-place ice creams had very different overruns—26 percent and 100 percent, with 100 percent being the legal limit. Our conclusion? In general, low overrun is preferable, although butterfat content is a better measure of quality. (We also noted that some tasters preferred the fluffier high-overrun ice creams—it is, to some degree, a matter of personal preference.)

The last component we researched was emulsifiers, such as mono- and diglycerides, which are used to control the behavior of fat in ice cream by keeping it from separating out of the ice cream mass. These emulsifiers give an ice cream rigidity and strength, so even if it doesn't have much butterfat or added gums, the ice cream will maintain its round, scooped shape for a prolonged period of time. The only ice cream in our tasting with emulsifiers was also the least favored sample: Edy's Grand. So, according to our taste test, it seems that emulsifiers are not desirable.

The winner of our tasting, as mentioned above, was Edy's Dreamery, with Double Rainbow coming in second and Breyer's third. The real news, however, was the poor showing of the two best-known premium brands, Häagen-Dazs and Ben & Jerry's, which rated fourth and seventh, respectively, out of the eight brands sampled.

EQUIPMENT CORNER: Ice Cream Scoops

WE GATHERED 10 READILY AVAILABLE SCOOPS AND DIPPED OUR WAY THROUGH 20 PINTS OF VANILLA TO FIND THE BEST. We tested three basic types of scoops: classic, mechanical-release (or spring-loaded), and spade-shaped. Testers were unanimous in assigning first place—in both its own category and overall—to the Zeroll Classic Ice Cream Scoop ($22). Its thick handle was comfortable for large and small hands, and its nonstick coating and self-defrosting liquid (which responds to heat from the user's hand) contributed to perfect release, leaving only traces of melted cream inside the scoop.

Although we frequently use a mechanical-release scoop to measure out even portions of cookie and muffin batters, we found these scoops less than ideal for ice cream. They are designed for right-handed users only, and their thin, straight-edged handles were distinctly uncomfortable when considerable pressure was applied. If you need to work your way through multiple gallon-sized containers of ice cream, a spade might be for you. Our preferred model is the Zeroll Nonstick Ice Cream Spade ($19.60).

CLASSIC

These scoops sport a thick handle and curved bowl. They can be used by lefties and righties with equal comfort.

MECHANICAL-RELEASE

These scoops operate with a spring-loaded, squeezable handle (or thumb trigger) that connects to a curved steel lever inside the scoop.

SPADE-SHAPED

With their flat, paddle-type heads, spades are useful when you need to scoop a lot of ice cream for an ice cream cake, but they are too big to fit into pint containers.

CHILLED SUMMER
puddings

CHAPTER 25

For most American cooks, pudding is something you make on the stovetop and thicken with cornstarch. Think chocolate pudding or butterscotch. When you replace the cornstarch with eggs and bake the dessert in the oven, you have something French, a custard such as pot de crème or crème brûlée. Whether made on the stove or in the oven, these desserts are rich and probably best suited to the cooler months.

But puddings don't have to be thickened with eggs or cornstarch. There are lighter options—made with or accompanied by fruit—that are perfect for summer eating.

Summer pudding is an English classic, a sort of trifle without the custard and whipped cream. Stale bread and superripe berries are layered together to create a stunning, refreshing ode to summer.

Panna cotta is the Italian "pudding" of the moment. Unlike crème brûlée or crème caramel, this cream-based, custard-like recipe doesn't contain eggs. Gelatin is the thickener in this bright white, wobbly pudding. Without any eggs, the focus remains on the dairy and vanilla. Raspberry sauce dresses up panna cotta and adds a bracing contrast in color and flavor.

"Fools" have a long history in Britain. Nothing more than cooked fruit and whipped cream, this chilled summer dessert is as simple as it is elegant. With its cool, creamy texture, fool is the perfect way to end a summer meal.

In the busy test kitchen, there's always an extra pair of hands to steady a strainer.

SUMMER PUDDING

WHAT WE WANTED: Sweet-tart berries melded with sliced bread to form a cohesive pudding.

Summer pudding doesn't fit the rich, creamy, silky pudding archetype. In this classic English dessert, ripe, fragrant, lightly sweetened berries are gently cooked to coax out their juices, which are used to soak and soften slices of bread to make them meld with the fruit. This mélange of berries and bread is usually weighted down with heavy cans, then chilled overnight until it is cohesive enough to be unmolded.

We have always been intrigued by this "pudding," drawn in by its rustic, unaffected appeal. Unfortunately, many summer puddings are sweet, and the bread often seems to stand apart from the fruit, as if it were just a casing. We wanted sweet-tart berries and bread that melded right with them.

In a typical summer pudding, berries fill a bowl or mold of some sort that has been neatly lined with crustless bread. Some recipes say to line the bowl with full slices, laying them flat against the bottom and sides of the bowl. Others have you cutting the slices down into triangles and rectangles and arranging them such that when unmolded they form an attractive pattern. Well, trimming the crusts is easy, but trimming the bread to fit the bowl, then lining the bowl with the trimmed pieces, is a bit fussy. After making a couple of puddings, we quickly grew tired of this technique; it seemed to undermine the simplicity of the dessert.

We came across a couple of recipes that called for layering the bread right in with the berries instead of using it to line the bowl. Not only is this bread-on-the-inside method easier, but a summer pudding made in this fashion looks spectacular—the berries on the outside are brilliant jewels. Meanwhile, the layers of bread on the inside almost melt into the fruit.

Our next adjustment to this recipe was to lose the bowl as a mold. We switched instead to a loaf pan. Its rectangular shape requires less trimming of bread slices, and, once unmolded, the pudding better retains its shape. Besides, this version was simply more beautiful than a round one made in a bowl. When we tried making individual summer puddings in ramekins, we found them to be hardly more labor-intensive in assembly than a single large serving. Sure, you have to cut out rounds of bread to fit the ramekins, but a cookie cutter makes easy work of it, and individual servings transform this humble dessert into an elegant one. The individual puddings are also easily served. You simply unmold them into bowls; there's no slicing or scooping involved.

With the form set, we moved on to the ingredients. For 4 pints of berries we were using, ¾ cup sugar was a good amount of sweetener. Lemon juice, we found, perked up the berry flavors and rounded them out. We then sought alternatives to cooking the fruit in an attempt to preserve its freshness. We mashed first some and then all of the berries

with sugar. We tried cooking only a portion of the fruit with sugar. We macerated the berries with sugar. None of these methods worked. These puddings, even after being weighted and chilled overnight, had an unwelcome crunchy, raw quality. The berries need a gentle cooking to make their texture more yielding, more puddinglike, if you will. But don't worry—five minutes is all it takes, not even long enough to heat up the kitchen.

So far, we had been using a mix of strawberries, raspberries, blueberries, and blackberries and were pleased with the variety of flavors, textures, and colors. Strawberries made up the bulk, contributing the most substance and sweetness. Raspberries easily break down with the gentle cooking, providing much juice along with their distinct flavor. Blackberries and blueberries are more resistant; they retain their shape and unique textures. And their deep color is a beautiful addition, like sapphires in a pool of rubies.

The next obvious ingredient to investigate was the bread. We tried six different kinds as well as pound cake (for which we were secretly rooting). Hearty, coarse-textured sandwich bread and a rustic French loaf were too tough and tasted fermented and yeasty. Soft, pillowy sandwich bread became soggy and lifeless when soaked with juice. The pound cake, imbibed with berry juice, turned into wet sand and had the textural appeal of sawdust. A good-quality white sandwich bread with a medium texture, somewhere between Wonder bread and Pepperidge Farm, was good, but there were two very clear winners: challah and potato bread. Their even, tight-crumbed, tender texture and light sweetness were a perfect match for the berries. Challah, available in the bakery section of most grocery stores, is usually sold in unsliced braided loaves and therefore makes for irregular slices. We decided to sidestep this complication and go with potato bread, which tastes every bit as good as challah in this recipe but comes in convenient bagged and sliced loaves.

Most summer pudding recipes call for stale bread. And for good reason. Fresh bread, we found, when soaked with those berry juices, turns to mush. You might not think this would be so noticeable with the bread layered between all those berries, but every single taster remarked that the pudding made with fresh bread was soggy and gummy. On the other hand, stale bread absorbs some of the juices and melds with the berries while maintaining some structural integrity. We tried different degrees of staleness. A day-old loaf was still too fresh, but bread left out long enough to become completely dry easily cracked and crumbled under the cookie cutter or bread knife. We found that simply leaving slices out overnight until they were dry to the touch but still somewhat pliable resulted in bread that was easy to cut and also tasted good in the pudding.

We encountered a few recipes with instructions to butter the bread. Since pound cake doesn't work in a summer pudding, we thought that this might be a nice way of adding a subtle richness. Wrong. The coating of butter prevented the juices from thoroughly permeating the bread and also dulled the vibrant flavor of the berries.

Probably the oddest thing about summer pudding is the fact that it is weighted as it chills. What, we wondered, does this do for the texture? And how long does the pudding need to chill? We made several and chilled them with and without weights for 4, 8, 24, and 30 hours. The puddings chilled for 4 hours tasted of underripe fruit. The bread was barely soaked through, and the berries barely clung together. At 8 hours the pudding was at its peak: The berries tasted fresh and held together, while the bread melted right into them. Twenty-four hours and the pudding was still good, though a hairsbreadth duller in color and flavor. After 30 hours the pudding was well past its prime and began to smell and taste fermented.

No matter how long they chilled, the summer puddings without weights were loose. They didn't hold together after unmolding, the fruit was less cohesive, and the puddings less pleasurable to eat.

WHAT WE LEARNED: **Cook the berries lightly to release their juices, layer the berries with slices of stale potato, challah, or white bread, then weight the pudding to create the proper texture.**

INDIVIDUAL SUMMER BERRY PUDDINGS

serves 6

Stale the bread for this recipe by leaving it out overnight; it should be dry to the touch but not brittle. Otherwise, put the slices on a rack in a single layer into a 200-degree oven for 50 to 60 minutes, turning them once halfway through. For this recipe, you will need six 6-ounce ramekins and a round cookie cutter of slightly smaller diameter than the ramekins. If you don't have the right size cutter, use a paring knife and the bottom of a ramekin (most ramekins taper toward the bottom) as a guide for trimming the rounds. Challah is the second choice for bread but will probably need to be cut into slices about ½ inch thick. If both potato bread and challah are unavailable, use a good-quality white sandwich bread with a dense, soft texture. Summer pudding can be made up to 24 hours before serving, but any longer and the berries begin to lose their freshness. Lightly sweetened whipped cream (page 294) is the perfect accompaniment to summer pudding.

    2   pints strawberries, rinsed, hulled, and sliced
    1   pint raspberries
    ½   pint blueberries
    ½   pint blackberries
    ¾   cup (5.25 ounces) sugar
    2   tablespoons juice from 1 lemon
    12 slices stale potato bread, challah, or other
        good-quality white bread (see note)
        Nonstick vegetable cooking spray

1. Heat strawberries, raspberries, blueberries, blackberries, and sugar in large nonreactive saucepan over medium heat, stirring occasionally, until berries begin to release their juice and sugar has dissolved, about 5 minutes. Off heat, stir in lemon juice; let cool to room temperature.

2. While berries are cooling, use cookie cutter to cut out 12 bread rounds that are slightly smaller in diameter than ramekins (see illustration 1 for individual summer puddings on page 325).

3. Spray six 6-ounce ramekins with vegetable cooking spray and place on rimmed baking sheet. Following illustrations 2 through 6 for individual summer puddings on page 325, assemble, cover, and weight summer puddings and refrigerate for at least 8 and up to 24 hours.

4. Remove weights, cookie sheet, and plastic wrap. Run paring knife around perimeter of each ramekin, unmold into individual bowls, and serve immediately.

VARIATION

LARGE SUMMER BERRY PUDDING   serves 6 to 8

To ensure that this larger pudding unmolds in one piece, use a greased loaf pan lined with plastic wrap. Because there is no need to cut out rounds for this version, you will need only about 8 bread slices, depending on their size.

Follow recipe for Individual Summer Berry Puddings through step 1. While berries are cooling, remove crusts from bread slices and trim so slices will fit in single layer in 9 by 5-inch loaf pan (see illustration 1 for large summer pudding on page 325). (You will need about 2½ slices per layer and a total of three layers.) Coat loaf pan with vegetable cooking spray and line with plastic wrap. Make sure wrap lays flat against surface of pan, leaving no air space. Place loaf pan on rimmed cookie sheet, and use slotted spoon to place about 2 cups of fruit into bottom of pan (see illustration 2 for large summer pudding on page 325). Lightly soak enough bread slices for one layer in fruit juices and place on top of fruit. Repeat with two more layers of fruit and bread (see illustration 3 for large summer pudding on page 325). Top with remaining juices, cover loosely with second sheet of plastic wrap, and weight with second cookie sheet and several heavy cans. To unmold, remove outer plastic wrap and invert onto serving platter. Lift off loaf pan, remove plastic wrap lining, slice, and serve.

TECHNIQUE: Assembling Summer Berry Puddings

FOR INDIVIDUAL SUMMER PUDDINGS:

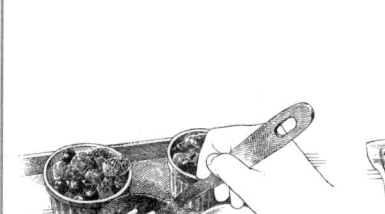

1. For individual puddings, cut out rounds of bread with a cookie cutter.

2. With a slotted spoon, place about ¼ cup of fruit into the bottoms of greased 6-ounce ramekins that have been placed on a cookie sheet.

3. Lightly soak a round of bread in the juices and place on top of the fruit in the ramekin.

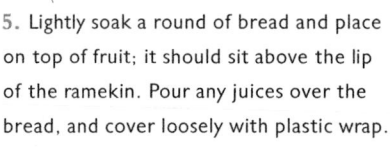

4. Divide the remaining fruit among the ramekins (about ½ cup more per ramekin).

5. Lightly soak a round of bread and place on top of fruit; it should sit above the lip of the ramekin. Pour any juices over the bread, and cover loosely with plastic wrap.

6. Place a second cookie sheet on top, then weight the sheet with several heavy cans.

FOR LARGE SUMMER PUDDING:

1. Remove the crusts from the bread slices and trim the slices to fit in a single layer in the loaf pan.

2. Line the greased loaf pan with plastic wrap. Place about 2 cups of fruit into the bottom.

3. Lightly soak one layer of bread slices and place on top of fruit. Repeat 2 more times. Top with juices, cover with wrap, and weight with another loaf pan. Unmold and serve.

PANNA COTTA

WHAT WE WANTED: A delicate cream pudding that would be sturdy enough to unmold from ramekins yet delicate enough to quiver at the touch of a spoon. The flavor should scream cream (lightly sweetened) and vanilla.

Panna cotta seems to have entered the world on tiptoe—or on wing. It is included in neither Waverley Lewis Root's book *The Food of Italy* (Vintage, 1971) nor in Marcella Hazan's *Classic Italian Cook Book* (Knopf, 1973). In fact, no one seems to know much about it. Yet from virtual anonymity 25 years ago, panna cotta has achieved star status in restaurants around the country, becoming the popular successor to tiramisu.

Though its name is lyrical, the literal translation of panna cotta—"cooked cream"—does nothing to suggest its ethereal qualities. In fact, panna cotta is not cooked at all. Neither is it complicated with eggs, as is a custard. Instead, sugar and gelatin are melted in cream and milk, and the whole is then turned into individual ramekins and chilled. It is a virginal dessert, a jellied alabaster cream. It forms a richly neutral backdrop for everything it touches: strawberry coulis, fresh raspberries, light caramel, chocolate sauce.

That, we should say, describes the ideal panna cotta. There are others.

Panna cotta is about nothing if not texture. The cream must be robust enough to unmold but delicate enough to shiver on the plate. Our mission, therefore, was to find correct proportions for four simple ingredients and the most effective way to deal with the gelatin.

We began by preparing five recipes from well-known Italian cookbooks. Each of them used like ingredients in varying proportions and dealt with the ingredients similarly. Two called for powdered sugar (favored in Italian confections). A couple simmered the cream; others merely warmed it. One recipe whipped half the cream and folded it into the base. Procedurally, the recipes were extremely straightforward.

Upon tasting the different recipes, it was clear they fell into two groups. Those with higher proportions of milk were slippery and translucent, their flavor elusive and flat. Those with more cream had a rich mouthfeel and a creamier, more rounded flavor. What united these recipes most noticeably, however, was a toothsomeness, a slight rubbery chew. It was the result of too much gelatin.

It would be practical, we decided, to design the recipe around a single packet of gelatin. Given this amount, we knew we would need to establish the volume of liquid required to set up the cream. But before that we had to determine the best proportion of cream to milk, critical in terms of mouthfeel. Preliminary tastings put us on the side of a 3:1 ratio of cream to milk.

Over the next week we made dozens of panna cotti in the test kitchen. We were surprised to find textural inconsistency between batches that should have been identical. Some were flabby, others stalwart. Serendipity saved the day when we realized that the amount of gelatin included in a packet is not consistent but in fact varies widely from one packet to another. Using a gram scale, we weighed more than 50 individual gelatin packets and found weight discrepancies as great as 20 percent. In fact, in two separate packages of four we found eight different weights. As soon as we began measuring gelatin by the teaspoonful, things began looking up.

In addition to proportions, there was chilling time to consider. Preparation and chilling times should be brief and the dessert quick to the table. Our first priority, therefore, was to create the best dessert to emerge within the shortest chilling time, a panna cotta that would be firm, say, in the space of a few hours. By increasing the amount of gelatin in increments of ⅛ teaspoon, from 2 to 3 teaspoons, we found that 2¾ teaspoons produced a firm enough, yet still fragile, finished texture after four hours.

Yet we wanted the option of an overnight version as

well. Knowing that gelatin grows more tenacious over time—transforming what was a lilting mousse one evening into a bouncing sponge the next—we figured there must also be a statute of limitations on its grip. At what point would the gelatin stop advancing? Research indicated maximum rigidity was reached after about 18 hours. (See the Science Desk on page 330.) At this point we recorded the textural changes occasioned by incremental decreases in gelatin and discovered that an implausibly small decrease (⅛ teaspoon) put the overnight version on par with the texture of the four-hour version.

With flexible time options in place, we moved on to technique. Because gelatin's response is hastened by cold temperatures, it seemed reasonable to keep most of the liquid cold. Why heat all the milk and cream when we only needed hot liquid to melt the gelatin and sugar? We gave the milk this assignment, pouring it into a saucepan, sprinkling the gelatin over it, then giving the gelatin five minutes to swell and absorb liquid. Knowing that gelatin sustains damage at high temperatures, we heated the milk only enough to melt the gelatin—a couple of minutes, stirring constantly—then added the sugar off heat to dissolve. The gelatin did not melt perfectly, and we thought we might have to increase the milk's temperature. Instead, we doubled the softening time to 10 minutes, and the problem was solved.

To do its job of firming the liquid to a gel, melted gelatin must be mixed with other recipe ingredients while its molecules have enough heat energy to move through the mixture. By combining ingredients hastily in the past, we had often precipitated gelatin seizures, causing the melted gelatin to harden into chewy strings, which ruined the texture of the dessert rather than enhancing it. So we stirred the cold cream slowly into the milk to temper it.

In cooking school, several test cooks in the kitchen had learned to stir gelatin-based desserts over an ice bath—allowing the gelatin to thicken somewhat under gentle agitation—before refrigerating them to set. Besides supporting nuts, fruit, or vanilla bean throughout, this process was said to produce a finer finished texture. Hoping to avoid

this step in a recipe that was otherwise so easy, we presented tasters with side-by-side creams, one stirred first over ice, one simply refrigerated. They unanimously preferred the texture of the panna cotta chilled over ice, describing it as "lighter, creamier, and smoother." Given the results, the extra 10 minutes required did not seem unreasonable.

Now it was fine-tuning time. First place for flavor accents went to vanilla, particularly in the company of fruit sauces. We preferred whole bean to extract and Tahitian to Madagascar (see the Tasting Lab on page 329).

This is a gorgeous anytime, anywhere dessert, proving that you don't have to be flocked, layered, filigreed, or studded—you don't even have to be chocolate—to win.

WHAT WE LEARNED: **Panna cotta requires more cream than milk for proper texture and richness. Soak the gelatin in cold milk, heat it briefly, and then cool it down with the cream and a quick trip to an ice bath. Measure gelatin by the teaspoon, not the packet, for accurate results. Use less gelatin if you plan on letting the panna cotta set up overnight in the refrigerator.**

PANNA COTTA serves 8

Serve panna cotta very cold with strawberry or raspberry sauce or lightly sweetened berries. Though traditionally unmolded, panna cotta may be chilled and served in wine glasses and sauced on top. If you would like to make the panna cotta a day ahead, decrease the gelatin to 2⅝ teaspoons (2½ teaspoons plus ⅛ teaspoon), and chill the filled wine glasses or ramekins for 18 to 24 hours. For more information about how gelatin works, see the Science Desk on page 330.

1	cup whole milk
2¾	teaspoons gelatin
3	cups heavy cream
1	piece vanilla bean, 2 inches long, slit lengthwise with paring knife (or substitute 2 teaspoons extract)
6	tablespoons (2.6 ounces) sugar
	Pinch salt
	Raspberry or Strawberry Coulis (recipes follow)

1. Pour milk into medium saucepan; sprinkle surface evenly with gelatin and let stand 10 minutes to hydrate gelatin. Meanwhile, turn contents of two ice cube trays (about 32 cubes) into large bowl; add 4 cups cold water. Measure cream into large measuring cup or pitcher. With paring knife, scrape vanilla seeds into cream; place pod in cream along with seeds and set mixture aside. Set eight 4-ounce ramekins on baking sheet.

2. Heat milk and gelatin mixture over high heat, stirring constantly, until gelatin is dissolved and mixture registers 135 degrees on instant-read thermometer, about 1½ minutes. Off heat, add sugar and salt; stir until dissolved, about 1 minute.

3. Stirring constantly, slowly pour cream with vanilla into saucepan containing milk, then transfer mixture to medium bowl and set bowl over ice water bath. Stir frequently until thickened to the consistency of eggnog and mixture registers 50 degrees on an instant-read thermometer, about 10 minutes. Strain mixture into large measuring cup or pitcher, then distribute evenly among ramekins. Cover baking sheet with plastic wrap, making sure that plastic does not mar surface of cream; refrigerate until just set (mixture should wobble when shaken gently), 4 hours.

4. To serve, spoon some raspberry or strawberry coulis onto each individual serving plate. Pour 1 cup boiling water into small, wide-mouthed bowl, dip ramekin filled with panna cotta into water, count to three, and lift ramekin out of water. With moistened finger, press lightly on periphery of panna cotta to loosen edges. Dip ramekin back into hot water for another three-count. Invert ramekin over your palm and loosen panna cotta by cupping your fingers between panna cotta and edges of ramekin. Gently lower panna cotta onto small serving plate with coulis. Repeat process with remaining ramekins of panna cotta. Serve immediately.

TECHNIQUE:
Making Raspberry Coulis

Pour the cooked berries into a fine-mesh strainer and use the back of a large spoon or a rubber spatula to push the puree through the strainer and into a bowl. Discard the seeds.

RASPBERRY COULIS makes about 1 ½ cups

24	ounces frozen raspberries (6 cups)
⅓	cup (2.3 ounces) sugar
¼	teaspoon lemon juice
	Pinch salt

1. Place frozen raspberries in 4-quart nonreactive saucepan. Cover, turn heat to medium-high, and bring to simmer, stirring occasionally, for 10 to 12 minutes. Add sugar and raise heat to high. Boil for 2 minutes.

2. Strain berries through fine-mesh strainer into bowl, using rubber spatula to push berries through strainer; discard seeds. Stir in lemon juice and salt. Cover and refrigerate until chilled, at least 2 hours and up to 3 days.

VARIATION
STRAWBERRY COULIS
Follow recipe for Raspberry Coulis, replacing raspberries with equal amount of frozen strawberries and increasing sugar to ½ cup (3.5 ounces). Increase simmering time in step 1 to 12 to 14 minutes.

TASTING LAB:
Vanilla Beans and Extracts

ALMOST TWO-THIRDS OF THE WORLD'S SUPPLY OF VANILLA beans comes from Madagascar, an island off the eastern coast of Africa. Significant amounts of vanilla beans are also grown in Mexico and Tahiti. Tahitian beans are a hybrid that originated spontaneously on several islands in the South Pacific. Beans grown everywhere else in the world, including Mexico and Madagascar, are from the same species.

Although vanilla beans are convenient to use in custards (the pods are split lengthwise, the seeds scraped into the liquid, and the pods usually added to infuse more flavor), extracts make the most sense for baking jobs, including cakes and cookies. (You could make vanilla sugar by nestling a split bean in some sugar, but this process takes about a week.)

When shopping for extracts, you have two basic choices—pure extract and imitation. Pure vanilla extract is made by steeping chopped vanilla beans in an alcohol and water solution. Imitation vanilla extract is made from vanillin, a product extracted from conifer wood pulp.

When developing our panna cotta recipe, we tried several kinds of beans and extracts. Tasters preferred the flowery flavor of the Tahitian vanilla beans to other vanilla beans. Most experts believe that Tahitian vanilla beans have a more intoxicating aroma, which we found really shines in an eggless custard. That said, tasters preferred panna cotta made with any kind of vanilla bean to those made with extract, so feel free to use other beans. We should note that the presence of black specks is a visual clue that may have influenced tasters when comparing panna cotti made with beans to those made with extracts. In the photo on the opposite page, Chris wears a sleeping mask to prevent him from picking out the samples made with vanilla beans.

If using extract, we wondered if the brand matters, or if you can tell the difference between real and imitation extract. We made panna cotti with nine extracts (seven real, two imitation) and gathered eighteen tasters. We also followed a standard tasting protocol in the vanilla business and mixed each extract with milk at a ratio of 1 part extract to 8 parts milk. Although you would never use so much extract in a real application, this high concentration makes it easier to detect specific characteristics in extracts.

The results of this tasting were so shocking that we repeated it, only to come up with similarly surprising findings. Tasters couldn't tell the difference between real and imitation vanilla. In fact, in the panna cotta tasting, the imitation extracts took first and third place, with Nielsen-Massey and Penzeys leading the pack among real extracts. In the milk tasting, the imitation extracts took the top two spots, followed by real extracts from Nielsen-Massey and Penzeys. Further tests in shortbread confirmed these results. Although we are loath to recommend an imitation product, it seems that most people don't mind imitation extract and, in fact, many tasters actually like its strong flavor.

SCIENCE DESK: How Gelatin Works

GELATIN IS A FLAVORLESS, NEARLY COLORLESS SUBSTANCE derived from the collagen in animals' connective tissue and bones, extracted commercially, and dehydrated. Most culinary uses for gelatin rely on a two-step process—soaking and then dissolving. Gelatin is usually soaked in some cool or cold liquid so it can swell and expand. It is then dissolved in a hot liquid and finally chilled to set.

This dual process results from the fact that when unsoaked gelatin is added directly to hot liquid, the outside edges of each granule expand instantly and form a gel coating, preventing the inside from becoming hydrated. The center of each gelatin particle then remains hard and undissolved. The resulting gelatin mixture doesn't set properly and is full of hard, granular bits.

In contrast, soaking gelatin in cold or cool liquid allows the particles to expand slowly so that they can tie up the maximum amount of liquid (up to three times their weight). Maximum rigidity in gelatin is reached after 18 hours. After that time, desserts will begin to soften again.

RHUBARB FOOL

WHAT WE WANTED: A dessert in which the tartness of the rhubarb was tamed but its true flavor and bright red color were preserved.

Fool is a quick, everyday dessert that just so happens to have a quaint and quirky British name. When we decided to try our hand at this simple dessert—essentially cooked fruit with sweetened whipped cream folded in—we sided with tradition and used rhubarb as the cooked fruit foundation. Although fool is in itself no culinary feat, working with rhubarb can prove tricky. First, its sourness can be overpowering. Second, if boiled, or cooked too hard and fast, it breaks down into a watery, porridge-like mass. Finally, its vivacious red color leaches out easily, leaving the rhubarb a drab gray. We knew that before we could finalize a fool, we would have to tame the rhubarb.

To begin our testing we tried baking the rhubarb, stewing it for a long time, sautéing it in butter, and simmering it for a short time. Baking and sautéing turned the rhubarb pulpy, chalky, and bland, while stewing produced a watery cream-of-rhubarb soup. And in each case the rhubarb lost its attractive red color, presenting instead hues that varied from gray-lavender in the baked version to pale, watery yellow in the stewed. The simmered batch, on the other hand, had a nice pinkish red color, a sweet/tart flavor, and a thick, toothsome texture.

The simmered rhubarb was not ideal, though; it was still too tart for most tasters. Looking further, we found an interesting precooking approach that purported to subdue its acidity: soaking 6-inch pieces in cold water for 20 minutes prior to cutting and simmering. When we gave this trick a try, we were surprised to find the rhubarb much less acidic, with a flavor that was more round and full. But this approach had one drawback: the color had dulled to a pale mauve.

To figure out what happened, we called Barry Swanson, a confirmed rhubarb enthusiast who is a professor of food science at Washington State University in Pullman. Swanson explained that a water-soluble pigment called anthocyanin is responsible for rhubarb's somewhat chalky, tannic mouthfeel as well as its bright pinkish red color. When we presoaked the rhubarb, a portion of the anthocyanin escaped from the rhubarb's cut ends into the water, muting the color as well as the harsh bite.

Swanson also explained that anthocyanin is sensitive to the acidity of its environment. When the pH is high (low acidity), the color shifts to the bluish gray range; when the pH is low (high acidity), the color is red. Thinking about this, we wondered what would happen if we reintroduced an acid with no bitter or tannic qualities, such as the citric acid in orange juice, while the rhubarb simmered. This test was successful. The juice added just enough acidity to restore the rhubarb red without having any ill effects on flavor. Fifty pounds later, we had finally figured out how to cook rhubarb.

We now turned our attention from the rhubarb to the whipped cream and the assembly of the fool. We tried whipping the cream to various degrees of stiffness, and everyone in the test kitchen concurred that a soft-to-medium peak was just right. It gave the fool just enough body without making it sliceable and stiff.

Fool-making tradition dictates that the cream be folded into the fruit, but this gave the dessert a somewhat dull, monochromatic texture and flavor. Arranging the fruit and cream in layers produced a more interesting result. The natural tanginess of the rhubarb played off the sweetness of the cream, and the alternating texture of fruit and cream made for a pleasing contrast.

WHAT WE LEARNED: To remove some of its bitterness, soak rhubarb in cold water for 20 minutes. To keep the color bright, simmer with orange juice. For best presentation and flavor, arrange the rhubarb and whipped cream in layers rather than folding the two elements together.

RHUBARB FOOL serves 8

For more information about buying and whipping heavy cream, see page 293. For a fancier presentation, use a pastry bag to pipe the whipped cream into individual glasses. To make one large fool, double the recipe and layer rhubarb and whipped cream in a 12-cup glass bowl.

2¼   pounds rhubarb, trimmed of ends and cut into
      6-inch lengths
⅓   cup juice from 1 large orange
1   cup plus 2 tablespoons (7.9 ounces) sugar
      Pinch salt
2   cups heavy cream, chilled, preferably
      pasteurized or pasteurized organic

1. Soak rhubarb in 1 gallon cold water for 20 minutes. Drain, pat dry with paper towels, and cut rhubarb crosswise into slices ½-inch thick.

2. Bring orange juice, ¾ cup sugar, and salt to boil in medium nonreactive saucepan over medium-high heat. Add rhubarb and return to boil, then reduce heat to medium-low and simmer, stirring only 2 or 3 times (frequent stirring causes rhubarb to become mushy), until rhubarb begins to break down and is tender, 7 to 10 minutes. Transfer rhubarb to nonreactive bowl, cool to room temperature, then cover with plastic and refrigerate until cold, at least 1 hour or up to 24.

3. Beat cream and remaining 6 tablespoons sugar in chilled bowl of standing mixer on low speed until small bubbles form, about 45 seconds. Increase speed to medium; continue beating until beaters leave trail, about 45 seconds longer. Increase speed to high; continue beating until cream is smooth, thick, and nearly doubled in volume and forms soft peaks, about 30 seconds.

4. To assemble fool, spoon about ¼ cup rhubarb into each of eight 8-ounce glasses, then spoon in layer of about ¼ cup whipped cream. Repeat, ending with dollop of cream;

serve. (Can be covered with plastic wrap and refrigerated up to 6 hours.)

VARIATIONS
STRAWBERRY-RHUBARB FOOL

Clean and hull 2 pints strawberries; quarter each berry. Follow recipe for Rhubarb Fool, substituting strawberries for 1¼ pounds rhubarb.

BLUEBERRY-RHUBARB FOOL WITH
FRESH GINGER

Follow recipe for Rhubarb Fool, reducing rhubarb to 1½ pounds, adding 1 teaspoon grated fresh ginger to orange juice along with sugar and salt, and gently stirring 1 pint blueberries into rhubarb after it has simmered 2 minutes.

CHOCOLATE desserts

CHAPTER 26

There's a reason why chocolates are a favorite gift on Valentine's Day. What better way to say you really care? Making a great chocolate dessert, such as a soufflé or roulade, says you really, really care.

Of course, a showy dessert that falls flat (which can happen, literally, to a soufflé) also says a lot about the cook (or recipe writer)—not much of which is probably very nice.

But never fear—the test kitchen has figured out how to make a chocolate soufflé that's nearly foolproof. You can even make the batter days in advance, spoon it into individual ramekins, freeze the batter, and then bake off the ramekins as needed. A great after-dinner soufflé without beating an egg white or melting chocolate in front of guests or loved ones—it's a minor culinary miracle.

A chocolate sponge roll cake, filled with coffee-flavored cream and covered with dark, rich chocolate ganache, is a festive way to celebrate almost any holiday. But a sponge cake that won't roll or a frosting that's gritty won't put anyone in a holiday mood. Our test cooks have figured out how to make a showy chocolate dessert with minimum fuss and maximum flavor.

Jack won't give Chris any hints as he weighs the pros and cons of four bittersweet chocolates and tries to pick out the brand that won the group tasting.

CHOCOLATE SOUFFLÉ

WHAT WE WANTED: A soufflé with big chocolate flavor, a dramatic rise above the rim, a crusty but airy outer layer, and a rich, loose center that was not completely set.

A great soufflé must convey a true mouthful of flavor, bursting with the deep, rich taste of the main ingredient. In a chocolate soufflé, the chocolate high notes should be powerful.

A primary consideration when trying to create such a soufflé is what to use as the "base," the mixture that gives substance and flavor to the soufflé as opposed to the airiness and "lift" provided by the whipped egg whites. The base can be a béchamel (a classic French sauce made with equal amounts of butter and flour, whisked with milk over heat), pastry cream (egg yolks beaten with sugar and then heated with milk), or a bouillie (flour cooked with milk or water until thickened). After trying several versions of each of these options, we found that we consistently preferred the béchamel base. It provided the soufflé with decent chocolate flavor and a puffed yet substantial texture. By contrast, the versions made with pastry cream and bouillie were too dense and puddinglike.

After a week of refining a recipe using a béchamel base, we thought the soufflé was good but that the chocolate was muted by the milk used in the béchamel. We removed the milk and flour from our recipe (which meant, essentially, no more béchamel), separated a total of six eggs and whipped the whites separately, more than doubled the amount of chocolate, and reduced the amount of butter. This approach resulted in a base of egg yolks beaten with sugar until thick, giving the soufflé plenty of volume. The result was fantastic—the most intense chocolate dessert we had ever tasted.

Our chocolate soufflé now had the intense flavor we had been looking for, but we still weren't completely happy with the texture because the outer layer was a bit cakey.

After several more experiments, though, we discovered that adding two egg whites resolved the problem, giving the soufflé more lift and a better texture.

For most recipes, a 25-degree variance in oven temperature is not crucial, so we were surprised to discover the dramatic impact it had on our soufflé. Our initial oven temperature was 400 degrees, but to be sure this temperature was optimum, we tested both 375 and 425 degrees. The higher oven temperature resulted in an overcooked exterior and an undercooked interior, while the lower temperature did not brown the exterior enough to provide as much flavor and also produced a texture that was too even, given that we were looking for a loose center at the point at which the exterior was nicely cooked. We decided to stick with 400 degrees.

A water bath was a truly awful idea. When we tested it, the outer crust of the soufflé turned out wet, with a gelatin-like appearance, and the soufflé did not rise well.

One factor we found to be of surprising importance was the baking dish. We tried using a standard casserole dish for one of the tests, and the soufflé rose right out of the dish onto the floor of the oven! The problem was that the dish did not have the perfectly straight sides of a soufflé dish. It pays to make sure that you are using a real soufflé dish.

We also tested the theory that a chilled soufflé dish improves the rise and discovered that it did cause our chocolate soufflé to rise higher. During the course of all this testing, we also found that a chocolate soufflé will give you three indications of doneness: when you can smell the chocolate, when it stops rising, and when only the very center of the top jiggles when gently shaken.

WHAT WE LEARNED: Don't block chocolate flavor by using milk or flour in the soufflé base. Just beat the yolks and sugar together and then fold in the melted chocolate and butter and, finally, the beaten egg whites.

CHOCOLATE SOUFFLÉ serves 6 to 8

See the Tasting Lab on page 343 for recommendations about specific brands of chocolate.

5	tablespoons unsalted butter (1 tablespoon softened, 4 tablespoons cut into ½-inch chunks)
1	tablespoon plus ⅓ cup (2.3 ounces) sugar
8	ounces bittersweet or semisweet chocolate, chopped fine
6	large egg yolks
½	teaspoon vanilla extract
⅛	teaspoon salt
8	large egg whites
⅛	teaspoon cream of tartar

1. Adjust oven rack to lowest position and heat oven to 400 degrees. Grease 1½-quart soufflé dish with 1 tablespoon softened butter, coating all interior surfaces. Coat bottom and sides evenly with 1 tablespoon sugar; refrigerate until ready to use.

2. Bring 2 inches water to simmer in small saucepan over medium heat. Combine chocolate and remaining 4 tablespoons butter in small heatproof bowl and cover tightly with plastic wrap. Set bowl over pan, reduce heat to medium-low, and heat until butter is almost completely melted and chocolate pieces are glossy, have lost definition, and are fully melted around edges, about 15 minutes. (Do not stir or let water boil under chocolate.) Remove bowl from pan, unwrap, and stir until smooth and glossy; set aside.

3. In bowl of standing mixer fitted with whisk attachment, beat yolks, 3 tablespoons sugar, vanilla, and salt on high speed until smooth, thick, and pale yellow, 8 to 10 minutes. Transfer mixture to medium bowl; wash mixer bowl and whisk attachment and dry with paper towels. (If you have 2 mixer bowls, leave yolk mixture in mixer bowl; wash and dry whisk attachment, and use second bowl in step 4.)

4. In clean mixer bowl with clean whisk attachment, beat whites, 1 teaspoon sugar, and cream of tartar at medium speed until combined, about 10 seconds. Increase speed to medium-high and beat until frothy and no longer translucent, 1½ to 2 minutes. With mixer running, add 1 tablespoon sugar; continue beating until soft peaks form, about 30 seconds. With mixer still running, add remaining 2 tablespoons sugar and beat to combine, about 10 seconds. Do not overbeat (if whites look dry and granular, they are overbeaten). While whites are beating, stir chocolate into yolks.

5. With rubber spatula, stir one quarter of beaten whites into chocolate mixture. Fold in remaining whites until no streaks remain (see illustrations on page 338). Gently pour mixture into prepared dish; to help soufflé rise properly, run index finger through mixture, following circumference of dish about ½ inch from edge. Bake until exterior is set, center jiggles slightly when shaken, and soufflé has risen 1½ to 2 inches above rim of dish, 20 to 25 minutes. Serve immediately.

VARIATION
INDIVIDUAL MAKE-AHEAD CHOCOLATE SOUFFLÉS serves 6

We had heard of recipes for soufflés that are prepared ahead of time, then refrigerated or frozen, and baked at the last minute. We tried both refrigerating and freezing the batter in individual ramekins. When we baked them, the refrigerated soufflés were a disaster (they hardly rose at all and were very wet inside), but the frozen version worked extremely well.

Follow recipe for Chocolate Soufflé, greasing each of six 1-cup ramekins with about ½ teaspoon softened butter and sprinkling bottom and sides of each with 1 teaspoon sugar. After folding whites into chocolate mixture, divide mixture between ramekins, set ramekins on baking sheet, cover baking sheet with plastic wrap, and freeze at least 3 hours or up to 4 days. Uncover and bake (do not defrost before baking) until exterior is set and soufflés have risen ½ to ¾ inch above rims of ramekins, 18 to 20 minutes. Serve immediately.

TECHNIQUE: Folding Beaten Egg Whites

Numerous recipes, everything from cakes to soufflés, call for beaten egg whites, which are usually folded into the batter just before it is baked. If you beat the eggs in too vigorously, the cake or soufflé may not rise. If you don't incorporate the eggs properly, you may be left with eggy patches in your baked goods. Here's the best way to fold beaten egg whites into a batter. Start by vigorously stirring a portion of the beaten whites (most recipes will call for a quarter or third of the whites) into the batter. This lightens the texture of the batter so the rest of the whites can be folded in more gently.

1. After stirring in a portion of the whites (see text above), scrape the remaining whites into the bowl. Starting at the top of the bowl, use a rubber spatula to cut through the middle of the whites.

2. Turn the edge of the spatula toward you so it moves up the sides of the bowl.

3. Continue this motion, going full circle, until the spatula is back at the center of the bowl again.

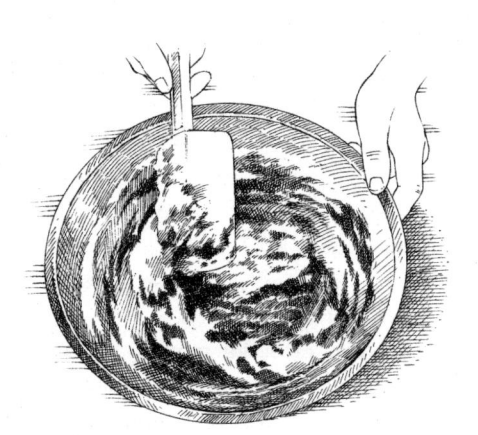

4. Follow this procedure four more times, turning the bowl a quarter turn each time. Finally, use the spatula to scrape around the entire circumference of the bowl.

SCIENCE DESK:
How to Beat Egg Whites

EGG WHITES ARE 88 PERCENT WATER AND 11 PERCENT protein; the remaining 1 percent consists of minerals and carbohydrates. When egg whites are beaten, they produce a foam. Beating an egg white relaxes its tightly wound protein molecules, which begin to unfold and stretch. With continued beating, the stretched proteins begin to overlap and bond together, creating a long, elastic surface. This is the soft-peak phase—the air bubbles are large and the foam is unstable because the proteins have not unwound and bonded to form a stable supporting structure.

With continued beating, the proteins further bond and envelop the air bubbles, trapping and separating them. This creates smaller bubbles and a more stable foam. Continuing to beat the foam after this point will cause it to become too rigid, and the liquid will be squeezed out of the whites.

When baked, these three types of foam will produce dramatically different results. Heat causes air inside the bubbles to expand, which in turns causes the entire structure to rise. The volume of stable, trapped air bubbles in the foam is what determines the success or failure of the rise. The none-too-stable foam that results from underwhipped whites will quickly deflate when combined with flour (for a cake) or a soufflé base, and the resulting baked good will be much shorter. A mixture made with overwhipped whites will suffer a similar fate when baked. The liquid squeezed out of the whites during overbeating signifies a corresponding loss of stable air pockets. In this case, a cake will appear to be fluffy and risen at first, but the overall structure will not be supported by the burst air pockets, and the structure will collapse. This is what happens when a soufflé falls.

There are other measures that can be taken to ensure a perfectly risen soufflé or cake. Adding sugar to the egg whites delays water evaporation by attracting moisture. The protein structure has more time to set up and thus can be beat longer without harmful consequences. Sugar also separates protein molecules, slowing the bonding process and guarding against overbeating. Cream of tartar, an acid, also slows down the bonding process. Acids donate hydrogen ions that interfere with the normal bonding patterns of proteins. The proteins remain more elastic, and the air cells encounter less resistance as they expand under the influence of the heat, resulting in a higher rise.

The conclusion: Smaller air bubbles that are formed slowly make the most stable foam. Beating the egg whites with sugar and cream of tartar results in a foam that is more stable and moist and will therefore rise better in the oven.

EQUIPMENT CORNER:
Fine-Mesh Strainers

A FINE-MESH STRAINER IS COVERED WITH THE SAME MATERIAL used in window screens. This mesh will trap all solid material or break up lumps in dry ingredients such as cocoa powder.

We put five fine-mesh strainers through a series of tests. We poured pureed pea soup through the strainers to test their ability to remove large solid bits. We pushed a raspberry puree through them to see how they would withstand scraping and moderate pressure. Finally, we passed pastry cream through the strainers to test their ability to catch small particles. (All fine-mesh strainers can sift dry ingredients like cocoa and flour, so we did not run this test.)

Based on these tests, we think it's imperative to buy a stainless steel strainer (aluminum can discolor acidic foods) with some heft. You don't want the strainer to buckle under moderate pressure, as several did in our tests. The finer the mesh, the better. Several strainers let solids pass through, which is unacceptable. Other strainers had handles that were uncomfortable, another no-no in our book.

Testers preferred the Williams-Sonoma Piazza 18cm Strainer ($26), which yielded perfectly smooth soup, raspberry puree, and pastry cream. The Küchenprofi 22cm Classic Strainer ($29.99) was the second choice in the test kitchen.

BITTERSWEET CHOCOLATE ROULADE

WHAT WE WANTED: A cake that would be easy to roll yet still moist, tender, and full of chocolate flavor.

A chocolate sponge cake roll—or roulade—begins life as a thin sponge cake baked quickly on a rimmed baking sheet, unmolded, and rolled up around a creamy filling. A rich frosting or glaze is often added to complement the cake and soft filling.

A sponge cake by definition contains little or no butter, and its (usually) separated eggs are whipped with sugar before the dry ingredients are folded in. Structurally speaking, a sponge cake sheet must be thin, even, and "rollable." Given the demands of its form, this cake cannot be fudgy, buttery, or rich. But it must pack serious chocolate flavor, remain moist, tender, and fine-pored, and refrain from being overly sweet.

To begin, we made five chocolate roulade recipes. Several things were immediately evident: Chemical leaveners were superfluous; cakes with more sugar failed to set the filling off to its advantage; and a rich, dark color was key to the cake's overall appeal. Only one of the cakes we baked used chocolate rather than cocoa, and that cake possessed by far the best flavor. Where every last cake fell from grace was in textural terms. We nibbled sheets of thick chocolate felt and soggy chocolate omelets. We wanted a texture that ventured to neither of these extremes.

Having chosen chocolate as the chief flavoring agent, we needed to determine which kind to use. We rejected unsweetened chocolate as too heavy-handed for this light, airy cake. Anything less than six ounces of semi- or bittersweet chocolate rendered a flavor too mild. One-third cup sugar tasted good with both semi- and bittersweet. We also added 2 tablespoons of butter to the melting chocolate. Though not enough to weigh down the cake, this small amount contributed to flavor and tenderness.

Because eggs are usually the sole liquid ingredient in a sponge cake—crucial for lightness of texture and ease of rolling—their number is key. Too few and our cake was not supple. Too many and we got either a wet chocolate sponge (if there was no flour in the recipe) or dry chocolate matting (if the proportion of eggs was too high). Six eggs provided the support necessary to blend the ingredients, the lift required to rise the cake, and the flexibility needed to roll it.

Still, even with chocolate contributing some structure, the fragile egg-and-sugar foam needed more support. We tested ¼ cup flour against the same amount of cocoa and ended up giving them equal partnership. The flour offered structural support, which kept the cake from becoming too moist after it was filled; the cocoa added a chocolatey undercurrent, which dramatically improved the overall flavor of the cake. Because the flavor of cocoa becomes more intense when it is mixed with water, we added 2 tablespoons of water to the recipe. The water helped to deepen the chocolate flavor and made the batter glossy and beautiful.

Recipes offer several techniques for coaxing sheet cakes into their customary cylindrical shape. Our cake responded best when cooled briefly in the pan on a cooling rack and then unmolded onto a kitchen towel rubbed with cocoa to prevent sticking. The cake, still quite warm, was then rolled up, towel and all. Allowed thus to cool briefly, the roll could be unrolled, retain its rolled memory, then be filled and re-rolled.

The roulade was now delectable, with a yielding, melting texture and intense chocolate flavor. It needed a rich but adaptable filling. Not wanting to crack open the cupboards and make a big mess, we decided to use a modified tiramisu filling made with lightly sweetened mascarpone and some ground espresso. A glossy layer of dark chocolate ganache put the final flavor layer in place and made the cake beautiful to gaze upon.

WHAT WE LEARNED: Use bittersweet chocolate and cocoa powder for real chocolate flavor. Butter adds some tenderness to sponge cake, while flour provides some structure.

BITTERSWEET CHOCOLATE ROULADE

serves 8 to 10

We suggest that you make the filling and ganache first, then make the cake while the ganache is setting up. Or, if you prefer, the cake can be baked, filled, and rolled—but not iced—then wrapped in plastic and refrigerated for up to 24 hours. The roulade is best served at room temperature.

6   ounces bittersweet or semisweet chocolate, chopped fine

2   tablespoons cold unsalted butter, cut into two pieces

2   tablespoons cold water

¼   cup Dutch-processed cocoa, sifted, plus 1 tablespoon for unmolding

¼   cup (1.25 ounces) unbleached all-purpose flour, plus more for baking sheet

⅛   teaspoon salt

6   large eggs, separated

⅓   cup (2.3 ounces) sugar

1   teaspoon vanilla extract

⅛   teaspoon cream of tartar

1   recipe Espresso-Mascarpone Cream (recipe follows)

1   recipe Dark Chocolate Ganache (recipe follows)

1. Adjust oven rack to upper-middle position and heat oven to 400 degrees. Spray 12 by 17½-inch rimmed baking sheet with nonstick cooking spray, cover pan bottom with parchment paper, and spray parchment with nonstick cooking spray; dust surface with flour and tap out excess.

2. Bring 2 inches water to simmer in small saucepan over medium heat. Combine chocolate, butter, and water in small heatproof bowl and cover tightly with plastic wrap. Set bowl over pan, reduce heat to medium-low, and heat until butter is almost completely melted and chocolate pieces are glossy, have lost definition, and are fully melted

around edges, about 15 minutes. (Do not stir or let water boil under chocolate.) Remove bowl from pan, unwrap, and stir until smooth and glossy. While chocolate is melting, sift ¼ cup cocoa, flour, and salt together into small bowl and set aside.

3. In bowl of standing mixer fitted with whisk attachment, beat yolks at medium-high speed until just combined, about 15 seconds. With mixer running, add half of sugar. Continue to beat, scraping down sides of bowl as necessary until yolks are pale yellow and mixture falls in thick ribbon when whisk is lifted, about 8 minutes. Add vanilla and beat to combine, scraping down bowl once, about 30 seconds. Turn mixture into medium bowl; wash mixer bowl and whisk attachment and dry with paper towels. (If you have 2 mixer bowls, leave yolk mixture in mixer bowl; wash and dry whisk attachment, and use second bowl in step 4.)

4. In clean bowl with clean whisk attachment, beat whites and cream of tartar at medium speed until foamy, about

30 seconds. With mixer running, add about 1 teaspoon sugar; continue beating until soft peaks form, about 40 seconds. Gradually add remaining sugar and beat until whites are glossy and supple and hold stiff peaks when whisk is lifted, about 1 minute longer. Do not overbeat (if whites look dry and granular, they are overbeaten). While whites are beating, stir chocolate mixture into yolks. With rubber spatula, stir one quarter of whites into chocolate mixture to lighten it. Fold in remaining whites until almost no streaks remain (see illustrations on page 338). Sprinkle dry ingredients over top and fold in quickly but gently.

5. Pour batter into prepared pan; using an offset icing spatula and working quickly, even surface and smooth batter into pan corners. Bake until center of cake springs back when touched with finger, 8 to 10 minutes, rotating pan halfway through baking. Cool in pan on wire rack for 5 minutes.

6. While cake is cooling, lay clean kitchen towel over work surface and sift remaining tablespoon cocoa over towel; with hands, rub cocoa into towel. Run paring knife around perimeter of baking sheet to loosen cake. Invert cake onto towel and peel off parchment.

7. Roll cake, towel and all, into jelly roll shape. Cool for 15 minutes, then unroll cake and towel. Using offset spatula, immediately spread filling evenly over surface of cake, almost to edges. Roll up cake gently but snugly around filling. Set large sheet of parchment paper on overturned rimmed baking sheet and set cake seam-side down on top. Trim both ends on diagonal. Spread ganache over roulade with small icing spatula. Use fork to make wood-grain striations on surface of ganache before icing has set. Refrigerate baking sheet with cake, uncovered, to slightly set icing, about 20 minutes.

8. Carefully slide 2 wide metal spatulas under cake and transfer cake to serving platter. Cut into slices and serve.

ESPRESSO-MASCARPONE CREAM makes about
2 ½ cups, enough to fill baked cake

Mascarpone is a fresh Italian cheese that is supple and spreadable. Its flavor is unique—mildly sweet and refreshing. It is sold in small containers in some supermarkets as well as most gourmet stores, cheese shops, and Italian markets.

½	cup heavy cream
4	teaspoons whole espresso beans, finely ground (about 2 tablespoons ground)
6	tablespoons (1.5 ounces) confectioners' sugar
16½	ounces mascarpone cheese (generous 2 cups)

1. Bring cream to simmer in small saucepan over high heat. Off heat, stir in espresso and powdered sugar; cool slightly.

2. With spatula, beat mascarpone in medium bowl until softened. Gently whisk in cooled cream mixture until combined. Cover with plastic wrap and refrigerate until ready to use.

DARK CHOCOLATE GANACHE
makes about 1 ½ cups, enough to cover filled roulade

Rose Levy Beranbaum, author of *The Cake Bible* (William Morrow, 1988), acquainted us with the technique of making ganache in a food processor, a method that beats all others for ease and consistency. If your kitchen is cool and the ganache becomes too stiff to spread, set the bowl over a saucepan of simmering water, then stir briefly until smooth and icing-like. We especially like Hershey's Special Dark for this recipe.

¾	cup heavy cream
2	tablespoons unsalted butter
6	ounces high-quality bittersweet or semisweet chocolate, chopped
1	tablespoon cognac

Microwave cream and butter in measuring cup on high until bubbling, about 1½ minutes. (Alternatively, bring to simmer in small saucepan over medium-high heat.) Place

chocolate in bowl of food processor fitted with steel blade. With machine running, gradually add hot cream and cognac through feed tube and process until smooth and thickened, about 3 minutes. Transfer ganache to medium bowl and let stand at room temperature 1 hour, until spreadable (ganache should have consistency of soft icing).

TASTING LAB: Bittersweet Chocolate

ACCORDING TO THE U.S. FOOD AND DRUG ADMINistration, there is no distinction between bittersweet and semisweet chocolate. Most chocolate manufacturers, however, follow the European tradition and produce bittersweet with a higher percentage of cocoa solids (resulting in a lower percentage of sugar) than semisweet. Therefore, bittersweet chocolate has a savory edge and a more intense flavor than sweeter and mellower semisweet chocolate. We generally prefer bittersweet chocolate in desserts, although good-quality semisweet chocolate can be used with good results.

To find out how various bittersweet chocolates perform in the kitchen, we sampled a mix of 10 American and European brands in a chocolate sauce as well as in our chocolate roulade. We found a strong correlation between results from these two tests.

Callebaut, a famed Belgian brand, took top honors. Lindt Excellence, a Swiss brand, also scored well, landing in fourth place. Several American chocolates also performed surprisingly well. The real shocker was the second-place finish of Hershey's Special Dark, a chocolate sold in many drug stores and supermarkets. Merckens Yucatan Dark, a hard-to-find American brand used by professionals, took third place, and Ghirardelli, a widely available brand from California, came in fifth.

Not all American brands did well, though. Baker's, the leading brand in supermarkets, finished last. Tasters complained about off flavors and gritty texture. Several brands with strong followings in the trade also showed poorly. Valrhona and Scharffenberger finished near the bottom of the pack, in part because these chocolates contain very little sugar and tasters found them too potent.

The top four chocolates, both European and American, all have a fairly clean, predictable flavor and smooth texture. No funky flavors, nothing too roasted, too potent, or too complex.

INDEX

A

Almonds
  in pesto, 14
  Sautéed Tender Greens with
    Raisins and, 213
Almost-As-Good-As Buttermilk Waffles, 257
American Garlic Bread, 33
American Pie Dough
  basic recipe, 300–301
  best ingredients/techniques, 300
  for free-form tarts, 301
  for lattice-top pies, 301
Apple Pie
  best ingredients/techniques, 302
  classic recipe, 303
  with Crystallized Ginger, 304
  with Dried Fruit, 304
  with Fresh Cranberries, 304
Apple Tartlets, Free-Form
  basic recipe, 307
  best ingredients/techniques, 306–8
  single tart recipe, 308
Apples
  and Currants, Tuna Salad with, 51
  for pies, choosing, 302
  and Raisins, Curried Coleslaw with, 96
  for tarts, choosing, 306
Arugula
  Crisp Thin-Crust Pizza with, 45
  and Red Onion, Flank Steak Sandwiches
    with, 56
  Salad, with Walnut Vinaigrette, 22
Asparagus, Broiled, and Smoked Mozzarella
  Filling, for chicken cutlets, 123
Astaxanthin, in cooked shrimp, 63
Avocados
  guacamole recipes, 155
  how to handle, 155

B

Baba Ghanoush
  best ingredients/techniques, 146
  charcoal-grill method, 147–48
  gas-grill method, 148
  oven method, 148
  with sautéed onion, 148
Baby carrots, 198

Bacon
  American, 18
  in guacamole recipe, 155
  in greens recipe, 214
  oven-fried, 244–46
  pancetta, 18
  in short rib recipe, 191–92
  in spaghetti alla carbonara, 18
Baking powder, in waffle recipes, 258
Balsamic vinegar, 21
  and Grapes, Tuna Salad with, 51
  vinaigrette using, 21–22
Bar cookies
  Brownies, 266–68
  Raspberry Squares, 269–70
Basil
  preparing for pesto, 14, 16
Beef
  aging, 179–80
  grades of, 77
  hamburgers, 126–29
  labeling practices, 126
  in meatballs, 26
  Prime Rib, 176–78
  resting, after cooking, 158
  steaks
    best cuts for, 76
    flank, 55–57, 156
    flat, comparisons among, 158
    pan-seared, 76–79
Beef broth, commercial, 180–81
Belgian Endive, Grilled, 136
Bell pepper, red
  omelet filling, 249
  tough greens with, 214
Biscuits, Cream
  best ingredients/techniques, 207, 209
  Cheddar, 208
  with Fresh Herbs, 208
  recipes for, 208
Bittersweet Chocolate Roulade, *239*
  basic recipe, 341–42
  best ingredients/techniques, 340
  Dark Chocolate Ganache for, 342
  Espresso-Mascarpone Cream
    for, 342
Blanching green beans, 186
Blenders, 8

Blueberry Muffins
  basic recipe, 220
  best ingredients/techniques, 218–19
  Cinnamon Sugar-Dipped, 220
  Ginger- or Lemon-Glazed, 220
Blueberry-Rhubarb Fool with Fresh
  Ginger, 333
Bow-Tie Pasta with Pesto, 15
Box graters, 46–47
Braising short ribs, 190
Brandy, Porter-Braised Short Ribs with, 192
Bread
  crumbs, homemade, 120
  croutons, buttered, 7
  for French toast, 252
  for garlic bread, 31
Bread knives, 33–34
Breaded Chicken Cutlets, *103*
  basic recipe, 119–20
  best ingredients/techniques, 118
  with Garlic and Oregano, 120
Breading
  for chicken cutlets, 118
  for crispy fried chicken, 87
Breakfast dishes
  Breakfast Strata, 260–63
  Cheese Omelet, 248–49
  Diner-Style Home Fries, 242–44
  French Toast, 252–55
  orange juice, taste test, 247
  Oven-Fried Bacon, 246–47
  Waffles, 256–58
Breakfast Strata
  best ingredients/techniques, 260–61
  with Potatoes, Rosemary, and Fontina, 263
  with Sausage, Mushrooms, and Monterey
    Jack, 262–263
  with Spinach, Shallots, and Gruyère, 225,
    262
Breasts of chicken. *See* Chicken: chicken cutlets
Brining
  chicken cutlets, 118
  fried chicken, 86
  ham, 202–3
  how it works, 171
  turkey, 166
Broiled Asparagus and Smoked Mozzarella
  Cheese Filling, 123

Flour *(cont.)*
    in French toast batter, 253
    for pizza dough, 43
    taste test, 208–11
Fond, in pan sauces, 117
Fontina cheese, Breakfast Strata with
    Potatoes, Rosemary, and, 263
Food mills, 197
Food processors, grinding meat
    in, 127
Fools
    Blueberry-Rhubarb, with Fresh
        Ginger, 333
    Rhubarb, 333
    Strawberry-Rhubarb, 333
Fra diavolo
    defined, 64
    Monkfish, with Linguine, 66
    Scallops, with Linguine, 66
    Shrimp, with Linguine, 65–66
Free-Form Apple Tartlets, *235*
    best ingredients/techniques, 306–8
    dough for, 301
French Fries, *107*
    basic recipe, 83
    best ingredients/techniques, 82
French tarts, pastry for, 274–76
French Toast
    best ingredients/techniques, 252–53
    Challah or Sandwich Bread, 254
    Firm European-Style Bread, 254
Fresh Fruit Tart with Pastry Cream
    basic recipe, 284
    best ingredients/
        techniques, 282–83
Fresh Pineapple Margaritas, 159–60
Fresh Raspberry Margaritas, 160
Fresh Roast Ham, choosing/cooking
    techniques, 202–3
Fresh Sour Cherry Cobbler, 317–18
Fresh Tomato Topping with Mozzarella and
    Basil, 40
Fruit(s). *See also specific fruits*
    dried, in apple pie, 304
    for fresh fruit tarts, 284–85
    in coleslaw, 96
    in tuna salad, 51
Frying
    crispy fried chicken, 87
    French fries, 82
    oils for, 90
    pots for, 90

G

Garam Masala, Garlic and Cilantro Marinade
    with, 144
Garlic
    basting oil, for grilled vegetables, 138
    blanching, 15
    butter, 135
    controlling flavor of, 34, 68
    in chicken cutlet recipes, 120
    in grilled shrimp recipes, 72–73
    in mashed potatoes, 195–96
    in pesto, 14
    in shrimp scampi, 63
    in spaghetti alla carbonara, 18
    marinades using, 144
    mincing technique, 67–68
    presses, 67–68
    -Soy Mayonnaise, 56–57
    toasting, 32, 33
    with hamburgers, 129
Garlic Bread
    American, 33
    best ingredients/techniques, 31–32
    Chipotle, 33
    Herb, 33
    Parmesan and Asiago Cheese, 33
Garlic Mashed Potatoes, 195–96, *228*
Gas grilling
    grills, choosing, 138–39
    hamburgers, 128
    shish kebab, 143–44
    shrimp, 72
Gelatin, how it works, 330
Ginger
    Blueberry-Rhubarb Fool with, 333
    Crystallized, Apple Pie with, 304
    Fresh, Cranberry Sauce with Pears and, 173
    -Glazed Blueberry Muffins, 219
    -Orange Glaze, Roasted Carrots with, 199
    Scones, 224
    Spicy Pineapple-, Glaze, 205
    Warm-Spiced Parsley Marinade with, 144
Glazed Scones, 224
Glazes
    for carrots, 199
    for fresh fruit tarts, 284–85
    for ham, 205–06
Golden Cornbread, 169
Gorgonzola Cheese Filling with Walnuts and
    Figs, 123
Graters, box, 46–47
Gravy, Turkey, 169–70

Green Beans
    cooking methods, 184–85
    with Sautéed Shallots and Vermouth, 187
    with Toasted Hazelnuts and Brown
        Butter, *110*, 187
Green-Topped Roasted Carrots, 199
Greens
    best ingredients/techniques, 212–13
    Quick-Cooked Tough, 214
    Sautéed Tender, 213
Griddles, 254–55
Grill tongs, 148
Grilled Cheese Sandwiches, 53–54
Grilled Cheeseburgers, 129
Grilled Fresh Mozzarella Sandwiches with
    Black Olive Paste and Roasted Red
    Peppers, 54, *102*
Grilled Hamburgers, *106*
    best cuts/techniques for, 126
    charcoal grilling, 128
    Cheeseburgers, 129
    gas grilling, 128–29
    with Cognac, Mustard, and
        Chives, 129
    with Garlic, Chipotles, and
        Scallions, 129
    with Porcini Mushrooms and
        Thyme, 129
Grilled Hot Dogs, 132–33
Grilled Shrimp
    with Lemon, Garlic, and
        Oregano Paste, 73
    with Spicy Garlic Paste, 72
Grilled Vegetables
    basting oils for, 138
    best ingredients/techniques, 134
    corn, 135
    eggplant, 147
    endive, 136
    fennel, 137
    Portobello mushrooms, 137–38
    radicchio, 136
Grilling techniques/tools
    grill tongs, 148
    judging temperature of fire, 132–33
    oiling the grilling rack, 129
Gruyère cheese, Breakfast Strata with
    Spinach, Shallots, and, 262
Guacamole
    best ingredients/techniques, 154
    Chunky, 154–55
    with Bacon, Scallions, and Tomato, 155

Potatoes
    browning of, reason for, 184–85
    French Fries, *107*
        basic recipe, 82–83
    Home Fries, 242–44
    in breakfast strata, 263
    Mashed, 194–96
    Pommes Anna, 182–84
    starch in, 197
    storing, 83
    with roasted carrots and
        shallots, 199
Prime Rib
    basic recipe, 178
    best ingredients/techniques, 176–77
    taste test, 178
    tying and carving, 178
Prosciutto, Quick-Cooked Tough Greens
    with, 214
Provolone Cheese, Filling with Rosemary,
    Roasted Mushrooms and, 123
Prunes, Brandy, and Lemon Essence, Porter-
    Braised Short Ribs with, 192
Puddings, chilled
    Panna Cotta, 326–30
    Rhubarb Fool, 332–33
    Summer Berry Puddings, 322–24

Q

Quick-Cooked Tough Greens, 214
    with Bacon and Onion, 214
    with Prosciutto, 214
    with Red Bell Pepper, 214
Quick Tomato Sauce for Pizza, 45

R

Radicchio, Grilled, 136
Raisin(s)
    and Almonds, Sautéed Tender Greens
        with, 213
    Curried Coleslaw with Apples
        and, 96
    Scones, Oatmeal-, 224
Raspberry(ies)
    Coulis, 329
    fresh, margarita using, 161
    preserves, taste test, 270–71
    Squares, *231*
        basic recipe, 270
        best ingredients/techniques, 269

Red bell pepper
    omelet filling, 249
    tough greens with, 214
Red Onion, Flank Steak and Arugula
    Sandwiches with, 56
Red wine
    for cooking, selecting, 79–80
    in spaghetti alla carbonara, 18
    in steak sauces, 78
    Sauce, 79
    Short Ribs Braised in, 191–92
Red wine vinegar, 21
Refrigerators, 255
Resting meat, 158
Rhubarb Fool, *237*
    basic recipe, 333
    best ingredients/techniques, 332
    Blueberry-, with Fresh Ginger, 333
    Strawberry-, 333
Rice
    cooking techniques, 149–50
    Pilaf
        basic recipe, 151
        best ingredients/techniques, 149
        Indian-Spiced, with Dates and
            Parsley, 151
        with Currants and Pine Nuts, 151
    types of, 149
Rice vinegar, 22
Roast Fresh Ham, *229*
    basic recipe, 204
    Coca-Cola Ham, 204–5
    glazes for, 205–6
Roasted Carrots
    basic recipe, 199
    best ingredients/techniques, 198
    Green-Topped, 199
    Maple, with Brown Butter, 199
    with Ginger-Orange Glaze, 199
    with Potatoes, and Shallots, 199
Roasted Mushrooms and Provolone Cheese
    Filling with Rosemary, 122
Roasting
    fresh ham, 203
    prime rib, 177
    turkey, 168–69
Roasting pans, 181
Rolling pins, 277
Root Vegetables, Mashed Potatoes with, 196
Rosemary
    and Fontina, Breakfast Strata with
        Potatoes, 263

Rosemary *(cont.)*
    Mint Marinade with Garlic and Lemon, 143
    Roasted Mushroom and Provolone
        Cheese Filling with, 123
Rubs, for shish kebab, 142

S

Salad spinners, 22–23
Salads, 13
    best ingredients/techniques, 20
    coleslaws, 94–96
    Leafy Green, 22
    Tuna, 50–51
Salt, effects of, on vegetables, 96
Sandwiches, 48
    Flank Steak, 55–57
    Grilled Cheese, 54
    Tuna Salad, 50–51
Saucepans, 173
Sauce(s)
    carbonara, 12–13, 19
    cocktail, for shrimp, 60–61, 62
    cranberry, 173
    for pan-seared steaks, 78–79
    pan, fond in, 117
    pesto, 14
    raspberry coulis, 329
    strawberry coulis, 329
    tomato, for pasta, 25–26, 27, 30
    tomato, for pizza, 45
Sausage
    in breakfast strata, 262–63
    dressing, for turkey, 166
Sautéed Tender Greens, 213
    with Raisins and Almonds, 213
Sautéed Wild Mushrooms, 10–11
Sautéing techniques, 114, 149–50
Scales, digital, 211
Scallions
    Bacon, and Tomato, Guacamole with, 155
    Garlic and Chipotles, Grilled
        Hamburgers with, 129
Scallops Fra Diavolo with Linguine, 66
Scampi, Shrimp, 65
Scones, Cream
    basic recipe, 224
    best ingredients/techniques, 223
    Cakey, 224
    Ginger, 224
    Glazed, 224
    Oatmeal-Raisin, 224